COLLECTED ECONOMIC ESSAYS

Volume 4

ESSAYS ON ECONOMIC POLICY II

COLLECTED ECONOMIC ESSAYS

by Nicholas Kaldor

ESSAYS ON ECONOMIC POLICY II

IV. Policies for International Stability
V. Country Studies

NICHOLAS KALDOR

HOLMES & MEIER PUBLISHERS, INC.
New York

Second impression published in the United States of America 1980 by
Holmes & Meier Publishers, Inc.
30 Irving Place
New York, N.Y. 10003
First edition published 1964

Library of Congress Cataloguing in Publication
Data

Kaldor, Nicholas, 1908–

Essays on economic policy.
(His Collected economic essays; v. 3-4)
Includes bibliographical references.
CONTENTS: v. 1. Policies for full employment.
The control of inflation. The problem of tax reform.
– v. 2. Policies for international stability. Country
studies.
    1. Economic policy – Addresses, essays, lectures.
2. Full employment policies – Addresses, essays,
lectures. 3. Inflation (Finance) – Addresses, essays,
lectures. 4. Taxation – Addresses, essays, lectures.
5. Economic stabilization – Addresses, essays,
lectures. I. Title. II. Series.
HD82.K3   1980   338.9   80–18155

ISBN 0 8419 0454 5 (v. 2)

Printed in Great Britain by The Anchor Press Ltd
and bound by Wm Brendon & Son Ltd
both of Tiptree, Essex

CONTENTS

INTRODUCTION

THE first six essays of the present volume are concerned, in one way or another, with what are probably the most important economic policy issues facing the world. In contrast to domestic economic policy, where a fair consensus of views has gradually emerged since the Keynesian revolution, the economics of international trade and payments still exhibits a bewildering variety of opinion, both as to objectives and methods. The complexity of the issues involved, and the intricate ways in which they interact, is such that few economists would claim to have reached a consistent set of views over the whole field, or to be fully confident about the merits of rival policies or techniques for dealing with the different aspects of the problem.[1]

Even to formulate the most important issues is a formidable undertaking. There is first of all the conflict, or potential conflict, between pursuit of national policies of full employment and economic growth and the simultaneous pursuit of international economic policies conducive to the interests of the world community. International trade is not amenable to control through instruments of national economic planning. Is it justifiable to follow policies of economic nationalism in order to reduce this area of potential instability? Or to seek escape by creating economic blocs (whether through customs unions or currency blocs) which hold the promise of greater stability for the insiders but only at the cost of throwing a greater burden of adjustment on outsiders?

There is the problem of reconciling internal economic stability with external balance. If each trading nation desires to maintain both full employment *and* the stability of its internal price-level, is the maintenance of international balance consistent with a

---

[1] It is not surprising that it is in the field of international trade and payments that diagnosis and prediction are most apt to go wrong. It was when everybody predicted a permanent dollar shortage that the U.S. balance of payments began to slide into a persistent deficit; when everybody had come to expect a steady worsening of the terms of trade of manufacturing countries the opposite trend began to reassert itself; the recent improvement of commodity prices (since 1962) has again occurred at a point of time when most economists had come to expect a chronic over-production in primary commodities accompanied by falling prices.

system of fixed exchange rates—particularly when the rate of growth of productivity and the movement of efficiency wages of individual countries differ markedly from one another?[1] Is a universal system of floating exchange rates a feasible alternative —considering that exchange rate variation can be deliberately engineered as a potent instrument of trade warfare?

More important than either of these is the problem of how to redress the balance between the smaller part of the world's population that is rich and is growing steadily richer and the greater part that is desperately poor. Can the tremendous handicap resulting from the inherent disadvantages of the producers of primary products in their trade with manufacturing countries be offset or compensated for? More generally, can we counteract the forces of "circular and cumulative causation",[2] making for concentration of development in the most successful areas, whose very progress creates a stumbling block for the development of the others? More important still, are we ready to do so? Whereas in the national field it has come to be generally accepted that economic welfare depends not only on the size of the national income but also on its distribution, few people are yet prepared to advocate major policy measures (a rise in raw material prices, for example) whose main effect would be to secure a more equal distribution of income between rich and poor countries.

This principle of "circular and cumulative causation" seems to operate moreover at all levels: between different regions of a single country (e.g. the north and south of the U.S.A., the north and south of Italy, and more recently, the north and south of England); between the different industrialised countries; as well as between the "developed" and the "under-developed" countries. Between the industrial countries, it takes the form of the tendency for an initial competitive advantage to become cumulative

---

[1] That surpluses or deficits in balances of payments must not be allowed to cause inflationary or deflationary trends in the domestic economy has now become universally accepted doctrine. Thus the 1964 Report of the U.S. Council of Economic Advisers says: "The United States has no reason to expect surplus countries to accept inflation, just as they have no reason to expect the United States to accept unemployment and unused capacity because of its payment deficit" (p. 133). It is not explained how the mechanism of adjustment is supposed to function in the absence of these effects, under a régime of fixed exchange rates.

[2] Cf. Gunnar Myrdal, *Economic Theory and Underdeveloped Regions*, London, Duckworth, 1957, Ch. 2.

through the link between the rate of growth of exports and the rate of growth of productivity. An industrial country which is able to enlarge its share in world trade—so that its exports and imports grow at a faster rate than its domestic product—may, through the consequential effect on its productivity growth, thereby enhance its competitive advantage at the expense of others whose productivity growth is slowed down in consequence.[1] The same kind of disequilibrating forces operate, more powerfully between the developed and the under-developed countries, handicapping the industrial development of the latter through their inability to compete with established exporters in the world markets.

Yet in a more fundamental sense, the different regions of the world are complementary rather than competitive: an increase in productivity and real income in any one area also tends to enlarge the trading opportunities for the others, and in so doing, to promote their own development. It is the simultaneous operation of opposing forces—those that tend to diffuse the benefits of economic progress and those that tend to concentrate it in the hands of a few—which makes the formulation of "ideal" policy prescriptions in the field of international trade and monetary arrangements so difficult. It is easy to identify circumstances in which unrestricted trade operates as a drag on the development of particular areas. It is also easy to show how, in other circumstances, economic nationalism, by restricting the scope of trade, slows down the rate of economic progress, both of the protecting country and of others. But it is extremely difficult to evolve a workable set of rules that allows each country the degree of freedom necessary for its own development, and at the same time allows maximum scope for the international division of labour.

The post-war international arrangements concluded at Bretton Woods, Havana, etc., were the first conscious attempt to formulate

[1] This is due partly to the behaviour of money wages in industrial countries, and partly to the existence of both static and dynamic economies of scale, which make the rate of productivity growth in any particular sector dependent on the rate of growth of total output. It is as a result of the latter factors that the disproportionate growth of output in the export industries raises the average productivity growth for the economy as a whole; which may only be partially offset by a higher rate of growth in money wages. Cf. A. Lamfalussy, *The United Kingdom and the Six*, London, Macmillan, 1963; W. Beckerman, "Projecting Europe's Growth", *Economic Journal*, December 1962, pp. 912–25.

an international code of behaviour in matters of trade and exchange policies. But, as they were evolved by the statesmen and economists of the developed nations, they were tailored to fit the economic circumstances of the advanced industrial countries, with little recognition of the special needs and requirements of the others. The virtues of stable and uniform exchange rates, convertibility, bound tariffs, non-discrimination, the prohibition of export subsidies, etc., may be genuine enough when applied to the conduct of the industrialised countries in their trading relations with each other. They are far from evident when applied to the under-developed countries. On the other hand, in matters of vital interest to the under-developed countries—such as the stabilisation of commodity prices, access to markets in agricultural products and raw materials, the abolition of discrimination against low-wage exporters of manufactured goods—the rules and obligations are not nearly so far-reaching or explicit.

Growing dissatisfaction with the one-sided character of existing international trading arrangements led, on the initiative of the under-developed countries, to the recent United Nations Conference on Trade and Development. Though in terms of concrete results its achievements were meagre, this Conference seems to have succeeded in promoting a new consciousness among the under-developed nations of their community of interest, and in creating a forum through which their needs and requirements will receive more continuous and systematic attention in the future. Sooner or later this is bound to lead to a new set of rules and of institutional arrangements that gives more adequate recognition to the differing requirements of countries in different stages of development.

At the moment expert opinion is far from agreed on what the exact character of these rules should be, whether in the field of monetary arrangements, financial aid, or trading relations —and even if agreement were reached, it is far from clear how the powerful countries of the West could be induced to adopt them. Indeed, nothing contributes so much to the general sense of hopelessness in formulating international economic policy as the knowledge that in matters requiring binding agreements between sovereign nations any far-reaching reform is "unnegotiable" except under the stress of grave emergency.

The six papers reproduced here illustrate the changing climate of opinion concerning international economic problems, as well as their manifold implications. The first two essays, written in the early 1950's, reflect the then overriding concern with the "structural dollar problem" and with the threat of instability to the world economy arising out of the fluctuation in the supply of dollars to the outside world. The first paper analyses the problem of how to offset, or minimise, the international propagation of cyclical fluctuations, and was partly intended to provide the theoretical background for a scheme of "compensatory financing" which was put forward in a U.N. report two years earlier.[1] That report recommended that each country should guarantee a certain annual supply of its own currency to the outside world—offsetting by long-term loan or gifts any short-fall of its disbursements on current account. Since that time, at least three other expert committees of the U.N. have recommended schemes of a similar kind[2] but, until recently, none of these have received serious consideration at the inter-governmental level.[3]

The second paper, "Foreign Trade and the Balance of Payments", has not been published before. It was written as a contribution to a projected volume of *Fabian Essays* which in the event was never completed. It presents a review both of the British balance of payments problems and of the trade and payments situation of the world as a whole, as they appeared in the early 1950's. On re-reading it after twelve years, I find very little to disagree with on the theoretical plane—the analysis of multilateralism versus discrimination (pp. 30–47) and the analysis of the circumstances

[1] *National and International Measures for Full Employment*, by J. M. Clark, N. Kaldor, A. Smithies, P. Uri, E. R. Walker, United Nations, Sales 60, 1948, II, A. 3.

[2] Cf. *Measures for International Economic Stability*, by J. W. Angell, G. D. A. Mac-Dougall, J. Marquez, H. Myint, T. Swan, U.N. Sales No. 1951, II, A. 2.; *Commodity Trade and Economic Development*, by C. F. Carter, D. Sumitro, J. Goudriaan, K. Knorr, F. G. Olano, U.N. Sales No. 1954, II, B. 1.; *International Compensation for Fluctuations in Commodity Trade*, by I. H. Abdel-Rahman, A. C. Flores, Sir John Crawford, A. G. Hart, S. Posthuma, M. L. Qureshi, U.N. Sales No. 1961, II, D. 3.

[3] The policy announced by the International Monetary Fund in 1962 recognised that a fall in export earnings entitles a member to special loans of up to 25 per cent. of its quota; and recently the U.K. and Sweden proposed a scheme at the Geneva Conference for special long-term loans to countries which suffer a fall in export earnings.

in which discriminatory restrictions on trade with countries with scarce currencies appear to be justified in the interests of the world economy. However, in the light of subsequent developments, I clearly underestimated the efficacy of the price mechanism as a means of altering the pattern of world trade, at any rate as between the developed industrial countries. The whole analysis rested partly on the premise (*vide* pp. 35–39) that the U.S. balance of payments surplus had deep structural causes and was intractable to adjustment by the ordinary market processes. In fact, this "structural surplus" was fast disappearing even at the time the paper was written—partly as a result of the economic recovery of Europe, and partly also as a result of the devaluation of the European currencies which left the dollar relatively over-valued in relation to other industrial exporters. The U.S. economy has shown itself far less prone to cyclical fluctuations than in pre-war days; the amplitude of fluctuations in U.S. import demand have been even smaller; and when contractions in U.S. demand did occur, they did not generate the expected deflationary tendencies in the outside world: they tended to be offset by a simultaneous expansion in import demand by the countries of Continental Europe.

In fact it was the countries of Continental Europe, particularly Germany, which exhibited a chronic balance of payments surplus during the 1950's. If this did not involve a contractionary pressure on the world economy it was because it coincided with a deficit in the U.S. balance of payments; and the U.S. was able, owing to her very large gold reserve, and to the readiness with which a dollar-hungry world absorbed, for a prolonged period, an accumulation of dollar claims, to finance this deficit without contracting her own purchases from, or her loans and grants to, the outside world. When at last, at the end of the decade, the "reserve-creating potential" of the U.S. dollar was nearing exhaustion[1] (because the Continental central banks found themselves

---

[1] The "reserve-creating potential" of sterling was exhausted much earlier—by the end of the war—since when there has been no further increase in official sterling balances. The examples of both sterling and dollar have shown that the creation of reserves through the "gold-exchange standard" is essentially a transitory phenomenon: it can only happen when a currency which was traditionally very "strong" becomes a "weak" one (through persistent balance of payments deficits), and whilst the "weakness" is still regarded as a temporary phenomenon by the reserve-currency holders.

with larger dollar balances than they bargained for) the unstable and unsatisfactory character of the existing international monetary system became manifest. There was then a strong revival of interest in creating more satisfactory institutional arrangements for the smooth functioning of international trade and payments.

However, in one respect, the gloomy prediction of my 1952 paper proved only too true: in suggesting (pp. 24–28) that Britain's own balance of payments problem would not be soluble without a *large* expansion of her exports, and this in turn would not be attainable without a far greater expansion of the basic metal and engineering industries than was then contemplated. In fact, the volume of our exports which increased by 16·5 per cent. a year in the period 1947–51, increased by only 1·8 per cent. a year in the subsequent eight years (in 1951–9) and by 3·7 per cent. a year in the following four years (in 1959–63). Despite the unexpected bonus of a 15 per cent. improvement in the terms of trade, our balance of payments remains just as precarious as it was twelve years ago. If we wished to attain the "strong balance of payments position" necessary for steady growth, we should still need an expansion of exports relative to our imports which could only be attained by an appreciable expansion of our manufacturing production *relative to* the expansion of domestic consumption and investment.

The next paper and the following one deal with the subject of commodity agreements as a means of stabilising incomes of primary producers. In the immediate post-war years tremendous hopes were placed on such agreements as an instrument for promoting economic stability. However, after numerous negotiations only a few definite agreements have been reached and, of these, few proved successful in stabilising prices or incomes for more than a limited period. The hopes placed by economists on the creation of internationally financed buffer stocks, advocated by Keynes shortly before the war,[1] proved abortive: the willingness

---

[1] "The Policy of Government Storage of Foodstuffs and Raw Materials", *Economic Journal*, September 1938, pp. 449–60. One of its early (and persistent) advocates was Mr. L. St. Clare Grondona (*National Reserves for Safety and Stabilization*, London, 1939). Later, the League of Nations report *Economic Stability in the Post-War World* (Geneva, 1945), and the report of the U.S. President's Materials Policy Commission *Resources for Freedom* (Washington, 1952) put forward proposals for the operation of buffer stocks on an international scale.

to provide finance for such schemes was lacking and, with the exception of tin, no buffer-stock scheme came actually into existence. There were many advocates of another type of scheme —a multilateral contract between governments which guarantees certain maximum prices by the exporters and certain minimum prices by the importers for the major portion of trade, irrespective of the fluctuations in market prices, and thereby reduces the instability of incomes associated with fluctuations in market prices. The only instance of this kind of agreement is the International Wheat Agreement of 1949, and the report which I prepared at the request of F.A.O. on the subject in 1952 (pp. 61–111 below) was intended to assist in the forthcoming negotiations for the renewal of that agreement in the following year. This paper contains a review of the various kinds of commodity agreements as well as an elaborate analysis (in Appendix A) of the economic effects of a multilateral contract of this type. It contains various suggestions for improving the efficacy of the agreement—an automatic formula for adjusting prices; incentives for the adjustment of production by the adoption of a dual price system in payments to farmers; the establishment of publicly-owned stocks by both the exporting and the importing countries. None of these suggestions was found acceptable; and although the Agreement was renewed in 1953, the major importing countries refused to participate, and they were only willing to re-enter, in 1959, after the Agreement was further weakened by the omission of any obligation on importing countries to pay minimum prices. Indeed the International Wheat Agreement, though formally still in force, ceased to be a significant factor in the world wheat trade after 1953.

The failure to secure stable prices or markets for primary producers by means of either international buffer stocks or multilateral contracts left only one other avenue open: the creation of producer cartels which influence prices through the direct regulation of supplies coming on to the world market. This type of agreement was generally frowned on in post-war discussions since it involved a restriction of production and trade which could not be justified in the context of an expanding world economy, or could only be justified when the price mechanism was not capable of restoring a balance between supply and demand except by a "slow and painful process."[1]

When, however, I came to review this problem afresh after a ten-year interval, this type of agreement appeared to me to be the only promising method capable of arresting the steady deterioration in the terms of trade of the primary producing countries. Accordingly, the paper entitled "Stabilising in the Terms of Trade of Under-developed Countries", which I wrote in 1962 at the request of Dr. Raoul Prebisch (then Executive Secretary of the Economic Commission for Latin America) was largely devoted to an examination of the necessary prerequisites for the successful operation of agreements of this type. These prerequisites, analysed on pp. 123–9 below, turned out, however, to be pretty stringent. Their fulfilment would require a degree of co-operation and self-discipline among the producing countries which may be just as difficult to attain as the degree of far-sightedness or financial *largesse* among the importing countries which is presupposed in commodity agreements of the other types.

Indeed, subsequent discussions with economists of under-developed countries have convinced me that the mechanism I recommended in that paper for adjusting the level of production of each producing country by means of variable export levies, and then adjusting the export quotas of the different producers in accordance with the pattern of export levies, is not one that is politically likely to be a "starter" in most producing countries. Yet without it no scheme of quantitative export regulation is likely to succeed for more than a temporary period. This is partly because without production controls export restriction is likely to lead to the accumulation of excess stocks which the financially weak producers are unable to carry; but mainly because without some built-in mechanism for changing the pattern of export quotas in favour of low-cost producers, any agreement is likely to be exposed to a steadily increasing stress which will cause it to break down sooner or later.

And here the matter rests. An intellectual exploration of the various techniques by which the prices of *individual* commodities

---

[1] Cf. *Measures for International Economic Stability, op. cit.*, para 71, also Article 62 of the Havana Charter, quoted in note 3, p. 116 below.

could be stabilised by international agreement leads to the sad conclusion that, whatever the potential benefits of such schemes, the *political* prerequisites for their realisation do not yet exist. Importing countries are not willing to undertake far-reaching commitments which may involve them in near-term financial sacrifices for the sake of conjectural long-run benefits. Exporting countries are not likely to be financially strong enough or disciplined enough to do the job themselves—particularly when this involves an effective control over their own agricultural producers. In cases where such control is feasible—as for example in the case of petroleum or copper, where control over world production is largely concentrated in the hands of a few business firms—the objectives of market and price regulation are largely attained without any inter-governmental agreement.[1]

I thus came to the conclusion that if the problem is to be solved, it must be tackled on entirely different lines—by a multi-commodity buffer-stock scheme that is directly linked to the creation of an international reserve currency. There have been many advocates, since the nineteenth century, of a composite-commodity reserve currency. Its advantages over a currency system based on gold, or of some symmetallic combination of precious metals, have been recognised by numerous economists from Jevons onwards.[2] But, despite the careful consideration given to this proposal in the U.N. report on *Commodity Trade and Economic Development* in 1954, it has played almost no role in the recent discussions—at the academic or the official level—for reforming the international monetary system. Yet I came to the conclusion, when studying the world liquidity problem last year, that the institution of an international currency based partly on gold and partly on a composite-commodity reserve offers a solution to the

[1] At the recent Geneva Conference on Trade and Development, commodity price-stablisation by means of individual commodity agreements figured high on the agenda as one of the principal objectives, yet the lengthy discussions on the subject did not succeed in producing any fresh idea as to how such agreements could be more effectively promoted. France alone, among the governments of the developed countries, came out in favour of the "organisation of markets" as a means of securing remunerative and stable prices to producers: but the actual methods for securing "organised markets" were left distressingly vague.

[2] The most prominent advocates in the 1930's were J. Goudriaan, Frank D. Graham and Benjamin Graham. For a review of earlier commodity currency proposals cf. B. Graham, *Storage and Stability*, New York, 1937, Ch. xviii, and the U.N. report, *Commodity Trade and Economic Development, op. cit.*, pp. 35 ff.

threatening problem that has emerged as a result of the un-
planned and haphazard growth of the "gold-exchange standard"
—a solution which alternative proposals based on the extension of
reciprocal credit arrangements among Central Banks, or the
creation of a world central bank with power to create credit, are
not likely to provide.

I circulated my preliminary ideas on this privately among a
group of economists in April 1963, and while I encountered a
great deal of scepticism and some hostility, I found that some of
my colleagues, notably Professor A. G. Hart of Columbia and
Professor Jan Tinbergen of Holland, had both been thinking
independently along the same lines. Encouraged by Professor
Hart, we decided to prepare a joint submission to the forthcoming U.N. Conference on Trade and Development on the
subject, which is reproduced with my co-authors' permission, on
pp. 131–77 below.[1]

In submitting this scheme, none of us was under any illusion
that the central bankers of the main industrial countries would be
prepared to give serious consideration to a plan of this kind at the
present time. But we were anxious that, at a time when the financial experts of the "Paris Club" were considering methods of
monetary reform that would yield little benefit to anyone outside
that Club, the case for alternative schemes which would produce a
more powerful and more widely diffused benefit to the world
economy should not go wholly by default. A commodity reserve
currency is not a substitute for some elaborate scheme for mutual
support among the leading Central Banks—it is more an alternative to a large-scale revaluation of gold, or better still, to an
increase in gold production resulting from a geographically well
diffused set of gold discoveries.[2] It would generate the necessary
increment in world monetary reserves through income-account
transactions which represent added earnings of the producing

---

[1] The paper was written jointly by Hart and myself in New York around Christ-
mas, 1963, and owes as much to Hart's ideas as to my own. While we kept in touch
with Tinbergen, he was not able to participate in the work of the actual drafting;
he was, however, sufficiently in agreement both with the scheme and its presentation
to be able to add his signature subject to a few minor changes which were acceptable
to Hart and myself.

[2] This aspect of the plan is far better brought out by a further paper by A. G.
Hart, "Monetary Reform to Further Economic Development", which is to appear in
the September 1964 issue of the *Political Science Quarterly*.

countries, and would thus directly stimulate a healthy development of world trade. Through its effect on the structure of demand, it would also tend to step up the rate of industrial growth in the world economy to the limits permitted by the growth of productivity in primary production. It is the one method of generating expansion through "favourable" balance of payments situations which does not require anyone to get into debt as a counterpart to the creation of added reserves. If this idea can be kept alive, I am confident that *some day* the world will come to accept some variant of it—though I am equally sure that this will not come about until numerous other schemes have been explored and found wanting.

The last, and most recent, paper in this section, "Dual Exchange Rates and Economic Development", examines the long-term balance of payments problems of the under-developed countries and comes to the not very surprising conclusion that only the development of their export trade in manufactures can relieve them of an ever-increasing dependence on economic aid. This conclusion is independent of whether the terms of trade of the primary producers remain stable in the future or not. To the extent that the prices of primary products continue to deteriorate, the problem of developing alternate sources of export earnings becomes all the more urgent. But even if these prices remained stable (or even if they improved above their current levels) the rate of growth of export earnings from the sale of primary products over longer periods would still lag behind the rate of growth of import requirements, owing to the relatively slow rate of growth of world consumption of primary products. The paper explores the implications of this conclusion; and while the conclusion would probably command general acceptance, the implications are not likely to be palatable to the developed countries, given their present dogmas. For they involve recognition of the need to stimulate manufactured exports of under-developed countries through the manipulation of exchange rates, or through other forms of export subsidisation, which are prohibited practices in the trade relations of the developed countries; they also require that the developed countries should be willing to face up to the structural adjustments necessitated by unrestricted imports from the low-wage countries in the same spirit in which they face up to the structural adjustments necessitated by the flow of inventions or innovation, whether domestic or international.

The last group of essays, under the heading "Country Studies", contains a selection of papers arising out of specific assignments in various countries. The first of these, on "The German War Economy", is of purely historical interest—it is reproduced here because, even at this distance of time, it makes a bizarre story. It shows the inhibitions from which even the most ruthless aggressor must suffer in pursuing his objectives. Hitler wanted to conquer the world, but he was anxious to do so with as little inconvenience as possible to the civilian population of Germany. This meant that the German economy was never fully mobilised for war until it was much too late. To have done it earlier would have meant admitting that the conception of victory on the cheap, or victory by "lightning war"—which alone, in Hitler's thinking, justified his policies in the eyes of the German people—had failed. Britain, Russia and the United States, once involved in the war, suffered from no such inhibitions.

The long essay on the "Economic Problems of Chile" was the result of a three-month study as a consultant to the Economic Commission for Latin America in 1956. Though the paper was never published in Chile, mimeographed copies of this "confidential" report found their way to Chilean political circles where they created considerable stir. Passages from the report were freely quoted in Parliamentary speeches, and, during the elections, by politicians of opposing sides. (There is nothing like having one's writing classified as a confidential document to ensure that it receives widespread attention.) The reasons for this, I presume, were mainly the analysis of income and expenditure distribution in Chile in comparison with Western countries, and the analysis of the trend of income distribution which showed a diminishing share accruing to wage-earners and an increasing share to property-owners.[1] The figures also showed that in Chile a

[1] The source of the figures used in this paper were the detailed national account statistics of the Corporación de Fomento which had only just become available (after a ten-year preparation) and the results of which had not yet been analysed. These estimates have been regularly published since, but the publication of the series relating to distribution by types of income has since been discontinued.

disproportionate part of the burden of taxation falls on wage and salary-earners, while the property-owners consume a surprisingly large proportion of their incomes.[1]

The explanation of these phenomena is hinted at (though not fully developed) in the final section of this paper dealing with the inflationary process. This puts forward a "structural" explanation of the Chilean inflation, in terms of the disproportionality between the increase in non-agricultural employment and incomes and the growth in marketable food supplies. The policy of import substitution has led to a considerable increase in urban employment; since agricultural production has remained relatively stagnant, this has led to a chronic shortage of food which was only partially offset by increased food imports. This process has involved not only a rise in food prices relative to other prices but a diminishing share of wages in the output of the secondary and tertiary sectors. Thus both the continued inflation and the increasing inequality in the distribution of incomes have been a reflection of the increasing shortage of wage-goods relatively to other goods, which could not have been remedied except by a higher rate of growth in agricultural production, or by a higher rate of increase in food imports, which, in turn, would have required a higher rate of growth in export earnings.[2]

The two short papers on problems of economic development in Ceylon and on the approach to economic planning in India were written during visits to these two countries in 1958, and in each case were a by-product of other activities (connected with fiscal

---

[1] The conclusion that the share of the G.N.P. taken up by property-owners' consumption was nearly three times as high in Chile as in the U.K. (and probably the U.S.) was received with some scepticism by economists outside Chile. However, subsequent investigations by an American research student based on a direct sample inquiry of property-owners' incomes and expenditure budgets supported these findings. (Cf. Marvin J. Sternberg, *Chilean Land Tenure and Land Reform*, a doctoral dissertation submitted to the University of California, 1962.)

[2] The countries in Latin America which have avoided these large and long-continuing inflations (such as Mexico, Peru and Venezuela, in contrast to Chile, Brazil or the Argentine) have been invariably those which succeeded *either* in raising the productivity of domestic agriculture (as Mexico did) or those (such as Peru and Venezuela) which succeeded in increasing their export earnings fast enough to allow the relatively free importation of food and other necessities. Monetary and fiscal policies had very little to do with the occurence of these inflations—a point which Western economists were slow to recognise, with the result that the stabilisation policies repeatedly urged on them by the I.M.F. and other organisations proved abortive in halting these inflations, though they frequently involved contractions in the level of production and employment.

matters) and not the result of any prolonged study. On re-reading the paper on Ceylon, I feel that I have not given enough emphasis to the dangers inherent in the policy of food subsidies which has since come to absorb a disproportionate part of the financial resources of that country, to the detriment of developmental expenditures; and I may have been too optimistic about the prospect of increasing foreign exchange earnings through a further development of the plantation economy.

With regard to my comments on the Indian plan, I feel that subsequent developments have justified my critical attitude to the methods adopted—i.e., planning in financial terms, with insufficient regard to the availabilities of different kinds of resources. The failure of agriculture in recent years has undoubtedly been the main factor in slowing down the progress of the Indian economy—though I am not competent to judge how far this was the result of a succession of bad harvests and how far a consequence of insufficient investment, or an inappropriate scale of priorities, in the agricultural sector. However that may be, unless India succeeds in making her agriculture far more productive, her future development can only be envisaged in terms of making her industry far more export-oriented—a matter which requires not only a progressive policy by India herself, but, even more, the readiness of the developed countries to provide access to her products in their markets.

The last paper on "Prospects of a Wages Policy for Australia" was prepared at the request of Dr. Coombs, the Governor of the Reserve Bank, during a sojourn in Australia last year. It deals with issues which are very much in the forefront of interest not only in Australia but also in Britain, and should perhaps be read in conjunction with my 1950 paper on the subject which is printed in the previous volume.[1] I found, in the course of preparing this paper, that the intriguing problem of the economic effects of Australia's centralised arbitration system of wage determination already preoccupied Australia's best economic brains; and I am far from certain whether I succeeded in advancing the subject much beyond the point it had reached before I arrived on the scene. Nevertheless I decided to include this essay for the benefit

[1] Cf. vol. I of these *Essays*, pp. 111–27.

of British readers, if not for Australians. The analysis of the effects of the arbitration system highlights the difficulties which a successful "incomes policy" must encounter—difficulties which have not been properly appreciated by the many recent converts to this policy in Britain.

Five of the eleven essays printed in this volume have not been published before in the English language (one of them has appeared in Spanish), while three others appeared in publications which are not easily accessible to British readers. I am indebted to the editors or publishers of the papers which have already appeared in print (as indicated in the footnote at the beginning of the essays) for permission to reprint them.

NICHOLAS KALDOR

KING'S COLLEGE,
CAMBRIDGE.
July 1964

PART IV

POLICIES FOR INTERNATIONAL STABILITY

THE INTERNATIONAL IMPACT OF
CYCLICAL MOVEMENTS[1]

THE problem of the international propagation of cyclical movements can be considered from two aspects: that of the balance of payments, and that of the level of employment and economic activity. In practice these two aspects are intricately related. The repercussions of external changes on the internal employment levels of a particular country are directly associated with their repercussions on that country's payments balance; while the need to restore equilibrium in the balance of payments of a particular country may entail further repercussions on levels of employment, both internal and external. For purposes of analysis, however, it is best to treat the two aspects separately.

I. DETERMINANTS OF BALANCE OF PAYMENTS EQUILIBRIUM

The first difficulty in any analytical treatment of the balance of payments problem arises from certain ambiguities in the definition of a "balance of payments equilibrium." If international capital movements could be ruled out altogether as being the symptoms of disequilibria of one kind or another, the definition of a state of equilibrium would be a simple one; it would involve a zero balance on current account (i.e. equality between the value of exports and imports of goods and services). It is generally agreed, however, that an equilibrium of this type—like the stationary state of classical economics—is much too long-run to be of much practical use. Hence the usual procedure is to divide capital movements into two kinds: those which can, and those which cannot, be treated as an independent variable; and to define "balance of payments equilibrium" as a state of affairs where net capital movements of a compensatory kind (including

---

[1] Paper presented to the Oxford Conference of the International Economic Association in September, 1952, and published in *The Business Cycle in the Post-War World*, ed. by E. Lundberg, London, Macmillan, 1955.

movements of gold) are zero, so that the balance on current account equals the net capital movements of an "independent" character. The trouble with this kind of definition is the impossibility of drawing any sharp and clear-cut distinction between "independent" capital flows and others. A sound distinction clearly could not rest on the financial character of the capital movement in question—i.e. whether it consists of short-term or long-term funds, private or public funds, etc.—partly because, within considerable latitudes, funds of different types are substitutes for one another; partly, also, because—to an unknown and indeterminate extent—long-term capital flows of an apparently spontaneous character are themselves conditioned by the nature of the current account balance. A third type of definition, according to which balance of payments equilibrium exists whenever, "in the opinion of the monetary authorities, the state of the current balance is not such as to call for corrective action of some kind" is equally question-begging, since it makes the definition of equilibrium dependent both on the degree of wisdom of the monetary authorities and on the extent of liquid resources at their disposal. It also fails on the test of consistency: since on this particular definition, it is perfectly possible for a given balance on current account between, say, two countries, to be treated as a state of equilibrium from the point of view of A and a state of disequilibrium from the point of view of B.

Owing to my inability to offer any improvement I shall ignore, in the rest of this essay, the difficulties inherent in a definition of the second type, and shall assume that there are certain capital flows between different countries the amount of which can be regarded as given independently of the other constituent items of international payments, so that each country is said to be in equilibrium whenever its current balance assumes the particular value that is numerically equal to its net (independent) capital flow (so that the sum of its current balance and its capital flow adds up to zero). On this definition the absence of equilibrium in the accounts of one particular country with the rest of the world involves the simultaneous lack of equilibrium in the accounts of at least one other country with the rest of the world; while the sum of positive and negative imbalances (i.e. the deviations from "equilibrium") for the world as a whole, must add up to zero.

Assuming, for the present, a purely multilateral system (i.e. general inter-convertibility of currencies) the only factor that is significant, from the point of view of any particular country, is its balance of payments with all other countries taken as a group. This, of course, will vary, to a greater or lesser extent, with every economic variable both of that country and of all other countries. Assuming, however, that for the problems in hand a certain number of these variables can be treated as given—in particular the technical conditions of production (the supply functions of commodities) and the demand functions of final consumers in-cluding, of course, the consumption function as a whole—we can select three particular sets of determinants of the payments balance: (i) the relative price levels of the different countries, measured in terms of gold (which depend both on the level of wages in terms of domestic currency and the rates of exchange); (ii) the relative levels of home investment in the different countries (again measured in terms of gold or some other common unit); (iii) the relative extent of the trade restrictions operating in the various countries—the "trade restriction ratio"—measured, in the case of each particular country, by the proportionate differ-ence between actual and "potential" imports—i.e. the level of imports that would obtain if, at the given values of all other variables, all restrictions on imports (whether by tariff or quan-titative regulation of any kind) were abolished.[1]

Of these three determinants, the role of the first is obvious and needs no further elaboration. A rise in the relative gold-price level of country A—whether brought about by a rise in money wages or a rise in the exchange rate—will cause a reduction in

[1] This summarisation of the relevant factors under the above three heads, while adequate for some purposes, is only intended as a rough first approximation; a more detailed analysis would require a further sub-division of determinants. In particular, treating the level of home investment as a single variable assumes that the net budget-ary deficit of public authorities (which is here regarded as a constituent item of home investment) can be treated as an independent variable, and that "passive investment" (the unintended accretion or diminution of stocks) can be ignored. Further, treating the relative levels of home investment as a variable assumes that the consumption functions of the various countries are treated as constants. A shift in the consumption function in any country (caused, e.g., by a shift in income distribution) would play the same role as a change in its home investment.

its net balance on current account and vice versa.[1,2] But the current balance—given the relative price levels—will also vary with the relative levels of employment and activity in the various countries, since an increase in employment in one country in relation to others will, *ceteris paribus*, increase its imports relatively to its exports and vice versa. The levels of employment in the various countries, on the other hand, given the demand functions (i.e. both the savings functions and the propensities to import) are a function of the level of home investment plus the level of exports in each country. But since (given relative price levels, etc.), each country's exports will be a function of the level of income of other countries, the relation of exports to imports of any particular country will depend on the rate of its own domestic investment in relation to the level of investment in other countries (and also, of course, on its distribution between these other countries). An increase in home investment in *A*, in relation to the home investment in other countries, will have the same effect as an increase in the price level of *A* in relation to others—it will increase imports relatively to exports. An increase in investment in countries other than *A* will increase *A*'s exports in relation to its imports. Trade restrictions—which reduce imports at given price levels and home-investment-relations—have the same influence on the balance of payments as the other two factors, though with a reverse sign. An increase in the trade restrictions imposed by *A*, in relation to those imposed by others, has the same effects as a (relative) fall in the price level of *A* or in its domestic investment; a reduction in restrictions as a rise in its price level or in its home investment.

[1] I am ignoring here the possibility that, if the elasticities of the relevant supply and demand functions are sufficiently small, changes in relative price levels may have a "perverse" effect on the current balance—i.e. a rise in relative price levels may cause an increase in the net balance, and vice versa. I think it could be shown that such "perverse" effects can only operate within certain ranges of price-level relations, and are always indicative of conditions of multiple equilibria—i.e. that the net balance could always be reduced by a sufficiently large increase, or increased by a sufficiently large fall, in the relative price levels, although with smaller movements in either direction the effects may be the other way round.

[2] To say that the net balance on current account will vary with the relative price levels so that it requires a particular constellation of price levels to secure zero balances is not, of course, the same thing as saying that the balances will become zero when the relative price levels are *equal*. The latter (which is the so-called purchasing power parity theory) is a far more ambitious doctrine, but is subject to such severe qualifications that it is better abandoned altogether.

International payments equilibrium therefore presupposes a particular constellation of price levels, investment levels and trade restrictions—or, rather, given the international pattern of any two of these sets of variables, there will (normally) be one particular constellation of values for the third set which secures equilibrium. Similarly, any change in the constellation in any one of these sets could be compensated by a change in the constellation of either one or both of the others. Hence, in principle, each country possesses, as regards the balance of payments, three degrees of freedom—the extent of its freedom depending in each case on the extent to which it can regard the price levels, domestic investment levels and trade restrictions of other countries as being determined independently of its own. (A small country therefore possesses a much greater "freedom" than a large one.) It can alter its price level by changing the exchange rate of its own currency in terms of gold, or by changing—though normally this is not within its competence—the general level of money wages; it can alter the level of domestic investment by means of monetary or fiscal policies or direct controls; and finally, it can change the extent of its own trade restrictions through a change in import duties, import quotas or licensing procedures.[1] Apart from the latter—which is always exclusively a matter of government policy—the values of the other two variables may also alter as a direct result of international pressures (in the case of investment, also of domestic pressures) rather than as a result of deliberate governmental action. To the

---

[1] It also follows that for a small country—i.e. to the extent to which a country is capable of altering the values of its own variables relatively to those of others—there will normally be one particular combination of values of the three variables which maximises the real income of its inhabitants. This is because (i) an increase in the level of domestic investment—up to a certain maximum, at any rate—will increase real income; (ii) a fall in the price level, through the associated changes in the terms of trade, will normally reduce real income; (iii) an increase in trade restrictions, by reducing the scope of internal exchanges, will reduce productivity and real income, Hence the point of optimum income is determined by the condition that the increase in real income brought about by a marginal increase in domestic investment is just offset by the reduction of real income associated with the compensatory reduction in the price level (given the extent of trade restrictions) or the compensatory increase in trade restrictions (given the price level). Similarly, at the optimum point, trade restrictions are carried to a point where the reduction in productivity caused by a marginal increase in restrictions is just balanced by the improvement in the terms of trade associated with a compensatory increase in the price level, etc. Hence the so-called "theory of the optimum tariff" exhibits only one of the facets of a more comprehensive theory of "optimum balance of payments policy."

extent that international payments equilibrium is maintained, as a matter of fact, this can only partly be ascribed to the various governments pursuing a consistent set of policies; partly it is the direct result of market forces tending to enforce a consistent set of values in the variables.

Finally, it should also be borne in mind that the purposes of international agreements aiming at the creation of a "code of international behaviour" (such as the statutes of the International Monetary Fund or the Havana Charter) could be looked upon as the elimination of certain of these "degrees of freedom" at the disposal of governments. To the extent that the freedom to vary exchange rates or trade restrictions is effectively eliminated by international agreements, governmental action for the preservation of balance of payments equilibrium is confined to the variation of the level of domestic investment or the general level of money wages; and since the latter is not normally regarded as an instrument of governmental policy—owing to the very limited power of governments in enforcing downward variations, and the inflationary risks inherent in deliberately contrived upward variations—the policies of governments are effectively confined to deliberate variations in domestic investment levels in accordance with the requirements of international equilibrium.[1]

This method of maintaining the international payments equilibrium—which may be termed, perhaps, the "classical method," though classical theories are far from clear as to its true mode of operation—necessarily involves, however, that each country should be prepared to vary the general level of its own production and employment in accordance with the requirements of its international balance. The elimination of a deficit, with this method, must involve a reduction in income and employment; while a deliberate policy aiming at the elimination of a surplus presupposes an expansion of income and employment. The use of the weapons of "monetary policy"—barring the

[1] This was, in effect, the method in operation under the international gold standard; except that, owing to the elasticity of supply of international funds with respect to changes in relative interest rates, the need to adjust domestic investment levels was considerably lessened by the ability of countries to alter the flow of international lending or borrowing. The re-establishment of the rules of the international gold standard without the simultaneous recreation of an interest-elastic international capital market would therefore impose a far more severe burden on countries than they in fact carried under the pre-1914 gold standard.

possibility of varying the general level of money wages by this means—must therefore be capable, in order to be successful, not merely of changing the existing distribution of resources between different uses, but of changing the level of employment and real income in general.

It is sometimes suggested that if the so-called "rules of the game" of the international gold standard were properly kept —so that the burden of maintaining the international equilibrium of payments was appropriately shared between surplus areas and deficit areas, rather than being unilaterally thrown on the latter—this would not be so. For in that case the increase in home investment in the surplus countries would exactly offset the decrease in the home investment of deficit countries, leaving world investment and (ignoring local differences in saving and import propensities) world production and trade unchanged. However, it can be shown[1] that even in that case the improvement in exports of the deficit countries—following upon the expansion of domestic investment of the surplus countries—must necessarily be less than the reduction in domestic investment of the deficit countries, so that their total income and employment must fall in consequence. (In other words, assuming that any reduction in investment in a deficit country, A, is matched by an equivalent increase in investment in other countries, it still remains true that the elimination of a given imbalance in international transactions will require a quantitatively greater shift in the local distribution of investments.[2]) The fall in income and employment in A will, of course, be greater if, in the face of a reduction of its own investment, the rates of investment in other countries are maintained unchanged;[3] a fortiori if the rates of investment in other countries—owing to the decrease in import demand of A—tend to be reduced in consequence.

In view of this, it may be doubted whether the "classical

---

[1] For a demonstration of this proposition, see Appendix, p. 19.

[2] The only exception to this is perhaps the case of "suppressed inflation" where, at the existing price relationships, there is an unsatisfied demand for the exports of a particular country, so that the reduction in home demand will "release" goods for export, in which case exports might be substituted for home investment, without any loss in total income.

[3] As is shown in the Appendix, p. 21, the reduction in domestic investment in this case needs to be more than twice as large as the amount of the imbalance if the propensities of the different countries are assumed to be the same.

method" of maintaining balance of payments equilibrium—
which may thus be defined as establishing that pattern of distribution of local investments which will establish the pattern of
current account balances required by the flow of international
capital funds, and of so altering the pattern of investments as
to maintain the required pattern of current-account balances
under changing conditions—has any superior merit, even from a
purely international point of view, in comparison with, say, a
method of varying the degree of trade restrictions in accordance
with requirements—i.e. of increasing restrictions in the face of
deficits, and reducing them in the face of surpluses. In the latter
case, adjustments might be brought about with less disturbance
to production and employment levels; and from the point of
view of securing a fair distribution of the burden of adjustment,
it might be easier to induce (surplus) countries to relax trade
restrictions wherever the international payments situation requires
it than to induce them to follow a policy of internal expansion
in such times, even when their domestic situation does not warrant
such an expansion.

II. CYCLICAL MOVEMENTS AND INTERNATIONAL EQUILIBRIUM

The trade cycle is essentially the result of the tendency of the
investment cycles of individual industries to become synchronised
on account of the powerful influence of the level of demand on
investment plans. It is as a result of this that the variegated investment requirements of particular industries tend to be swamped by
the common factor of the general level of demand. Since the
general level of demand in turn depends on the general level of
investment in the economy, this means that the investment cycles
of major industries (which account for the larger share in the total
of investment) determine the timing of investment in the others.
This tendency acts both nationally and internationally: to the
extent that the trade cycle is a world-wide phenomenon, it consists
of the simultaneous variation of the domestic investment levels of the
various countries, where the investment cycles of the less important
countries are synchronised with those of the major countries as
a result of the impulses received through international trade.

If this synchronisation were complete the domestic investment levels of the various countries would fluctuate in unison without altering their relation; and the international trade cycle might consist merely in fluctuations in the volume of goods traded, without upsetting international payments equilibrium. Balance of payments disequilibria might still arise, however, as a result of (*a*) differences in the demand functions for commodities in the various countries, and/or their non-linearity which could cause a given percentage reduction in the level of domestic investment to bring about a greater reduction in the income of some countries than of others; or a given percentage reduction in income to bring about a greater reduction in the demand for some of the internationally traded goods or of some countries, than of others; and (*b*) differences in the elasticities of the supply of different commodities which could cause a given reduction of demand to be associated with a greater fall in the price of some commodities than of others. In other words, even with complete synchronisation in the movement of domestic investment levels, some countries may still develop deficits, and others surpluses, in the course of cyclical movements if (i) their own demand for imports varies more or less than the world demand for their exports; or (ii) there are associated changes in their terms of trade, export prices falling either more, or less, than import prices. It was mainly for the latter reason that cyclical depressions in the past were associated with a tendency towards balance of payments deficits in the primary producing countries; while the former reason is probably an important contributory cause of a world-wide cyclical down-swing being usually associated with a tendency towards a balance of payments surplus in the United States.[1]

The disequilibria in international payments associated with cyclical movements become much more important, however, when the synchronisation in the movement of domestic investment levels is not complete. This may simply be a result of ordinary time-lags in the operation of market forces; or it may be the result of differences in the "economic climate" of the different countries—in monetary and fiscal policies, and so on. The latter factor becomes all the more important the more the regulation of

[1] In the case of Britain, a relatively low income elasticity of imports tended to offset the effect of the movements in the terms of trade, leaving the balance of payments without any clear cyclical pattern.

domestic investment levels in the interests of the domestic economic situation becomes a deliberate aim of government policies.
In the limiting case the international propagation of investment
fluctuations may thereby be entirely prevented, and the domestic
investment levels of the various countries be determined independently of each other.

The assumption of independently determined domestic investment levels in itself does not, of course, eliminate the international
propagation of cyclical influences in so far as incomes, employment levels and payments balances are concerned. For a
fall in the domestic investment level of one particular country,
A, the investment levels of other countries remaining unchanged,
will involve a surplus in the current balance of A and a corresponding deficit in the current balance of the other countries; so
that the *net* investment of A (i.e. its domestic investment plus its
foreign balance) will rise relatively to (i.e. falls to a lesser extent
than) its domestic investment, while the *net* investment of other
countries falls relatively to their domestic investment. This means
that incomes and employment levels will be higher in A and lower
in the other countries than would correspond to the domestic
investment levels under conditions of balance of payments equilibrium. (This is only a different way of saying that the fall in the
demand for imports of A, consequent upon a fall in its domestic
investment, will transfer some of the impact of A's reduction
in domestic investment on income and employment from the
inhabitants of A to those of other countries.) In order to prevent
incomes and employment from being reduced it is not sufficient
therefore for the governments of countries other than A to maintain their domestic investment levels undiminished; the maintenance of internal economic stability would require them to
maintain the levels of their *net* investment undiminished—which
means that they would have to compensate for any reduction in
their foreign balance by an increase in their domestic investment.
Such a policy would, of course, in itself involve a further reduction in their foreign balance, and would thus tend to improve
the income and employment position of A. In the final result the
increase in investment in countries other than A would have to
equal A's reduction in imports consequent upon a reduction of

its own investment and thus be quantitatively equal to the imbalance in international payments.

The balance of payments problems associated with cyclical fluctuations can be considered therefore on at least three different 'levels." The first of these proceeds on the assumption that the investment cycle is internationally synchronised; imbalances in international payments would arise in this case only on account of the factors mentioned on page 11. The second assumes that the domestic investment levels of the various countries are independent of each other; the cyclical movement in this case would involve a surplus in the balance of payments of those countries whose investments fall in the course of the cycle, in relation to the others, and vice versa. The size of the surpluses and deficits generated is a fraction of the change in relative home investment levels; the fraction depending (as shown in the Appendix) on the relation of the marginal propensities to import and save in each of the trading countries and on their relation to each other. The third "level" might proceed on the assumption that the different countries aim at maintaining domestic full employment policies, and that some countries succeed in doing so, even in the face of the failure of others. This, as was shown, requires that the reduction in the foreign balances of countries other than A should be offset by corresponding increases in their domestic investments, in which case the size of the imbalances generated will depend entirely on the relation of the marginal propensities to import and to save in country A, and on the amount by which its domestic investment has fallen.

Two conclusions emerge from this. This first is that the extent to which investment fluctuations in one country affect the employment and income levels of the others is inversely related to the extent to which that country creates balance of payments difficulties for the others. At one extreme, with a sufficient compensating increase in the domestic investment of other countries, reductions in their employment and income levels may be entirely avoided.[1] In that case the international impact of cyclical move-

---

[1] I am ignoring here the complications that arise owing to the specificity of particular industries, as a result of which a rise in domestic investment, however large, may not fully compensate (in terms of employment or output) for a fall in the output of export industries.

ments will be entirely confined to changes in current account balances; a fall in real incomes in other countries will only occur as a result of their inability (or unwillingness) to finance the resulting imbalances out of their liquid reserves and to maintain their customary scale of imports.[1] At the other extreme, balance of payments disequilibria may be entirely avoided, but only at the cost of magnifying the investment fluctuations of some countries into proportionate fluctuations in world investment as a whole—i.e. by allowing incomes and employment to fluctuate in all countries to an equal degree.[2] From the point of view of any particular country the desire to reduce the internal impact of external fluctuations in demand must always run counter to the desire, or need, to preserve external payments equilibrium.

The second, and rather obvious, conclusion is that the "classical" method of maintaining international payments equilibrium by means of domestic investment variations—whatever views one may hold of its appropriateness in a world where total world investment is maintained constant—is wholly inappropriate as a means of combating the balance of payments problem arising out of cyclical fluctuations. This is not only because it is bound to be inconsistent with the requirements of internal economic stability. It is mainly because the very use of the method is bound to increase the severity of the cyclical movement in the countries which suffer from it, and hence must be creative of added balance of payments disequilibria in the process of trying to eliminate them. If the domestic investments of the different countries could be regarded as being determined independently of each other, this of course would not be so. The balance of payments effects of a fall in domestic investment in A could then be eliminated by a

[1] This, in a sense, is the exact reverse of the situation postulated by the classical mechanism where the pattern of local investments is continually so adjusted as to preserve international payments equilibrium. Here the changes in the pattern (caused by endogenous variations in the local investments of some countries coupled with the desire of the others to maintain internal economic stability) are the cause of the disequilibria in international payments. It is worth pointing out, however, that the *maximum* international imbalance that may be generated as a result of a successful stabilisation policy can only be a fraction of the fall in domestic investment of those countries whose domestic investment has fallen.

[2] For reasons mentioned on p. 11, the preservation of balance of payments equilibrium may for some countries require a more than proportionate contraction in domestic investment.

reduction in the domestic investments of *B, C, D* . . . that would restore the appropriate relations between investment levels necessary for the preservation of payments equilibrium. But the very assumption of the domestic investment of *A* being subject to cyclical influences *implies* that it must be sensitive to changes in the general level of demand; so that any reduction in the total of world investment must exert a further depressing influence on the rate of domestic investment in *A*. The attempt to use the classical method in this case might therefore lead to an indefinite process of contraction (or in the reverse case, expansion) of world investment without fully re-establishing international payments equilibrium at any particular stage. The reduction in domestic investments of *B, C, D* . . . *enforced* by the fall in domestic investment in *A*, might in turn *induce* a further contraction of investment in *A*, that would in turn *enforce* a further reduction in *B, C, D* . . . and so on. Even in the absence of such a chain reaction, the effect of enforced variations would clearly be additive to the effects of induced or spontaneous variations, and the attempt to preserve international payments equilibrium in the course of the cycle would be bound to make the magnitude of the world cyclical movement far greater than if the disequilibria in payments balances generated by the cyclical movement had been allowed to develop freely.

III. METHODS OF COMBATING THE PROPAGATION OF CYCLICAL MOVEMENTS

From the point of view of the maintenance of stable employment and income levels the international character of the business cycle does not raise problems different from those which arise when the cycle is considered in relation to a single "economy." The nature and the effectiveness of counter-cyclical devices may be pretty much the same, irrespective of whether the cyclical tendencies originate from forces endogenous to the national economy, or are propagated from outside. The novel feature arising out of the division of the world into different political areas is that the effective use of counter-cyclical policies involves the ability of the stabilising authority to incur debt in terms of other currencies, and not only of its own. If governments had the same power to borrow in terms of foreign currencies as in terms of their own, the finance of cyclical balance of payments deficits would be fully analogous to that of the finance of cyclical budgetary deficits. Lacking such power, the pursuit of stabilisation policies by any single country presupposes an adequate international currency reserve which is operated counter-cyclically— i.e. allowed to run down in depression years and replenished in boom years. The size of the problem confronting any particular country depends of course on its size in relation to the world economy as a whole, and on the extent to which the cyclical movement it is confronted with embraces the others. Contracyclical policies pursued by large countries are far more effective in preventing or minimising the international spread of the cycle than the policies of small countries.

Thus it would not be disputed that in present circumstances a policy by the United States of maintaining income and employment levels stable within its own territory would, if pursued effectively, alone suffice to confine possible fluctuations in world trade to minor dimensions. This is not to suggest that in that case investment fluctuations would not occur at all in other areas; but with the United States "holding out" against their spread, destabilising movements emanating from particular areas could hardly gather any great international momentum. Moreover, any variation in the level of domestic investment necessary to compensate for the impact of possible fluctuations elsewhere could be carried out without undue strain on the American economy;[1] and without any strain on U.S. monetary reserves.[2] A similar policy pursued by any other country in isolation would be far less effective in combating the international spread of the movement; while, with the present distribution of the world's

[1] Since it is estimated that two-thirds of world investment (outside the U.S.S.R.) is accounted for by U.S. domestic investment, a 20 per cent. reduction in the level of domestic investment by all countries other than the United States could be compensated (from the point of view of the U.S. economy) by a less than 10 per cent. expansion in U.S. domestic investment.

[2] The effects on the U.S. balance of payments of a 20 per cent. reduction in investment in all countries other than the United States could not exceed 3–4 billion dollars annually, while U.S. gold reserves are around 20 billion. (This ignores, of course, that since the war the U.S. balance of payments was in a continual surplus of around 6 billion dollars annually—financed largely through U.S. Governmental aid—so that fluctuations in the current balance of the above magnitude would be within the range of that surplus and would not necessarily involve a recourse to reserves.)

gold reserves, the policy might be impracticable even if all other countries acted in concert.[1]

The problem of combating the international propagation of cyclical movements cannot therefore be sensibly discussed, even on a purely theoretical plane, without specifying whether the kind of problem to be considered is that of the United States combating cyclical influences emanating from other countries (such as Britain, Belgium or Germany) or whether it is that of the other countries (singly or in co-operation) attempting to combat cyclical influences emanating from the United States. The former (from a U.S. point of view) does not really give rise to problems different from those generally involved in domestic economic stabilisation. The latter presents an extremely intricate problem. In fact, it would be generally agreed that the outside world could not possibly avoid being adversely affected by a cyclical down-swing in the U.S. economy; the question is merely by what methods and policies its impact could be minimised.

This question can be considered in two stages: from the point of view of minimising the loss of production and trade within the other countries as a group; and from the point of view of minimising the loss of real income arising out of the diminished ability to purchase goods from the United States.

The first problem is that of preventing, or minimising, reductions in the level of domestic investment in the non-dollar countries and of avoiding unnecessary restriction of trade. If the level of domestic investment could be maintained, and trade restrictions between the various countries of the group avoided, the loss of employment and output would be confined to the reduction of exports to the United States, and the loss of real income to the reduction of imports from the United States made necessary by the reduction of dollar receipts from trade, plus such "dollar aid" as may be forthcoming.

In principle these results could be secured by a simultaneous devaluation of all non-dollar currencies in terms of dollars that would be adequate to restore equilibrium in the accounts of the non-dollar with the dollar world, at the given domestic

[1] The total monetary gold stocks outside the United States are not much greater than the estimated short-fall in the supply of dollars in a single year that might follow a medium-sized U.S. recession.

investment levels of non-dollar countries. The required degree of devaluation, however, might have to be extremely severe; and it might well involve a reduction in the total dollar value of exports to the United States, so that its buying power in terms of U.S. goods might be even smaller than before. In other words, the balances in the dollar accounts might only be achieved at a very low level of U.S. exports, involving both additional losses in output to the United States and added losses of real income to the outside world. It must also be borne in mind that large-scale devaluations of the non-dollar currencies might easily set up perverse speculative movements in funds to the Dollar Area (which governmental controls of capital movements are not able wholly to prevent) especially if the requisite degree of devaluation, necessarily a matter of trial and error, could not be achieved at one stroke, but only in stages.

The alternative is some system of discriminatory[1] restriction on imports from the Dollar Area that cuts down the level of imports to the available supply of dollars without restricting trading conditions between the other countries. If each country aimed at restricting its dollar imports to its own dollar income, and renounced the possibility of obtaining dollars through triangular trade, such discriminatory restrictions could be operated without causing a downward pressure on the trade between other countries. But as long as the settling of balances between other countries continues to involve some form of ultimate settlement in gold or dollars, it is difficult to see how a generalisation of restrictionist pressure could be entirely avoided, even though with various devices it might be minimised. A detailed consideration of these questions is, however, beyond the scope of this essay.

It only remains to point out that a system under which each country guaranteed a certain annual supply of its own currency to the outside world (offsetting, by long-term loans or gifts, any short-fall of its payments on current account) is greatly superior to all other conceivable devices for minimising the international impact of business cycles. But for reasons advanced above, the

---

[1] The term "discriminatory" is used here in a purely technical sense, since in an economic sense the alternative of a simultaneous devaluation of non-dollar currencies is of course equally "discriminatory." (It implies a change in trading conditions with the Dollar Area without a corresponding change in trading conditions between other areas.)

introduction of such a system would involve a far more genuine additional obligation by the United States than by any of the other countries which might formally assume it: a defect which makes its persistent advocacy by countries or persons outside the United States somewhat difficult!

APPENDIX

The proposition that the change in trade balances following upon a given international shift in investments will necessarily be smaller than the shift in the distribution of investments, so that the elimination of a given imbalance will require a (quantitatively) larger shift in investments, can be demonstrated as follows.

(1) Let us assume two countries, A and B (where B can also stand for all countries other than A taken together). A's foreign balance with B (F_A) will be affected both by the reduction in A's investment (ΔI_A) and the increase in B's (ΔI_B), each of which will react on B's balance. (These reactions will be denoted as ΔF_{A1} and ΔF_{A2}). The problem is to show that if

$$\Delta I_A = -\Delta I_B,$$
$$\Delta F_{A1} + \Delta F_{A2} < \Delta I_A.$$

(2) We shall first examine the change in A's balance with respect to an isolated change in A's home investment (B's investment being given). Writing c_1, m_1, s_1, for A's marginal propensities to consume, import and save respectively, so that

$$c_1 + m_1 + s_1 = 1,$$

the change in A's income, ΔY_A, according to the multiplier formula, is

$$\frac{1}{1 - c_1}\Delta I_A, \quad \text{or} \quad \frac{1}{m_1 + s_1}\Delta I_A.$$

Consequent upon the change in income, ΔY_A, there will be a change in imports, $m_1\Delta Y_A$, so that *assuming A's exports as given*, the change in A's balance as a function of the change in investment becomes

$$\Delta F_{A1} = \frac{m_1}{m_1 + s_1}\Delta I_A, \quad \text{or writing} \quad k_1 = \frac{m_1}{m_1 + s_1},$$
$$= k_1\Delta I_A. \qquad \cdot \qquad \cdot \qquad \cdot \qquad \cdot \qquad \cdot \quad (1)$$

The magnitude of k thus depends on the relation of m and s; it will approach unity as s approaches zero, and it will be all the smaller, the larger is s in relation to m.

(3) The change in A's imports, $k_1 \Delta I_A$, implies however an equivalent change in B's exports which, *assuming B's home investment to be given*, will cause a change in B's income (writing c_2, m_2, s_2, for B's propensities)

$$\Delta Y_B = \frac{1}{m_2 + s_2}(k_1 \Delta I_A),$$

the reaction of which on B's imports can be written

$$\frac{m_2}{m_2 + s_2}(k_1 \Delta I_A), \quad \text{or, writing} \quad k_2 = \frac{m_2}{m_2 + s_2},$$

$$k_2(k_1 \Delta I_A) \quad . \qquad . \qquad . \qquad . \quad (2)$$

which evidently implies a secondary change in A's foreign balance of a reverse sign. This in turn causes a tertiary change in A's income (assuming A's investment to be given) and so on. The total change in A's balance, following a change in A's investment, ΔI_A, is therefore given by the following series:

$$\begin{aligned}
\Delta F_{A1} &= k_1 \Delta I_A - k_2(k_1 \Delta I_A) + k_1[k_2(k_1 \Delta I_A)] - \ldots \\
&= \{k_1 - k_2 k_1 + k_1 k_2 k_1 - k_2 k_1 k_2 k_1 + \ldots\} \Delta I_A \\
&= \{k_1 + k_1 k_2 k_1 + \ldots\} \Delta I_A - \{k_1 k_2 + (k_1 k_2)k_1 k_2 + \ldots\} \Delta I_A \\
&= \frac{k_1(1 - k_2)}{1 - k_1 k_2} \Delta I_A. \qquad . \qquad . \qquad . \qquad . \quad (3)
\end{aligned}$$

(4) Assuming that A's and B's propensities are equal, so that

$$k_1 = k_2 = k,$$

the above equation (3) can be written

$$\Delta F_{A1} = (k - k^2 + k^3 - k^4 + \ldots)\Delta I_A = \frac{k}{1+k}\Delta I_A . \qquad . \quad (4)$$

The latter expression must be less than $\frac{1}{2}$, if $k < 1$; in fact it approaches $\frac{1}{2}$, as k approaches unity.[1] Hence *whatever the value of* k,

$$\Delta F_{A1} \leq \frac{1}{2}\Delta I_A. \qquad . \qquad . \qquad . \quad (5)$$

[1] The evident reason for this is that the sum of the negative items in equation (3) must always be less than the sum of the positive items, if $k < 1$; but they must exceed $k/2$, if $k > \frac{1}{2}$.

(5) The effects of a change in investment in B must be analogous (with a reverse sign) to that of a change in investment in A. By analogous reasoning,

$$-\Delta F_{A_2} = \{k_2 - k_1 k_2 + k_2 k_1 k_2 - \ldots\}\Delta I_B$$

$$= \frac{k_2(1 - k_1)}{1 - k_1 k_2}\Delta I_B \qquad . \qquad . \qquad . \qquad . \qquad (6)$$

(6) Assuming, again, that $k_1 = k_2 = k$,

$$-\Delta F_{A_2} = \frac{k}{1 + k}\Delta I_B < \tfrac{1}{2}\Delta I_B$$

so that if

$$\Delta I_A = -\Delta I_B,$$

$$\Delta F_{A_1} + \Delta F_{A_2} < \Delta I_A \qquad . \qquad . \qquad . \qquad (7)$$

(7) This conclusion has only been demonstrated so far on the assumption that A's and B's propensities are identical. It can easily be shown, however, that differences in these propensities cannot affect the result. In the general case (as shown by equations (3) and (6)), if

$$\Delta I_A = -\Delta I_B,$$

$$\Delta F_{A_1} = \Delta F_{A_2} = \left\{\frac{k_1(1 - k_2)}{1 - k_1 k_2} + \frac{k_2(1 - k_1)}{1 - k_1 k_2}\right\}\Delta I_A \qquad . \qquad (8)$$

If k_2 is large relatively to k_1, the second term in this expression (representing ΔF_{A_2}) becomes larger than it would be under the assumption that the propensities are equal; in fact, as k_1 approaches 0, the second term approaches k_2. At the same time, the first term of the expression (ΔF_{A_1}) becomes correspondingly smaller; and its decrease must necessarily offset the increase in the second term. Similarly, if k_1 is large relatively to k_2, the first term of the equation can be larger than $\tfrac{1}{2}$, but the second term becomes correspondingly smaller; as k_2 approaches zero, the first term approaches k_1 and the second term approaches zero. Hence the validity of equation (7) cannot be affected by differences in the propensities of A and B.

If B maintains its investment constant, in the face of a change in home investment in A, the change in the balance is that given in equation (3), which, as we have seen, can be greater than $\frac{1}{2}$ (if A's and B's propensities differ) though it must necessarily be less than 1.

If B follows a "full employment policy"—i.e. expands its domestic investment by whatever is necessary to maintain income and employment in B constant, then

$$\Delta I_B = -k_1 \Delta I_A,$$

since this is the change in home investment which just offsets the primary decrease in exports. In this case the consequences of B's change in investment on A's balance must be numerically equal (with a reverse sign) to the secondary and further terms of equation (3), so that

$$\Delta F_{A1} + \Delta F_{A2} = k_1 \Delta I_A.$$

If k_1 and k_2 are both positive and less than unity, this will be necessarily greater than the change in balance under the assumption that B's investment is constant, and also necessarily less than that shown in equation (7)—i.e. assuming a change in home investment in B that exactly offsets the change in investment in A.

15

FOREIGN TRADE AND THE BALANCE OF PAYMENTS[1]

THE problem of Britain's international economic position has two aspects. One concerns the structure of the British economy and the other the nature of her external economic relations. Britain is vitally interested in stable trading conditions, in expanding markets for her goods and expanding supplies of raw materials, without which her internal economy could not prosper. She is therefore concerned in securing the best political framework for international economic relations for the sake of the development of the British, as well as the world, economy.

But the most ideal trading conditions are unavailing if we are not in a position to produce and deliver sufficient goods to cover our import needs. There is, therefore, the complementary and equally vital problem of adapting the internal economic structure to the need for sufficient exports.

A. THE INTERNAL PROBLEM

Few would dispute the fact that the major reason for Britain's external problem since the war has been that our post-war exports have been inadequate. Over the six post-war years, 1946–51, our balance of payments on current account was effectively in surplus only in one year (1950) and over the six-year period the aggregate deficiency on current account amounted to £1,658 million or over 10 per cent. of the imports of goods and services during the whole period. In 1951, which was an exceptionally unfavourable year, the current account deficit amounted to over 13 per cent. of imports and would have required a 17 per cent. higher export volume to cover it.

This was despite the fact that the performance of our export trade, judged by pre-war standards, was very impressive. The target of an increase of 75 per cent. over the pre-war volume of

1 An essay written for the Fabian Society in 1952 and not previously published.

exports was attained by 1950. At the same time the volume of imports, despite the much higher rate of national income, has never exceeded pre-war levels. The main reason why even these high export figures were insufficient was the deterioration in the terms of trade since the war which was much greater than anyone had expected and was in marked contrast to the experience after the First World War. This was fundamentally due to the fact that the world supplies of food and raw materials failed to keep pace with the tremendous expansion in world industrial production, causing a considerable shift in the relation of world prices of foodstuffs and raw materials to those of manufactures.

It is important to bear in mind the world-wide character of these changes in price relationships which had nothing to do with the policies pursued by Britain or any other single country. In fact, owing to Britain's policies of bulk buying and long term contracts, she had been buying foodstuffs and raw materials at considerably lower prices than she would have had to pay in free markets. The deterioration in Britain's terms of trade was therefore considerably less (and probably still is less) than would correspond to the changed relationship in world prices.

It should also be borne in mind that the mere avoidance of balance of payments deficits is by no means enough. We must aim at a surplus; partly because our present reserves are inadequate, but mainly because we must assist in the development of under-developed areas. It is only through the continuous expansion of the world economy that progress in Britain's own economy can be ensured. The growth in Britain's economy over the past 150 years, and her present high density of population, was only made possible through the continued expansion in the exportable surpluses of food and raw materials of the rest of the world—which was only secured, in turn, by a continuous process of foreign investment. There is no reason to suppose that the need for foreign investment to secure this continued expansion is any less today than it was in the past; or that Britain's former role as a financier can now be handed over to other nations, such as America. American foreign investment since the war—if we disregard the special measures of economic assistance to Europe —has been largely concentrated in fields where it served her own particular interests (as e.g. in oilfields). Even if American foreign investment for development were to be much greater in the future than in the past, there is no reason to suppose that it will be so directed as to suit the particular interests of the British economy. Added to this is the important consideration that the trade policies which would best serve Britain's interests (discussed below) can be promoted far more easily in conditions in which Britain is again an important source of long-term international lending.

In the past, in good years, Britain's balance of payments surplus available for foreign investment amounted to as much as 20 per cent. of her imports or more. If we were to aim at a 10 per cent. surplus, this would require a current account surplus of £400 million (the target aimed at in the long-term plan of 1947, but never carried out owing to the deterioration in the terms of trade); but it would be far more desirable to aim at a surplus of at least 15 per cent. of imports, or some £600 million. This means—assuming that the terms of trade remain at the average of the last two years—that the volume of our exports should be not 17, but at least 33 per cent. higher: the necessary export target should have been not 175 per cent., but 230–40 per cent. of pre-war.

Now whatever may be the situation in the future, our exports since the war have generally (except in the current year) not been limited by markets, but by the capacity of British industries to supply goods. This is certainly true of the metals and engineering industries, (which now account for about a half of the total exports), whose order books in some cases extend to years. But it was also true, until recently, of the light industries, though to a much lesser extent.

Greater exports would only have been possible, therefore, by higher production or reduced domestic consumption. But, in the fields of metals and engineering, lower domestic consumption would have meant lower domestic investment; and since our domestic investment had already been less than adequate for maintaining or improving the competitive efficiency of British industry, a further restriction of domestic investment for the sake of exports would have been a rather shortsighted policy. In the field of light industries, particularly textiles, a reduction in domestic consumption would no doubt have made higher exports possible in the years 1947–50—although it is difficult to say by how much, since the potential demand for these products has never been so much in excess of supply as in the case of engineering products. But this is certainly no longer true today; and it is doubtful, in view of the development of light industries everywhere and the emergence of new exporters, whether it would be possible to raise the volume of exports in these fields at all significantly in the future. We must mainly rely, therefore, for the necessary increase in exports on the heavy industries, particularly coal, steel and engineering.

The main cause of the insufficiency in exports must be sought therefore not so much in excessive domestic consumption or insufficiently restrictive monetary policies, but in the inadequate adaptation of the structure of the British economy to the changed character of world trade and the changed trading conditions of Britain.[1] A more restrictive monetary policy could only have improved the situation fundamentally through a drastic curtailment of domestic investment, but for that very reason it would have retarded, rather than accelerated, the necessary adaptation in the British economic structure. For, apart from the case of coal, where production was essentially limited over most of the post-war period by the shortage of miners, increased export capacity is primarily a matter of capital investment in the heavy industries. It requires more steel for increasing the production capacity of the steel industry, for increasing the capacity of the engineering industries, and for increasing the through-put of these industries.

Britain's steel producing capacity has expanded by some 25 per cent. since the war, from 12 to 16 million tons. This is not a very impressive figure when account is taken of the fact that American steel capacity has expanded by some 70–80 per cent. over the same period, Russian steel capacity has probably doubled, and even Germany plans to produce some 25 per cent. more

---

[1] This is not to say that lower domestic consumption would not have been necessary in order to increase investment. But this is different from the suggestion sometimes put forward that a reduction of domestic consumption would have directly promoted exports.

steel next year than her pre-war output (on the present territory).

To make Britain's international economic position secure means having sufficient export capacity to provide for a large surplus in the balance of payments. This requires in essence nothing short of doubling the present export capacity in the heavy industries. In turn this requires an annual steel output (for both domestic requirements and exports) which is not much short of 25 million tons a year and a correspondingly large concentration of our manpower resources in the steel-using industries.[1] An increase in steel and engineering production of this dimension would also require 250–60 million tons of coal—or rather, an annual output of near 300 million tons, if the valuable export market for British coal in Europe is to be fully exploited.

The main criticism that can be made therefore against the post-war economic policies of Britain is not that she travelled on the wrong road, but that she travelled on the right road far too slowly. The sights of post-war economic planning were not raised high enough.[2] There has been a great deal of investment in steel and in the engineering industries and the changes in manpower distribution show a much greater concentration on these industries than before the war. But there can be little doubt that if investment had been larger and the shift in man-power distribution greater, our position today would be far stronger; and

[1] Britain's steel industry concentrated in the past more on the finishing stages, so that our rolling mill capacity was (and still is) greater than that of crude steel, relying on imports for the difference. But the experience of the post-war years has shown that where steel is generally short, steel imports are difficult to obtain. It would be very unwise to make our export capacity in engineering products dependent on large-scale steel imports—quite apart from the loss of foreign exchange involved.

[2] In the case of steel, this was not due to any general shortage of resources, but simply to the fact that the Government accepted the development plan put forward by the steel industry without wishing to impose a more ambitious scheme of expansion than the steel industry deemed appropriate. Steel industrialists are notorious for a conservative estimation of future requirements, since they normally want to avoid excess capacity more than anything else. The reasons for this are to be sought not so much in the fact that the existence of excess capacity in itself lowers the *rate* of profit earned on capital, but in the far more serious factor that despite cartel-arrangements of various kinds, only full capacity operation affords any real protection against the danger of price cutting. From a national point of view, on the other hand, there is much to be said in favour of, and very little against, the maintenance of considerable excess capacity in the industry: since this permits a flexibility of adjustment not attainable otherwise. In the case of the U.S., Canada and many other countries, the expansion in steel capacity was sometimes only brought about at the insistence of the Government, and against the wishes of the industry; and this factor provides the most important argument in favour of the nationalisation of the steel industry.

it is not easy to think of any other method by which the position could have been strengthened.

Steel and engineering must remain the mainstay of British exports, not only because they make proportionately far greater use of indigenous materials than other industries, but because it is the one field where continued expansion in the world export markets can be relied upon. With the industrialisation of the less developed areas, the markets for light industries are bound to shrink, but for that very reason the markets for steel and machinery are bound to expand; moreover, the export demand for these products can be *stimulated* by foreign investment. This is not to deny that in the case of a recurrence of a general economic depression of the kind of the 1930's the demand for these products might not collapse to a far greater degree than the demand for the products of the consumer goods industries. But the point is that with sufficient export capacity in these industries, we should be in a position to prevent such a collapse of our customers' effective demand. Hence only a large increase in the capacity of these industries offers a chance of carrying out an effective economic stabilisation policy, both for Britain and for her trading partners.

B. THE PROBLEM OF TRADE POLICIES

While an enlarged export capacity is thus the *sine qua non* of any lasting solution of Britain's balance of payments problem, its actual solution will greatly depend also on the trading and monetary policies followed by Britain and her trading partners. It is to the second aspect of the question that we must now turn.

The world-wide economic depression of the 1930's witnessed a severe shrinkage in the volume of world trade, and was accompanied both by the breakdown of the traditional international monetary mechanism, the gold standard, and the growth of restrictions on trade (in the form of new or higher tariffs or quantitative import quotas) of various kinds. Some countries, (such as Britain), adopted the policy of freely variable exchange rates modified only by the operation of an Exchange Equaiisation Fund. Others (such as Germany) maintained fixed exchange rates, but introduced controls on exchange transactions and permitted the purchase of currency at special and varying discounts for particular purposes. These amounted to the adoption of discriminatory restrictions on imports, according to the country of origin of the commodities; and also discriminatory subsidies on exports, according to the country of destination. With the outbreak of the war, measures of exchange control, and the quantitative control of imports by means of a licensing system, became fairly general throughout the world.

These new discriminatory trading practices which emerged in a rather haphazard manner in the course of the 1930's were often regarded as a direct cause of the shrinkage in world trade and of the general instability in trading conditions. In fact, they should have been looked upon as the consequence, rather than the cause, of the shrinkage in trade. Many of these devices served the purpose of minimising the impact of world-wide deflationary pressure; of enabling particular groups of countries to maintain their volume of trade at a higher level than would have been possible otherwise, and to engage in internal expansionary policies. However that may be, there emerged during the war a fairly general desire among the Western belligerents to evolve a new set of rules governing international trade—a new code of economic behaviour—which would secure the framework for an orderly expansion of world trade in the post-war period. The Bretton Woods agreement (which set up the International Monetary Fund and the International Bank) and the proposed International Trade Charter (which has never reached the stage of ratification, though it led to the adoption of tariff arrangements under G.A.T.T.) were the products of this. The purpose of these agreements was to re-establish, more or less, the trading system as it existed prior to 1929—but with certain safeguards to minimise its shortcomings, and to rule out certain practices which were thought to have a disruptive and destructive influence on international trade. The main provisions of these agreements were to re-establish the general convertibility of currencies on current transactions; to establish a new international régime of fixed exchange rates (subject, however, to the proviso that an adjustment of the exchange rate of particular countries can be authorised by international consent); the abolition of all quantitative import restrictions; the stabilisation and, if possible, the reduction of import duties; the elimination of differential duties (such as Imperial Preference) and of discriminatory measures of all kinds.

In Britain these agreements were not accepted without considerable controversy. There was general agreement that Britain, as a great trading nation, stood to benefit pre-eminently from any set of measures designed to facilitate international trade. It was a matter of doubt, however, whether the policies of multilateralism—i.e. the general inter-convertibility of currencies and the absence of discriminatory measures of all kinds—were appropriate ways of increasing the volume of international trade or of creating the pre-conditions of stability and progress in the international field.

In the intervening six years, the provisions of the Bretton Woods agreement and of the Havana Charter have remained very largely a dead letter. Britain, like other countries, has remained formally wedded to the philosophy embodied in these agreements as a long-run aim of her economic policy. She, like others, has pleaded the absence of "normality" in international economic relations for the failure to put the provisions of these agreements into force. But the conditions of "normality" which would permit or justify their adoption were never properly defined; and it is questionable whether the fiction of the ultimate desirability of these objectives should be maintained since its very existence tends to block the way to the creation of alternative policies of a more permanent character. It is important therefore to re-examine the issues of the "multilateralism versus bilateralism" controversy and to attempt to answer the question: what are the appropriate international trading policies which Britain should endeavour to promote?

The Advantages of Multilateralism

The philosophy of multilateralism is the philosophy of universal free trade: both rest upon the same premises. If it is correct to say that it is advantageous to a country to import commodities from abroad in all cases in which commodities would in fact be imported in the absence of any impediment, it equally follows that it is advantageous for that country to trade "multilaterally"

—i.e. to buy in the cheapest market and to sell in the dearest market—without any regard to the relation between purchases and sales in the trade with any particular foreign country. It is thus the policy of "freely multilateral" trade which, according to this theory, maximises the advantages of the international division of labour. Moreover, if the ideal of completely free trade is for some reason or other unattainable, it remains true, that it is according to this theory, better, from the point of view of any particular trading country, if the restrictions on trade are applied in a universal and non-discriminatory manner, than if that country discriminates in the application of restrictions as between commodities coming from different areas. For in the latter case trade will not merely be restricted but also diverted from its most profitable channels. Any discriminatory measure therefore, whether it is the result of preferential treatment in the matter of import duties or of currency allocations (under exchange control) must result in an additional loss of wealth over and above the loss caused by the existence of restrictions as such.

The shortcomings of this doctrine partly arise from the basic limitations of free trade theory as such and partly from its particular application to the problem of multilateral trade.

It was known for a long time that the theory of free trade is subject to at least two large qualifications—though the advocates of the theory tended to minimise their practical importance.

The first qualification amounts to saying that where an economically less highly developed country A trades freely with a more developed country B, this may put obstacles to the development of A without any compensating advantage to the world as a whole. Let us suppose that under free trade A exports raw cotton and imports cotton goods manufactured by B, since such cotton goods are cheaper in terms of raw cotton than similar goods would be if manufactured in A. The theory of free trade presupposes that under these conditions both A and the world as a whole (meaning in this case A and B together) will be better off—in the sense of having more of both raw cotton and cotton goods—than if A restricted her imports from B and manufactured cotton goods herself. This will be so because the manufacture of cotton goods in country A will involve a transference of resources from the making of raw cotton to that of cotton goods that will reduce the output of raw cotton for any given quantity of cotton goods produced by more than the amount of raw cotton that would have had to be given up in exchange for procuring the same amount of cotton goods from B. It is quite possible, however, that the production of cotton goods in A would not, in fact, reduce the output of raw cotton at all or it might reduce it, but only by very little—something very much less than what would be indicated by the money costs relationship for cotton goods and raw cotton, in country A. This would be the case, for example, if the output of raw cotton in A were limited by the area available for cultivation rather than the amount of labour available for its production. The production of cotton goods may require a great deal of labour, but very little land, so that if labour is freely available to cotton goods production, the output of cotton goods will not result in a reduction in raw cotton production at all. Free trade theory pre-supposes that the money costs of production accurately reflect the real cost in terms of foregone alternatives. But for any country that suffers from disguised unemployment in the form of surplus population on the land, free trade is by no means the best policy and restrictions on imports are thoroughly justified from the point of view of the world as a whole, and not only of that of the protecting country. This is particularly true in cases where the trade consists of the exchange of products of pre-capitalist enter-prise (i.e. primary products) for products of capitalistic enter-prise (i.e. manufactures), for as between the products of the capitalist and the non-capitalist sector, comparative money cost is a very poor guide to comparative real cost.

The second qualification relates not to the imperfection of the price mechanism for allocating resources to the best uses, but to its consequences as regards the changing distribution of income between various areas. Even if the price mechanism registered correctly the true attractiveness of various alternatives, it is per-fectly possible that its unimpeded operation would from time to time impoverish some areas and unwittingly enrich others. It is of course a well-known feature of the functioning of capitalism that the price changes in the market that are necessary for main-taining a continued balance between supply and demand cause haphazard shifts in the distribution of income between various individuals or economic groups. When such shifts take place within the economy of a single nation, and when they are none too violent, they are accepted as part of the ordinary give-and-take of the operation of free markets—as the inevitable consequence of using the market mechanism as the directing agent in the use and allocation of resources. But when the market mechanism induces such shifts in the economic relations between different nations, it is likely to produce queer results. If a particular country happens to have large exportable surpluses of certain essential goods, but has no corresponding deficiencies of such goods, the free market can only produce a balance in the economic relations with the rest of the world in one of two ways: *either* by raising the price of its exportable commodities to the point where the outside world, however desirous of having them, can no longer afford to buy them; or by lowering the price of importable commodities coming from the outside world to the point where the country, although not particularly desirous of having them, is nevertheless induced to buy them. Depending on the urgency of the need on the one side and the absence of such need on the other, the equilibrium resulting from the free operation of market forces may be arbitrary or artificial—in the sense that the resulting ratio in which commodities exchanged with one another need bear no relationship to either the amount, or the productivity, of the resources involved in producing them.

To put the same point in another way: the operation of free trade may be said to produce *reasonable* results whenever the resulting "terms of trade" (i.e. the ratio of prices of the commodities bought and sold in international trade) fairly reflect the differences in the productivity of labour between the different trading areas. If, for example, the product of one hour's labour in country *A* exchanges for the product of three hours' labour of country *B*, the result may be said to be reasonable if the output per man-hour over the field of industry in general is about three times as high in *A* as in *B*. In the trade between structurally balanced economies this result may by and large tend to be satisfied. But if there is no such structural balance—if a genuine complementarity of needs is lacking—reliance on the free market might produce absurd results—e.g., in terms of the above example, if the product of one hour's labour of A were to be exchanged for the product of ten or twenty hours' labour of B. Moreover in such cases B's capacity to buy A's goods out of the proceeds of its own exports to A might well be considerably less, under a régime of free trade, than it would need to be otherwise. If a reduction in B's price failed to raise the demand for B's goods sufficiently to increase the *total* proceeds from exports, B may have to reduce its demand for A's goods by more than if it had not reduced its own price at all. Clearly it is more sensible in such cases for B to restrict its imports directly from A than to rely on the free price mechanism to bring about a reduction.[1]

A third important consideration, related to the above, is the high degree of sensitivity, under free trade, of the internal economy of any particular country to fluctuations in demand emanating from others. If A buys less from B on account of a general contraction of demand in A, B may be forced to buy correspondingly less from A (unless it possesses adequate liquid resources to finance the difference). Under free trade this may happen to some extent automatically since the very reduction in the demand for these goods may set up similar tendencies to contraction in B's economy. But to the extent that the induced contraction in B's demand is not sufficient to restore the balance automatically, B may be forced to impose on itself, by measures of monetary policy, a degree of deflation similar to that experienced in A. Here again it would be a more sensible policy for B to cut down its imports from A to whatever amount it could continue to afford, rather than to rely on the forces of deflation (spontaneous or induced) for bringing about the same result. Moreover, if we assumed the existence of three or more countries, one of which is subject to a spontaneous contraction of demand,

[1] This is not to deny a particular country might improve its real income through a policy of import restrictions, even if under free trade the terms of trade are "reasonable" in the above sense—i.e. lead to an equalisation of efficiency wages; in the latter case, however, there is a far greater presumption that the beneficial effects of protection may be nullified by retaliation on behalf of other countries. Where the effect of protection is merely to bring efficiency wages into equality, the scope for retaliation is less—in the same way in which a cartel formed to maintain prices need have much less fear of inviting competition by outsiders when the effect of its action is merely to prevent uneconomically low prices, than when it attempts to raise prices above costs of production.

it is clearly far better from the point of view of the other countries if such import restrictions are applied in a discriminatory manner (i.e. directed only on goods coming from A) than in a non-discriminatory manner (i.e. are applied indiscriminately to goods coming from all sources), for in the latter case the unavoidable reduction in the volume of trade with A is unnecessarily extended to the trade between the other countries. In these cases, it is therefore only by means of discriminatory restrictions that a loss of trade following A's contraction of activity can be minimised. It would be a mistake to suppose, moreover, that A suffers any additional damage as a result of discriminatory restrictions applied to her goods, since in the final result A's exports will be limited by her imports and will be cut down in much the same way irrespective of whether the restrictions are of a discriminatory or non-discriminatory kind. It is only from the point of view of the other countries—which can maintain a higher level of trade among themselves in the one case than in the other—that the adoption of discriminatory policies makes a difference.

The Role of the United States in the World Economy

These propositions, but particularly the second and the third, have important applications when considered in the background of the world economic situation as it has developed since the war. The dominating influence of the United States in the world economy is too well known to require stress. From the point of view of the present analysis the most important consideration is the fact that the United States possesses large exportable surpluses in vital categories of primary products (such as cotton, wheat, tobacco, etc.). At the same time she is the world's largest supplier of manufactured goods, the greater part of which consists of vitally needed engineering products. Her import needs are confined, on the other hand, to a limited number of staple commodities.[1]

Given the fact that her import requirements in primary products are largely structurally determined, a balance in her trading relations could only be attained through America becoming an

[1] Over two-thirds of U.S. imports are concentrated on a dozen or so basic commodities, i.e. coffee, sugar, rubber, tin, copper, newsprint, etc.

importer of manufactured goods on a considerable scale. But American manufacturing capacity is in excess of domestic requirements in most fields of manufactures, so that from a structural point of view, America has no real deficiency in such products. Any considerable importation of manufactured goods—unless it could induce a corresponding increase in total domestic consumption, which is unlikely—must therefore be at the expense of domestic production. Such imports therefore are not only "nonessential" but may be positively harmful, since they may cause a net loss in national wealth. If the American public were to be induced to buy, say, foreign motor-cars to a point where it curtailed the production of domestic motor-cars, it would be a *sensible* policy for the American Government to erect additional barriers against their importation. This is because, although the foreign motor-cars may be cheaper in terms of *money cost* to the American consumer, they are bound to be dearer in terms of *real cost* to the American economy; since the labour and other resources which would no longer be required in domestic motor-car production would not be likely to be absorbed in alternative employments, but would be likely to remain idle (particularly since the same factor would be likely to restrict output not only in the motor-car industry, but in other related fields as well). In fact, bearing in mind the mode of operation of the economic system, it should be obvious that the importation of manufactured goods is only really advantageous to a country in situations in which the requirements of domestic consumption exceed domestic manufacturing capacity; and there can be little doubt that the bulk of the world trade in manufactures is subject to these conditions—it goes to countries where it *supplements* supplies from domestic sources rather than where it *replaces* them.

For these reasons it does not appear likely that America will become an important market for foreign manufactured goods in the foreseeable future. No doubt the sales of such goods could be extended by cheapening their price, but it is doubtful whether the sales would rise sufficiently to achieve a significant increase in the total dollar proceeds from such exports. The restoration of equilibrium through the free market process (which presupposes, in this case, that the non-dollar currencies are devalued in terms of the dollar to whatever extent found necessary to restore the balance), would therefore tend to operate mainly through inducing a contraction in the world's purchases of U.S. goods, rather than through increases of its sales in the U.S. In other words the free market mechanism could only bring about a balance by making American goods so expensive in terms of domestic incomes that people could no longer afford to buy them, however much they needed them. To the extent that the cheapening of prices of foreign goods would actually reduce the dollar proceeds of exports to the U.S., the ultimate reduction in purchases of U.S. goods, and the necessary "dearness" to secure this result, would have to be all the greater. The problem of an economic equilibrium between the U.S. and the rest of the world may provide a case therefore where reliance on the free market mechanism would not produce sensible results—since not only would the outside world be made poorer, but its ability to buy American goods might be considerably less than it would need to be, if the balance had been achieved through the imposition of discriminatory restrictions on the importation of U.S. goods on behalf of other countries. The latter kind of policies may therefore be basically justified if they secure a more healthy economic relationship between the U.S. and the rest of the world that is sure to redound in the long run to the benefit of the U.S. as well as to the benefit of the others.

That the use of such methods is in fact so justified has in recent years been increasingly recognised by the U.S. Administration itself—as revealed by its actions, if not its formal pronouncements. There have been several instances (as, for example, in connection with the creation of the European Payments Union) where the U.S. authorities have deliberately encouraged the development of discriminatory trading policies as a means of attaining "dollar viability." Since the war the world as a whole has been in a persistent deficit of about 6,000 million dollars a year in its current transactions with the U.S. This was financed largely through American generosity—the provision of financial aid by the U.S. Government to other governments in the form of the British Loan, Marshall Aid, the Mutual Security Aid, etc. Nobody desires these purely emergency arrangements to continue. They were vital to Europe at a time when the necessity for any sudden and large scale curtailment in purchases from America would have wrought havoc in the European economies; but they are symptoms of a fundamentally unhealthy situation, and their continuance is apt to postpone, rather than facilitate, fundamental adjustments which must sooner or later become necessary.

With the cessation of Extraordinary Aid, the world's purchases from the U.S. may have to be sharply curtailed. There can be little doubt that a deliberate and orderly policy of economising on dollar imports—of confining purchases from America to the most essential goods—is likely to produce far better results than reliance on "nature's cure," the price mechanism, which may cause a highly disturbing (and, to the U.S., embarrassing) shift in the world terms of trade with America, as a by-product of effecting this curtailment.[1]

There is, of course, the alternative view which regards this 6 billion surplus in the U.S. balance of payments as a reflection of the inability of the rest of the world "to live within its income," and not of any structural disharmonies between the U.S. economy and other countries. The dollar gap, on this view, is merely the consequence of inflationary tendencies in other countries (fostered by the very existence of discriminatory policies) which would disappear once these inflationary policies were halted. It is difficult, however, to reconcile this view of the situation with the facts; nor do the advocates of this view give any coherent account of how the cessation of inflationary tendencies would act to rectify the balance. It is rather naïve to suppose that the relatively low level of American imports merely reflects the inability of the rest of the world to withdraw commodities from domestic use. Anti-inflationary or deflationary measures in the rest of the world are not likely to have any appreciable effect on America's imports; nor could it be suggested that American exports consist largely of goods the demand for which is sensitive to inflationary or

---

[1] It is possible, of course, that America may wish to increase foreign investment for developmental purposes on a large scale, thus rendering a downward adjustment of trade unnecessary. But under present conditions foreign investment on any large scale is unlikely to come about automatically as a result of private enterprise; while public foreign investment will need to be carefully elaborated and its purpose clearly stated, if it is not to be regarded as the continuance of emergency aid under another guise.

deflationary tendencies. The world needs American wheat, cotton, tobacco, machinery, etc., not because it tolerates inflationary conditions, but because it is essentially short of them; and it would need very large doses of deflation—involving serious reductions in the level of production and employment in these countries—if the effective demand for these commodities were to be adequately curtailed by means of monetary measures.

There is, finally, the factor of cyclical instability. It is a well-known fact that since the beginning of this century at any rate, if not earlier, the character and timing of cyclical fluctuations in world trade and prices have been determined by the movement of the business cycle in the United States. To find an explanation for this there is no need to assume that the American economy is inherently more prone to cyclical fluctuations than the economies of other industrialised countries; it may simply have been due to the fact that owing to the very much greater size of American industry, the investment cycles of other countries have tended to get synchronised in time with the investment cycle of American industry. It does appear to be the case, however, that the extent to which the policy of internal economic stabilisation, by means of counter-cyclical economic policies, is likely to be carried, is less in the United States than in Britain and a number of other countries, because the extent of Government interference which a higher degree of stabilisation would involve is not likely to be approved of by the American public. Although imported commodities account for only a small proportion of America's national income, they amount to a large proportion (around 15 per cent.) of world trade, so that the fluctuations in American import demand cause significant changes in the total world demand for staple commodities.

Moreover, fluctuations in the general level of effective demand in America tend to have a disproportionate effect on the demand for imported goods, on account of the marginal character of import requirements in total supplies. Thus when, for example, the total demand for wool in America falls off, the reduction tends to be largely concentrated on that part of supplies which comes from abroad. This explains why fluctuations in American imports tended to be so much more violent in the past than the fluctuations in her national income. Thus between 1929 and 1932 a 52 per cent. reduction in the U.S. national income was associated with a 68 per cent. fall in the value of imports of goods and services; between 1937 and 1938 a 10 per cent. fall in the national income caused a 35 per cent. fall in the dollar value of imports, and so on. Since the war the fluctuations in the national income and the level of employment in the United States have been confined within relatively narrow limits; but even these relatively narrow fluctuations were associated with sizeable variations in the demand for imports. Thus, between the second half of 1948 and the first half of 1949 the value of imports fell by 20 per cent.; between the first half of 1949 and the first half of 1951 it rose by 100 per cent.; between the first half of 1951 and the second half of 1951 it fell by 20 per cent., and has since risen by 10 per cent. According to a recent estimate,[1] a medium-sized economic recession in the United States (such as that experienced between 1937 and 1938) would reduce the annual supply of dollars to the outside world by 10,000 million.

If countries outside the United States possessed ample gold reserves, they might be able to take such fluctuations in their stride without being forced to contract their imports in consequence. In fact, the world's total monetary gold stocks outside the United States hardly amount to one-quarter of the value of their annual imports. The biennial dollar crises since the war—which were partly caused by the fluctuations in the world demand for American exports—have invariably necessitated more or less immediate measures of import restriction. Owing to the existence of non-convertibility, such measures (until recently) were largely concentrated on imports from the dollar area; but with a system of convertible currencies they would have to be generalised and would thus exert a far greater unsteadying effect on the world economy. In fact, a system of convertible currencies, even if reintroduced, would hardly be able to stand up for long to the strain of such fluctuations in the world dollar requirements which are bound to recur from time to time.

The problem of the re-establishment of multilateral trade and general currency convertibility thus centres around two questions:

[1] *Measures for International Economic Stability*, United Nations, 1952.

the problem of attaining a reasonable balance in transactions with the dollar area, and the problem of the instability in the supply of dollars.

So long as the world's dependence on dollar goods is as great as at present, the continuance of *some form* of discrimination against dollar imports appears unavoidable as a means of restricting the demand for dollars to the available supply. For if such discrimination were to cease, the demand for dollars would have to be curtailed *either* by means of a general curtailment of demand— i.e. deflation—with all the additional loss in production and employment that it would involve; *or* by making dollar goods sufficiently expensive in relation to non-dollar goods—i.e. general devaluation of currencies in relation to the dollar—with all the additional loss that it would involve in the form of a deterioration of the terms of trade. Since both deflation or devaluation would have to be pretty far-reaching to be effective, discrimination certainly appears to be the lesser evil for dealing with the problem of structural imbalance.

It may be thought, however, that the problem of structural imbalance is only a temporary one and will gradually disappear with the attainment of better balanced production in the rest of the world. The world's dependence on dollar goods is certainly not as great at present as it was in the immediate post-war years; and this tendency is likely to continue with the further development of resources in the sterling area and elsewhere.

But even if the structural problem were to be solved, it is questionable whether it would be wise to re-establish conditions of freely multilateral trade until a better balance is attained in the distribution of the world's monetary reserves. For with the present dearth of gold and dollar reserves in most countries, fluctuations in current dollar income are bound to lead to enforced variations in dollar expenditure; under a multilateral system, the effects of such enforced variations are bound to be magnified, so that world trading conditions would be subjected to an unnecessary degree of instability.

A redistribution of the world's monetary reserves is bound to be a slow process, since it could only be attained through a persistent surplus of the outside world with the United States.

Failing this, the re-establishment of multilateralism and general currency convertibility could only be recommended if some system were established—such as that recommended in the U.N. report on full employment—whereby each country guaranteed a certain annual supply of its own currency to the outside world.

Problems of Discriminatory Policies

If an early re-establishment of multilateralism and general currency convertibility is thus only to be envisaged in rather unlikely eventualities, this still leaves the question open as to the kind of currency and trading arrrangements that would best serve the interest both of Britain and of other countries. The absence of general non-discrimination is consistent with a number of alternatives, ranging from "strict bilateralism" at one end, to a freely multilateral system embracing a wide group of countries and with no currency and trade restrictions within, at the other.

A strict bilateral system is one where a country's imports from any particular other country are entirely financed by its exports to that country. This may be ensured by trade agreements of a barter type—like the trade arrangements between the Iron Curtain countries—where the governments directly exchange goods with one another, or it may also be ensured by means of trade and clearing agreements of a kind that was used by various European governments in the immediate post-war years. This method envisages that the trade between the partners to the agreement is regulated by means of import licences which the trading partners promise to grant to each other, normally for equal total amounts; payments for imports (on both sides) are made into a special clearing account out of which payments are made to exporters. In order to facilitate the flow of trade, it was usual for each country to grant a certain clearing credit to the other, but no provisions were made in such agreements for the liquidation of such credits except through the purchase of goods. Hence each country aimed at a bilateral balancing of accounts; to the extent that in any particular period, the trade in one direction failed to balance the trade in the other direction, an automatic pressure was put on the creditor country to increase its purchases, and on the debtor country to reduce its purchases—the pressure being all the greater on the creditor and all the smaller on the debtor, the greater the maximum amount of credit allowed in relation to the trade turnover.

The disadvantage of such a strictly bilateral system is that since the proceeds of exports to any particular country can only be used for purchases in that country, the possibilities of "triangular trade"—where country A uses the proceeds of its exports to B to pay for purchases in C—are excluded. This eliminates such trading opportunities, but it also creates "artificial" trading opportunities, in that it may induce countries to buy goods from their trading partners which they would not have bought at all had they been able to use the proceeds of their exports elsewhere.

These disadvantages of bilateralism are all the more serious, of course, the smaller the size of the individual "countries" with separate currency systems and trading policies.

These disadvantages of bilateralism may be greatly reduced, however, though not eliminated, if the restrictions on convertibility are not applied universally, but only in the trade between fairly large groups of trading countries, while each country is free to use the proceeds of its exports for purchases anywhere within each group. This means that each country need only attain an overall balance in its trade with each of these trading groups, instead of with each country, taken individually. Provided that the number of such separate trading groups is small, and the possibilities of multilateral compensation within each group are unrestricted, the losses of beneficial trading opportunities due to the restrictions on convertibility might be relatively unimportant.

The purpose of such arrangements is to enable greater freedom in trading relationships, and a greater volume of trade to be maintained between the members of a trading group, than would be consistent with the requirements of an overall balance, in the case of universal convertibility. An adverse balance of payments with a particular trading group, which could not be financed by drawing on reserves, need only involve restrictions of imports from that particular group and not universal restrictions of imports; and need have no unsettling effect in the trade relations with other groups. Restrictions of trade can be progressively relaxed, or even entirely abolished, in the trade with members of those groups which have a high degree of import responsiveness to changes in exports—which are prepared to increase their purchases in response to an increase in their sales.

The operation of such "restricted-multilateral systems" involves, however, a number of difficult technical problems. The foremost among these concerns the financial arrangements for the settlement of balances of the members of the group. Relatively free and stable trading arrangements presuppose the existence of reserves which can be drawn on to finance temporary imbalances in the flow of payments. If such reserves do not exist—in other words if payments need to be in exact balance, month by month, or even day by day, and not only over longer periods—stable relationships become impossible, since countries would be forced to take immediate or violent measures whenever for any reason their external balance were disturbed with no opportunity for an orderly adjustment in trading relations. If on the other hand the system provides for the automatic creation of "compensatory finance" to cover such imbalances, the danger always exists of some members of the group falling into a persistent deficit with the others—which must sooner or later lead to a break-up of the arrangements, as no country is normally willing to extend compensatory credit to others indefinitely. If, finally—as would be the more usual situation—the financial arrangements provide only for a limited amount of compensatory finance, the danger exists that the advantages provided by the arrangements will prove only temporary; as the credit limits initially provided become exhausted, and balances require to be settled in gold or hard currency, the pressure to restrict imports is bound to become generalised. Moreover, the very prospect of being able to earn gold and dollars, once a certain cumulative credit position is reached, might induce countries to restrict imports from the other members of the group in the hope of attaining such a position.

A second problem, closely related to the first, concerns the methods employed for maintaining balance-of-payments equilibrium between members of the group. If some members tend to have persistent deficits in their trade with the group, clearly remedial measures need to be applied to re-establish the equilibrium. Such remedial measures—in a manner completely analogous to the case of general convertibility—might take the form of important restrictions, internal deflation, or possibly an alteration of the exchange rate on behalf of the deficit country. The last of these alternatives might perhaps be left out of consideration altogether in this context, since changes in exchange rates that are not universally applied but only in the trade with a certain group of countries raise almost insoluble technical problems. But the manner of application of either of the two other methods is clearly not a matter of indifference to the other members of the group, since such measures could have a serious destabilising effect on their economies if employed in an indiscriminate way. In order to illustrate this problem, we might suppose a multilateral trading group consisting of only three countries, A, B and C, where A is in surplus and B is in a corresponding deficit with the other members of the group, while C is in balance. If B, the deficit country, reduces its imports from the others to the extent necessary to eliminate its own deficit, this might well result in the appearance of a deficit in the account of C, as well as a reduction in the surplus of A. If C in turn is forced to reduce its imports from the others, this might involve a re-emergence of the deficit of B, as well as a further reduction in the surplus of A. The re-establishment of equilibrium in the flow of payments would then ultimately only be attained as a result of a chain process in the course of which the volume of trade was reduced to a far greater extent than the amount of the initial imbalance in the accounts of A and B. In other words, the operation of a "restricted multilateral system" might suffer from the same defects as we have examined in connection with full multilateralism, of magnifying any tendency towards contraction in the volume of trade. But these are far less likely to arise if the members of the group operate their trading policies in a co-operative spirit; if the burden of adjustment is not thrown unilaterally on deficit countries, but is shared equitably between surplus and deficit countries alike; if steps are taken by some countries to facilitate purchases from the other members at the time when others are forced to reduce them.

A third problem concerns the relations of members of a trading group with the world outside. Since the logic of such a system requires that each member should seek to attain an overall balance with the other members of the group taken together (except in so far as it is a net lender, or borrower, on long-term capital account) it also requires that each member should attain an overall balance in the trade with non-members. It may happen, however, that owing to the character of trade, some members would tend to have persistent surpluses with the group and a deficit with countries outside, while with others it may be the other way round. It would be reasonable in such cases if the surpluses earned by some members could be made available to finance the deficits of others, thus avoiding the need for an enforced adjustment in the pattern of world trade. Yet such arrangements would hardly be consistent with the operation of such a system unless it involved also a complete pooling of reserves.[1] The pooling of reserves on the other hand removes the direct responsibility for maintaining balances with outside areas from the shoulders of any particular member country. It could hardly be made to work, therefore, unless the monetary and trading policies of the various members were subordinated to some central authority; or unless there were sufficient solidarity and community of interest between the members to pursue co-ordinated policies even in the absence of such compulsion.

To appreciate the nature of these problems some account needs to be given of how these questions were faced in the case of the two multilateral trading systems which have actually developed

---

[1] The reasons for this are not perhaps immediately apparent. If some countries maintained a persistent surplus with other members of the group, in order to finance their deficit with countries outside the system, they would require to be paid in terms of gold or convertible currency. This involves, however, that the other members which incur the corresponding deficit should (sooner or later) also settle their balances in terms of gold or convertible currency, with the result that the *raison d'être* of the whole arrangement (to be able to indulge in freer trading policies than would be possible under full convertibility) disappears. When reserves are pooled the situation is different inasmuch as any particular country's ability to draw on the reserves is not directly linked (in the short run at any rate) to its current account position.

It would be possible, however, to devise schemes (as discussed further below) under which creditor members of the system would have the right to draw a *proportion* of their credit balance in gold and convertible currency, while debtor countries would have a similar obligation to settle a *proportion* of their current debit in this manner (irrespective of their cumulative position as creditors or debtors). This would provide a continued incentive to discrimination while permitting continuing surplus and deficit positions.

since the war, namely the Sterling Area and the European Payments Union.

Mode of Operation of the Sterling Area

The Sterling Area arrangements, like the British Constitution, are the product of gradual historic growth, rather than of explicit and comprehensive agreements on principles between the partners. The habit of British Commonwealth countries (other than Canada) of keeping their international reserves in sterling originates from the 1920's; it acquired added significance with the abandonment of the Gold Standard in 1931, when it became the means of maintaining fixed parity of local currencies with sterling, while sterling itself fluctuated in value in terms of the dollar and other currencies. With the institution of exchange control in 1939, the free convertibility of sterling currencies with each other was maintained, while members of the area agreed to impose controls on capital movements with outside areas and to regulate their import controls with due regard to the state of reserves of the area as a whole. The right of members to convert their sterling balances into dollars or other currencies was maintained, however, though *ad hoc* arrangements were made from time to time by which members agreed to keep their drawings within more or less definite limits. The Bank of England acted as a banker for the area as a whole in outside transactions; and the Sterling Area is automatically included in any payments arrangements made by Britain with non-sterling countries.

The implication of these arrangements is that Britain, as the banker of the area, can automatically obtain finance for any increase in payments to other members through an increase in her sterling liabilities. This is not true of the other members of the area; however, partly as a result of the large accumulation of credit balances during the war period, most members possessed large sterling reserves, which tended moreover to be continually replenished through the free movement of capital from Britain to the other members of the area. Hence, until recently, payments difficulties did not arise in transactions between the various members of the area, and intra-sterling area trade proceeded almost entirely without restrictions. In a world drained of liquid reserves,

these arrangements thus conferred the benefits, as also the disadvantages, of a high state of liquidity for the conduct of trade
within the group.

Since Britain continues (with certain exceptions) to manage
the gold reserve for the whole area so that the net gold or dollar
earnings of members are automatically converted into sterling
balances, the arrangements also provide full multilateral compensation between members in transactions with the outside world:
dollars earned by certain members of the group are freely available to finance the deficits of others. The system of pooling of
reserves, combined with the existence of large sterling balances,
means moreover that the members' ability to obtain gold or
dollars is not directly dependent on their current sterling earnings;
fluctuations in current dollar receipts exert no influence on sterling
trade.

On the other hand, the individual members are under no
direct incentive to ensure that the area as a whole maintains an
adequate balance in its transactions with the outside world.
There are no special incentives to dollar exports—other than
those provided by the market—while the degree of restraint
exercised in dollar imports is normally left to the discretion of
each member. While Britain can exercise a direct influence on the
import policies of dependent territories, this is not so with the
independent members. Nor are there any clear principles governing access to the central reserves. Formally each member has
the right to convert into gold or dollars to the limit of its own
sterling resources. In practice they are asked to exercise restraint
in doing so, and on some occasions members agreed to keep
their net drawings within certain limits. There can be little
doubt that the effective degree of restraint on dollar imports
(i.e. the effective degree of discrimination in favour of sterling and
other soft currency imports) varied widely between different areas;
and in general, Britain and her dependencies have borne a disproportionate share of the economies in dollar purchases. That
the arrangements have worked as well as they did may have been
partly due to the fact that it was the dependent territories which
have provided a net surplus of dollars, while the independent
members (with the exception of Ceylon) were dollar deficit areas.

The history of the recurring dollar crises of 1947, 1949 and 1951 provides plenty of evidence, however, of the inadequate character of the arrangements for maintaining a satisfactory balance with the dollar area. These biennial crises were partly caused by fluctuations in the dollar income of the area, which can be traced to fluctuations in the American demand for imports. But they were at least equally caused by the biennial fluctuations in dollar expenditure, both by Britain and the overseas sterling countries. These fluctuations were partly the direct consequence of alternating tightening-up and relaxation in import controls, which mirrored, with a considerable time-lag, the changing impact of the dollar shortage itself. But for the independent members of the area they were in part the automatic consequence of fluctuations in domestic incomes due to the changing levels of export prices.[1] Since the changes in import demand followed the changes in export income with about a one-year lag, years of high dollar outlay by the Sterling Area tended to coincide with years of relatively low dollar income, which accounts for the sharp changes in the net dollar balance. The net dollar surplus of the "good years" was far from sufficient, however, to compensate for the dollar deficit of the "bad years," which indicates that the measures taken for economising on dollar spending were insufficient in scope as well as being badly out in timing.

The dollar crisis of 1951, like its predecessors, was overcome in greater part through cuts in spending and, to a lesser extent, through a recovery in earnings. It left the central reserves, however, far too low to withstand another similar shock which, if past experience is any guide, is bound to recur in a year or so. If the Sterling Area arrangements are to be preserved, it is urgently necessary to make some fresh arrangements that would improve its manner of functioning and strengthen its ability to withstand the dollar crises of the future.

One obvious suggestion that has often been made is to improve

[1] Thus the large increase in dollar imports in the second half of 1951 was partly the consequence of unduly low imports, and hence destocking, in earlier periods; partly the delayed effect of the rise in raw material prices in the six months following Korea. In the last quarter of 1951 U.S. exports to the Sterling Area, at 780 million dollars, were 122 per cent. higher than in the corresponding quarter of the previous year. Of this total, the value of exports to the U.K. increased by 90 per cent., to the dependent territories by only 10 per cent., and to the independent members of the Sterling Area by no less than 175 per cent.

the co-ordinating machinery. If instead of *ad hoc* meetings at the Ministerial level called together under the stress of acute crisis (like those of July 1949 and January 1952) permanent organs of co-ordination were created at the policy-making level, decisions to deal with the constantly changing situation could be made far more smoothly, and the delays which so much aggravated events in the past could be greatly reduced. The very absence of such permanent co-ordinating machinery may be an indication, however, that the independent members of the area, though ready to rally round in times of crisis, are not willing to subordinate their economic policies, as a continuing measure, to the decisions of some central body; and that any such deliberate attempt to bring their policies more closely together would strengthen, rather than weaken, the centrifugal tendencies.

A more promising method might be the creation of automatic economic incentives that would discourage dollar spending, and encourage dollar earning, in proportion to the varying pressure of the dollar shortage. One suggested way to bring this about is a return to the system of the "floating rate" as it existed in the 1930's. Assuming (as would undoubtedly be the case) that the rate was not really left to be determined by the day-to-day constellation of market forces, but was "managed" behind the scenes by the Bank of England through an Exchange Equalisation Fund, this suggestion is really tantamount to a more frequent— and less formal—application of the weapon of exchange-rate variations. In recent years this weapon has only been employed on two occasions: in connection with the devaluation of the pound from 4·89 to 4·04 dollars in 1939, and from 4·04 to 2·80 dollars in 1949. If variations in the exchange rate are to be resorted to at all, the method of a formally "floating rate" is certainly a far less clumsy and cumbrous way of giving effect to such variations, than changes in the "official rate." It requires no formal consultations; it can give effect to the desired changes gradually rather than suddenly; it is capable of being used for the purpose of revaluing (rather than devaluing) the currency, as circumstances permit, in a way that is hardly feasible with a formally fixed rate; and for this very reason, it is capable of neutralising the operation of speculative forces that would otherwise act as a constantly aggravating factor. With a fixed rate of exchange, where the rate is only altered under the stress of grave emergency, the danger exists that the public will come to regard currency devaluation as the inevitable outcome of a crisis, so that any unfavourable trend in the balance of payments will tend to get exaggerated by speculative movements against the currency, which the methods of exchange control (as past experience has shown) are by no means wholly able to prevent.

There can be little doubt that a policy of counter-cyclical variation in exchange rates (i.e. allowing the value of the pound to fall in times of falling dollar earnings and causing it to rise in times of rising dollar earnings) could go a long way in neutralising the effect of such fluctuations—particularly in situations in which the monetary authorities do not possess sufficient reserves to permit a passive attitude towards such fluctuations. Nevertheless a policy of this kind is not without its difficulties and disadvantages. For one thing, the abandonment of fixed rates of exchange—though this is not perhaps of decisive consequence—is contrary to the obligations assumed in the I.M.F. Charter.[1] A more important objection lies in the difficulty of combining floating rates with the maintenance of discrimination. In the 1930's the system of floating rates was introduced under conditions of full currency convertibility; and it is questionable whether members of the Sterling Area would consent to the maintenance of present restraint on convertibility if the notion of fixed exchange rates was abandoned. The reintroduction of floating rates is thus bound to lead to increased pressures for the restoration of multilateralism and of full convertibility; it may well cause the premature abandonment of existing measures of discrimination against dollar imports. This, as we have seen, is bound to aggravate greatly the long-term problem of attaining a dollar balance, and might involve a serious further deterioration of the terms of trade. If a manipulated floating rate could be combined with the maintenance of discriminatory measures against dollar imports, and of exchange control, there may be much to be said for it; but the

[1] There were several occasions—the most recent one being that of Canada—in which the Fund has permitted member countries to abandon fixed exchange rates; and it could perhaps be argued that rigid adherence to a system of fixed exchange rates, under present conditions, is not likely to promote the basic objectives of the Fund.

case for such a policy is greatly weakened if account is taken of the fact that the introduction of the one is likely to lead, in practice, to the abandonment of the other.

But continuing incentives to dollar saving and dollar earning could be introduced into the system without abandoning the fixed rate of exchange. Without interfering with the right of individual members to convert their sterling balances into gold or dollars, it is possible to provide such an incentive (and a powerful one) by means of a system of graduated fines collected from, and graduated premia paid to, members, according to whether their net drawing from (or net contribution to) the central dollar pool exceeds or falls short of some "normal" standard. To the extent that the fines collected under the scheme exceeded the premia paid out, the net gain would accrue to the collective benefit of members; and similarly, to the extent that the premia exceeded the fines, the net loss involved in the operation of the scheme would be a collective charge on members.

A scheme of this kind (capable of numerous variations) could be instituted on the following lines:

(i) Each member of the Sterling Area is allocated an initial (quarterly or annual) dollar quota which can be either positive or negative—i.e. representing a net surrender of dollars to, or a net drawing of dollars from, the central pool. These quotas are to be determined by mutual agreement between the members, and should represent the "normal" dollar surplus or dollar deficit of each; they should thus represent a kind of target fixed on the basis of the actual payments results of the last few years, modified in accordance with special factors. These quotas should be capable of adjustments from time to time by mutual agreement between the members.[1] It would be advisable (though not essential) to fix the quotas in such a way that the sum of the positive and negative quotas of individual members adds up to zero or some positive sum.

(ii) Premia are payable to members at quarterly intervals with respect to any dollars surrendered to the pool in excess of their quota (if positive) and any short-fall of drawings of dollars

[1] The agreement might provide for such adjustments specifically in cases in which the (gross) dollar receipts of particular countries change owing to circumstances beyond their control (e.g. a fall in the world prices of the main export commodities).

below their quota (if negative). Similarly fines are collected from members for any short-fall of dollars surrendered below the quota (if positive) and any drawings in excess of the quota (if negative). Both premia and fines should be graduated—e.g. 10 per cent. of the sterling paid or received for any excess or short-fall of 10 per cent. or less of the quota, 20 per cent. of the price for any excess or short-fall between 10 and 20 per cent. of the quota, and so on. (The scale of graduation could of course be varied in numerous ways.)

(iii) Premia and fines, payable in sterling, are to be paid through a special fund instituted for the purpose. This fund should be created by a special contribution in sterling, apportioned among members in accordance with the relative values of their foreign trade turnover. In view of the fact that a net gain in dollar reserves is expected to accrue from the scheme, its operations over the years are likely to involve it in a net loss. It would be advisable therefore to make the initial size of the fund rather large—say, of the order of £500–600 million. The net balance of the fund, on liquidation, should be divided among the members in proportion to their original contributions.

(iv) The initial arrangement might be for a trial period of, say, three years, at the end of which members would be free to liquidate the arrangement altogether, or to renegotiate it with new quotas adjusted to the circumstances. In addition, the scheme should be made subject to renegotiation if the central dollar reserves rose so rapidly that the fund was exhausted (or fell below some minimum balance) prior to the expiry of the trial period.

An arrangement of this kind would obviously involve some rather delicate negotiation, in connection with the fixing of quotas, etc. Its advantages, however, might make the effort well worth while. It would provide immediate and automatically graduated pressure to economise on dollars whenever the dollar deficit were rising; in place of the slowly-operating and generally very belated attempts to achieve dollar economies by *ad hoc* negotiation. And it would provide the strongest continuing incentives to all members to increase their net dollar earnings. It would thus secure all the advantages that might be gained from a freely variable exchange rate but without the disadvantages of the latter that were indicated earlier. In effect, it would cause the marginal cost of dollar imports and the marginal return on dollar exports to vary without changing the cost, or return, on the bulk of transactions. The incentives provided by the scheme are primarily directed to the participating governments; and it could be left to the discretion of each government how far, and in what manner, it desired to pass on these incentives to the individual traders.

It would certainly appear desirable that continued access to the central dollar pool should be made conditional on the willingness of individual members to participate in some scheme of the kind described. For without it, it is highly doubtful whether it will be possible, or even desirable, to continue over longer periods with the present pooling arrangements. In the light of postwar experience, a strong case could be made out for throwing back the responsibility of maintaining a balance on dollar account to the individual members, and restricting the existing convertibility of sterling balances into gold and dollars. It would be a mistake to think that the liquidation of the central dollar pool would necessarily mean a break-up of the Sterling Area; even without the pooling arrangements, members would have a strong common interest in maintaining more intimate trade and currency relationships with one another. But the abandonment of the pooling arrangements would undoubtedly necessitate some additional controls; in particular, restrictions might have to be introduced on the movement of capital funds. In the light of the very substantial advantages of the present system for the freedom and stability of trade within the area, the possibilities of strengthening the economic unity of the area by supplementary arrangements ought to be thoroughly explored therefore before the present arrangements are even partially abandoned.

The European Payments Union

The European Payments Union is the other "restricted-multilateral" trade and payments system created since the war. But, unlike the Sterling Area, it came into being as a result of prolonged and intricate formal negotiations between the participating governments. It had its origin in the administration of Marshall Aid which involved that the countries of Western

Europe granted "drawing rights" to each other, in partial *quid pro quo* for the dollar aid which was apportioned among them according to their dollar needs, rather than the overall requirements of their balance of payments. From mid-1950 onwards these arrangements were replaced by a system of multilateral payments according to which each country's consolidated net balance with all the other countries participating in the scheme are settled at monthly intervals in accordance with the rules of the Payments Union. More or less simultaneously with the introduction of this system, the governments participating in the scheme agreed to lift import restrictions on the major part of their trade with each other though any particular country was to be entitled to reimpose restrictions if it became involved in serious deficits with the Union.

Compensatory finance was provided under this scheme in the form of a basic quota allotted to each country and which was calculated as some percentage of its past turnover in intra-European trade. These quotas govern both the extent of the credits which participating countries are obliged to provide to the system and also the credits which they can receive from it. In either case the mechanism provides for fractional gold payments in settlement of current balances once a certain initial proportion of the quota is exceeded. Thus a country whose balance of payments shows a surplus with the rest of E.P.U. grants a multilateral credit to E.P.U. corresponding to 20 per cent. of its quota; but once its cumulative monthly surplus exceeds this figure, it needs only grant credit with respect to 50 per cent. of its monthly surplus, while it is entitled to receive gold for the remaining 50 per cent. A country whose balance of payments shows a deficit with E.P.U. can incur a cumulative deficit of up to 20 per cent. of its quota without making any gold payments, but for each subsequent slice of 20 per cent. of the basic quota gold payments are required on a sliding scale until 80 per cent. needs to be paid in gold for the last slice of 20 per cent.[1] The

---

[1] The lack of immediate correspondence between the inflow and outflow of gold payments was made possible by an initial fund of 350 million dollars provided to the Union out of Marshall Aid. In cases where a debtor country's cumulative deficit exceeds its quota, the agreement requires that the monthly settlement will have to be covered by 100 per cent. gold payments, but there are no stipulations laid down with regard to a creditor country which has exceeded its quota.

idea behind the provision of a gradually rising percentage of gold payments is to provide increasing pressure on debtors to rectify their balance of payments' position. Similarly the idea behind the provision of creditors receiving only 50 per cent. of their credit balance in the form of gold is to induce them to apply measures of discrimination in favour of imports from the other members of the Union if they are in a surplus position. The multilateral character of the credits received or granted reduces the total amount of credits required to finance a given pattern of trade. In fact, the consolidation of the bilateral surpluses and deficits under the scheme automatically eliminated about 50 per cent. of the previous credit requirements through the compensating machinery of the system. With the multilateralisation of payments, moreover, the motive for the application of discriminatory measures as between different member countries disappears.

The purpose of the scheme, however, is not only, or even mainly, to eliminate discrimination between member States, but to promote the degree of economic co-operation within the area. Its success must be judged therefore by the extent to which it permits member countries to abstain from restrictionist policies in their mutual trading relations; and this, in turn, depends on the degree to which credit or debit balances with the Union involve a gain or loss of gold and dollars. Since the credits extended to member countries depend on their cumulative position, it is evident that the advantages of the scheme in promoting trade must gradually disappear as the initial credits tend to become exhausted. The system therefore can only function satisfactorily in so far as (a) the initial credits provided are reasonably large in relation to possible short-term requirements; (b) member countries renounce the possibility of financing their deficits with outside areas through the surpluses earned with the Union and aim, in effect, at maintaining an overall balance with the area.

In the actual case neither of these conditions was satisfied. The credits provided (amounting to some 9 per cent. of the intra-European trade turnover) proved to be much too small to avoid the need for violent counter-measures. Thus Germany ran through her initial quota within four months of the introduction of the scheme and had to be authorised to suspend trade liberalisation after eight months; Britain, after running up a surplus equal to over half of her quota in a period of ten months, ran through her quota in the following nine months, and had to restrict liberalisation at the end of 1951. Similarly France had to reintroduce quantitative restrictions, of an even more severe character, in February 1952. Belgium on the other hand accumulated a credit position equal to 250 per cent. of her quota by the middle of 1952 and was only willing to extend fresh credit to the Union on condition that the previous credit would be repaid in gold over a period of years. Italy and Portugal had also exceeded their credit quotas by the end of 1951.

However, it has proved to be an important advantage of the continuing inter-governmental consultations provided by E.P.U. that the application of corrective measures by the deficit countries was allowed to proceed without giving rise to retaliatory measures by the others; in fact, efforts were made to balance the contractive measures taken by the debtors by expansive measures of the creditors. Thus Italy was induced to remove all quantitative restrictions on European imports, and even to lower customs duties, despite the danger of adverse effects on home industries. Similarly Germany was pressed to restore liberalisation when she changed over to a net creditor position. In the case of Belgium, since suggestions for raising her imports through an internal expansionary policy proved unavailing, efforts were made to get her to discourage exports through the imposition of (rather moderate) export taxes and a tightening up of the export licensing system. In the interest of maintaining the economic stability of member countries, the Union was even obliged to recommend discriminatory measures—as in suggesting that Germany should exempt certain debtor countries from her import restrictions or that surplus countries, such as Belgium, should provide particular facilities for imports from deficit countries.

In so far as the deficits of particular countries arise from an abnormal increase in their own imports (as in the case of Germany in late 1950 and early 1951, and Britain in the later part of 1951) the method of permitting deficit countries to impose import restrictions while preventing others from doing so is probably the most appropriate one for restoring the payments balance—without causing an undue contraction in the volume of trade. When, however, the deficits of the debtor countries are merely the reflection of an abnormal decrease in imports by others, or are simply the counterpart of the growing surpluses of the so-called "structural creditors" (such as Belgium), the application of non-discriminatory import restrictions by the debtor countries is not an appropriate method of adjustment, since it causes a general curtailment of trade and thus necessitates further contractive measures by others. It is essential therefore that the "structural" surplus countries—or countries which desire to maintain a surplus position with the Union indefinitely, as a means of offsetting their deficits with other areas—should also be content to receive fractional gold payments indefinitely—i.e. to extend matching credits without limit—and not only up to the limit of their quotas. If they refuse to do so, they ought not to continue to receive the benefit of non-discriminatory treatment and the necessary import restrictions, which are ultimately caused by them, should be organised on a discriminatory basis.[1] Similarly, some provision needs to be embodied in the agreement to protect deficit countries from having to restrict imports when their deficits have their origin in an undue fall of imports of countries suffering from deflationary tendencies. This case has not so far arisen; but when it does arise on any large scale it might well wreck the whole structure—precisely at the time when the need for its continued existence might be the strongest.

If the E.P.U. is to function satisfactorily—or even to survive, for any length of time—it is essential therefore that the present inadequate credit arrangements should be revised. This could be done in various ways; but probably the most advantageous method is along the lines originally suggested by Professor Kahn[2] which gets rid of the idea of "quotas" altogether and suggests instead that balances should be settled part in gold and

[1] The E.P.U. agreement left the problem of countries which exceeded their credit quotas to *ad hoc* negotiation. The only instance so far where new arrangements became necessary on account of this was that of Belgium. The solution in the Belgian case—where the repayment of past credits was made a precondition of the extension of fresh credit—certainly does not augur well for the future.

[2] "A Possible Intra-European Payments Scheme," *Economica*, November 1949; "The European Payments Union," *Economica*, August 1950.

as to the rest cancelled as they arise. The fraction of the current deficits and surpluses that are payable or receivable in gold could be varied from time to time in accordance with the varying pressure of the dollar shortage. The advantage of this method is that it provides steady incentives in favour of substituting imports from the area for dollar imports and of dollar exports in preference to exports in the area; whereas under the present system, the strength of such incentives is made to depend on the wholly irrelevant consideration of the cumulative net debtor or creditor positions of individual countries. Further, this method makes it possible also to vary the extent of the incentives provided in accordance with the overall balance of dollar trade of the area— by varying the rate of discount of gold payments—in a manner that is not possible under the present system. It would therefore be analogous in its effects to, and would complement the operation of, the arrangements suggested above in connection with the sterling area.

CONCLUDING REMARKS

The results of the above review suggest the need for strengthening and under-pinning the trade and payments arrangements that have developed since the war, rather than for any radically new departure. The danger in the present situation is rather that the dissatisfaction with the repeated balance of payments crises of the past will lead to a premature abandonment of existing protective and discriminating devices—as a result of a rather naïve *post hoc ergo propter hoc* reasoning, according to which it is the continuance of currency restrictions and discriminatory trade arrangements which makes it possible for countries to continue with all-too-inflationary internal policies; and it is the continuance of inflationary tendencies which in turn causes the balance of payments crises.

It is not to be denied, of course, that a policy of maintaining full utilisation of resources greatly aggravates the problem of maintaining equilibrium in the balance of payments. A country with surplus resources of manpower, equipment and materials can respond to outside stimuli in a far more flexible manner than one without such idle reserves; and an economy that is prepared to tolerate wide fluctuations in its production and employment levels has far less need of the use of quantitative or discriminatory controls. Given a sufficiently restrictive and adaptable monetary policy, balance of payments crises could no doubt be avoided— but only at the cost of converting them into internal crises of production and employment.

The restoration of general currency convertibility and the abandonment of import controls—without adequate safeguards in the form of large liquid reserves, or of automatic compensatory finance—would undoubtedly enforce the use of far more stringent monetary controls and without regard to the requirements of internal economic stability; in this way it would unquestionably powerfully aid the anti-inflationary forces and thereby alleviate the problem of maintaining balance of payments equilibrium.

But the converse of these propositions is certainly not true. It would be wrong to suggest that without the aid of such restraints it is impossible to guard against inflation effectively; or that a country pursuing internal full employment policies could not build up a strong external financial position. Britain may have erred in past years both in the insufficient use of financial controls and in the inadequate concentration of her resources on the development of export industries. But the remedy to these defects should be sought in more powerful restraint over private spending, and in a more comprehensive planning of industrial development, and not in a hasty return to the methods of *laissez faire*.

16

A RECONSIDERATION OF THE ECONOMICS OF THE INTERNATIONAL WHEAT AGREEMENT[1]

Summary and Recommendations

1. In this study the International Wheat Agreement is examined as a means of securing greater stability of income to producers and consumers of wheat and of protecting the national economies of both importing and exporting countries from the fluctuations normally associated with the operation of a free market, while preserving the mechanism for an orderly adjustment to variations in supply and demand.

2. The efficacy of the Agreement in attaining these objectives is shown to depend on:

(*a*) the degree to which participating countries succeed in bringing a reasonably high proportion of their normal transactions within the scope of the Agreement and the extent to which the Agreement succeeds in limiting the range of prices on guaranteed transactions;

(*b*) the appropriateness of domestic policies of participating countries for preserving normal incentives to adjustment to changes in the balance of world supply and demand;

(*c*) the degree in which participating countries succeed in distributing among themselves the quantities of wheat guaranteed under the Agreement in fair proportion to their normal supplies and normal requirements;

(*d*) the extent to which participating countries are willing to maintain publicly owned stocks above the levels required by the normal period of turnover and to operate these stocks so as to prevent undue fluctuations in market prices.

---

[1] A report prepared for the Food and Agriculture Organisation of the United Nations and published as *Commodity Policy Studies*, No. 1, F.A.O., Rome, Italy, September 1952. (Appendix C containing a description of the domestic price and output policies of various countries and Appendix D giving a historical account of the operation of the International Wheat Agreement in 1949–51 are not reproduced here.)

3. The above objectives raise the following considerations:

(*a*) The willingness of importing and exporting countries to enter into commitments clearly depends on a fair distribution of gains and the effective protection of the interests of both parties (paragraphs 14, 28–29). This cannot be attained—and certainly there cannot be any guarantee that it will be attained—by the method of fixing the minimum and maximum price under the Agreement for long periods in advance without introducing into the Agreement itself some principle by which prices can be automatically adjusted in accordance with requirements (paragraph 30). It is therefore recommended that when the Agreement comes up for renegotiation, the contracting parties consider the following proposals:

(i) The Agreement should incorporate a formula by which minimum and maximum prices are automatically changed by some fraction of the difference between prices paid on non-guaranteed transactions and the mean price laid down in the Agreement for the previous year (paragraphs 32, 34). By means of this adjustment mean prices laid down in the Agreement would tend to be equal, over a period of years, to the moving average of market prices (paragraphs 33, 35). In this connection it is recommended that in the interests of preserving the value of the Agreement as a stabilising instrument the fraction used for the adjustment should be relatively small and the margin between minimum and maximum prices should be narrowed (paragraphs 31, 32).

(ii) In order to protect the contracting parties from the risks of major instability in the world price level of commodities generally, the mean price laid down in a future agreement should also be adjusted in accordance with major changes in the price level of world trade as a whole; for this purpose an adjustment should be made in the mean price, each year, to the extent of one-half of the change in the unit value of

world exports in the previous year, whenever the
change in the unit value of world exports, as computed by the Statistical Office of the United Nations,
changes by more than 10 per cent. (paragraphs
34–39). Any such adjustment in the mean price
should be taken into consideration whenever the
mean price is adjusted in accordance with the formula
suggested in (i) above (paragraph 36). These two
principles of adjustment complement each other and,
together, would ensure the equitable protection of
the interests of both parties (paragraph 40).

(b) The objectives of the Agreement may be partially de-
feated by a greater tendency towards instability in the
free market if internal policies of the participating countries
put the incentives to adjustment, provided by the normal
market mechanism, partially or wholly out of operation
(paragraphs 13, 16; Appendix A, 3). This will not be the
case if (i) the producers continue to receive the current
market price for their crops—in which case, however, the
benefits of the Agreement accrue merely to the national
economies of producing countries and not to the producers
as such (paragraph 17); or (ii) the governments of the
producing countries operate a dual price system under
which farmers receive the guaranteed price up to a certain
quota, and the price corresponding to the market price
for quantities in excess of that quota (paragraphs 21–22).
It is therefore recommended that the two major exporting
countries which place the distribution of wheat under
government control adopt a dual price system for payments to farmers (paragraph 26).

(c) If the distribution of guaranteed quantities is not equal
among importing countries, some of these may have to
bear a disproportionate share of the burden of adjustment
resulting from some unforeseen reduction in available
supplies. This, in turn, may place a strain on the operation
of the free market (Appendix A, paragraphs 18–19). It is
further believed that an uneven distribution of guaranteed

quantities of wheat among exporting countries in relation
to normal supplies might make it difficult for particular
countries to preserve the normal incentives to adjustment
or even to fulfil their obligations under the Agreement
(paragraph 22). It is therefore recommended that when
the Agreement is renegotiated, the contracting parties
pay due regard to the even distribution of guaranteed
quantities of wheat both among importing and among
exporting countries in relation to normal requirements
and normal exportable supplies (paragraphs 22; Appendix
A, 19).

(d) The effective operation of the world wheat market and the
active implementation by the participants of the obligations
assumed in the Agreement both require that the participating governments normally carry reasonably large
stocks of wheat and that they endeavour to ensure that the
stocks of wheat carried in the economy (including both
publicly and privately owned stocks) be sufficiently varied
to exert a price-stabilising rather than a price-destabilising
influence (paragraphs 11, 27). To this end, it is recommended that some provision be incorporated in the new
Agreement to the effect that major exporting and importing countries normally carry publicly owned stocks in
excess of minimum requirements; and operate these stocks
so as to alleviate scarcities at times of high prices and
moderate the pressure of extra supplies at times of lower
prices. This would involve an obligation, in the case of
exporters, to release stocks in the face of upward price
movements when the prices themselves are above the
maximum price and a similar obligation for major importing countries to increase the size of publicly owned
stocks in the face of falling prices when market prices are
below the minimum price (paragraph 27).

4. It is believed that, subject to the above criteria being
satisfied, the conclusion of a new Wheat Agreement would secure
considerable benefits in the form of greater security and stability
to exporting and importing countries alike and would tend to

improve the normal functioning of the world wheat market. Such an agreement would have certain inherent advantages over other possible types of international commodity agreements (paragraphs 8, 12, 26–27, 40; Appendix A, 15–16, 20).

I. BASIC OBJECTIVES OF THE INTERNATIONAL WHEAT AGREEMENT

5. The main purpose of the International Wheat Agreement is to prevent—or at least to moderate—the instability in the income of producers and consumers which is normally associated with the operation of a free market, without, however, thereby rendering the allocative functions of the market mechanism inoperative. It is well known that the main objection to the use of the price mechanism as a regulator of economic activity (apart from cases where the Government desires to interfere with the consumer's choice on the grounds of social priorities or other grounds, which obviously do not arise in the case of wheat) is based on the fact that the changes in prices that are necessary to bring about a certain adjustment in the balance of supply and demand also imply a transfer of income between buyers and sellers, the magnitude of which is directly proportionate to the price change. These shifts in income cannot be considered a necessary part of the adjustment in the relations between supply and demand; they are an undesirable by-product of the use of the price mechanism as a market adjuster.

6. The economic function of a rise in price is to encourage producers and to discourage consumers; that of a fall in price is the opposite. If producers can be encouraged and consumers discouraged, without undue enrichment of the former at the expense of the latter (or vice versa), the price mechanism may be regarded as an efficient instrument for securing an equilibrium between production and consumption. In the opposite case, however, it is generally considered a crude and inefficient instrument, which causes disturbances disproportionate to the quantitative adjustments involved. This is particularly so when, because of the slowness with which producers or consumers react to price incentives, the initial price reaction following upon a particular change in demand/supply relations tends to be much greater than the price change that is ultimately necessary for the purpose.

Delayed reactions that are disproportionate to the genuine need for adjustment may thus be called forth. In fact, most government interferences with the free market mechanism may simply be regarded as attempts to secure adjustments between production and consumption with less disturbance to established social and economic relations and to economic stability generally than would be caused by the operation of a free market.

7. It follows from the above that in the case of a particular commodity, the efficiency of the price mechanism as a regulator of demand/supply relations depends entirely on the responsiveness of the market demand and supply with respect to price changes and the time lags involved for such responses to take place. When these responses (the so-called elasticities) are large and occur fairly promptly, relatively large adjustments in the balance of production and consumption can be secured with proportionately small changes in price; hence, the disturbance in income distribution, and thus in the general economic and social relations (both within and between different countries) is relatively small. In the case of primary commodities, however, past experience has shown that these elasticities are relatively small and/or the responses are slow, hence small marginal adjustments in the balance of production and consumption were associated with large fluctuations in prices. The precise reasons for this may have varied from commodity to commodity; certain specific reasons in the case of wheat and other agricultural commodities will be discussed in some detail below (see Appendix A). It should be noted here, however, that it was thus fundamentally the low values of the elasticities of market demand and supply— and/or the slowness with which producers and consumers react to price incentives—which gave rise to numerous demands for regulating the production and marketing of primary products, or for government control over prices, both in the inter-war period and since the war.

8. Apart from a large variety of national measures, three types of international measures were advanced to deal with the problem of instability of free markets. One type of proposal— which gave rise to numerous international arrangements of a greater or lesser duration in the inter-war period—was to limit

the exports and/or the production of a particular commodity, in times of abundant supplies and low prices. Pre-war experience with this type of arrangement has shown it, however, to be of limited value; partly, because in general it affords no adequate protection of the interests of consumers; partly also, because the problem of price and income instability is not confined to periods of excessive supplies. The second type of proposal, debated mainly during and since the war, was to confine price fluctuations in the world market of any particular commodity within certain limits, by means of an international agency willing to buy and sell the commodities at fixed prices and to keep a continuing store of them (creation of "buffer stocks"). The third, which underlies the International Wheat Agreement, was to ensure, by means of a multilateral contract between the governments of exporting and importing countries, that the greater part of the transactions in a particular commodity should be "guaranteed" between exporters and importers, to be undertaken within a stated price range, irrespective of the fluctuations in market prices.[1] In this way, the shift in income distribution corresponding to any given change in the market price, is reduced, if not entirely eliminated. Thus, if the Agreement stipulates for two-thirds of all transactions to fall within their "guaranteed" category, and the permitted price variation within the guaranteed category is a maximum of 10 per cent., the operation of the Agreement will reduce the income variation corresponding to a 30 per cent. price change to $16\frac{2}{3}$ per cent., and of a 50 per cent. price change to $23\frac{1}{3}$ per cent. In case 75 per cent. of all transactions fall within the guaranteed category, and the permitted range of price variation is only 5 per cent., the income variations in the two cases would be reduced from 30 per cent. to 11 per cent. and from 50 per cent. to 16 per cent.[2] By means of such an Agreement it is therefore possible to eliminate the greater part of the income variation that would otherwise be

[1] Long-term contracts between individual governments (such as those between the United Kingdom and the British Dominions as regards butter or meat, etc.) serve the same purpose. They differ from an international agreement of the I.W.A. type chiefly in being bilateral and not multilateral in character.

[2] In the case of I.W.A. two-thirds of normal transactions between participating countries are "guaranteed" but the permitted range of price variation, in the final year, is 33 per cent. downwards or 50 per cent. upwards. Hence in the case of a 50 per cent fall in price the operation of the Agreement might only reduce the income effects from 50 to $38\frac{2}{3}$ per cent.

associated with the operation of a free market, while preserving
—to a greater or lesser degree, depending upon the nature of
the domestic policies of participating countries—the resource-
allocative functions of the latter.

9. In the case of the buffer stocks proposal, price fluctuations
outside a permitted range are to be completely avoided. This
eliminates, however, not only the income instability arising out
of price changes but also the use of the price mechanism as a
means of securing adjustments between production and consumption—except in so far as the Agency operating the scheme
is able to fix, and to vary from time to time, its buying and selling
prices so as to secure a balance between production and consumption over longer periods. The Agency, however, would have
no means of knowing in advance the "long-run equilibrium
price" of any particular commodity; this can only be discovered
gradually, through a prolonged accumulation or decumulation
of the Agency's stocks. Past experience with national agencies
of this type has shown, however, that downward price adjustments are strongly resisted by the interests concerned; they would
be even more difficult to obtain on an international plane. Hence
a buffer stock arrangement might be said to have an inherent
bias toward keeping prices above long-run equilibrium levels. The
corresponding problem in the I.W.A. type of agreement—fixing
the maximum and minimum prices on guaranteed transactions—
though certainly difficult, should not, as will be seen in paragraphs
31–39 below, give rise to complications of the same extent.

10. It should be noted also that in the case of a number of
agricultural commodities, where the instability in price is due
to fluctuations in supply, rather than in demand (i.e. changes in
crop yields), the buffer stock device does not eliminate instability
in the income of producers, since it would involve a fall in income
in years of poor harvest and a rise in income in years of good harvest.
Under a free market system the situation tends to be the opposite.
In the I.W.A. type of agreement, a fall in the free market price in
years of good crops and a rise in price in years of poor crops, tends
to offset the variation in income arising out of variations in yield
—provided only that in the case of a short crop, production is
still large enough, in relation to the quantities guaranteed under

the Agreement, to enable producers to benefit from the relatively high prices on non-guaranteed transactions prevailing in such periods.

11. It must be remembered, on the other hand, that buffer stock arrangements would also serve to prevent such unnecessary and disequilibrating movements in market prices as may be caused by temporary or random fluctuations in the relation of production to consumption. In theory, it is the function of the market mechanism to absorb the effects of such fluctuations through corresponding variations in the amount of stocks carried by inter- mediaries, i.e. traders and speculators. When, however, the market does not respond to such short-period variations in the appropri- ate manner (and, *a fortiori*, when it responds in a perverse manner by tending to increase stocks in the face of a rise in price or *vice versa*) movements in prices occur that cause fresh inequalities between supply and demand, rather than serve as a remedy for existing inequalities. This is mainly the consequence of the large differences between the short- and the long-period elasticities of supply and demand. A purely temporary shortage, for example, caused by a short crop, may have an altogether disproportionate effect on prices—particularly when the anticipated magnitude, or the effect of the shortage, is exaggerated by speculators—with the result that the producers are induced to expand production (e.g. in the case of wheat by expanding the acreage) in a way that causes an unwarranted fall in price in a future year. The purpose of government-operated buffer stocks arrangements is to eliminate such price variations and ideally to ensure that only such price movements are transmitted to producers and consumers as pro- vide the needed incentives for adjustment. The provisions of an I.W.A. type of agreement do not in themselves ensure the elimi- nation of such disequilibrating price fluctuations, though they are by no means inconsistent with the adoption of policies at the national level serving the same purpose. In particular, it is highly desirable that the operation of the agreement should be combined with the provision of publicly-owned stocks in both exporting and importing countries. These stocks should be operated so as to reduce the possibilities of undue price fluctuations in the free market without, however, attempting to stabilise prices.

12. To sum up, the principles underlying the International Wheat Agreement appear to have certain inherent advantages—particularly for agricultural commodities—over an international buffer stock scheme. Moreover, there are practical difficulties involved in creating, under conditions of limited currency convertibility, an international buffer stock requiring large international capital investment.

13. The practical achievement of the objectives of an international agreement of this type depends, however, predominantly on two factors. It depends, first, on the internal policies of participating countries which determine, on the one hand, the extent to which the benefits of greater stability are passed on to the ultimate producers and consumers; and, on the other hand, the extent to which the incentives to adjust the level of production and consumption to the changing requirements of the situation remain unaffected by international arrangements. It is evident that unless variations in the current market price are adequately reflected in the price which producers obtain on their marginal output and—though, in this particular instance, it is not nearly so important—consumers pay on their marginal purchases, the mere existence of a fluctuating price on non-guaranteed transactions would not be effective for securing adjustments in the balance of production and consumption. If, by virtue of a given internal policy, producers received a fixed price on all sales and consumers paid a fixed price on all purchases, irrespective of the market price, the agreement would break down sooner or later under the growing pressure of inequalities between supply and demand; if, however, changes in market prices were partially reflected (that is if producers received, or consumers paid, the *average* price on guaranteed and non-guaranteed transactions, with regard to the whole output) the benefits of the stabilised price on guaranteed transactions might be partially offset by a greater instability in market prices. It is equally clear, on the other hand, that if the internal arrangements were such that the producers received (and/or the consumers paid) the current market price with respect to the whole output, the agreement—while leaving incentives unaffected—would mainly serve the interests of the national economies of participating countries as

a whole and not the particular interests of the producers or consumers of the commodity in question. The effects of such an international scheme greatly depend, therefore, on the internal policies which participating countries adopt for its implementation; its basic objectives are not likely to be achieved unless national measures taken by participating countries are adequate for the purpose and reasonably consistent.

14. The practical achievement of the objectives of the agreement depends, in the second place, on the degree to which participating countries succeed in bringing a reasonably high proportion of their total transactions within the scope of the agreement and the extent to which the agreement itself manages to stabilise the price of guaranteed transactions. It is obvious—subject only to the qualification mentioned in paragraph 10 above—that the higher the ratio of "guaranteed" transactions in relation to the total, and the lower the range of permitted price variations within the guaranteed category, the more effective is the agreement as a stabilising instrument. The problem here is one of finding a price range for the guaranteed transactions satisfactory to both exporters and importers as being near the true average of the market prices expected to prevail during the period in the absence of agreement, so that neither side feels it is paying an excessive price for the elimination of uncertainty. In the experience of the immediate post-war years—characterised by scarcities which were known to be largely temporary—there was little to go on for establishing such a price, so that the prices selected as the basis of such an agreement were necessarily "shots in the dark." At the same time, because of the change in the economic climate in the course of 1949, and the wide uncertainties concerning the future connected with it, the time was particularly propitious for the conclusion of such an agreement. Thus, I.W.A. came into being—for a four-year period—with guaranteed transactions extending to over two-thirds of the expected total transactions of participating countries, and an arbitrarily chosen price range that permitted gradually rising variations from around ±10 per cent. of the mean in the first year to ±20 per cent. of the mean in the final year. Experience since 1949 seems to indicate, however, that unless some new principle for the determination of

prices on guaranteed transactions can be introduced—making the prices selected appear less arbitrary, and less a matter of pure bargaining between exporters and importers—it may not be possible to renegotiate an agreement of the same scope.

15. In the following sections, the problem of internal policies will be discussed first, and the question of finding a more suitable basis for stabilising the prices of transactions under the Agreement will then be discussed. Appendix A presents a more detailed theoretical discussion of the effects of arrangements of this type on the fluctuations in market prices. In Appendix B, the effects of certain proposals concerning prices are examined, in relation to the existing Wheat Agreement.

II. THE PROBLEM OF IMPLEMENTATION IN EXPORTING AND IMPORTING COUNTRIES

16. As was pointed out in paragraph 13 above, it depends on the domestic policies of participating countries how far the objective of greater stability of income envisaged in the Agreement will prove consistent with the effective functioning of the price mechanism for maintaining equilibrium between production and consumption over longer periods. In actual fact, policies regarding distribution and marketing of wheat differ in various countries for reasons that may be largely independent of the International Wheat Agreement; some governments desire to retain competitive private trade, while others prefer public control of distribution. The effective operation of the Agreement may be possible under either system provided that adequate supplementary measures are introduced to ensure that the benefits of more stable prices under the Agreement do not risk being wiped out through the greater instability of prices in the free market.[1]

17. To illustrate the nature of the problem, let us suppose,

[1] The question as to whether the operation of an agreement of the I.W.A. type would in itself tend to enlarge the range of price fluctuations in the free market (thereby partially nullifying its benefits) is one that has received considerable attention in economic literature. The problem has various aspects and raises rather involved issues, which are discussed in some detail in Appendix A. The results of that analysis indicate, however, that while there might be a tendency towards greater price fluctuations in the free market, this is not inherent in the principles of the Agreement, but depends on the domestic policies operated in conjunction with it and also on the uneven distribution of the guaranteed quantities among exporters and importers, in relation to normal supplies and requirements.

first, that both production and distribution of wheat are entirely uncontrolled and in the hands of competitive private trade in both exporting and importing countries. It is technically perfectly conceivable that the Agreement should be operated so as to leave the conditions of production and marketing completely unaffected, while merely maintaining a central record of individual transactions. In that case, the implementation of the Agreement would consist solely of periodic payments between the governments of participating countries. These would annually pay each other the difference between prices actually paid for individual transactions and the guaranteed maximum or minimum price, for transactions up to the guaranteed amount; plus the total guaranteed price on the short-fall, if any, of their total transactions below the guaranteed amount (assuming, of course, that the actual price paid on transactions is below the minimum guaranteed price of buyers, or above the maximum guaranteed price of sellers; otherwise no obligations would arise). To preserve the multilateral character of the Agreement, it may be supposed that under these arrangements payments are made through a central pool. Countries which happen to be debtors in the transactions of any particular year would pay their debts in their own currencies to a central pool, which would then apportion these payments among the creditor countries according to their credits. These intergovernmental payments would constitute credit or debit items in the general budgets of participating countries; and it may be supposed that they would involve offsetting changes in general taxation. In this way the income-stabilising effects of the Agreement would be passed on to the general body of taxpayers of the participating countries; if the actual price were below the minimum guaranteed price, there would be some reduction in the general level of taxation of exporting countries; and if the actual price were above the maximum price, there would be some reduction in the general taxation of importing countries. But for this very reason the Agreement would only have a very limited effect on the actual producers or consumers of the particular commodity—unless the economy of a given country happened to be largely specialised in the production of that commodity, or unless the consumption of that commodity were fairly general and evenly distributed among the body of taxpayers. It is evident, however, that under these arrangements the Agreement would still secure definite benefits to participating countries: on the national plane, there would be protection against the balance-of-payments effects of market instabilities, while individual producers and consumers would still derive some personal benefit through resulting changes in taxation. On the other hand, the efficacy of the Agreement as a stabiliser, under such arrangements, would clearly be more limited. The functioning of the price mechanism would hardly be affected; the fluctuations in market prices, and the incentives to adjustment to both producers and consumers in consequence of price changes, would be much the same as in the absence of any agreement.

18. We may suppose, next, that participating governments, while leaving private trade uncontrolled, desire directly to recompense traders (and through them, the ultimate producers and consumers) rather than other participating governments. This involves the payment of a subsidy by exporting countries to their traders in periods when the actual market price is above the maximum guaranteed price; and a subsidy paid by importing countries to their traders, when the actual price is below the minimum guaranteed price; in both cases, provided that the traders receive or pay the guaranteed price on transactions for which a government subsidy is paid. This system presupposes some quota allocation of guaranteed transactions among traders of countries benefiting through the operation of the Agreement —that is a quota allocation among traders of importing countries when the actual price is above the maximum guaranteed price (and when, therefore, the governments of exporting countries pay a subsidy), and a quota allocation among traders of exporting countries when the actual price is below the minimum guaranteed price (and when, therefore, the governments of importing countries pay a subsidy).[1] In both cases, this would merely lead

[1] A system analogous to the one outlined here is actually in force in at least one exporting country (U.S.A.) and several importing countries (e.g. Belgium, Guatemala, and Venezuela). Since at present the actual price is above the maximum guaranteed price, the United States Government pays a subsidy to exporters, while the Government of, say, Belgium allocates a quota of guaranteed transactions among importers. But if, on the contrary, the price were below the minimum guaranteed price, the Government of Belgium would have to pay a subsidy and the United States Government would have to institute a system of quota allocation among its traders.

to exceptional gains by traders receiving a quota allocation unless special steps were taken to ensure that the traders passed on these benefits to the ultimate producers and consumers. It is difficult to see how this might be done, except by some method of price control which would force traders of importing countries to sell at a fixed maximum price, and traders of exporting countries to buy at a fixed minimum price.[1] Even so the price received by producers or paid by consumers would, at best, reflect the average price paid on guaranteed and non-guaranteed transactions taken together. This, of course, would considerably reduce (though not wholly eliminate) the incentive effect of the preservation of a variable market price. It should be noted that the problem of instituting a system of price control only arises (a) in importing countries when the actual price is above the maximum guaranteed price, and (b) in exporting countries when the actual price is below the minimum guaranteed price. In these cases, however, the fixed maximum or minimum price in a given participating country would have to be continually adjusted (according to changes in the market price) if the desired effect of passing on the benefits to producers or consumers were to be ensured.

19. We may next suppose that participating governments, while leaving private trade uncontrolled, attempt to stabilise the internal price in each country by means of government-operated buffer stocks.[2] When this is done by major exporting countries it may, of course, in itself exert a strong influence on the world price of the commodity. Subject to this, however, the result of such a system—assuming that in each country the domestic price is determined within a narrow range—is that the domestic price in individual countries would differ from the world market price (that is, the price currently obtainable in non-guaranteed international transactions) and the governments of both exporting and importing countries would have to institute a special system of subsidies or levies, both for exports and imports, to equalise the difference between internal prices and the world market price. In the absence of such a scheme, either the internal price

---

[1] In Belgium, a scheme of this kind is in operation, with a Government-fixed maximum retail price of bread.

[2] This is partially the case in the U.S.A. where the Government must buy wheat whenever the actual price falls below the support price.

stabilisation scheme would break down (through the depletion of publicly-owned stocks), or the normal flow of international trade would be disturbed (through the diversion of supplies from exports to stock accumulation in exporting countries or, conversely, through abnormally large imports with resulting stock accumulation in importing countries, etc.). Such subsidies or levies on exports and imports (added to any subsidies paid, or payments made, under the Agreement) would have to be constantly varied to equalise the difference between the fluctuating market price and the stable internal price. This alone renders such a scheme, in the absence of other controls (particularly controls over international trade), wholly impracticable; except perhaps in the United States where, because of that country's dominant position in world exports, internal price policies may exert a primary influence on world prices. It should be noted also that a scheme of this kind, while achieving the object of stabilising incomes of both producers and consumers, would almost entirely eliminate the incentive effects of a fluctuating world price on producers and consumers. In such a scheme all the problems arising out of the buffer stock proposal which were indicated in paragraphs 9 and 10 above would be present.

20. It is a different matter when participating governments (of both exporting and importing countries) build up publicly-owned stocks, not so much to stabilise prices within a narrow range, as to ensure that the movement of stocks in the economy as a whole operates in a price-stabilising rather than in a price-destabilising direction—that is, to ensure that in times of exceptional scarcity, the situation is improved by releasing stocks, and in times of glut it is equally improved by absorbing stocks. The operation of such a policy of stock-variation—provided no attempt is made to prevent price changes within normal ranges—would, for the reasons advanced in paragraph 11 above, greatly contribute to the efficient functioning of the price mechanism, since it would facilitate the orderly adjustment of production (or consumption) to genuine variations in supply/demand relations. It would also help both exporting and importing countries in the effective fulfilment of obligations assumed under the Agreement.

21. Let us now suppose (this is actually the case in some of

the exporting and importing countries, though for reasons largely unconnected with the acceptance of the Wheat Agreement) that participating governments place the distribution of wheat entirely under government control through an official agency which becomes the sole buyer of wheat both in the domestic and foreign markets, and the sole seller of wheat, both to foreign countries and to domestic consumers. In principle, there are two methods which the government agency might follow in determining the price of purchases and sales:

(a) The government agency might set the price so as to cause —in the case of exporting countries—the producer to receive the *average* price obtained on all types of sales and —in the case of importing countries—the consumers to pay the *average* price paid on all types of purchases.[1] It is assumed here that the government agency desires to balance its receipts and expenditure. It is possible, of course, that for reasons unconnected with the operation of the Agreement, the government should not desire to balance the purchasing agency's accounts—e.g. when it desires to subsidise the price to the consumer, or to subsidise the producer, or to withhold part of the receipts of producers to build up a stabilisation fund, etc. So long, however, as the prices paid to producers (or charged to consumers) constitute a simple average, this makes no real difference to the principle at operation.[2]

(b) The alternative method would be a dual pricing system under which the difference in price, if any, between the prices received (or paid) in the case of guaranteed transactions, and the prices received (or paid) in transactions outside the Agreement, are directly reflected in the manner of payment to producers and in the manner of charges to consumers:

[1] The methods current in Canada or Australia, among exporters, and, to some extent, in the United Kingdom, among importers, correspond to this, except that for purely administrative reasons both in Australia and in Canada the government board fixes a provisional price and makes a final payment afterwards on the basis of its actual receipts.

[2] The system actually in force in the United Kingdom differs from this in so far as the prices fixed for domestic producers are largely governed by domestic costs of production and are independent of movements in world prices; while the prices charged to consumers reflect the Government's cost-of-living subsidy policy.

(i) In the case of exporting countries, this method requires the following technique. The producers should initially receive a basic payment per bushel on all produce sold to the government agency. Each farmer should then be allotted a "basic quota" (in terms of so many bushels) which bears the same relation to his total output in a representative year as exports guaranteed under the Agreement bear to the total production of wheat in the country.[1] (When the quota is initially determined in this way it should, of course, remain fixed during the period of operation of the Agreement, irrespective of subsequent variations in production.) Finally, when the crop is disposed of by the government agency, the farmers should receive two separate and distinct final payments: one, on the "quota" sales which, together with the basic payment already made, should reflect the price received by the government agency on guaranteed transactions; and another, a final payment on "non-quota" sales, which should reflect the actual price received by the government agency on domestic sales and on foreign sales outside the Agreement.[2] (In order to ensure that farmers receive a price on non-quota sales reflecting this, even in cases where the price of such sales is well below the price on guaranteed transactions, it would be necessary to fix the initial or basic payment per bushel well below the guaranteed price.) Thus, the whole benefit from greater income stability is passed on to producers, while at the same time their receipts fully

[1] Depending on the policies adopted with regard to domestic sales (see below) this quota might also reflect some proportion of the output destined for domestic consumption.

[2] The prices charged in many countries on domestic sales of wheat are determined by considerations of general economic policy and the desire for cost-of-living stabilisation, rather than by considerations of production policy. In the interests of production policy it would, of course, be desirable that all actual subsidies paid to wheat consumers constitute a charge on general taxation, so that prices received by producers would not be affected by them. If, on the other hand, governments desired to fix a price on domestic wheat as a means of securing a more stable overall price to farmers, it would also be desirable—for reasons advanced in the text—that they operate, with respect to such sales, a dual price system, i.e. that they extend the principle of the basic quota so as to comprise not only the guaranteed sales under the Agreement but also the greater part of the output destined for domestic consumption.

reflect the variation in market prices on marginal output; the incentives to adjustment afforded by market price changes are thereby maximised.

(ii) In the case of importing countries the adoption of an equivalent principle is more difficult, but at the same time—at any rate, in the case of wheat—less important, owing to the fact that bread consumption would in any case be highly irresponsive to price changes. One method by which the government could discriminate between the prices paid on marginal and non-marginal purchases is by means of a rationing system of flour or of bread, under which the rationed part of the supply would be sold at a fixed price, while the non-rationed part at variable prices. It is highly doubtful, however, whether the results would justify the adoption of such a scheme, even if the obvious political and social objections to it could be ignored. However, it would always be open to governments of importing countries to vary the price charged for wheat for purposes of non-human consumption, in accordance with prices paid on non-guaranteed transactions. Practically, the latter is by far the more important aspect of the problem, since the elasticity of demand for wheat used for animal feed is much greater than the elasticity of demand for wheat intended for human consumption.[1] (It is in any case mainly through the change in consumption for non-human uses that wheat consumption normally adjusts itself to changes in available supplies.)

22. This last method—which we may briefly call the "dual pricing method"—is unquestionably the most effective one for implementing, on the national level, the basic principles of an international agreement of this type. Its advantage over the method first described (in paragraph 17) is that the benefits

[1] A similar dual pricing method could also be introduced for the domestic produce of importing countries, although in their case this may not be nearly so important; partly, because in most importing countries some arrangement is already in force which maintains prices paid to producers at a fairly stable level; also, because the elasticity of supply of wheat in deficit areas is frequently small.

deriving from the Agreement devolve on the producers (and perhaps also on the consumers); its advantage over the second and the third methods (described in paragraphs 18 and 19) is that it gives the maximum incentive to adjustment to the changing requirements and, at the same time, avoids the administrative difficulties involved in ensuring that the benefits are passed on from intermediaries to ultimate producers or consumers. This method also presupposes that international transactions are concluded between government agencies, which are thus directly responsible for ensuring that the terms of the Agreement are observed. The method presumes that in normal circumstances there is a fair margin of supplies available for export in each exporting country over and above the exports guaranteed under the Agreement. This, of course, is a criterion of the successful implementation of the Agreement itself—since countries might not be able to fulfil their obligations in years of short crop if they guaranteed an unduly high proportion of their normal supplies —but it is important that it should be kept in view when the distribution of guaranteed quantities under the Agreement among the various exporting countries is considered. It is desirable that, as far as possible, guaranteed quantities should be so distributed among the different exporters that they constitute a fairly uniform proportion with regard to normal supplies available for export.[1, 2]

23. Actual methods in force at present in the various countries participating in the International Wheat Agreement contain elements of most of the methods enumerated above, or combinations of them. Thus, in the case of the United States, domestic producers receive either the prevailing market price, or the so-called "support" price fixed by domestic legislation, whichever is the higher. When the prevailing market price is above the price fixed for guaranteed transactions, the government pays the difference. (The domestic market price could fall below the minimum price on guaranteed transactions only if the latter were above

[1] For reasons advanced in paragraphs 18–19 of Appendix A, it is equally desirable that the distribution of guaranteed quantities among importers should bear a fairly uniform relation to their normal requirements.

[2] The ratio of guaranteed transactions to normal supplies, as was argued in paragraph 14 above, must be fairly high if the agreement is to be effective as a stabilising instrument; though, for reasons advanced in paragraph 10, not so high as to prevent exporters from deriving any benefit from high prices in years of relatively short crop.

the domestic "support" price, which is not the case at present.) The methods adopted in the United States imply therefore that (*a*) the income-stabilising features of the Wheat Agreement do not directly affect the producers of wheat, whose income is protected only through the "floor" provided by domestic legislation; (*b*) variations in market prices are effective in providing inducements to producers at the margin of production, so long as the actual price is above the "support" price. Producers have the same incentives in this case, as they would have in the absence of an agreement; (*c*) if, however, the price paid in international transactions were to fall below the guaranteed minimum price (which, as far as can be foreseen, would mean *ipso facto* that it is below the domestic support price) the acceptance of the agreement would merely benefit the United States Treasury rather than individual wheat producers (who would in any case obtain the support price under domestic legislation). The methods in force in the United States, therefore, appear to be adequate for maintaining producers' incentives when the actual market price is above the domestic "support" price, though, in that case, they are not effective in stabilising the income of producers relative to fluctuations in market prices. When, on the other hand, the market price is below domestic support levels, the arrangements in force are effective in stabilising the income of producers but do not afford incentives to adjust production to changing requirements.[1]

24. In Australia and Canada, a government board buys the whole crop at a price that is provisionally fixed and is supplemented afterwards by final payments varying with actual receipts of the board from sales. This corresponds to the method described under paragraph 21 (*a*) above, the prices received by farmers simply reflecting the average prices received on all transactions. This, as explained above, does not render price incentives entirely inoperative, but it greatly reduces their efficacy. (In the case of Australia the actual situation is aggravated by the fact that prices fixed for domestic sales are greatly below prices obtainable for

---

[1] It is, however, provided in United States domestic legislation, that if market prices fall below domestic support levels for prolonged periods (while the government corporation continues to accumulate stocks in consequence) additional measures will be taken (by means of acreage restrictions or marketing quotas) to secure an adjustment of production.

exports, and also because the government board withholds part of the receipts for the purpose of building up a stabilisation fund, with the result that the average price received by farmers is greatly below the average price received from exports, not to mention the price on non-guaranteed transactions. The reduction in the Australian wheat acreage over the last two years was undoubtedly largely caused by this policy.)

25. In the case of importing countries, there are corresponding differences between countries where all wheat trade is under public control (such as the United Kingdom) and others where it is in private hands (such as Belgium, etc.). As indicated in paragraph 18, there is always a danger, in the latter case, of intermediaries retaining all internal benefits from the Agreement instead of passing them on to final consumers. A general feature of the policy of many countries, on the other hand, is the subsidy paid on bread, introduced for reasons of internal monetary stabilisation, or on grounds of general economic and social policy. In this case the benefits accruing from the Agreement go to the national budget, since they are reflected in the net budgetary cost of subsidies.

26. It is evident that the methods adopted by different countries with regard to the price and distribution of wheat will continue to vary because of differences in general economic philosophy and basic attitudes toward public control. It cannot be expected that governments should be willing to depart from such general principles for the sake of more effective implementation of international commodity agreements. It is also evident, however, that within the existing framework of policies in force in particular countries, there is room for considerable improvement from the point of view of effective implementation of the Agreement. The most important concrete recommendation that can be made in this connection is that exporting countries having already a government monopoly of wheat purchasing (such as Canada and Australia) should attempt to operate the dual price system described in paragraph 21 (b) above. This would increase considerably the elasticity of the wheat supply in relation to changes in the market price, and would thus tend to narrow the range of price fluctuations over longer periods in the non-guaranteed sector of the market. Since, in the United States, price changes

are already fully reflected in the value of marginal output (when the price is above the support price, while other means are available to restrict production when it is below), the adoption of this proposal by Australia and Canada would mean that the market price would become an effective incentive to producers in the three exporting countries which together are responsible for most of the guaranteed supply of wheat under the Agreement.

27. In addition, participating countries could contribute to the efficient operation of the world wheat market and the effective implementation of the Agreement if they maintained publicly-owned stocks above the levels required by normal periods of turnover and operated them so as to prevent undue fluctuations in market prices in either direction. Proposals to this effect were embodied in the original draft of the Wheat Agreement (Article IX of the draft), which provided that exporting and importing countries both operate special price-stabilising reserves (up to 10 per cent. of their respective guaranteed quantities) to be utilised whenever the free market price rose above the maximum price in the Agreement, and to be accumulated whenever it fell below the minimum price. Though the assumption of such formal obligations by all participating countries did not prove acceptable, it would be desirable to incorporate rather less rigid arrangements in a new agreement, to the effect that publicly-owned stocks, which are in any case carried by the governments of major exporting and importing countries, should be operated so as to alleviate scarcities in times of high prices and to moderate the pressure of excess supplies in time of low prices. This would involve an obligation on the exporting countries to release stocks in the face of an upward movement in prices when the prices themselves are above the maximum price; and a similar obligation on major importers to accumulate stocks in the face of falling prices when these are below the agreed minimum.

III. PRINCIPLES FOR THE DETERMINATION OF PRICES

28. It cannot be emphasised too strongly that the success of stabilisation schemes of the Wheat Agreement type depends predominantly on the agreement operating over longer periods to the advantage both of exporters and of importers, rather than

to the exclusive or overwhelming advantage of one side or the other. Unless a fair division of long-term gains between the two parties can be guaranteed, the principle embodied in the existing Wheat Agreement is doomed to failure, since the willingness of parties to enter into commitments, and to renegotiate the Agreement from time to time, will rapidly diminish.

29. Since the future course of prices (particularly over longer periods) cannot be foretold, it is essential that the terms of the agreement should themselves embody such provisions as would carry a certain assurance to the contracting parties that any advantage accruing from the agreement to one side is likely to be temporary and would automatically tend to compensate itself by a corresponding advantage to the other side in a later period.

30. The Wheat Agreement concluded in 1949 fixed maximum and minimum prices rather arbitrarily and without the introduction of any definite principle for the determination of prices. That participating countries nevertheless succeeded in coming to an agreement may have been chiefly due (as was indicated in paragraph 14) to the peculiar circumstances of the time when the Agreement was concluded. Wheat prices had been steadily falling since the post-war peaks reached in late 1947 and early 1948; and since the general economic situation in leading industrial countries showed symptoms of a growing economic recession in the course of 1949, there was a general expectation on both sides that prices of primary products would continue to fall. Under these conditions, exporters were willing to agree to a maximum price appreciably below the prices then prevailing and also to a minimum price that was to be lower in each subsequent year of operation of the Agreement. The willingness of importing countries to conclude an agreement may be attributed to the fact that the Agreement offered the certain prospect of paying less for wheat than the prices prevailing until then; they were thus merely confronted with the choice between the prospect of an uncertain gain of unknown dimensions or a limited, but certain, gain. Since the outbreak of the Korean war, however, a general inflationary movement in prices has set in and the prices of wheat, though they have risen far less than prices of most other

primary products, have been consistently above the maximum price laid down in the Agreement. This experience does not augur well for the prospects of renewing the Agreement unless the new arrangement embodies some fresh principle of price fixing which, together with the assurance of greater stability, would also give some assurance to producers that over longer periods they will not fare badly, and that the contract prices under the Agreement will not be significantly different—in an average of good years and bad—from the prices they would have obtained in the absence of an agreement.

31. The only way such an assurance can be incorporated in an arrangement is by framing the agreement itself so as to provide for such automatic adjustments of minimum and maximum prices as would maintain these prices, in the long run, around some long-term average of market prices. This means that the prices in the agreement should themselves constitute some moving average of past prices. If the period chosen for obtaining the average is fairly long (say, six to ten years), the main benefit of greater stability will still be preserved, since the *year to year movement* in contract prices under the agreement could only amount to a fraction of the year to year price movements on transactions outside the agreement.

32. The adoption of such a principle of price fixing would require the application of a procedure on the following lines:

(*a*) The prices should basically be determined in terms of a "mean price." Maximum and minimum prices would then be expressed as simple percentage additions or deductions from the "mean price." (As indicated in paragraph 8, the efficacy of the agreement would depend on these percentages being fixed rather narrowly. It would be far more advantageous if a minimum and maximum price could be fixed at ± 5 per cent. of the mean price, than at ± 10 per cent. or ± 15 per cent.)

(*b*) The "mean price" should be automatically adjusted each year by a proportion—laid down in the agreement—of the difference between the previously prevailing mean price and the average prices that were obtained in the previous year in transactions outside the agreement among partici-pating countries. (If this proportion is fixed at one-sixth, this means that the mean price will become a moving average of market prices over a six-year period; if it is fixed at one-eighth, it means it will become a moving average of market prices prevailing over an eight-year period, etc.). The value of the agreement as a stabilising instrument greatly depends, of course, on this proportion being *low*; it is preferable to establish an average over an eight or ten-year period rather than over a six-year period.

(i) For this purpose, *all* transactions (not only transactions under the agreement) between participating countries are to be recorded by the International Wheat Council together with actual prices paid. These prices are then translated by the Council into terms of their "standard equivalent."

(ii) On the basis of this information the Council annually computes and declares the average price paid in trans-actions between participating countries in the pre-vious twelve months (*a*) on guaranteed quantities; (*b*) on non-guaranteed quantities. It then states the new "mean price" for the current year, on the basis of the difference between (*b*) and the mean price of the previous year, multiplied by a coefficient laid down in the agreement. (The fact that there will be an inevitable time lag before the necessary adjustment in the mean price can be computed and stated would not be an in-superable difficulty, since it would be quite possible for the amended price to be deemed to have been in force from the beginning of, say, each crop year. Alterna-tively, the Council could declare a provisional mean price at the beginning of each crop year, subject to final adjustment when all information is available.)[1]

---

[1] Another, administratively simpler, but less reliable, method would be to take the average market prices of a particular quality of wheat in the previous crop year (say, Manitoba No. 1 ex-bulk in store Port Arthur/Fort William, as published week by week by the Canadian Wheat Board) as an indication of the prices relating to non-guaranteed transactions and use this as the basis for computing the annual adjust-ment in the mean price. (In Appendix B, the annual adjustments that would have been involved, had this provision been in operation in the case of the existing Agree-ment, are worked out on this assumption.)

33. It is evident that, subject to the situation described in paragraph 34 below, this method would ensure that over a sufficient number of years the gains and/or losses accruing to one side or the other in the operation of the Agreement would tend to cancel each other out, while at the same time the benefit of greater income stability would be largely retained. As Fig. 1 indicates, if the course of market prices (or more precisely, the prices paid on outside transactions) were to move as shown in curve A, the

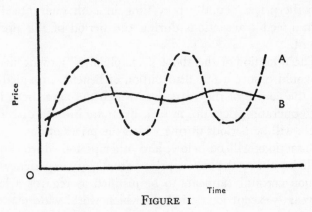

FIGURE 1

prices applicable for transactions guaranteed under the Agreement would move in the manner of curve B.[1]

34. A problem to be faced in connection with this procedure is how the initial "mean price" is to be fixed when the agreement embodying the principle first comes into operation. It should be evident that this initial mean price could not be constructed in

[1] An alternative method of attaining a similar result—which may be termed the method of "half-spread adjustment"—would be to take as the "mean price" of any particular year the maximum price fixed under I.W.A. for the previous year, if market prices in the previous year were at or above the guaranteed maximum price, or the respective minimum price of the previous year if market prices were at or below the guaranteed minimum price. The maximum and minimum prices for the given year would then be fixed around this new mean price, the spread between them remaining constant. This method, though administratively simpler, has, however, the disadvantage that, once there is sufficient discrepancy between supply and demand to bring the agreement into effective operation (i.e. when the market price is at or above the maximum, or at or below the minimum price), the adjustment of the agreement prices from year to year is exactly the same, whether the discrepancy is great or small. The stabilising effects of the agreement may therefore be practically lost. In the "moving average" formula given in the text, the annual adjustment in guaranteed prices is a constant fraction of the difference between market prices and guaranteed maximum or minimum prices; the adjustment in guaranteed prices is therefore directly related to the magnitude of the disturbance without, however, sacrificing the stabilising influence of guaranteed prices.

a similar manner as an average of past prices, primarily because initially there would be no records available from which such a computation could be made; but also partly because conditions in the immediate post-war period were admittedly so abnormal that the parties would hardly accept them as a basis for the computation of such a starting point. It is suggested therefore that, taking into account the interests of both exporting and importing countries, the initial mean price be conceived as some average between the prices actually prevailing in both guaranteed and non-guaranteed transactions during the period of the previous agreement.

35. The adoption of the above principle of a "moving average price" would ensure a fair distribution of benefits provided only that, in the course of the years over which the agreement is designed to operate, prices do, in fact, fluctuate in both directions: that there will be periods during which the prices of non-guaranteed transactions will be below, and other periods during which they will be above the mean price. From past experiences this supposition certainly appears to be justified as regards a longer run of years—except for periods in which world wide monetary instabilities occur. In such periods the general price instability might outweigh the normal fluctuations in the prices of wheat or other primary products, so that the price movement, even over longer periods, might be predominantly in one direction. Thus a continuance of world inflationary tendencies might lead over the years to a continued increase in the dollar price of wheat; a prolonged deflationary movement would lead to the opposite. In this case the adoption of the moving average principle would not be sufficient to ensure *over any given period* an equitable price, since the annually adjusted contract price would steadily lag behind the current market price. To guard against this danger it may be necessary to supplement the principle of a moving average price with the adoption of some formula (which, for the sake of brevity, might be termed a "parity formula," though clearly it will not serve the same purpose as the parity legislation in the United States) which would secure further adjustments in the mean price in accordance with any major movements in the general level of world prices.

36. It might be thought at first that the introduction of any such formula would tend to vitiate the stability accruing from the agreement and to diminish the efficacy of the formula based on a moving average of market prices. This, however, is by no means the case. The basic purpose of the agreement is to shield both exporting and importing countries against the instability of incomes generated by price fluctuations. An adjustment in contract prices in accordance with major movements in world prices in general could never make the *real* income of producers or consumers *less* stable than it would be without it; it is the stability of real incomes, and not merely of money incomes, which is the general interest of both exporters and importers. (The adoption of such a formula appears to be mainly in the interest of exporters at present only because inflationary movements have predominated in the recent past and because the fear of inflation is far more prevalent now than the fear of deflation. But if a prolonged deflationary movement were to recur, the incorporation of such a parity formula would equally operate to the benefit of importers.) At the same time it clearly could not be suggested that a parity formula of this kind should supersede the formula for adjusting the contract price with the moving average of market prices— since the former is only applicable when world prices are unstable and does not in itself ensure that the contract prices in the agreement do not operate, over longer periods, to the one-sided advantage of either the producing or the consuming countries. The two formulae complement each other and should be used jointly.[1]

37. While there is thus no logical difficulty in incorporating such a parity formula in the agreement, its practical consideration depends on finding some index of world prices that would be sufficiently comprehensive to serve as a measure of the general change in the value of money and which, at the same time, might be acceptable to both importing and exporting countries. Since the agreement refers to international transactions, clearly only the general price level applicable to international transactions is relevant to the problem; and it may be thought that the relevant prices here are those of goods which the wheat-importing countries

---

[1] *See* Appendix B, where the application of the two formulae is illustrated in relation to the existing Agreement.

sell to the exporting countries in the normal course of trade in exchange for wheat bought from them. However, there is no adequate reason for restricting the price changes to be taken into consideration to any particular category of goods or to the price prevailing in any particular group of countries, as the wheat-exporting countries may wish to use the proceeds from the sale of wheat for the purchase of commodities from all parts of the world, not only from the importing countries.

38. The most satisfactory measure, from this point of view, would therefore be the price level applicable to world trade as a whole, that is, comprising all countries and all commodities with the possible exception of wheat itself, though the importance of wheat in the aggregate quantum of world trade is not such as to make any appreciable difference by its exclusion or inclusion. While there is no method by which the change in the world price level applicable to world trade as a whole could be measured with any accuracy, annual computations are now made by the Statistical Office of the United Nations of both the current dollar value and the volume (i.e. its value at constant dollar prices) of world trade—that is, they compute the "unit value" of transactions applicable to world trade as a whole. The results of this computation for the last few years, given in Appendix B, show the results to be not unsatisfactory in the light of known movements of prices in recent years. It must, of course, be borne in mind that the results of such a computation would serve only as a rough guide rather than as a price measure; as such, however, it is probably more reliable than any other single indicator that could be devised.[1]

39. The fact, however, that this indicator could provide only a rough approximation to changes in world prices means that no precise significance could be attached to *small*, as distinct from larger, changes in the index; and further, that the *exact magnitude* of any change is subject to considerable uncertainty. For these reasons it would be advisable to apply the formula only (*a*) at given intervals, say, at the beginning of each crop year; (*b*) when

---

[1] In particular the fact that the resulting index indicates the "unit value" of world exports (or imports) rather than average prices—i.e. that it does not exclude changes due to the composition of trade—is not likely to be of any significance when world trade as a whole is considered as a single series.

the change in world prices indicated by a comparison between the value and quantum of world trade exceeds a certain proportion (say, 10 per cent. in either direction as compared with a base year); and (c) when the actual adjustment to be applied to agreement prices is itself some proportion (say, 50 per cent.) of the change in prices indicated by the index. Although these provisions would prevent the contract prices under the agreement from being fully adjusted to the change in world prices, they would leave little room for uncertainty as to whether any particular adjustment was really justified or not; they would therefore prove far more acceptable to the contracting parties than if either no adjustment were made, or the index were used for continuous and full-scale adjustments.

40. The adoption of the two principles suggested above—the principle of moving average price and the parity formula—would ensure that the benefit of greater economic stability deriving from the agreement is consistent with the equitable distribution of gains and the effective protection of the interests of both parties. Their inclusion would undoubtedly add to the technical difficulties of negotiating an agreement of this kind and to its actual operation; but these difficulties are unavoidable if the principles embodied in the first Wheat Agreement are to yield their fruit in creating a more stable international economic order. It may be expected that by the inclusion of these two principles, the willingness of both importing and exporting countries to enter into commitments would in time be so increased as to enhance considerably the value of the agreement as a stabilising instrument—through a high proportion of total transactions coming under it, and through a reduction in the margin between the minimum and maximum prices. It would also be possible, then, to extend these principles to other commodities.

APPENDIX A

THE PROBLEMS OF PRICE FLUCTUATIONS

(1) Since the coming into operation of the International Wheat Agreement, there has been considerable discussion in various economic periodicals[1] as to whether the operation of the Agreement itself would tend to enhance the instability of prices in the non-guaranteed sector of the market and thereby offset—partially or fully—the benefit of more stable prices on guaranteed transactions. This problem has various aspects, some of which raise complex issues; but as the analysis presented here indicates, the charge is not, in general, justified; or rather it is justified only when it relates to particular domestic policies adopted by the participating countries, or results from a disproportionate allocation of the guaranteed quantities among them, rather than to any inherent feature of the Agreement itself.

(2) In the following paragraphs, the problem will be examined from three angles: how far it affects the normal incentives to adjustment provided by the market mechanism; how far it affects the elasticities of supply and demand; and finally, how far the reduction in the size of the "free market" may in itself cause greater instability.

Effect on Incentives

(3) As was argued in paragraph 13 above, the principles underlying an I.W.A. type of agreement presuppose for their efficient operation that the effects of variations in market prices are passed on to the ultimate producers (and, though this is less

---

[1] The following articles on the subject of the International Wheat Agreement deal, *inter alia*, with the more specific question of its effects on the free market price of wheat: Golay, F. M., "The International Wheat Agreement of 1949," *Quarterly Journal of Economics*, August 1950, pp. 442–63; Johnson, H. G., "The De-stabilising Effect of International Commodity Agreements on the Prices of Primary Products," *Economic Journal*, September 1950, pp. 626–9; Harbury, C. D., "Commodity Agreements and Price Fluctuations," *Economic Journal*, September 1951, pp. 652–5; Maiden, A. C. B., Orlando, Giuseppe: Pedersen, Jorgen; Burgess, Clare; and Strange, M. G. L., "International Wheat Agreements, Symposium," *International Journal of Agrarian Affairs*, No. 3, September 1949; Niehans, Jürg, "Das Internationale Weizenabkommen auf halbem Wege," *Aussenwirtschaft*, September 1951, pp. 181–95; Tyszynski, H., "Economics of the Wheat Agreement," *Economica*, February 1949, pp. 27–39; "A Note on International Commodity Agreements," *Economica*, November 1950, pp. 437–47; "Commodity Agreements and Price Fluctuations," *Economic Journal*, September 1951, pp. 655–9.

important in the present context, to the ultimate consumers). For, unless the value of the producer's marginal output varies with the price on non-guaranteed transactions, he will have no incentive to expand or to contract output, following upon a change in price—the normal incentives provided by the market mechanism will be inoperative. The preservation of these incentives can be rendered consistent, however, with the operation of the Agreement by the dual pricing method described in paragraph 21 (b) above; this is also the case (as was shown in paragraph 17) when domestic producers receive simply the current market price, though in this latter case, the benefits derived from the Agreement consist only in a stabilising effect on the national income and the balance of payments of participating countries, rather than on the income of wheat producers as a group. However, under arrangements whereby domestic producers receive the *average* price on all transactions (guaranteed and non-guaranteed), the incentives provided by the market are transmitted only with diminished amplitude; and when producers receive a fixed price quite independent of the market price, the incentives will be entirely absent. In the last two cases—assuming that these arrangements are a result of the international agreement, and would not have been introduced without it—the agreement would tend to increase the instability of market prices, since a greater variation in price would be neccessary to secure any given adjustment in supply/demand relations.[1]

Effect on Elasticities

(4) An entirely different argument, that is independent of the particular form of compensation paid to producers or of charges to consumers, and applying equally under the dual price system, is based on the supposition that the very diminution of the income effects of price changes will affect the responsiveness of consumers and producers—that is, will alter the elasticities of the con-

---

[1] This remains true, even though the argument of paragraph 11, above, suggests that the price fluctuations in the free market are often "excessive" from the point of view of giving the right incentives to adjustment to producers. While it is true to say that the moderation of abnormally large and rapid price changes facilitates the orderly adjustment of production to changing conditions, the "averaging" of agreement and non-agreement prices serves to attenuate the effect of price variations of a normal kind equally with the others.

sumers' demand curves and the producers' supply curves. In order to deal with this question it is necessary, first, to analyse the factors which determine the elasticities of supply and demand. This, in turn, necessitates a somewhat lengthy excursion into the field of economic theory. This analysis, however, may also prove useful in throwing additional light on the causes of price instabilities in commodity markets. In order to isolate this problem from the one discussed earlier, it will be assumed for the purposes of the argument that the "dual price system" is operated as regards both producers and consumers, so that the market price is effective as regards both marginal sales and marginal purchases.

(5) Economists group the forces influencing the elasticities of both demand and supply under two heads, which are normally termed "income effects" and "substitution effects." The "substitution effect" is that part of the change in production or in consumption following upon a given change in price which can be attributed to the desire of producers or consumers to substitute that particular commodity for other commodities (or vice versa) as the result of the change in the price of that commodity relative to others. The substitution effect always works in the same direction—that is, it will cause an expansion of production and contraction of consumption following upon a rise in price, and vice versa in case of a fall in price—its magnitude depending in any particular case on the extent to which substitutes can be found for the commodity in question, either in the sphere of consumption or of production. On the production side, if a particular commodity, such as wheat, is taken in isolation, the substitution effects might be considerable, since the producers (i.e. the farmers) generally have extensive possibilities of substituting other crops (such as coarse grains or pasture) for wheat, but if, as more usually happens, the change in the price of wheat is only a part of a more general change in agricultural commodities (i.e. the prices of various kinds of grains, etc., move more or less in sympathy) the substitution effect may be rather low, since the farmer has no appreciable opportunities (either for his labour or the material resources he employs) of substituting non-agricultural for agricultural products—except, of course, that he may be tempted to

work harder or less hard as, with the change in agricultural prices, the real reward of his effort changes. On the consumption side, wheat used for human consumption (bread) has no easy substitute; that part of the demand, however, which comes from the use of wheat as feedstuff, may have an appreciable elasticity of substitution, this again depending on whether the price of wheat moves in isolation or whether it is part of a general movement of the prices of crops.

(6) The "income effect" consists of that part of the change in supply or demand following upon a given change in price which is due to the change in real income (of both buyers and sellers) associated with the change in price. A change in price, as described in paragraphs 5 and 6 above (see p. 65) in itself implies a change of income of buyers and sellers, the magnitude of which depends on the proportion of the total income of producers which is acquired through the sale of the commodity in question and the proportion of the total income of consumers which is spent on the commodity in question. Hence, a change in a particular price in a given proportion is equivalent to a change in income of a correspondingly lesser proportion, the difference depending on the proportionate importance of that particular commodity in total sales or purchases. To the extent that price changes cause a change in income, they have much the same effect on the demand (or supply) of the commodity, as if the income of producers or consumers had been changed, prices remaining unchanged. These income effects are therefore only important in the case of those commodities which take up a considerable proportion of the consumer's budget, or which represent a major source of income to producers.

(7) Since producers normally acquire their income through the sale of a more limited number of various commodities and services, than the number of such commodities and services into which the consumer's budget is divided, these income effects are normally a more important factor on the side of supply than on the side of demand. Here, however, it is important to bear in mind that income effects on the side of supply are only relevant in those cases where production clearly involves the sacrifice of some non-monetary alternative to the producer. They are not relevant,

therefore (or only to a very minor extent), in the case of manufactures where the producer's costs consist of wages paid to hired
labour and the raw materials purchased, and where the entre-
preneur's own effort in production is not a significant element in
cost. In the case of primary products, however, these income effects
may be very important; precisely because, with the family farm
still remaining the dominant type of producing unit in agriculture, output is directly dependent on the magnitude of personal
effort of the producers—though to a lesser extent in countries
where agriculture is highly mechanised.

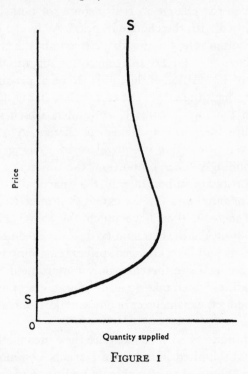

FIGURE I

(8) Finally, it must be borne in mind that the income effect
of a change in price may operate in either direction. There are
commodities the consumption of which would increase with a
rise in income, and others the consumption of which would
decrease following on such a rise; accordingly, it is usual to classify
commodities as "normal" and "inferior" goods, respectively.

Further, it should be remembered that an income effect operates in a reverse direction on buyers and sellers, precisely because a rise in price implies a *fall* in income to the one and a *rise* in income to the other. Thus in the case of "normal" goods, the income effect reduces the elasticity of supply and increases the elasticity of demand; in the case of "inferior" goods, it increases the elasticity of supply and reduces the elasticity of demand.[1]

In other words, the effects might cause the supply curve of agricultural products to be "backward rising" (as shown in Fig. 1), a phenomenon which has frequently been associated with the marketable produce of primitive economies, but sometimes also with the agricultural output of economically advanced countries. The basic reason, in either case, is that the producer has no easy alternative occupation to turn to, and therefore is ultimately sacrificing only his own effort when he is producing agricultural commodities. When prices go up, he will be inclined to spend some part of his increased real income on increased leisure—in other words, he will prefer to work less hard.

(9) The implication of this analysis, in the case of agriculture, is that the income effects of a change in price operate to *reduce* the elasticity of supply. In fact, these effects may even prove more powerful than the substitution effects and thus cause—within certain price ranges—a reduction (rather than an increase) in supply following upon a rise in price, and an increase in supply (instead of a reduction) following upon a fall in price—whereas with the "substitution effect" it is necessarily the other way round. In other words, the effects might cause the supply curve of agricultural products to be "backward rising" (as shown in Fig. 1), a phenomenon which has frequently been associated with the marketable produce of primitive economies, but sometimes also with the agricultural output of economically advanced countries. The basic reason, in either case, is that the producer has no easy alternative occupation to turn to, and therefore is ultimately sacrificing only his own effort when he is producing agricultural commodities. When prices go up, he will be

---

[1] For reasons mentioned below, however, the case of "inferior" goods does not normally arise on the side of supply.

inclined to spend some part of his increased real income on increased leisure—in other words, he will prefer to work less hard rather than to increase in the same proportion the supply of commodities at his disposal. It must be borne in mind, of course, that this backward rising supply curve is far more likely to apply to agricultural produce in general than to any particular crop taken separately; or rather, that it is likely to apply to the latter in so far as the prices of various commodities move together; if not, then only as far as a single commodity is responsible for a large part of the farmer's total income. But even when the supply curve is forward—and not backwards—rising, it remains true that the elasticity of supply will be less, as a result of income effects, than it would be otherwise.

(10) In the particular case of wheat, it is possible that the income effect may also operate to reduce elasticity on the side of demand. It is well known that bread is an "inferior" commodity because its consumption per head varies inversely with real income per head. Moreover, in the low income groups and in communities with a low average income per head, bread also takes up an important proportion of total consumers' expenditure. Hence, in these cases, the income effect of a change in the bread price is significant and may operate so as to out-balance the substitution effect. This gives rise to the well-known "Giffen paradox," that —within certain price ranges—a rise in the price of bread is followed by an increase in consumption and a fall in the price by a decrease. In such cases, the income effects cause the demand curve to be "backward falling," as shown in Fig. 2. In more advanced communities, where bread is no longer an important factor in expenditure, the "Giffen paradox" as such does not apply; but bread remains, of course, an "inferior" commodity, and the income effect reduces the elasticity of demand. On the other hand, in parts of Europe and Latin America, in Asia and in Africa, wheat competes with other food grains in consumption, and often forms only an insignificant part of the diet. In some geographical areas wheat is considered a "superior" bread grain, in others, e.g. in the Far East, it seems to hold an intermediate position between coarse grains and rice. If world demand for wheat imports as a whole is taken into consideration, it is

doubtful that the income effect is at all important. In so far, however, as it may be of significance, it is possible that, in view of the importance in wheat trade of countries where wheat is the staple bread grain, it will operate to reduce the elasticity of demand rather than to increase it.[1] In the case of the non-human uses of wheat (as feed-stuffs), on the other hand, only the substitution effect, and not the income effect, appears to be relevant in determining the elasticity of demand. This is because wheat used as feedstuff is in competition with numerous other feeds, and

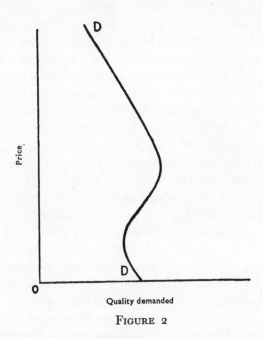

FIGURE 2

amounts to only a small proportion of the total cost of animal products on which the consumers' demand directly depends.

(11) It is the combination of inelastic (or even backward rising) supply curves with inelastic (or even backward falling) demand curves that is the basic reason for the inherent instability

---

[1] Thus in the case of wheat, unlike in many other cases, the income effects may operate so as to reduce the elasticity of both demand and supply. This is because the income effects themselves are different in the case of producers and of consumers; for consumers, bread is an "inferior" commodity but for producers it is not wheat itself that is relevant but the effort involved in producing it, which in turn is a "normal" commodity.

of prices of staple agricultural commodities. Situations in which
the supply curve is backward rising (and/or the demand curve
is backward falling) always involve the possibility of multiple
equilibria as illustrated in Figs. 3 (a) and 3 (b). As is shown in
Figs. 3 (a) and 3 (b), demand and supply can be equal at three
different prices of which the middle position (C) is totally unstable. Demand exceeds supply at prices higher than (C) and
supply exceeds demand at prices lower than (C); thus, there can
never be a position where market prices come to a rest. (A) and
(B), however, represent a stable equilibrium and it should be
noted that when, as in Fig. 3 (a), a backward rising supply curve
is matched by a backward falling demand curve, supply and
demand can become equal either at a high price or a low price,
without the quantities traded being necessarily different in the
two cases. The importance of this is not confined, of course, to
situations where several possibilities of equilibrium occur simultaneously. As is evident from Fig. 4, the question whether the
two curves actually cut several times or only once, is purely
a matter of their relative position. (In Fig. 4, three different
positions for the demand curve are shown—representing proportionately small shifts in demand—the position of the supply
curve remaining constant. In case of D_1 Point B_1, in case of D_2
Points A_2 and B_2 and in case of D_3 Point A_3 represent the positions
of equilibrium.) The significance of potentially multiple equilibria, deriving from a particular market situation, lies always in
the fact that relatively small changes in conditions of supply or
demand may necessitate a switch from a high-price to a low-price
equilibrium or vice versa, thus causing disproportionate changes
in prices. Such shifts in the relative position of the demand and
supply schedules are continuously occurring in most markets (in
the case of agricultural commodities they may, of course, be
merely due to variations in the weather), but as is shown by comparison with Fig. 5 (presuming the same proportionate shifts in
the relative position of demand and supply curves, as are shown
in Fig. 4, they could never lead to such disproportionate price
variations when the demand and supply curves are of a normal
shape.

(12) The peculiar nature of the elasticity of demand and

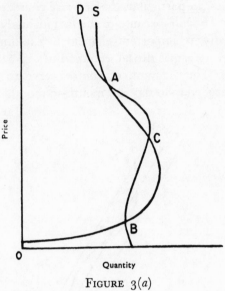

FIGURE 3(a)

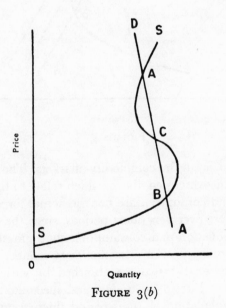

FIGURE 3(b)

supply schedules (in particular, the perverse character of the producers' supply schedule because of the factors analysed above) is
thus undoubtedly an important element in explaining the wide
price variations of agricultural commodities, particularly over
longer periods. They cannot, of course, serve to explain adequately the large day-to-day or month-to-month variations in

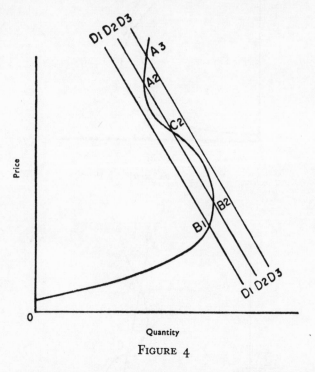

FIGURE 4

prices liable to occur in commodity markets. The supply and
demand schedules discussed above, which relate to the behaviour
of producers and consumers, are not the actual forces determining market prices over very short periods, since the market does
not equate production and consumption continuously, from day
to day, so to speak, or even from month to month; short-period
differences between the two are absorbed by variations in the
amount of stocks carried by traders and speculators or governments. The explanation of short-period fluctuations in market
prices is rather to be sought in the changing attitudes toward stock-

holding. Speculation, when acting in a price-stabilising direction, should smooth the transition from one equilibrium position to the other (i.e. in adjusting the level of consumption to changes in the level of production or vice versa); but as the behaviour of commodity markets in the past has amply shown, speculation also acts in a price-destabilising direction—at any rate within

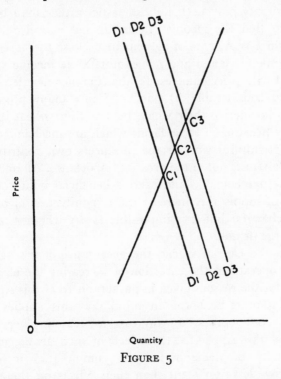

FIGURE 5

certain ranges of price oscillation—so that it is impossible to say how far, on all counts and viewing the matter over longer periods, speculation causes the range of price fluctuations in the market to become narrower.

(13) We are now in a position to answer the question as to how the operation of an agreement of the type of the International Wheat Agreement affects the elasticities of supply and demand. The effect of the agreement is to reduce the income effects of price changes. This will necessarily operate in the direction of increasing the elasticity of supply; and if the income effects of

price changes were entirely eliminated by it, any supply curves that were previously backward rising would necessarily become forward-rising. This in itself, as is evident from a comparison of Figs. 4 and 5, would tend greatly to reduce the possible magnitude of price variations corresponding to a given proportionate shift in the relation of the two curves. It must be remembered, however, (*a*) that supply may be merely inelastic, rather than backward rising; (*b*) that the income effects are not entirely eliminated through an I.W.A. type of agreement because the agreement in itself will merely lessen and not eliminate the income variations associated with price changes; (*c*) that the income effects are not necessarily considerable (i) partly because many producers of wheat do not derive their whole income from wheat itself, and (ii) partly because on those farms which are mechanised and/or engage agricultural workers the producers own contribution in terms of labour is not of the greatest importance. All one can say is that the agreement would exert a beneficial influence on the elasticity of supply (i.e. increase the responsiveness of producers to price changes) but it is impossible to say whether this effect will be large or not.

(14) In the case of wheat, the acceptance of the agreement may also operate in the direction of increasing the elasticity of demand, for the reasons given in paragraph 10 of this Appendix; although it must be borne in mind that this applies only to "inferior" commodities.[1] In any case, for reasons given in paragraph 7 of this Appendix, the effects of such arrangements on the elasticity of demand for the commodities in question should prove less significant than their effects on the elasticity of supply.

(15) The general conclusion of the above analysis therefore is that, to the extent that the International Wheat Agreement succeeds in eliminating the income effects of price changes, it increases the elasticity of supply and possibly also the elasticity

[1] H. G. Johnson, in "The De-stabilising Effect of International Commodity Agreements on the Prices of Primary Products," *Economic Journal*, loc. cit., argued that the elimination of income effects will operate so as to reduce the elasticity of demand and thereby cause an increased instability in market prices. Apart from the fact that he made an altogether inadequate allowance for the reverse influence on the side of supply, he did not consider that, in the case of "inferior" commodities, the elimination of the income effects would operate in the contrary direction, i.e. to increase the elasticity of the demand curve, and not reduce it.

of demand, although income effects on the side of demand are in any case not likely to be important. To the extent that in its overall effect this influence is significant, the Agreement tends to reduce the scope of price fluctuations in the free market. This stabilising effect on prices will, of course, be the more powerful the more comprehensive the scope of the Agreement and the more it will be possible to extend its principle to other related commodities. Agricultural prices, as well as agricultural incomes, could therefore be stabilised to a far more significant extent if agreements of this kind embraced several commodities (e.g. coarse grains, as well as wheat, etc.), rather than when they relate to a single commodity only.

(16) To the extent that, under a dual pricing system, the moderation of income effects increases the responsiveness of producers to changing requirements, the scope of price fluctuations will be further narrowed if the influence of speculative forces is taken into account. As is well known, the price stabilising effects of speculation are more likely to predominate over the destabilising effects, the smaller the likely range of price fluctuations caused by non-speculative factors. Hence the increase in the elasticity of producers' and consumers' supply and demand schedules would in itself tend to cause speculation to operate in a more price-stabilising direction. In the specific case under consideration, the Agreement might have a further stabilising effect on speculators because the mere knowledge that buyers can obtain a large part of their normal supply at guaranteed prices (and, vice versa, sellers can obtain guaranteed prices for a large part of their normal supply) might itself weaken any expectation that either buyers or sellers might be "squeezed"— particularly when, as was suggested in paragraph 27, the publicly-owned and operated stocks of both exporting and importing countries tend to become larger, as a result of the operation of the agreement.

Effects of the "Narrowing" of the Market

(17) A third argument[1] advanced in the contention that the I.W.A. type of agreement tends to increase the instability of

[1] Cf. Burgess and Strange, *International Journal of Agricultural Affairs*, loc. cit.

prices in the free market is based on the fact that the proportionate fluctuations in supply (caused by weather changes, etc.), in the non-guaranteed sector of the market will be much greater than the corresponding fluctuations in the whole market. Thus a 10 per cent. reduction in total exportable supplies will cause a 30 per cent. reduction in supplies to the free market when two-thirds of the supplies constitute guaranteed transactions under the agreement. Hence, it is argued, the price fluctuations in the non-guaranteed sector will be considerably greater as a result of crop changes in the one case than in the other. This argument ignores, however, the fact that in the partial market, not only the proportionate changes in supply are greater, but also the numerical value of the elasticity of demand; and in a homogeneous market, one should precisely offset the other (since both the variations in supply and the elasticity of demand must be multiplied by the same coefficient to translate the values applicable to the whole market to the values applicable to a partial market).

(18) However, the "free wheat market" is not homogeneous, since the demand comes from many different importing countries, with internal markets that are more or less isolated from each other. Hence, if the guaranteed quantities under the agreement are unequally distributed among the various importing countries in relation to their normal requirements, any reduction in world market supplies will affect those countries proportionately more that have a relatively low quota; this, in turn, would tend to enhance the effect of the reduction in supplies, on prices. In other words, if some countries are relieved of the need for economising in the use of wheat in times of scarcity because their requirements are largely guaranteed under the agreement, other countries will be forced to economise all the more; consequently, the market demand will prove less elastic, in relation to the variation in supplies, than if the effect of scarcity had been more evenly spread among the different importing areas.

(19) Thus the added instability in prices caused by the "narrowing" of the free market—if it occurs—must be the consequence not of the agreement as such, but of the uneven distribution of quotas (of guaranteed quantities) under it. It is highly desirable,

therefore, that the guaranteed quantities should be so distributed among the different importing countries as to constitute a fairly uniform proportion of their normal requirements. An analogous condition was shown to be desirable also (in paragraph 22 above) as regards the distribution of guaranteed quantities among exporters.

(20) It thus appears that the objection against an I.W.A. type of agreement on the grounds that it would tend to enhance the price fluctuations on non-guaranteed transactions must be based either on particular domestic arrangements of participating countries or on a disproportionate distribution of guaranteed quantities among them. Provided that the former are not such as to reduce the normal incentives afforded by the price mechanism, and provided the quotas are reasonably evenly distributed, the argument appears to be without foundation: on the contrary, the presumption is that agreements of this type might exert a stabilising influence on the prices of non-guaranteed transactions and thus provide added stability to the market.

APPENDIX B

NUMERICAL ILLUSTRATION OF PRICE FORMULAE

(1) In this Appendix the operation of the various proposals put forward in paragraphs 29–39 (p. 84–90) above for automatic adjustments in agreement prices are illustrated by means of an estimate of what the effect of these proposals would have been had they been in force in the case of the existing Wheat Agreement.

(2) For this purpose the guaranteed prices laid down for the first year of operation of the International Wheat Agreement of 1949 were taken as a starting point. Since the maximum price for that year was fixed at \$1.80 per bushel and the minimum price at \$1.50, the mean price was assumed to have been \$1.65 per bushel. It was assumed that the mean price was subsequently annually corrected in accordance with the following formulae:

(*a*) the moving average formula (paragraph 32);
(*b*) the parity formula (paragraphs 38–39);
(*c*) the combined operation of the moving average formula and the parity formula.

(3) For the purpose of the moving average formula, the price of Manitoba No. 1 Wheat in store Fort William/Port Arthur as published by the Canadian Wheat Board was taken as an indication of the price applicable to non-guaranteed transactions. This price and the mean price were expressed in terms of U.S. dollars converted at the current rates of exchange. The monthly quotations were averaged for the twelve monthly periods of August-July each year, the average quotations from August to December 1951 being taken as representative for the crop year 1951/52. The market prices thus calculated were as follows:

			U.S. $
1949/50 ..	..	..	2.01
1950/51 ..	..	..	1.99
1951/52 ..	..	..	2.29

The adjustment of the mean price was calculated on the assumption that the mean price, in the long run, should reflect the six-yearly average of market prices. Hence the mean price for each year (other than the first) was adjusted by taking one-sixth of the difference between the market price (as given above) and the mean price of the previous year.[1]

(4) For the purpose of the parity formula, the series employed was the "unit value index of world exports" as published by the Statistical Office of the United Nations.[2]

These indices are published quarterly and if the average for twelve monthly periods June-May is taken, the following results are obtained for the years relevant to the operation of the Wheat Agreement (1948 = 100):

---

[1] If P_1, P_2 ... are taken as the mean prices and π_1, π_2 ... as the market prices for successive years, the adjustment is described by the following formula:

$$P_2 = P_1 + \frac{\pi_1 - P_1}{6}; \quad P_3 = P_2 + \frac{\pi_2 - P_2}{6}$$

[2] *Monthly Bulletin of Statistics*, United Nations.

$$1948/49 = 99$$
$$1949/50 = 86$$
$$1950/51 = 97$$
Second Quarter $1951 = 107$

The figures for 1951/52 are not yet available, but for the purpose of calculation it was assumed that the figures for that year will be the same as those for the last quarter of the crop year 1950/51. In accordance with the proposals made in paragraph 36, the actual adjustment applied was one-half of the change in the index for the previous crop year.[1] This meant the following adjustments:

ADJUSTMENTS FOR CHANGE OF WORLD PRICES

			per cent.
1949/50	..	..	-6.5
1950/51	..	..	$+6.5$
1951/52	..	..	$+5$

(5) Finally, the effects of these two adjustments were combined by the method of first adjusting the mean price in accordance with the parity formula and then taking the difference between the market price and the adjusted mean price for the purpose of the moving average formula.[2]

The calculations were made under two alternative assumptions:

(*a*) that the spread between guaranteed minimum and maximum prices is ± 5 per cent. of the mean price;

(*b*) that the spread between guaranteed minimum and maximum prices is ± 10 per cent. of the mean price.

[1] As was shown above, the change in the index exceeded 10 per cent. (assumed to be the critical minimum for the adjustment) in each year.

[2] In other words, taking $P_1, P_2 \ldots$ as mean prices, $II_1, II_2, \ldots$ as market prices, $C_1, C_2, \ldots$ as coefficients of adjustments for the changes in world prices, $N_0, N_1, N_2, \ldots$ as the indices of unit value of world exports in successive years, the following formulae were applied:

$$C_2 = \frac{N_0 + N_1}{N_0} \; 0{\cdot}5; \quad C_3 = \frac{N_1 + N_2}{N_1} \; 0{\cdot}5$$

$$P_2 = P_1 \; C_2 + \frac{(\pi_1 - P_1 \; C_2)}{6}; \quad P_3 = P_2 \; C_3 + \frac{\pi_2 - P_3 \; C_3}{6}$$

The result of this method is that if the mean price were fully adjusted to the change in world prices, no adjustment would be called for on account of change in the market price of wheat in periods when the market price of wheat changes at the same rate as world prices generally.

The results of these calculations are given in Table A which shows both mean prices and maximum prices for successive years on the various assumptions. For the purpose of comparison, the table also includes a column showing the actual mean and maximum prices under the International Wheat Agreement.

(6) It was felt to be of interest also to compare the results of the application of the half-spread adjustment formula (mentioned in the footnote to paragraph 33) with the application of the moving average formula. For this purpose again, two alternative assumptions were made according to whether the spread between minimum and maximum prices were assumed to be ±5 per cent. or ±10 per cent. of the mean price. This is shown in Table B.

Table A

EFFECT OF THE APPLICATION OF VARIOUS PRICE FORMULAE ON THE
GUARANTEED PRICES OF THE WHEAT AGREEMENT

Year	Actual Price under I.W.A.	Price According to Moving Average Formula	Price According to Parity Formula	Combined Effect of Moving Average and Parity Formula
I Mean Price	*U.S. $ per bushel*			
1949/50	1.65	1.65	1.65	1.65
1950/51	1.60	1.71	1.54	1.62
1951/52	1.55	1.76	1.64	1.77
1952/53	1.50	1.85	1.72	1.93
II Maximum Price (Mean Price ±5%)				
1949/50	1.80	1.73	1.73	1.73
1950/51	1.80	1.80	1.62	1.70
1951/52	1.80	1.85	1.72	1.86
1952/53	1.80	1.94	1.81	2.03
III Maximum Price (Mean Price ±10%)				
1949/50	1.80	1.81	1.81	1.81
1950/51	1.80	1.88	1.69	1.78
1951/52	1.80	1.94	1.80	1.95
1952/53	1.80	2.03	1.89	2.12

Table B

COMPARISON BETWEEN THE EFFECT OF THE "MOVING AVERAGE"
AND THE "HALF-SPREAD ADJUSTMENT" FORMULAE

Year	±5% Spread		±10% Spread	
	Moving Average	Half Spread Adjustment	Moving Average	Half Spread Adjustment
Mean Price				
1949/50	1.65	1.65	1.65	1.65
1950/51	1.71	1.73	1.71	1.81
1951/52	1.76	1.82	1.76	1.99
1952/53	1.85	1.91	1.85	2.19
Maximum Price				
1949/50	1.73	1.73	1.81	1.81
1950/51	1.80	1.82	1.88	1.99
1951/52	1.85	1.91	1.94	2.19
1952/53	1.94	2.00	2.03	2.41

STABILISING THE TERMS OF TRADE OF UNDER-DEVELOPED COUNTRIES[1]

I. THE PROBLEM OF THE TERMS OF TRADE

Ever since the mid-fifties the terms of trade of the under-developed areas of the world (i.e. all countries excluding those of North America, Western Europe, Australia, New Zealand, South Africa, Japan and the centrally-planned economies) have suffered a steady deterioration, the rate of which has shown some signs of acceleration during the last two years.[2] Taking 1955 as a base, the deterioration up to the middle of 1962 was over 11 per cent. This refers to the total exports and imports of the under-developed countries, including their exports of manufactures and their imports of primary products from other countries. The deterioration of the terms of exchange between primary products and manufactures has been considerably greater: since 1955 it has amounted to at least 17 per cent. While the quantum of exports of under-developed countries increased by some 30 per cent., from 1955 to 1961 the value of their exports rose by only 16 per cent., and much of this reflects the rise of petroleum exports—which only benefited Venezuela and a limited group of countries in the Middle East. Excluding the exports of those countries, the increase in the value of the total exports of the remaining under-developed countries of the world was a little over 10 per cent. in the last six years, or only about two-thirds of their population increase during the same period.[3] The rise in the purchasing power of these exports *in terms of manufactures* has been only 5 per cent. Their foreign earnings have thus failed to keep pace with the growth of their populations, let alone to afford the basis for a rise

[1] A paper written for the U.N. Economic Commission of Latin America, and published in the *Economic Bulletin for Latin America*, March 1963.

[2] Some might suggest that this deterioration started even earlier, i.e. with the end of the short-lived boom in prices caused by the war in Korea in 1951, but the prices ruling in 1951 were exceptional in the light of the experience of earlier years; if one views the experience of the postwar period as a whole, the unfavourable turn in the position of the under-developed countries may be said to have started in 1954-5.

[3] Figures derived from the United Nations *Monthly Bulletin of Statistics*.

in imports *per capita*, which is an essential requirement for continued economic development.

II. PROSPECTS FOR THE 1960's

Various estimates made recently on the future trend of prices of primary commodities[1] agree in the view that if no special action is taken, the longer-run prospects for the under-developed countries will continue to be unfavourable. This is due to a combination of adverse circumstances:

(*a*) There has been a considerable increase in acreage yields due to technological improvements in the production of a large number of commodities which is likely to continue at an accelerated pace. Added to this, the favourable prices of the early 1950's have led to a large increase in plantings in many areas which are only now beginning to come into production.

(*b*) The world market prospects for many tropical products and for some of the raw materials produced by the under-developed countries are unfavourable, owing to the increasing substitution of synthetic materials and to a change in the pattern of industrial production in the developed countries, which has caused a decline in the relative importance of industries that are heavily dependent on imported materials.

(*c*) The consumption of many tropical foodstuffs (such as tea and coffee) seems to have reached saturation levels in some of the high income areas. There is considerable scope for increased consumption in the less prosperous and fast-growing areas (such as Japan) as well as in the U.S.S.R. and other communist countries, but it is uncertain how far the economic policies of these latter countries will permit greatly increased importation of such products.

(*d*) Finally, there is the further threat of a narrowing of markets

[1] See in particular *Agricultural Commodities-Projections for 1970*, F.A.O. Commodity Review, 1962; *Study of Prospective Production of and Demand for Primary Commodities. Prospective Demand for Non-agricultural Commodities*, United Nations, 1962 (E/3629-E/CN.13/49).

due to trade diversion resulting from the preferential arrangements of the European Common Market in favour of their overseas associates in Africa and the Caribbean. If these preferential agreements secure high export prices for the commodities produced inside the area, they are likely to lead to increases in production which may narrow considerably the market for other exporting countries.

Even without taking into account the additional production generated by measures of trade diversion, there can be little doubt that the under-developed countries are confronted with the danger of a structural over-production of a number of tropical products and raw materials. The only remedy to this situation is a change in the structure of production of the under-developed countries and the diversification of their economies, which lessens their dependence on the export of a small number of minerals or plantation crops. But this is clearly a long-term remedy and its effective application requires co-ordinated action by the under-developed countries themselves. This is because acting individually each country is under a strong temptation to increase the production of its own export crops, even of commodities whose prospects are known to be unfavourable, so long as this offers an immediate promise of increased export earnings for the particular country concerned. Moreover, the prospects of any planned diversification of the economies of the under-developed countries will be seriously compromised by the very fall in their export earnings which is likely to result from a continuation of the current trend of prices. The lower their earnings are, the less they will be able to undertake the investments necessary for any major change in their production structure.

In order to bring about such a planned re-organisation in the structure of production, two kinds of arrangements are therefore essential. The first is to stabilise commodity prices at a level which is in some reasonable relationship to the prices of manufactured goods. The current prices of primary products may be regarded as being already unduly low in this context. If the prices of primary products were stabilised at, say, 10 per cent. above their current level,the terms of trade would be about the same as in 1928 i.e. before the great depression of the 1930's.

The second requirement (which is of course closely connected with the first) is that satisfactory arrangements be made to limit the production and export of individual commodities to the extent needed to bring production and consumption into balance at a satisfactory level of prices.

Both these objectives could best be promoted by international commodity agreements—the type of instrument on which the main reliance has been placed by both developed and under-developed countries, ever since the end of the war. But despite all the effort which went into the making of such commodity agreements during the last seventeen years—as reflected in innumerable international conferences, consultations or study groups for a large number of commodities—only five operative agreements have been concluded—for wheat, sugar, tin, coffee and olive oil—and of these only two remain in effective operation at present (tin and coffee);[1] and there have been only three (those for sugar, tin and coffee) which could be said to have succeeded, at least during some part of their period of operation, in stabilising prices at a higher level than would have been attained without them.

As a result of a growing dissatisfaction with the very limited results attained in individual commodity agreements, attention has increasingly turned to alternative methods of remedying the situation in the form of compensatory financing schemes. These would not attempt to stabilise the prices or to regulate the trade of individual commodities but would provide instead some financial compensation (in the form either of gifts or of loans) for the fall in export earnings, financed by a universal levy on both exporting and importing countries.[2]

---

[1] Apart from the International Wheat Agreement which, though in force, no longer provides for purchases at guaranteed minimum prices.

[2] Details of two such schemes have been published recently. The first is by a group of United Nations experts (*International Compensation for Fluctuations in Commodity Trade*, United Nations Publications, Sales No. 61.II.D.31, New York, 1961), and the second by the Organisation of American States, which put forward a proposal for the establishment of an international fund for the stabilisation of export receipts. The United Nations report states that participants should be entitled to compensation of 50 per cent. of the fall in their export earnings as against the previous year in excess of a minimum reduction (for which no compensation would be payable) of 5 per cent., financed by contributions based on a percentage of the national income of

III. THE EXPERIENCE OF POST-WAR
COMMODITY AGREEMENTS[1]

Before we can discuss what is the most promising approach to the solution of this problem, it is necessary to analyse the causes of the very limited success of the numerous commodity negotiations since the war.

One of the reasons often cited lies in the limitations under which post-war commodity negotiations have been conducted. The guiding principles for commodity negotiations were laid down by the Havana Charter of 1948—a treaty which was never ratified but whose major provisions in this field have been, and still are, generally observed. The Havana Charter states that one of the main objectives of international commodity agreements is "to prevent or moderate pronounced fluctuations in the price of a primary commodity, with a view to achieving a reasonable degree of stability on the basis of such prices as are fair to consumers and provide a reasonable return to producers, having regard to the desirability of securing long-term equilibrium between the forces of supply and demand."[2] The Charter also specifies that "participating countries which are mainly interested in imports of the commodity concerned shall, in decisions on substantive matters, have together a number of votes equal to that of those mainly interested in obtaining export markets for the commodity."[3]

the high income countries and a percentage of the export receipts of the low income countries. The United Nations experts suggest that such compensation should take the form of non-repayable grants, and they estimate that, if this scheme had been in operation in the years 1953-9, the under-developed countries would have received a net annual transfer of 240 million dollars from the high income countries. The O.A.S. proposal is that compensatory finance should be available up to a maximum of 20 per cent. of previous exports to cover a proportion (up to a maximum of two-thirds) of any short-fall of export receipts below that of the average of the previous three years. It is proposed that the compensation should take the form of loans to be repaid in a maximum of five years, irrespective of the subsequent movement of export proceeds of the borrowing countries.

[1] The following owes much to Gerda Blau, *International Commodity Arrangements*, paper presented to the International Congress on Economic Development, Vienna, September 1962.

[2] Article 57 (c).

[3] Article 63 (b). The Charter also lays down (Article 62) that "commodity control agreements" (i.e. agreements which involve the regulation of production or the quantitative control of exports or imports, or the regulation of prices) may only be entered into after an international commodity conference, called specifically for the purpose, has found that (a) a "burdensome surplus" has developed or is expected to develop in a primary commodity which would cause serious hardship to small producers, and which could not be corrected by normal market forces; or (b) widespread unemployment or underemployment in connexion with a primary commodity has

In other words, the provisions of the Havana Charter prescribed that producers and consumers should have equal weight
in conducting the negotiations and in shaping the provisions of
any commodity agreement. They also laid it down (in effect)
that the main purpose of such agreements is to moderate any
pronounced fluctuations in prices; not to interfere with long-term
trends that may be necessary for securing "long-term equilibrium"
between the forces of supply and demand.

These guiding principles have been interpreted (at least by the
developed countries) in a manner that has unduly limited the
scope of such negotiations. The main interest of the producing
countries has been in obtaining both stable prices and satisfactory
terms of trade in respect of manufactures—in the same way in
which agricultural producers of the developed countries demand,
and generally obtain, such terms, either through guaranteed
prices (as in the United States or the United Kingdom) or through
measures of agricultural protection (as in Continental Europe).
But the Governments of the main importing countries were, not
unnaturally, unwilling to extend to the primary producers of
foreign countries the same kind of support as regards prices or
guaranteed markets which they were ready to grant to their own
agriculturists; and they also discouraged attempts by the producing countries to secure these ends by themselves through concerted
regulation and control of market supplies. Thus the pre-war type
of commodity agreement—which mainly relied on a restriction of
exports by producers—was at first frowned upon as contrary to the
liberal principles of the Charter, partly because it was held that
by restricting production and maintaining high prices such agreements tended in the long run to restrict consumption as well, and
partly because they inevitably tended to freeze the pattern of
production and trade in a commodity, and thereby prevent the
realisation of one of the objectives laid down in the Havana
Charter, that of "increasing opportunities for the satisfaction of
requirements from sources which can produce in the most effective
and economic manner." The only post-war agreement which
mainly relied on export restriction for its operation was the

developed or is expected to develop, which would not be corrected by normal market
forces owing to low elasticities of demand and the lack of alternative employment
opportunities.

International Sugar Agreement of 1953. But sugar has always been recognised as constituting a special case, and the 1953 Agreement was largely a continuation or renewal of a similar Agreement concluded in 1937. In the case of coffee an analogous agreement—comprising both exporting and importing countries— could not be concluded until 1962.

The authors of the Havana Charter evidently had two kinds of commodity agreement principally in mind which were thought to provide the possibility of "moderating pronounced fluctuations" in prices, but without necessarily interfering with the long-term operation of the free market. One of these was the creation of international buffer stocks for particular commodities and the other a multilateral contract or guarantee, by both exporting and importing countries, to buy or sell at least part of their normal requirements or supplies within a stipulated range of prices, irrespective of the level of prices in the free market. As it turned out, neither of these two types of agreement offered much scope for successful international negotiations.

(a) Buffer stock agreements proved extremely difficult to negotiate, as they would have required financial resources for their successful operation beyond the reach of producers and beyond the willingness of consumers. The only international buffer stock agreement which actually materialised was the international Tin Agreement of 1956, and as the subsequent history of its operations shows, its success was due not to the buffer stock scheme but to its provisions relating to export control, which were originally intended as subsidiary. The financial resources of the buffer stock authority were exhausted in less than two years after the inception of the scheme, and in the two following years the price was maintained by a heavy restriction of exports by the producers (a reduction of 41 per cent. in the first full year of export control and of 36 per cent. in the second full year; after that the world demand-and-supply situation changed so that it was possible to maintain the price above the support level without restrictions).

(*b*) The only known instance of a multilateral contract guaranteeing purchases and sales within a range of stipulated prices is the International Wheat Agreement, originally negotiated in 1949. In the four years covered by this Agreement the world price was consistently above the maximum price stipulated in the Agreement, so that the Agreement was effective in securing supplies to the participating importing countries at lower prices than they would have paid otherwise. This agreement thus operated entirely in the interest of the importers; and when the exporters insisted on some increase in the maximum price for the second four-year period (from 1.80 to 2.05 dollars per bushel) the largest importer, the United Kingdom, withdrew from the Agreement, and was later followed by other participating importers. The Agreement was re-negotiated for a third time in 1959, but its price-stabilising features were virtually abandoned. The history of the Wheat Agreement thus shows that it is unsafe to rely on the willingness of the high-income importing countries to guarantee to pay higher prices for their imports than they need to pay in the free market.

On the other hand, the International Sugar Agreement of 1953 was successful, during most of its period of operation, in stabilising world prices around 3.75 cents per lb. This Agreement, whilst it conformed to the formal requirements of the Havana Charter in giving equal voting rights to both exporting and importing countries, was essentially an agreement to restrict exports by means of quotas, on the same lines as its predecessor, the International Sugar Agreement of 1937. Each country was given a "basic quota," the actual quotas being expressed as a percentage of this, fixed in the light of estimated requirements each year. The main novel feature of the 1953 Agreement was that it provided for an *automatic* adjustment of the actual quotas upwards or downwards, whenever the price of sugar rose above a stated maximum, or fell below a stated minimum, for thirty consecutive days. (Later on, this was amended to allow for both automatic and discretionary adjustments of the quotas at various points within the initial zone of stabilised prices.)[1] The main obligation on importers (in both the 1937 and the 1953 Agreements) was to reserve a certain minimum percentage of their total import requirements for participating exporters. Exporting countries were obliged to take measures to restrict their production whenever their stocks exceeded 20 per cent. of their output, but the manner of implementing this obligation was left entirely to the particular Government concerned.

Although the International Sugar Agreement of 1953 covered only one-half of the world's trade (the rest was covered by special arrangements such as the United States preferential import arrangements or the Commonwealth Sugar Agreement) it was successful (except for a brief period after the Suez crisis) in stabilising prices within the stipulated range through the regulation of supplies. However, when after the cessation of United States purchases of Cuban sugar the pattern of world trade changed suddenly and drastically, the Agreement broke down owing to the inability of exporters to agree on a new distribution of export quotas, and its operative provisions are at present suspended.

The new International Coffee Agreement of August 1962 (which succeeds two earlier one-year agreements negotiated among producing countries only) follows, in its general outline, the provisions of the International Sugar Agreement, except that the adjustment of the actual quotas in relation to the "basic quotas" is not tied to the movements of the world price, but is left to the quarterly decision of the Council, the obligations relating to prices being confined to "assuring that the general level of coffee prices does not decline below the general level of such prices in 1962," and "assuring to consumers prices which are equitable and which will not hamper a desirable increase in consumption." The participating importers undertake to limit their imports from non-participants, whenever the exports of participants fall below 95 per cent. of the total world exports of the

---

[1] Apart from allotting a special quota as a reserve from which the Sugar Council could allocate additional quotas to new producers (or increased quotas to existing producers) and the automatic pro-rata re-allocation of unutilised quotas, this Agreement contained no provisions for a systematic periodic review of the distribution of "basic quotas."

calendar year 1961.[1] Exporting countries for their part undertake to limit their production to the amounts needed for domestic consumption, exports and stocks, but the policies and procedures to be adopted in this connexion are left entirely to the individual country concerned. There is provision for a review of the distribution of the basic quotas after three years, and for their revision by the Council subject to a two-thirds majority vote of the exporters and importers; failing that the initial quotas will remain in operation for the remaining two years of the Agreement.

IV. LESSONS AND POLICIES FOR THE FUTURE

The above outline of the post-war experience with commodity agreements suggests two main conclusions:

(a) Of the various types of international commodity arrangements that have been considered, international agreements for the regulation of the export and production of primary commodities provide the most promising instrument for stabilising the terms of trade of under-developed countries and assisting them in an orderly adjustment of their production structure. If it is objected that such agreements tend to create monopolistic conditions in the marketing of the commodities concerned, it should also be borne in mind that the under-developed countries are themselves confronted by such monopolistic markets in their purchases of manufactured goods, where prices are kept at higher than competitive levels by international private cartels or simply by the absence of price competition among producers operating in imperfect markets.

In fact the sellers of primary commodities suffer from two important handicaps in comparison with those who sell manufactured goods. The first is that, by and large, the primary producers are "price-takers", whereas industrial producers are "price-makers". A fall in demand for manufactured goods leads directly to a reduction of output; any reduction in prices occurs only indirectly and incidentally, depending on the extent to which producers are induced to lower profit margins. A fall in demand for primary commodities, on the other hand, leads directly to a

---

[1] This Agreement has still to be ratified, and its entry into force is dependent on at least 20 exporting countries, representing at least 80 per cent. of world exports, and at least 10 importing countries, representing at least 80 per cent. of total world imports, acceding to it.

fall in prices; it leads to a restriction of output only indirectly, in so far as the decline in prices causes producers to lower their output. The second handicap is that, whereas the benefits of technical progress in manufacturing are largely retained by the producers (in the form of higher real wages and profits), the benefits of technological progress in primary production are largely passed on to the consumers, in the form of lower prices, leaving little benefit to the producers in the form of higher real income.[1] (The exceptions to this are to be found in those cases—such as oil—where the distribution of the commodity is controlled by large international concerns.)

The creation of "producers' cartels" for primary commodities would serve to lessen the structural handicaps of under-developed countries resulting from differences in market structures and market organisation—a state of affairs which turns the terms of trade against them, and makes them poorer, without any compensating advantage from the point of view of the total wealth produced by the world as a whole. The prices resulting from the operation of unrestricted competition are commendable from the point of view of the optimum allocation of the world's resources only in a world where *all* markets are equally competitive.

(*b*) The second lesson to be drawn is that the prejudice, or opposition, of importing countries to export-restriction agreements *can* be overcome, once it is demonstrated that a sufficient number of the exporting countries are determined to come to such an agreement in any case (this was shown in the negotiations leading up to the International Coffee Agreement). Faced with the alternative of a one-sided cartel agreement of the producers, it is clearly in the interests of the importers to participate, and thereby acquire an influence in shaping the basic provisions as well as the policies of the Council operating the Agreement—quite apart from the wider interest in helping under-developed countries on broad humanitarian considerations. (It is also in the interests of the exporters to have the importers included, since they alone can guarantee access to markets and

---

[1] This is partly due to the prevalence of imperfect competition in manufacturing and partly to the fact that organisations of industrial workers are in position—unlike workers in the agricultural sectors of under-developed countries—to ensure that industrial wages increase at least as fast as industrial productivity.

ensure compliance among the exporters.) Hence the negotiation of export-quota agreements (of the type of the sugar and coffee agreements) for all the principal primary commodities produced by the under-developed countries is largely a matter of securing adequate co-operation and co-ordination of policies among the different exporting countries. Once the exporting countries are prepared to form a "trade union" of some kind, the opposition of importing countries will cease to be an effective obstacle.

However, if such export-control agreements are to become the major instrument for regulating and stabilising the terms of trade of under-developed countries, not just in times of "emergency" but as a more or less permanent measure, they must provide for more efficacious and flexible techniques for adapting both the structure of production to the requirements of world trade, and the structure and pattern of trade to the changing conditions of production than either past or existing agreements have succeeded in doing.

It is well known that export-quota agreements are difficult to negotiate and, if brought into being, are likely to break down sooner or later, for one of three reasons or a combination of them:

(a) *Failure to secure full participation by all the producing countries.* The larger the number of exporting countries which accede to an agreement, the greater the temptation for the remaining exporters to stay out, since the restriction of the exports of the others gives them the benefit of better prices, without their being restricted in the development of their own exports. On the other hand, as pre-war experience has shown, countries which are willing to participate in an agreement are not likely to tolerate for long encroachment by outsiders on their markets; if the agreement leads to a gradual reduction in the share of world trade of the participating exporters, it is likely to break down sooner or later.

(b) *Failure to regulate the domestic production of the exporting countries, leading to the accumulation of excess stocks which the participating countries are financially unable to carry.* If at the prevailing (domestic) price the production of any particular country exceeds its requirements for domestic consumption and exports, and the excess is purchased by a government agency which holds it in stock, the incomes generated by the production of the export commodity will exceed the export receipts; and this will be reflected in an adverse balance of payments, or in domestic inflation, or both. The maintenance of the domestic price will also militate against the structural adjustment and diversification of the economy which the agreement was designed to facilitate. The carrying of excessive and growing stocks imposes an increasing strain on the operation of the agreement, and an increasing temptation to evade or to abrogate it.

(c) *The impossibility of "freezing" the pattern of world production and trade for more than a limited period.* It is inevitable that the initial distribution of export quotas should follow more or less closely the actual distribution of exports in the year (or years) prior to the first negotiation of the agreement. But the pattern of world trade—which in the absence of international regulation would constantly tend to change, as the production and exports of low-cost areas, or areas showing a high rate of productivity growth, expand at the expense of other areas—cannot be artificially "frozen" in this way for more than a limited period.[1] Unless the agreement provides some mechanism for a steady adjustment in the distribution of the quotas in the directions in which the *pattern* of trade would have changed in the absence of regulation, the agreement is bound to break down at some point—at the point where the "low cost" producers feel that they have more to gain from the expansion in the share of their trade under free competition than they have to fear from the fall in prices that will accompany that process.

All these defects *can* be overcome, however, once the nature of the problem is sufficiently understood, and the participating

---

[1] The history of most commodities shows dramatic changes over longer periods in the distribution of the sources of supply and the channels of trade. The main centre of rubber production shifted from Brazil to Malaya; of coffee from Arabia to Brazil, and (lately) to Africa; of cocoa from Central America to West Africa; of tea from China to India and Ceylon, etc. The share of African countries in world coffee exports has increased from 3 to 20 per cent. in recent years.

exporting countries are fully apprised of both the requirements and the advantages of obtaining a solution.

(a) As regards the problems of securing full participation, this is partly a matter of "bringing home" the advantages of a commodity agreement to *all* (actual or potential) exporters, which of course partly depends on the provisions made in the agreement itself for securing in the long run a growing share of world trade to the fast-growing, low-cost areas. But it also depends on the extent to which the major importing countries are willing to participate in the scheme; as was pointed out earlier, if the importing countries are willing to limit their imports from non-participants to their existing share of such imports, the major obstacle to securing full participation is removed. The willingness of importers to participate and to undertake such obligations will depend, of course, on how far the exporters are ready to regulate the actual quotas so as to stabilise prices at levels which are "fair to consumers" as well as providing a "reasonable return to producers", and as the example of the Sugar Agreement has shown, it is possible to get agreement on the automatic variation of quotas so as to keep prices within the desired zone.

(b) With regard to the prevention of excessive accumulation of stocks, both the sugar and coffee agreements, as we have seen, impose an obligation on exporting countries to regulate their domestic production so that it does not exceed their requirements, but they leave the manner and method of such regulation entirely to the countries concerned; nor are there any sanctions on countries which fail to implement this obligation effectively. It would not be unreasonable to impose an obligation on exporting countries to the effect that such regulation should be by means of a *variable export duty or export levy*, or at least that such a variable export duty or levy should form *at least one* of the instruments of production control. Without prescribing what the level of such a duty should be, the participating exporters could be asked to increase this duty in the face of any persistent excess of production over requirements and to decrease the duty whenever there are persistent shortages (and/or the countries concerned are unable to utilise their full quotas) and to continue raising or lowering the duty until the disequilibrium is eliminated. For example, the obligation might be to increase the sum of export duties and levies[1] by an amount equal to 10 per cent. of the f.o.b. price of the commodity whenever domestic stocks increase by more than 10 per cent. of output over a period of, say, three years and when total stocks carried exceed, say, 30 per cent. of the average annual output of the previous three years; and there should be a similar obligation to decrease the sum of export duties and levies by, say, 5 per cent., of the f.o.b. price whenever the total stocks carried fall below 10 per cent. of the average output of the previous three years (any unutilised amount of the export quotas being reckoned as a deduction from stocks).[2]

These provisions would ensure that market forces were utilised to the maximum possible extent in securing the required adjustments in production. Market forces alone may not of course always be sufficient to bring about the degree and the kind of adjustment required, in the absence of other complementary instruments of regulation. For example, in the case of commodities with a long gestation period, short-period output may be quite inelastic with respect to price, and excessive price variations in the domestic price of the commodity may set up cobweb-type reactions. In such cases the export duty should be set so as to reflect the difference between the export price and the long-run domestic cost of production of the commodity, and other instruments should be employed for dealing with short-period maladjustments. To the extent that governments regulate production by methods other than changes in the internal price (acreage-restriction subsidies, for example) the need to vary the internal price through variations in the export duty will be correspondingly lessened, or may be

[1] The meaning of "export duties and export levies" will need careful definition. Apart from a formal export duty levied at the ports, fees charged for export licences should be treated as an export levy, as also should the profit on the operation of a government-owned marketing or purchasing agency; the losses, on the other hand, should count as a negative levy, or a subsidy, and should be deducted from other duties or levies charged. Allowance would also have to be made for differential exchange rates in cases where the proceeds of exports are converted into local currency at a different rate that from charged on imports.

[2] This scheme would thus allow for a considerable variation of stocks in relation to output without calling for remedial measures. It would allow for any bumper crop or any crop failure due to weather conditions which is likely to be reversed subsequently without any price incentives. The difference between the minimum increase of duty of 10 per cent. and the minimum decrease of duty of 5 per cent. is intended to take into account the greater responsiveness of producers (in the short run) to price increases than to price decreases.

avoided altogether. But a provision on the above lines would ensure that participating countries would be obliged to cut (or raise) the internal price in *the last resort*—i.e. if other methods of regulation failed to be effective.

Variable export duties or levies are already widely employed, mainly as a means of stabilising the internal price in the face of fluctuations of the external price, or simply as a method of collecting revenue. In the scheme envisaged here their function would be different. The external price would be stabilised by the operation of the export restriction agreement itself, and the purpose of the variable export duty would be to regulate internal supplies so as to keep pace with external requirements, and thus assist in the necessary structural readjustment of the economy. There may be a political objection to this—precisely on the grounds that it fails to maintain the internal purchasing power of the farming population (though this argument loses much of its force when the increase in production is itself the consequence of a rapid growth of productivity). But if high prices lead to excessive production, the desire to secure an adequate income for farmers by buying their crop at a high price and the desire to maintain satisfactory terms of trade in the world market are incompatible—as the recent example of Brazil has shown. If governments wish to maintain the farmers' purchasing power it would surely be much better to do this by means of subsidies administered in a manner that would promote the necessary re-organisation of agriculture instead of obstructing it—e.g. by subsidies on the acreage devoted to food production for home use, or on the produce of such acreage, or by developing alternative export crops for which there is still an unsatisfied world demand.[1]

(*c*) It is obvious that a scheme of this kind will only be found acceptable if the agreement also provides for a systematic

[1] It has also been suggested that instead of the exporting countries imposing export duties, the importing countries should impose a variable import levy on the imports of primary commodities—the levy being varied so as to stabilise the prices paid by the consumers of the importing countries—the proceeds of which, subject to suitable safeguards, would be remitted to the producing countries. From the point of view of the primary producing countries it would obviously be less satisfactory for responsibility for stabilisation to rest on the action of the importing countries, and to be dependent on the remission of the receipts from import levies which would be bound to be hedged round by various conditions. (A variable import levy forms of course the principal instrument for stabilising the common internal agricultural price of the E.E.C. countries. The Rome Treaty envisages however, that the proceeds of this levy are to be

redistribution of the basic export quotas by small and gradual steps in favour of the most efficient producers. The governments of the relatively efficient low-cost producing countries could hardly be expected to carry out the self denying ordinance of discouraging their farmers by low prices—and the more efficient their farmers the lower these prices must be—unless they can look forward, in the long run, to the prospect of raising their exports by obtaining a growing share of the world market. If such an adjustment in the distribution of quotas is to proceed in a smooth and orderly manner it must be based on *objective* criteria that are specified in the agreement itself and not left to subsequent *ad hoc* negotiation. Fortunately the scheme of variable export levies provides such a criterion: once each country attains the export duty which keeps its domestic production in balance with its requirements, the level of that duty (in relation to the f.o.b. price of the commodity) gives a clear indication of the domestic cost of production, or supply price, of the commodity, in terms of international currency. Hence the heavier that duty for any particular country in relation to the average, the lower the costs of production of that country in relation to the average costs of all producers.

It is suggested therefore that after the lapse of some initial period (say, three or five years) during which the "basic quotas" remain unchanged, there should be an annual re-distribution of quotas in favour of countries whose net export levies (reckoned either simply per ton or as a percentage of f.o.b. prices) are greater than the average, and at the expense of those countries whose net export levies are less than the average.[1] No country's basic quota should be increased by more than, say, 5 per cent. in any one year, the actual increase among the various countries being distributed according to some logarithmic formula, based on the percentage excess of their export duties over the average. Only countries which have been able to make full use of their existing quotas should be entitled to any increase in quotas.[2] Similarly, no

retained by the importing countries for subsidising their own agricultural producers; and to the extent that the levy encourages an increase in agricultural production inside the Common Market area, it will also reduce the size of the market of the exporting countries.)

[1] The average would need to be calculated as a weighted average—the export quotas serving as weights.

[2] This makes it impossible for countries to obtain higher quotas by raising their export levies to excessive levels.

country should have its basic quota cut by more than, say, 5 per cent. in any one year, the actual cuts being distributed in the same way in accordance with the short-fall of the level of export duties below the average, subject to the proviso that the total reductions of all countries whose quotas are cut should represent not less than (say) 2½ per cent. of their aggregate basic quota, the sums of the increases in quotas being equal to the sums of the reductions. (These adjustments in the *basic* quotas are of course additional to, and independent of, the change in the *actual* quotas, expressed as a percentage of the basic quotas, which are decided quarterly by the Council, and distributed on a *pro rata* basis.)

This system would give a strong incentive to each participating exporting country to rely on export duties (or levies) as the main instrument for regulating domestic production, since the higher its export duties are, the greater its chance of obtaining a gradually increasing share of world exports. At the same time, a country would not benefit by making its export duty excessive, since in that case, it would be unable to fulfil its existing quota, and would not be entitled to any increase in its quota.

Since the countries whose basic quotas are increased under this scheme would gradually be forced to reduce their export duties (otherwise they would be unable to make full use of their quotas) while the countries whose basic quotas are reduced would be forced to increase them (otherwise they would accumulate excessive stocks) the continued operation of the scheme would lead to a *gradual equalisation of the level of export duties among all partici-pants*—which means that it would tend to bring about the same distribution in the pattern of production and trade as would come about in an ideally functioning competitive market, but without the price fluctuations and uncertainties involved in the latter. It would thus combine the flexibility of a free market system with the maintenance of stable and remunerative world prices.

There is no reason why this system should not be extended to a wide range of commodities—including those (e.g. cotton) where different countries produce widely differing grades and qualities. It is less promising for those commodities (e.g. rice or wheat) which are mainly produced for domestic consumption, and where the exports are marginal to domestic requirements. It may therefore not be the ideal method for dealing with the problems of temperate-zone foodstuffs. But such commodities are largely produced by the developed, high-income countries; with the exception of rice, the commodity exports of most under-developed countries consist of commodities the bulk of which is destined for export, and only a relatively small part for domestic consumption.

One of the principal difficulties with international commodity arrangements since the war has been the lack of agreement among countries—particularly as between exporting and importing countries—as to the basic objectives which such arrangements should serve, and as to the techniques of regulation by which the objectives were to be attained. If the coming United Nations Conference on Trade and Development could come to an agreement on principles to be followed in the regulation of commodity trade and production that are both more explicit and more broadly conceived than the provisions of the Havana Charter, the way would be opened for tackling the problem of the terms of trade of the primary producing countries in a more comprehensive manner by arranging for the simultaneous negotiation of a large number of commodity agreements on parallel lines.

It is not suggested of course that the attainment of stable and satisfactory terms of trade is the only problem facing under-developed countries in the field of international trade. The restriction of the size of their markets through heavy revenue duties (or protective duties) in the importing countries, or as a result of discriminatory arrangements favouring particular groups of producers (as for example the preferences granted by the Common Market or the Commonwealth) represent further problems whose solution will no doubt form one of the principal subjects of discussion at the coming international trade conference. Another equally important problem is to secure relatively free access for the exports of manufactures of under-developed countries to the developed, high-income countries, which are bound to play an increasingly important role with the passage of time. These wider problems may require a recasting of the institutional arrangements in the field of international trade that were created after the war.

18

THE CASE FOR AN INTERNATIONAL COMMODITY RESERVE CURRENCY[1]

I. THE SETTING OF THE PROBLEM

IN the last few years, there has been a growing awareness that the present international monetary order constitutes an increasing threat to the maintenance of world prosperity. There has been a whole crop of proposals, emanating from academic economists, and also from business men, bankers and officials[2] for the reform of the existing international monetary arrangements. These arrangements are based partly on the formal agreements made after the war at Bretton Woods and are partly the result of *ad hoc* developments since that time.

It is evident that the international monetary system is part of the world trade mechanism, and that the way the monetary system is reshaped is bound to make a great difference to the future course of trade. In our view, this aspect of the monetary problem has not received adequate emphasis in public discussion in recent years. The last occasion on which problems of trade were made the starting point for proposals for a reform of the monetary system was in the report of the U.N. group of experts on *Commodity Trade and Economic Development*[3] in 1953. Since that time the most encouraging development has been the acknowledgment by the International Monetary Fund that it is appropriate for member countries to draw from the Fund when they fall into balance-of-payments difficulties because of a fall in commodity prices. The present world concern with monetary reform seems to us to present a rare opportunity to adapt the world monetary structure so as to foster the growth of world production and trade,

---

[1] A paper written in collaboration with A. G. Hart and J. Tinbergen and submitted to the United Nations Conference on Trade and Development, Geneva, March-June, 1964.

[2] For a systematic analysis and summary of such plans, see F. Machlup, *Plans for the Reform of the International Monetary System*, Special Papers in International Economics, No. 3, Princeton: Princeton University Press, 1962.

[3] United Nations Sales No. 1954, IIB, 1.

and in particular, so as to contribute to the stabilisation and expansion of trade in primary products.

Present Monetary Strains and Proposed Remedies

In the last decade, the volume of world imports has expanded by two-thirds—from $79·8 billion in 1952 to $131·5 billion in 1962. (These figures are in current values. There has been a slight rise in the prices of manufactured goods over the period and an appreciable fall in the prices of primary products, leaving the overall level of prices roughly constant.) The total reserves held by all central banks expanded over the same period by less than one-third—from $51·3 to $65·5 billion.[1] Of this expansion, gold contributed less than one-half; the remainder consisted of increases in foreign exchange reserves—in this case, of balances in U.S. dollars. If gold continues to be hoarded on the same scale as in recent years, the annual increase in central banking reserves from new gold production will amount to less than 1 per cent. a year.

If the world as a whole has not experienced an acute financial stringency during this period, it has been mainly because the United States has been able to release large amounts of gold and to carry a large increase in its foreign-exchange liabilities as a "key-currency country." For the world excluding the United States, the growth in imports (67 per cent.) and the growth in reserves (70 per cent.) were roughly proportional. But of the $21·7 billion by which the reserves of countries other than the United States have expanded, no less than $7·5 billion arose from the sale of gold by the United States and $7·2 billion from the increase of official dollar liabilities.[2] These reserve funds came into the hands of outside holders as a result of the "deficit" in the United States balance of payments.

There is a strong consensus of opinion that the deficit in the United States balance of payments (which has now lasted for ten years or more) must some time be brought to an end. Once it is

[1] *See* Appendix, Table 1, col. 1, p. 172, below.

[2] The "world excluding U.S.A.," of course, did not present a uniform picture. The countries of the European Common Market gained reserves much faster than their trade expanded, and must be presumed to hold some excess reserves at present; while a number of under-developed countries had absolute losses of reserves.

brought to an end, the main source of growth in the currency reserves of the rest of the world will disappear. So long as it is not brought to an end, the continued deterioration of the *net* reserve position of the United States is bound to undermine progressively the acceptability of the dollar as a reserve currency.

Widely-discussed Policy Alternatives

The monetary reform proposals which command most attention at present may be grouped under two heads, according to the way in which they propose to generate a growth in reserves. The first group aim at a further extension and formalisation of the "key currency system," by which the leading industrial countries hold at least part of their reserves in each others' currencies. The second group aim at the establishment of a supra-national central bank with credit-creating powers.

(*a*) *Broadening of the "Key-currency" System.* The common feature of plans in the first group is to bring about a change in central banking practices—making more currencies eligible for use as reserves, and establishing permanently, and as a matter of daily practice, the inclusion of such currencies in the reserves of other countries. Plans in this group range from extension of existing informal agreements for reciprocal credits among central banks to proposals which verge upon the international unification of currencies. They have in common a tendency to produce such a close network of relationships among individual currencies that both the prevailing structure of exchange rates and the monetary and credit policies pursued by individual countries in the group are bound together more tightly. The effectiveness of such devices in generating reserves depends on the degree to which the system is automatic in operation; and the more automatic the system, the greater is the loss of freedom in the internal monetary and fiscal policies of individual countries.

At any one time it is easy to identify some currencies which are so strong that they could readily become eligible as reserves. But this is not enough. If the extension of the key-currency system is to generate an increase in the world stock of monetary reserves, there must be a mechanism to get additional holdings of reserve currencies into the hands of other countries. Here we come up against a paradox inherent in the key-currency system. To be widely acceptable as an international reserve, a currency must be *strong*, in the sense that nobody seriously contemplates its devaluation. But to make a contribution to the stock of reserves owned by other countries, a currency must be *weak*, in the sense that the country in question must have a deficit in its balance of payments.[1] As the history of the dollar illustrates, these two conditions for contributing to the working of the world monetary system may be in conflict. If the balance of payments deficit is large enough over a long enough period to add much to outside monetary reserves, it tends to erode confidence in the currency. To be simultaneously strong and weak in the relevant way is an inherently transitory condition.

Making additional currencies *practically available* as well as eligible to serve as reserves is thus an essential part of this type of currency reform. Reciprocal arrangements offer a way to make more reserves available *provided that* members of the key-currency group maintain payments deficits. But if the United States deficit is to be eliminated and other key-currency countries do not develop deficits, it is hard to see how an actual expansion of world monetary reserves is to come about under such a mechanism.[2]

There is, of course, the possibility that a development of this kind might reduce the *need* for reserves, rather than increase their *size*. If a country could be *sure* that other countries would always welcome an accumulation of its currency as an addition to their own reserves, that country would have a reduced incentive to expand its reserves *pari passu* with growth of its trade; and it might be less worried about developments likely to weaken its own balance of payments—for example, about flotations of foreign issues in its domestic capital market. But a system of this kind is

[1] Such a "deficit" need not reflect a deficit in the current trade accounts; even though these show a surplus, they may be outweighed (as they have been for the United States) by capital exports and unilateral transfers.

[2] Countries may engage in "currency swaps." Suppose the central banks of countries A and B each start with $1 billion in gold, and agree that each will buy $500 million worth of the other's currency. Country A can now declare that its reserves are $1·5 billion, and so can country B. But it is hard to believe that if each country lost $500 million of gold and again reached a level of $1·0 billion (including $500 million of the other country's currency), either would feel that its reserve position was as strong as at the outset. Even if neither central bank had any reservations about the other's ability to make good its obligations, to hold *borrowed* reserves is not the same thing as to hold *owned* reserves.

necessarily based on mutual confidence—mainly, confidence in individual members *not* allowing their domestic policies to become expansionary to a point where it becomes burdensome on others. The maintenance of this confidence requires consultation and co-ordination in the credit and fiscal policies of individual countries, which may well create a general bias in favour of more conservative and less expansionist economic policies.

The problem is best seen in terms of the likely consequences of an increased rigidity of exchange rates. If a key currency becomes over-valued in the sense that the export costs of the country possessing the key currency are rising relative to its competitors, and its share in world markets is diminishing, that country may find itself confronted with unemployment, against which it cannot take corrective measure for fear of weakening its international monetary position. Since the progress of industrial productivity is not uniform as between the different competing countries, and since the movement of money wages is partly determined by forces other than the change in productivity, there is a probability that under a régime of fixed exchange rates, the countries with a lower growth of productivity are likely to become progressively over-valued in relation to others.[1] A moderate devaluation in such situations could serve to expand world employment and output, since the higher level of activity in the country which escapes from overvaluation would not be offset by an equivalent reduction in the rapidly advancing countries (whose output is apt to be limited by available resources rather than by demand).

[1] This appears to have been the case with the dollar and the pound in the period 1953-61. While world trade in manufacturing expanded at 8 per cent. a year, the volume of exports of the United States and the United Kingdom expanded only at 3 per cent. a year over the same period. Export prices (measured by "unit values") of the United States and the United Kingdom increased by 20 per cent. relative to the other major industrial exporters (Germany, France, Belgium, Italy and Japan), despite the fact that money wages increased more slowly than in the fast growing countries (cf. B. Balassa, "Recent Developments in the Competitiveness of American Industry and Prospects for the Future" in Joint Economic Committee, *Factors Affecting the United States Balance of Payments*, Government Printing Office: Washington, 1963). There was thus a tendency for wages to increase faster in the countries where productivity rose most; but the difference in wage increases was not nearly large enough to offset the difference in the growth of productivity, so that money costs per unit of output varied inversely with the rate of productivity growth. There is evidence, moreover, that a "feedback" exists, whereby productivity growth tends to be accelerated when production grows faster, and vice versa. In consequence, the balance of forces may operate for prolonged periods so as to enlarge the difference in "efficiency wages" between different countries, linked by rigid exchange rates, rather than to eliminate such differences.

If exchange rates are made more rigid, the duration and intensity of periods of unemployment tend to be increased. This entails not only a loss of potential industrial output but also a loss of markets for primary products.[1]

(b) *Establishment of a Credit-creating World Central Bank.* The second main group of proposals aim to create an institution—presumably by transformation of the I.M.F.—which on a world level would play much the same role towards national central banks which these central banks themselves play on a national level towards commercial banks within their own countries. The best known of these plans—that of Triffin[2]—proposes to cure the frailty of the key-currency system by converting the foreign exchange liabilities of the key-currency countries into reserve deposit balances with a reorganised I.M.F. For the creditor countries, this would mean that they held their liquid funds in I.M.F. balances rather than (for instance) with the Federal Reserve Bank of New York and in United States Government securities. For the key-currency countries themselves it would mean that their foreign exchange liabilities would be funded into a long-term obligation to I.M.F., and there would no longer be a threat of sudden withdrawals of the reserve funds of other countries. Member countries would be obliged by the reformulated I.M.F. agreement to maintain a stated proportion of their reserves as balances on deposit with I.M.F. This arrangement would protect the I.M.F. against a run on its gold, and guard all

[1] Jaroslav Vanek has estimated that the loss of world income from the United States over-valuation alone amounts to $20 to $30 billion yearly. (see his paper, "Over-valuation of the Dollar" in Joint Economic Committee, *Factors Affecting the United States Balance of Payments*, Government Printing Office: Washington, 1962.) The orders of magnitude of the effect on under-developed countries through primary-product markets may be sketched out as follows: Suppose that the United States takes a quarter of the primary products exported by these countries, with an income elasticity of (for illustration) two-thirds, and a price elasticity of about $-1/4$. Then for each percentage point by which United States income and output falls below its potential, its adverse income effect on the sales of these primary products tends to be $(1/4) \times (1 \text{ per cent.}) \times (2/3)$, or $1/600$. With a price elasticity of $-1/4$, the price concessions necessary to get into consumption an additional $1/600$ of the real volume will be $4/600$ or $1/150$ of the price. A 5 per cent. deficiency of United States output below potential tends to hold the terms of trade of under-developed countries producing primary products about $5/150$, or 3 per cent. below the level that would correspond to full employment in the United States. If we think of the proceeds of primary products exported by under-developed countries as of the order of $20 billion per year, this difference in terms of trade is equivalent to roughly $600 million a year.

[2] *See* Robert Triffin, *Gold and the Dollar Crisis*, Yale University Press, New Haven, 1961.

concerned against evaporation of what is now the foreign exchange component of the world's monetary reserves.

Under the plans of this group, the reorganised I.M.F. would have power to create credit by advances to national central banks, or by purchases of government securities in centres with organised financial markets. These operations—corresponding to the rediscount and open market operations carried on within individual countries by their central banks—would "create reserves" for central banks in the same way that central banks now create reserves for the commercial banks within their national systems.

Accordingly, the increment to the western world's monetary reserves furnished by gold production (diminished or augmented by changes in private hoards, and in the gold holdings of the Soviet countries) could be supplemented to whatever extent was necessary to avoid a stringency in world reserves. The rate of growth of reserves would no longer depend on the course of gold-production, the vagaries of gold-hoarders, and the variations in willingness of countries which gained reserves to hold balances in key currencies. It would depend on policy decisions by the governing board of the reorganised I.M.F.

As compared with reform plans of group (a), those of type (b) thus offer an arrangement whereby the course of total monetary reserves would be more definitely under control, and undesirable changes would not happen simply by accident. Furthermore, plans of group (b) avoid freezing the structure of exchange rates. We should visualise the reorganised I.M.F. as having its own currency unit, parities of national currencies being stated in that unit. If the United States (for example) found it desirable to raise the U.S. dollar price of the I.M.F. unit in order to correct its foreign balance, it would not be deterred from action by the network of obligations which characterise a key-currency system.[1]

---

[1] Presumably there would still be some "official" foreign holdings of dollars, but not of a type which would be an obstacle to readjustment of the dollar parity when appropriate. Unless official holdings of individual currencies were banned by the revised monetary agreement (and there would seem to be no sufficient reason for such a ban), some countries for which dollar trade is of predominant importance might well choose to align themselves with the dollar in much the same sense that members of the "sterling area" align themselves with the pound. For countries which make this choice (as for the countries of the sterling area which went through the 1949 devaluation with their eyes open and without regrets) there would be no need to worry about

Consequently, reforms of group (*b*) offer more national autonomy in the field of internal economic stabilisation than do reforms of group (*a*).

However, there are very real difficulties with reforms of this type—though they are of a more subtle character than those which apply to group (*a*). These difficulties hinge on the relationship between the credit operations of a central bank and the sovereignty of governments.

Within any one nation with a "managed paper currency"— and today the internal monetary arrangements of every country are "managed"—the acceptability of the obligations of the central bank is backed up by the power of the government to define the rules as to what consistutes "legal tender," and to put substance into those rules by deciding in what form to accept payment of taxes. The liabilities of a supra-national central bank, lacking such government backing, and holding only a fraction of its reserves in "real" form, might be vulnerable to a crisis of confidence. The ready acceptability of the obligations of such a bank would depend on the confidence of each member central bank that its fellow members are ready to maintain the monetary agreement and to fulfil its obligations; and also on the confidence of member central banks that the value of the underlying assets (consisting largely of loans to member countries, many of which may be loans on long-term) will protect them against undue loss in case of liquidation.

Another way in which the power to create credit supra-nationally may conflict with national sovereignty stems from the fact that to advance central-bank credit is to give the borrower a claim on resources. *Within* any one nation, the exercise of that power is normally accomplished without giving rise to sharp political or social conflict, largely because the allocation of credit

the gold value of their balances so long as their value in dollars—and their purchasing power in dollar merchandise—remained secure.

What makes a key-currency system fragile is the creation of holdings which are only semi-voluntary: the holders would prefer (say) gold to U.S. dollars, but nevertheless keep their balance in a form they regard as second best, out of a sense of international obligation. Under plans of type (*b*), no conceivable *obligation* to hold dollars rather than gold or I.M.F. balances would exist. There would be an obligation to hold part of reserves in I.M.F. balances, even though some holders might prefer to hold only gold; but this would be a recognised and defined obligation, rather than a vague one involving mutual accommodation between pairs of countries.

proceeds under more or less uniform commercial rules. Under these rules, the amount and terms of credit depend on the "credit-worthiness" of the borrower, as measured by the conventional yardsticks of the market. These command acceptance and are not regarded as excessively arbitrary or discriminatory. But if we think of the operation of a supra-national central bank, the normal situation will be that the potential borrower is the government or central bank of one country, and the resources over which the borrower will gain command are in a different country. The ordinary standards of credit-worthiness are scarcely applicable in such a case, and it is hard to visualise analogous rules which would give the bank the necessary discretion without leading to decisions that seem arbitrary and discriminatory either to borrowers or to the countries whose resources are at stake. If the world central bank operated chiefly in countries whose obligations were most marketable (which would be the natural extension of the traditions of "credit-worthiness" and would be the most acceptable policy from the standpoint of the bank's depositors), every country which failed to obtain credit might resent the policy as an apparent discrimination in favour of the "advanced" countries.[1] On the other hand, the country whose resources are to be drawn upon might well feel that its sovereignty was infringed by any loan whose "soundness" was debatable. If, for example, the proceeds of a loan to an under-developed country A are likely to be spent in some "advanced" country B, and if the loan is not so obviously attractive that it could have been directly financed through B's financial institutions, the authorities of country B might well feel that an unwelcome decision has been imposed upon them by the supra-national bank.

To have a credit decision imposed in this way would not present an issue as acute as the traditional grievance of "taxation without representation," but basically it is of the same character. The supply of an international paper currency—which is essentially what is involved in reform plans of type (b)—cannot be regulated by fully automatic rules. Yet it would involve a serious surrender of sovereignty for the member countries to endow the central

[1] It might be argued that any open-market purchases by the supra-national central bank were inherently discriminatory in this way, since the existence of organised financial markets is in itself a characteristic of highly developed countries.

authority with adequate discretionary powers. It is plain that responsible officials will feel bound to build precautions against "unsound" operations into the statutes of any reorganised I.M.F., and to use their authority as its directors to this end. Either a stringent limitation on the scale of credit-creation by the new organisation, or a persistent effort to restrict it to credit operations of the highest "quality" are almost unavoidable.[1] It is almost inevitable that any such organisation would be preoccupied with the problems of the industrial countries, at the expense of the problems of the under-developed countries, which can scarcely be expected to hold many voting shares, to own any large proportion of the funds on deposit, or to provide any large proportion of the "top-quality" obligations regarded as suitable for I.M.F. purchase.

Gold in the International Financial Structure

Despite the expansion of credit elements under the key-currency system in recent years, gold continues to constitute almost two-thirds of the world stock of monetary reserves. In view of the difficulties with devices to expand the credit element which we have just seen, would it not be feasible to accelerate the expansion of the gold element?

If it were possible to secure an adequate expansion of monetary reserves through an increase in the stock of gold alone, this would clearly possess considerable advantages. In the absence of a supra-national government, the deep-seated tradition of regarding gold as the ultimate medium for holding reserves and for settling international accounts is a great source of strength. It enables individual countries to possess a liquid reserve with which they can feel secure. The possession of gold in no way restricts their autonomy to pursue the internal monetary or fiscal

---

[1] Concern with "quality" may go beyond insisting on "credit-worthiness" of the borrower and consider the purpose of the advance. It is hard to imagine, for example that any director of such an organisation would challenge the certainty that if the I.M.F. buys securities of the United States Government, those securities will be redeemed at maturity with strict conformity to the contract terms. But one can visualise a situation where such a director might object to a purchase of United States Government securities on the ground that to buy them would be to "underwrite unsound policies," if the director in question felt (for example) that the United States was shirking its responsibility to help adjust an international balance-of-payments problem by holding down the rise in costs of production of dollar goods.

policies of their choice nor their autonomy to adopt fixed or flexible exchange rates. Furthermore, there is no occasion for differences of opinion over the "quality" of the credits extended —which, as we have just seen, are liable to make the creation of additional reserves through credit operations a source of political and economic tensions. Few tensions are set up by adding new gold to the monetary stock. Countries which put newly-produced gold into circulation do so as part of their ordinary trading; they do not need to be in the position (as are countries which put their liabilities into circulation as foreign exchange reserves for others) of suffering a "deficit" in the balance of payments. Neither the countries which produce the new gold nor those which acquire the corresponding increment of reserves run into debt. Nor do the countries which gain reserves have any need to assess the "quality" of the new assets which underlie the expansion of their monetary reserves.

An important aspect of monetary expansion through gold production—which has been prominent in discussion of the international monetary system at least since Ricardo—is the fact that the transactions which bring new gold into the system *yield income* to the producers. This fact, as Ricardo emphasised, introduces a stabilising factor into the world economy. If monetary expansion is excessive, the resulting inflationary drift tends to raise the cost of producing gold and thus to slow down the growth of the monetary stock. If gold-production is insufficient, the lag in the monetary stock tends to depress prices and business activity; hence the production of gold becomes more attractive and tends to expand. If only this stabilising effect had worked fast enough and on a large enough scale, it would have been a powerful factor in securing steady expansion of the world economy. But historically the low elasticity in supply of gold, and the small volume of annual production in relation to the outstanding stock of gold and to the total flow of income from all activity, made this mechanism much too weak to serve the purpose. Without the powerful growth of credit money, on which the world has become increasingly dependent, the economic history of the last century would certainly not have known the dramatic expansion which it did.

Revaluation of Gold as a Possible Adjustment Measure. There are many advocates of a revaluation of gold as a simple remedy to the present or prospective monetary problems. However, there are a number of serious objections that can be raised against such a solution. These justify the attitude of the major currency authorities of the world in not having recourse to this expedient as a method of ridding themselves of their difficulties. In order to effect a lasting cure, the necessary revaluation would have to be very large—of the order of 100 or even 200 per cent.—partly because any more moderate adjustment would give a powerful encouragement to private hoarding (by giving rise to the expectation of further increases) and partly because a lasting solution requires not only a rise in the value of the existing gold stock (in terms of commodities), but a rise in annual gold production in relation to the existing stock that is sufficient to generate an adequate rate of growth in monetary reserves. Such a large increase in the value of gold in terms of commodities would be highly undesirable. It would bring a large uncovenanted gain to private hoarders (the increase in private gold hoards since the Second World War has been estimated at $10 billion; the total size of these hoards is unknown, but may be twice this amount); it would benefit only the limited number of countries which own the great bulk of monetary gold reserves; it would increase the cost to the world community of maintaining the status of gold as a monetary reserve: since the commodity value of gold is in any case artificial—it is determined by its official price, and not by its intrinsic value—any large increase in the commodity value of current gold-production would be hard to justify, the more so since it would concentrate the benefit on the few countries which produce the great bulk of the world's gold output.

The Commodity-reserve Alternative

These considerations suggest that the world may ultimately find the best solution to the problem not along the lines of a further extension of the key-currency system, nor in the creation of a world paper currency backed by the obligation of member countries, nor in the revaluation of gold, but in the monetisation of real assets other than gold. For example, if Marshall's old proposal for a symmetallic currency were adopted (currencies were to be convertible into so many ounces of gold *plus* so many ounces of silver *plus*, if you like, so many ounces of other metals, such as platinum or even nickel), the available quantity of monetary assets would be increased, and what is more important, the collective elasticity of world supply of the currency media would be raised.[1]

The above line of reasoning inevitably leads to Benjamin Graham's old idea of an international commodity-reserve currency.[2] For there is no real case for restricting a symmetallic currency base to a limited number of precious or semi-precious metals: this idea is a historical survival from the days when the monetary asset was a universal medium of exchange, and not just a medium for storing *value*. Silver, and later gold, was selected on account of its high intrinsic value; but this situation has been perverted in that the high value of gold is now very largely dependent on its continuance as a reserve medium. If the medium were changed from a monometallic base to a symmetallic base, there is everything to be said for selecting a wide range of commodities which are universally used, and whose value therefore, taken individually, would not be greatly changed by their use as a reserve medium. There is everything to be said, in other words, for selecting a bundle of commodities wide enough to make the value of the store only a *fraction* of annual world production and consumption, instead of, as with gold, a very large *multiple* of it.

To include commodities which represent the bulk of the world's primary production in the symmetallic standard means multiplying the effectiveness of Ricardo's stabilising influence by a large factor. This is not only (or mainly) because such monetisation

---

[1] It would, of course, be quite unreasonable to expect the individual central banks to agree to store a collection of commodities (instead of just gold) in proportions which are uniform; or to undertake the necessary legislative reforms for expressing the par values of individual currencies in terms of a symmetallic standard. But this is not necessary. The *storage* of monetary assets can be entrusted to an international authority; the deposit certificates of the Authority could form the "backing" for individual currencies.

[2] B. Graham, *World Commodities and World Currency*, McGraw Hill, New York, 1944. In its original version (*Storage and Stability*, McGraw Hill, New York, 1937) Graham advocated a multi-commodity standard for national currencies. Earlier, W. S. Jevons (*Money and the Mechanism of Exchange*, 1875) put forward the same idea, and in 1932, Jan Goudriaan (*How to Stop Deflation*, London, 1932). In addition there have been and are, many advocates of linking the balance of a buffer stock in individual commodities to the monetary system.

would yield an annual increment of reserves (and thus a contribution to community income earned from the increment of reserves) that is several times as large as could be expected from gold (unless the price of gold were raised to fantastic levels). A far more important consideration is that the income-stabilising effect of the monetary standard applies not merely to that part of the output of the standard commodities which is actually added to the reserve,[1] but to the *entire output* of these commodities. Gold has so few non-monetary uses that its total production is valued at around one-tenth of 1 per cent. of world gross product. In contrast, the value of the total output of commodities which might reasonably be eligible for a commodity reserve would amount to something between 5-10 per cent. of world gross product. Instead of remaining a pale might-have-been, accordingly, the income-stabilising effect of the "real" monetary standard would become a major factor working towards economic stability and growth.

We have arrived at this conclusion in the search for a universal reserve medium which would command acceptance on account of its evident stability in *real value*. Graham arrived at the same conclusion by the opposite route—in the search for a method of stabilising the *money value*, or rather the money price-level, of commodities. The basic considerations may not be the same, but the two approaches are obviously consistent with one another.

It should also be emphasised that the advocacy of a commodity-*reserve* is not the same thing as the advocacy of commodity-*money*: any more than the gold reserve is the same thing as a gold currency. There is no suggestion that individual currencies should have a fixed and unalterable par value in terms of commodities: on the contrary, the proposal is advanced in order to make changes in par value (i.e. adjustments in exchange rates) easier to introduce than it is under the so-called "gold-exchange standard" at present.[2]

---

[1] As will be argued below (p. 164), the rate of addition to reserves under this system is likely to approximate, over a run of years, the rate of increase in the world production and consumption of the commodities included in the "standard."

[2] The proposal is therefore entirely free from the objection Keynes advanced against the commodity reserve proposal that in a world of rising money wages stabilising the price level by means of a commodity-money might lead to highly undesirable results since it would prevent the rise in prices that is necessary to compensate for the rise in money costs (cf. *Economic Journal*, June-September, 1943. p. 176). This would be true only if individual countries were not free to devalue in terms of an international

The best way of applying such a complicated idea as that of monetising a whole bundle of primary commodities must obviously be hammered out through long discussion, among people with many kinds of expertise and experience. Responsible policy-makers cannot be expected to accept such a novelty the first time that it is put forward; and there will be plenty of time to work out details in the future. Yet it is hard to come to grips with the full implications of such a proposal unless it is crystallised in fairly concrete form. Only by considering a proposal which has been worked out in a fair amount of detail can one form a reasonable judgement as to whether the difficulties raised by a plan of this nature are of the kind that can be overcome by straightforward adaptations, or whether they are of a kind that lead into a morass of further difficulties—with each adaptation to cope with some particular problem opening up a series of further problems. Accordingly, we shall proceed in Section II of this memorandum, to put a scheme forward in some detail.

When an idea is turned into a concrete scheme, it is necessary to take into account factors which would be important if the scheme were to be adopted in the near future but which would not necessarily enter into an "ideal" solution in the abstract, or if one were only considering its adoption at some remote future date. Thus account had to be taken of the present existence of large stocks of a number of commodities carried by various governments, which could not be ignored if, in the near future, the building up of stocks by the international authority were envisaged; and it was found that the absorption of these stocks into the commodity reserve would not only ease the problem which the very existence of these stocks present to the production and marketing of the commodities concerned, but it would make the initial introduction of a commodity reserve currency a great deal easier than it would otherwise be.

An even more important consideration is that, given the present status of gold as a reserve medium, it is essential to safeguard the

standard when their "efficiency wages" rose in relation to others. But since the movement of "efficiency wages" of different countries is far from uniform, the possibility of individual devaluations does not obviate the advantages of having a stable international standard in terms of commodities or the parallel advantages of stabilising the price level of commodities in terms of an international standard.

position of gold in any proposed reform of the system. This means that if commodities are to be monetised, gold and commodities must form two separate media of reserve, convertible into one another at fixed rates. There are of course well-known objections to a "bimetallic system." But it must be recognised (i) that whenever a new reserve medium is introduced, an orderly transition unavoidably involves some "bimetallism"—as was shown when countries changed over from a silver standard to the gold standard—(ii) since gold is an "artificial" commodity whose value resides *mainly* in its reserve-medium function, this particular kind of 'bimetallism' need not involve the same kind of problems which bimetallic standards presented in the past. Because the market for gold is dominated by its monetary role, whereas the market for primary commodities must be dominated (except for short period) by the balance between the production and use of such commodities, the maintenance of a fixed ratio between gold and a composite bundle of commodities would not raise the same kind of problems as would arise (for example) from the maintenance of a fixed price ratio between a bundle of metals and a bundle of fibres.

The manner of operation of the scheme will be further explained in Section III, while its major economic effects will be considered in Section IV.

II. OUTLINE OF A PROPOSAL

An I.M.F. Currency

1. It is suggested that, in line with other monetary reform proposals, the I.M.F. should establish its own currency—let us call it the "bancor"—which after an initial "build-up period" should be convertible into (*a*) gold, (*b*) a bundle of commodities consisting of the thirty or so principal commodities in world trade which combine a high degree of standardisation with reasonable durability in storage.

2. Bancor issued by the I.M.F. should be fully covered by gold and commodities, except for a fiduciary issue which should be fixed in amount (subject to possible revision by re-negotiation in later years).

3. Bancor operations should be held distinct from the existing

system of drawing rights of members to purchase each others' currencies out of holdings at the disposal of I.M.F.; such drawings should not lead to emission of bancor.

4. Bancor should be exclusively a deposit currency, and only the central banks of member countries should be entitled to hold bancor balances with I.M.F. The bancor unit should be distinct from the monetary unit of any member country, and should be assigned a gold par value that is large in relation to that of any national currency unit (equivalent, perhaps, to 100 or 1,000 U.S. dollars). Member countries should undertake to accept bancor in settlement of claims in the same manner as gold.

5. It is suggested (the figures are intended as illustrative) that initially the I.M.F. should aim at an issue of bancor of the order of the present equivalent of U.S. $30 billion, made up as follows:

(i) $5 billion in exchange for gold.
(ii) $20 billion in exchange for commodities of various kinds, according to the procedure described below.
(iii) $5 billion against loan obligations of member countries (constituting the fiduciary issue).

Commodity Bundles

6. The composition of the "commodity bundle" should be agreed upon at the outset, on the basis of the following principles:

(i) As many internationally traded commodities as possible should be included, provided that each commodity included satisfies four basic criteria:

(a) A high degree of standardisation (which means that it possesses a clearly defined world-market price, when quantity, grade, place and date of delivery are specified).

(b) Reasonable durability in storage (which means that the stock need not be turned over, to avoid physical deterioration, more often than say, once a year).

(c) Reasonable storage costs (which implies that in general commodities with low values per ton will not be eligible).[1]

(d) Reasonable freedom from price manipulation.[2]

(ii) Since the eligibility of commodities for inclusion cannot, in all cases, be decided beforehand—and some commodities may have to be excluded subsequently, in accordance with paragraphs 7 (ii) (d) and 13 below—the I.M.F. should be given discretion to *add* commodities to the reserve in addition to those initially agreed on, from among a list of such commodities specified in the initial agreement, provided that the inclusion of such additional commodities does not cause the size of the target reserve aimed at to increase by more than a certain percentage. (A reasonable rule would be that if the initial target reserve agreed on is $20 billion, the I.M.F. should have the authority to enlarge the reserve by adding further commodities in the required proportions—see below—provided this does not increase the target reserve by more than $5 billion.)

(iii) The weight of each commodity in the "bundle" should approximate a stated percentage of the tonnage of that commodity which moved in international trade in the three years prior to the agreement. In order to avoid undue delay in building up the required stock, the I.M.F. should be given a certain latitude to vary the exact composition of the ultimate "bundle"; rules to define this range of discretion should be part of the initial agreement. A reasonable rule might require the I.M.F. to build up its stock of each commodity to *at least* the equivalent of x per cent. of a year's trade, but in no case to *more than* the equivalent of

[1] This criterion may require the exclusion of solid fuels, iron ore, etc.

[2] Without laying down any firm rules, it would be wise to exclude commodities, the world price of which is highly artificial because of international private cartels (as in the case of petroleum) and to reduce the weight of commodities in which a substantial part of the world trade takes place under special concessional terms (as in the case of wheat). In general, however, price and market regulation by means of international commodity agreements concluded in conformity with the Havana Charter and registered with the United Nations should not prejudice the eligibility of commodities under this head.

$\dfrac{3x}{2}$ per cent.;[1] the value of x being so chosen as to yield the required figures for the target reserve, once the number of commodities to be chosen for the initial reserve is agreed upon.

(iv) When several varieties or "grades" of a commodity exists, the initial agreement must specify the different grades (according to quality and provenance) of any particular commodity which qualifies for inclusion, and it should also specify their value equivalent, expressed in terms of the grade which is taken as the standard. These equivalents should be based on the relative market prices of the various grades in the average of the last three years. The I.M.F. should have the right to purchase any one grade which is thus qualified in substitution for others so long as its current market price is below its value equivalent in terms of the standard grade; and its obligations to build up the required stock of any one commodity as described in (iii) should be deemed to be fulfilled when it acquires a sufficient stock of that commodity in terms of the standard grade, irrespective of the particular qualities or grades in which the physical stocks of that commodity are actually held. However, in so far as the relative market prices of the different grades correspond more or less closely to their value equivalents specified in the agreement, the I.M.F. should aim at building-up a stock containing all the various grades in the proportions in which they move in international trade.

[1] Since the total value of world trade in primary commodities amounted to $66 billion in 1963, the value of x would be around 0·3 for a target reserve of $20 billion, if *all* commodities so classified in international trade statistics could be included. However, a considerable part of such "commodities" would fail to meet the criteria laid down in (i) above—for example, the inclusion of petroleum would be difficult to justify, under several of these criteria—and the value of world trade in eligible commodities probably does not exceed one-half of the total, or may be appreciably less. In the Appendix (see Table 2) a range of thirty commodities was selected for illustrative purposes, the total annual trade of which amounted to $19 billion, and it was found that a target reserve of $20·5 billion could be built up on the criterion that no commodity is represented by less than 90 per cent. of a year's trade, or by more than 125 per cent. It must be remembered of course that for many commodities world trade accounts for only a fraction of total world production and consumption; thus for the thirty commodities specified in the Appendix, annual world production may be estimated at $80 billion, or four times the value of world trade.

(v) For commodities for which reliable future delivery con-
tacts can be obtained, future contracts should be substituted for physical commodities in all such cases in
which, owing to a shortage of stocks, the future price is
below the spot price by more than a reasonable margin.

The Build-up Period

7. For the purpose of the initial build-up:

(i) Member countries agree to accept bancor balances in
exchange for their current gold deposits with the I.M.F.
amounting to around U.S. $2 billion, and to deposit a
further $3 billion in gold in exchange for bancor, the
individual gold contributions being in proportion to their
present official gold holdings.

(ii) The I.M.F. undertakes to purchase commodities up to the
quantities required on the basis of the principles already
described:

(a) in the open market, at or below the "declared values"
(see below);

(b) from member governments, out of the stocks officially
held by them—

(α) at "declared values" in the case of commodities the
stocks of which are less than the equivalent of six
months' world trade;

(β) at 10 per cent. below "declared value" in those
commodities the stocks of which exceed six months'
world trade;

(γ) at 20 per cent. below "declared value" in the case
of those commodities the stocks of which exceed
twelve months' world trade.

(c) The "declared value" of any commodity is the highest
six-monthly average world price of the standard grade
of that commodity within the two years preceding the
initial introduction of the scheme. "Declared values"
should be revised upwards at six months' intervals
after a lapse of three years from the initial declaration,
if the required minimum stock was not acquired by
that time, subject to such revision *not exceeding* the

average price of the six months previous to the latest declaration.

(d) When the world market price of any commodity rises by 50 per cent. or more above its "declared value" for more than two consecutive months, the I.M.F. should have the right to sell such part of its stocks of that commodity (or if it holds contracts for future delivery, assign the contracts or sell the commodities at the delivery dates for such parts) as can be sold at or above such prices. Subsequent purchase in such cases should be in accordance with the rule suggested in (c) above.[1]

(iii) When two or more member governments carry stocks of a particular commodity, and when the amounts of a commodity which they are ready to sell to the I.M.F. on the terms specified under (b) exceed the amounts required, the purchase from the various governments should be in proportion of the stock offered by each.[2]

Use of Bancor Balances in Relation to Key Currencies

8. (i)   Member governments should undertake to apply the bancor balances acquired in exchange for the sale of commodities owned by them in the first instance to the repayment of short term debt owed to other member governments (but excluding debts to international institutions) who opt for this.

(ii) The fiduciary issue of bancor should be allocated in the first instance to countries which provide a reserve currency to other members, provided that their short-term liabilities exceed the bancor acquired through the sale of publicly-owned commodities, and provided that they undertake to apply the bancor thus acquired to the repayment of their official liabilities, at the option of the creditors.

---

[1] This provision (relating to the build-up period only) is in line with analogous provisions in paragraph 13, below.

[2] Since in many commodities very large stocks are held at present as a result of internal price support policies, or for strategic purposes, there are a number of commodities which could be purchased entirely from governmental stocks, and such purchases would probably cover two-thirds to three-quarters of the total initial requirements. Cf. p. 158, below.

(iii) If the amount of such liabilities which the creditors desire to transfer into bancor deposits with the I.M.F. exceeds the amount of bancor acquired by reserve currency countries as a result of the sale of publicly owned stocks or the fiduciary issue, reserve currency countries should also undertake to apply any subsequent increase (in gold and bancor) acquired in the course of trade, or as a result of private capital flows, to the repayments of their short term liabilities.[1]

(iv) Member governments who hold dollar or sterling balances as part of their official reserves should be encouraged to transfer such reserves—in excess of minimum working balances—into bancor deposits. If they do not opt for this, and in consequence the bancor holdings of the key currency countries rise by *more* than the bancor acquired against deposit of gold, the key currency countries should also undertake to *freeze* such additional reserves until they provide a 100 per cent. cover against their official liabilities; and they should also undertake to co-operate with the I.M.F. in encouraging the transfer of these balances by lowering short-term interest rates; or possibly by asking official holders to keep them in the form of non-interest-bearing deposits.[2]

Storage Costs and Interest Payments

9. Once the I.M.F. has acquired title to a particular stock of any particular commodity, it should become financially responsible for its storage and maintenance. It should be entitled to levy an annual charge on members, distributed in accordance with their total monetary reserves (including bancor balances held) to cover the

[1] Since the present size of such "official" liabilities of the two main reserve currency countries, the United States and the United Kingdom, is around $20 billion, an issue of $30 billion ought to be sufficient to transform the official reserves now held in dollars and sterling into bancor reserves, even when account is taken of the possibility of the initial acquisition of bancor—in exchange for commodities or as part of the fiduciary issue—by the two main reserve currencies being less than their current liabilities to foreign official holders.

[2] Assuming that the accession of bancor holdings in the hands of key-currency countries are thus "frozen" until they are transferred to their "official" creditors, the net increase in world currency reserves resulting from an issue of $30 billion of bancor would not exceed $5-$10 billion.

cost, in so far as costs are not covered by the profits made on commodity transactions during the build-up and subsequent operation.[1] The physical storage of commodities should be located in places which are suitable for the storage, taking account of cost, climatic conditions and the ease with which the proper care of the stocks can be supervised. Warehouses rented by the I.M.F. should enjoy extra-territorial status.

10. Each member country should receive interest on the first $100 million of its annual bancor balance.[2]

Full Operation of the Scheme

11. If within five years from the commencement of operations the initially agreed target reserve has been built up in accordance with the principles described in paragraphs (6) and (7), the I.M.F. should:

(i) cease purchasing individual commodities;

(ii) declare the final composition of the commodity bundle and the bancor value of the commodity unit.

(iii) appoint a day for commencing operations of the scheme. Since at the key date the actual number of tons of each commodity in the reserve (in terms of the standard grade) will be known, the make-up of a "Composite Ton" can be arrived at by simple arithmetic. Given the declared values in terms of bancor of each commodity the value in bancor of the composite ton can be determined by summing the value of the components. The size of a unit "bundle" should be that number of composite tons which is required to give a convenient unit for market dealings for each of

[1] Such profits will arise (a) because a considerable part of the initial stock will have been purchased below "declared values," (b) because, as described below, subsequent purchases will be made at some discount below the par value, and subsequent sales at some premium above it; (c) because in the case of commodities in short supply, future contracts may be substituted for actual commodities; (d) it may also arise in connexion with subsequent changes in the commodity bundle (see paragraph 19, below).

[2] Since something like 80 per cent. of the total issue of bancor will be covered by gold and commodity stocks which do not earn interest, and only around 20 per cent by interest-earning obligations, there is no case for the payment of interest on more than say, a fifth, of the outstanding balances. In order to assist the poorer member countries who are in need of earning interest on their reserves, and to encourage the widespread holding of bancor, it is preferable to pay interest on the amount held by *each* country up to a certain maximum, rather than to distribute interest-earning bancor according to the size of members' quotas, or in proportion to total reserves, etc.

the commodities in the bundle. Thus, supposing that the smallest convenient market unit for a commodity is a ton, the size of the "commodity unit" should be that number of composite tons which would enable the amount of each commodity in the bundle to be expressed in multiples of tons.[1]

12. If the build-up of the initially agreed target reserve has not been completed after the lapse of five years from the commencement of purchasing operations, the scheme should be put into operation on the basis of a provisional commodity unit as soon as the purchases for the "target reserve" have been completed for at least three-quarters of the commodities originally selected, provided that the total value of the stock of such commodities exceeds three-quarters of the value of the target reserve initially agreed on; the value and the composition of the provisional commodity unit being determined in the manner set out in paragraph 11 (iii) above. The commodities whose purchases have not been completed at that date should continue to be bought individually on the basis of their "declared values," as provided in paragraph 7 (ii) (c) above, until their "target stock" is complete, and they should then be added to the commodity bundle, the contribution of each added commodity to the par value of the "commodity unit" being on the basis of its latest "declared value," prior to its incorporation.[2]

Exclusion of Commodities

13. When the market price of any particular commodity in the commodity unit (as measured by the price of its standard grade)

[1] Thus, supposing the bundle contained thirty commodities and that the relative number of tons held of the various commodities varied at an even rate from 1 to 30 (i.e. there were thirty times as many tons of the "heaviest" commodity as of the "lightest") a commodity unit would contain 465 composite tons. Supposing that the par value of a composite ton is equal to 1·15 units of bancor (which may be assumed to be identical with $115 at the current parity) the par value of a "commodity unit" would be 534·75 bancor. The range of discretion at the disposal of the I.M.F. must evidently include authority to round off holdings in multiples of convenient trading units.

[2] Thus supposing (in accordance with the example given in the previous note) that the unit of the complete bundle of thirty commodities would have contained 465 tons and had a par value of 534·75 bancor, operations might commence with, say, a unit of 24 commodities only, containing 350 tons, with a par value of, say, 390 bancor. The total weight of the unit bundle and the par value of each unit would be gradually raised with the addition of further commodities, but as these commodities would enter on the basis of their latest "declared values" (which, according to paragraph 7 (ii) (c) cannot exceed the average price in the previous six months), the ultimate par value of the complete "bundle" would not be precisely known until this process was completed.

rises by 50 per cent. or more above its latest "declared value" prior to its incorporation, that commodity should be excluded from the commodity unit, and the composition of the official commodity unit, and its par value, be revised accordingly. If the market price stays at or above 150 per cent. of declared value for two consecutive months, the I.M.F. should have authority to sell such parts of its existing stock of that commodity (or if it holds contracts for future delivery, assign the contracts or sell the commodities at the delivery dates for such parts) as can be sold at or above that level. If a commodity has thus been excluded from the bundle, it should only be re-incorporated subsequently after a lapse of three years, and on the basis of a revised "declared value," fixed in accordance with paragraph 7 (ii) (c) above, at the end of that period, and only after the I.M.F. has acquired additional stocks by individual purchases on that basis sufficient to bring its stocks up to the target amount.

Convertibility of Bancor

14. (a) Member countries should be entitled, from the day the scheme is deemed to come into operation, to *purchase* bancor from the I.M.F.:

(i) in exchange for gold;

(ii) in exchange for the warehouse certificates of the currently declared bundle of commodities, in multiples of commodity units.

(b) Member countries should also be entitled to *sell* bancor to the I.M.F.:

(i) against commodities, by taking possession of the appropriate bundle of warehouse certificates in multiples of commodity units;

(ii) for a combination of commodities and gold, in the ratio four commodity units to one gold unit. (At a later stage, assuming that adequate gold is deposited with the I.M.F. by member countries, full two-way convertibility should be introduced in gold and in commodity units separately).

15. The I.M.F. should be obliged to purchase gold at 1 per cent. below par value and to purchase commodity units at 2 per

cent. below par value. It should be obliged to sell commodity units at 2 per cent. above par and gold and commodity units together at 1 per cent. above par in the case of gold and 2 per cent. above par in the case of commodity units. If the scheme is put into operation with an incomplete bundle (as provided in paragraph 12) the margin between the official buying and selling prices might well be widened to, say, 3 per cent. each way.

16. The par value of commodity units in terms of bancor should be expressed in terms of the standard grade of each commodity. The I.M.F. should be obliged to accept delivery of standard quantities in terms of any of the grade specified in the agreement and correspondingly should have the right to offer delivery in terms of any of such grades; the actual price offered or demanded being adjusted in accordance with the value equivalents of the different grades specified in the agreement.

17. The I.M.F. should undertake to maintain at all times parity between bancor and the world free market price of gold, if necessary through open market sales of gold whenever its price threatens to rise above its official bancor parity value. Member countries undertake, if it should prove necessary, to put sufficient additional gold at the disposal of the Fund to enable the I.M.F. to do this. For this purpose countries whose gold reserves exceed a certain agreed percentage of their total reserves should have the obligation to sell their excess gold holding (or such part of it as may be required) to the I.M.F., at the request of the organisation.

18. Parity between bancor and the current market price level of the commodities in the commodity bundle should in principle be assured by arbitrage operation of private traders who would buy commodities in the open market for the purpose of tendering to the I.M.F., or buy commodities from the I.M.F., for the purpose of tendering in the open market whenever there is a profit in doing so. Since, however, ordinary businesses are not in the habit of operating in many markets simultaneously or of dealing in composite bundles of commodities, it is possible that such arbitrage operations would not in fact proceed smoothly or quickly enough to maintain the current market value of the commodities entering into the commodity unit sufficiently near to

parity values. It is suggested, therefore, that the I.M.F. should set up its own marketing unit which would engage in open market operations in various commodity markets whenever the market value of commodities included in the bundle moves outside the official margins. (Such an arrangement could be guaranteed to make the official limits effective and thus increase confidence.)

Periodic Revision of the Official Commodity List

19. In order to keep the composition of the commodity bundle in reasonably close relationship to the pattern of world trade, the I.M.F. should be obliged to revise the weights of individual commodities at intervals of five years, on the basis of the tonnage of each commodity which moved in international trade in the three years prior to such revision; and it should also revise, on analogous principles, the scales of the "value equivalents" of individual grades of commodities in terms of the standard grade. When the "bundle" is thus revised, the I.M.F. should be free to buy or sell individual commodities in the open market (on the basis of a revised set of "declared values") so as to adjust the composition of its stock to the new requirements. The book profits or losses resulting from such operations should accrue to the collective benefit of, or be a collective charge on, members, and could conveniently assume the form of an appropriate scaling-up or scaling-down of the bancor balances of members.

Individual Exchange Rates

20. Individual members should be free either to maintain a fixed rate of exchange of their own currency in terms of bancor (which they should be free to adjust from time to time in accordance with agreed procedures) or a freely variable rate (a so-called "floating rate") but in the latter case, there should be penalties on members who deliberately keep the market value of their own currency low through open market *sales* of their own currency over prolonged periods, and thereby increase their reserves, in terms of gold and bancor, at an unduly fast rate. Such penalties may take the form of the invoking of the "scarce-currency clause" as originally envisaged, or some alternative form.

III. EXPLANATORY COMMENTS

(a) Until the range of commodities to be included in the bundle is specified, it is impossible to make any precise estimates as to how much of the target quantities could be obtained at the outset by the transfer of officially held stocks, and how much would be left to be acquired by way of purchases out of the annual flow of goods into the open market. In Table 2 of the Appendix an estimate is made of thirty commodities whose annual trade amounted to $19 billion in 1962, and whose total world production and consumption may be estimated at $80 billion annually.[1] As shown in Table 2 a reserve of just over $20 billion could be built up on the assumption that no commodity is represented by a target stock that is more than 125 per cent. of world trade or less than 90 per cent. of such trade. This would involve member governments turning over $14·7 billion worth of visibly held stocks to the I.M.F. (including $2·8 billion of metals from strategic stockpiles) leaving only $5·7 billion to be purchased in the open market. On the assumption that the purchases in the open market are divided among the various countries in the same proportion as total world trade, $3·5 billion or 62 per cent. would be purchased from under-developed countries and $2·2 billion or 32 per cent. from high-income primary exporters. Taking the thirty commodities as a whole, some 58 per cent. of the world exports come from under-developed countries and 42 per cent. from high-income primary exporters (i.e. North America, Western Europe, Japan and Oceania).[2]

(b) The provisions concerning the "build-up" of the initial reserve were motivated by the view that the I.M.F. operations should provide a "buffer" in times of declining prices, and should

[1] These commodities have been selected on the basis of their suitability in accordance with the criteria laid down in paragraph 6 (i) above; it was decided to include cereals in the list with reduced weight, despite possible objections on ground of criterion (d), since it was felt that an adequate allowance can be made for the element of artificiality in their prices by excluding non-commercial trade in calculating the weights.

[2] This gives a considerably higher weight to the under-developed countries than their share in the total world trade in primary products, which is only 38 per cent. ($25 billion out of a total of $66 billion in 1961). The reason for this is that under-developed countries have a higher share in the trade of those basic raw materials and foodstuffs which are suitable for inclusion in a commodity bundle on account of their grading and standardisation.

not aggravate shortages in times of rising prices. Hence the provisions that purchases in the open market should only proceed whenever the price of a commodity is below some average of prices which obtained previously; that the initial "declared values" should not be adjusted in the first three years; and that the extent of any subsequent adjustment should be left at the discretion of the authorities, subject to a clearly defined ceiling. Assuming that the plan is adopted in a period of declining commodity prices (such as occurred, on the evidence of Table 3, in the period 1955-62, for the group of thirty commodities selected), the "build-up" period should not exceed five years or so, provided that the I.M.F. is given powers to commence operations with an "incomplete" bundle as suggested in paragraph 12, while continuing its build-up of the remaining commodities on an individual basis.[1]

(c) If on the other hand, the plan were adopted at the time when the trend of commodity prices was upward, or if it turned upward soon afterwards, the whole scheme would "go into suspense," so to speak. The plan would go into action again once commodity prices came down to the level of declared values— which would have been revised upwards meanwhile, if the advance were long sustained. Clearly the need for additional reserves (or liquidity) cannot be pressing in a period of rising prices, and no great harm would be caused if the initially envisaged time-table for the introduction of the commodity reserve currency were stretched out. (This would not affect that part of the scheme which concerns the fiduciary issue of bancor, or its issue against excess stocks in the hands of governments, which would serve to transform the existing key-currency system.) On the other hand, if commodity prices turned upwards at a relatively late stage it might be possible to commence operations in accordance with paragraph 12, provided that the I.M.F. acquired a sufficient stock of a representative bundle of commodities.

(d) Once the scheme is in operation, the convertibility of bancor into both gold and commodities should ensure that the price level

[1] As Table 3 shows, even in a period such as 1955-62, when the average price of the thirty commodities declined by 20 per cent., at least five of the thirty commodities had shown a persistent rise, and five others a rising trend for the greater part of the period.

of primary commodities contained in the bundle should be stable in terms of gold (or conversely, that the value of gold in terms of these commodities should remain unchanged), irrespective of variations in the exchange rate of individual currencies. Any tendency for prices to fall would be met by an absorption of stocks by the Fund, an increase in the bancor income of primary producers and an increase in world liquidity; any tendency for world prices to rise would be met by a release of stocks, a limitation to the rise in the bancor income of producers, and a reduction in world liquidity.

(*e*) Unlike the "buffer-stock" schemes for individual commodities, the commodity-reserve scheme is not intended to stabilise the prices of individual commodities once the scheme is in operation. These prices would continue to move in relation to each other, in accordance with the changing supply and demand conditions for particular commodities, and to the extent that individual commodities continued to be liable to large fluctuations in prices or to instability in trading conditions, the scheme would not obviate the need for individual commodity arrangements for particular commodities. However, to the extent that price fluctuations reflect common influences—i.e., those originating in changes in the level of industrial activity, which were regarded as the major source of instability in the past—clearly the stabilisation of prices of a large group of commodities will also tend to stabilise the prices of individual commodities in the group. To the extent that the price fluctuation in any particular market reflects factors peculiar to that market, the price fluctuation in that commodity may also be reduced outside a certain range, since if the price falls far enough it will induce purchases of that commodity (in conjunction with the others) and vice versa.[1] However, it would clearly be undesirable if a shortage of some particular

[1] Owing to the margin between the buying and the selling price for the "bundle," this influence would only be operative, in one direction or another, when the price moved outside some critical range. Thus, if we supposed that the weight of a particular commodity in the bundle is 5 per cent., and the margin between the buying and the selling price of a "bundle" is 4 per cent., it will require a fall in price of 40 per cent. below "declared value" in order to induce additional purchases of the bundle (assuming for the purposes of the argument that the market value of all other commodities was around their par value), and thus induce an upward movement in the prices of other commodities. Similarly, it would require a rise in price of 40 per cent. above "declared value" to induce sales of the commodity bundle and thus exert a downward pressure on the prices of other commodities.

commodity, leading to a large rise in its market price, induced appreciable sales of all other commodities. The provision concerning the substitution of future contracts for the holding of physical commodities (paragraph 6 (v)) is intended as a safeguard against this (since the future price is often well below the spot price when the latter rises on account of a shortage that is expected to be only temporary) as well as the provision (paragraph 13) which calls for the exclusion of a commodity from the "bundle" when its price—which means the future price (if relevant) as well as the spot price—rises by more than 50 per cent. above "declared value."[1] There seems no need, however, for a corollary provision that would call for the exclusion of a commodity in the event of a large fall in price: since the major purpose of the scheme is to prevent a fall in aggregate income, it is thoroughly in accord with its purpose for a fall in the price of some commodities to induce increases in the prices of others.

(f) An important drawback of the scheme (in common with buffer-stock schemes) is the high cost of storage (including turnover, where necessary). The *gross* cost of this has been estimated at as much as $3-3\frac{1}{2}$ per cent. a year of the value of the stock.[2] However, account must be taken of the fact that the greater part of the stocks (two-thirds to three-quarters) are carried anyway, as a result of national price-stabilisation and stock-piling policies; and the governments concerned might reasonably be asked to offer continued use of their existing storage facilities at a token charge.[3] The net cost of storage to the world community (over and above the cost already incurred by governments) may amount to some $200 million annually by the end of the build-up

[1] If this scheme had been in operation since 1955, there would have been only one occasion which clearly called for the exclusion of a commodity under this provision— sugar, which would have gone "off the list" sometime in 1962. As is evident from an inspection of Table 3, the fantastic rise in the sugar price (which rose by more than 400 per cent. in twelve months, between January, 1962, and January, 1963) might have wrought havoc with the scheme otherwise, since the market-price index of the thirty commodities *including* sugar would have shown a rise of 20 per cent. between the average of 1962 and May, 1963; *excluding* sugar, the rise in prices had been only 2 per cent. As Table 3 shows, apart from the case of sugar, the price increases that occurred for other commodities in the years 1955-62 were not large enough to prevent a continued downward movement in the total index in each successive year.

[2] Cf. Elmer M. Harmon, *Commodity Reserve Currency*, Columbia University Press, New York; 1959, pp. 83-7.

[3] The scale of such contributions should be taken into account in determining an equitable scale of discounts, suggested in paragraph 7 (ii) (b) above.

period, a part of which at any rate would be covered by the profits arising from transactions.

IV. EFFECTS ON THE TERMS OF TRADE AND ON ECONOMIC GROWTH

It remains to consider what will be the effect of a scheme of this kind on the terms of trade and on the rate of economic development. The answer to these questions, as we shall show, also provides some indication on how fast commodity reserves will accumulate over longer periods and, therefore, how fast the world currency reserves are likely to grow.

The terms of trade, as W. A. Lewis[1] and others have shown, tend to fluctuate as the growth in world manufacturing production causes the demand for primary products to run ahead of the growth in the supply of primary products, and *vice versa*. On account of the low elasticity of demand for foodstuffs, and also the substitution of synthetics for many natural raw materials, a given rate of growth in manufacturing production generates a less than proportionate growth of demand for primary products. The rate of growth of primary production, on the other hand, follows, with a considerable time lag, the movement of agricultural prices relative to money costs. A period of high prices may lead to considerable new investment in the primary sector—which in turn is likely to accelerate the growth in production at a later date, through the opening up of new producing areas, through the expansion of existing facilities and also through accelerated technological progress (e.g., improved varieties of crops, etc.). When additional supplies eventually come to the market, primary product prices fall again, investment in primary production becomes unprofitable, and a prolonged period of low prices may set in before the rate of growth of supplies slows down sufficiently for the growth of demand to catch up again and restore prices to a remunerative level.[2]

[1] *See* Lewis, "World Production, Prices and Trade, 1870-1960," *The Manchester School*, Vol. 20 (1952), pp. 105-38.

[2] This period may be further prolonged because increases in productivity in the primary sector, instead of being retained in the form of higher money earnings per head, are likely to lead to a reduction in money costs, and so to be passed on to the consumers in lower prices. This is not the case in manufacturing industry, where money wages tend to rise as fast as productivity (and sometimes faster). The difference in the relative movement of money earnings per worker in the two sectors constitutes a further element which tends, in the long run, to turn the terms of trade against primary products.

The rate of growth of world manufacturing production thus exerts a strong influence on the level of primary prices and, in the long run, on the rate of growth of primary production. But with the market mechanism as it is, it cannot be asserted that there are any appreciable forces at work in the other direction—in causing *manufacturing production to expand* in response to increased availabilities of primary products. The fall in the prices of primary products, by releasing purchasing power, ought, in principle, to generate additional demand within the industrial sector. But the fall in the purchasing power of the primary producing sector—reflected in a reduced demand for manufactured goods—pulls the other way; and so does the fall in the scale of world investment in the primary sector which is normally also largely financed by the "industrial" sector. Thus the fall in exports of the industrialised countries, both on account of the reduction in foreign investment, and the reduction in the purchasing power of the primary producing countries, may more than offset any expansionary tendency resulting from the rise in real incomes per head in the industrialised countries. Indeed, allowing for these effects it seems quite likely that the *net* effect of a fall in the prices of primary products relative to manufactures is to depress, rather than to stimulate, the level of activity in the manufacturing sectors.

At any rate, there is no presumption that the balance of forces would operate in one direction more than in another. Historically, a period of falling raw material prices has more often been associated with a slowing down of the rate of industrial growth, rather than with its acceleration. Yet it is precisely when the supplies of primary products are rising relatively fast that there is scope for acceleration in the rate of growth of world manufacturing production. For the world as a whole (and internally for each under-developed country with prospects of industrialisation) the flow of primary products represents the materials necessary to operate industry, and the food necessary for the expansion of urban employment. While any given rate of expansion of primary production may be more than is required to support the industrial expansion of the countries which are *already fully industrialised*, it can be viewed as "excessive" only if we ignored the possibilities of accelerated industrialisation in all those areas which still have large labour reserves in the agricultural sectors, and whose industrialisation could be stepped up very considerably under favourable conditions. If an acceleration of agricultural production fails to induce an acceleration of industrial production it is primarily because it fails to generate the necessary increase in effective demand.

This in our view, is the central advantage of a scheme of commodity price stabilisation by means of an international commodity reserve currency. Under such an arrangement, an increase in primary production will generate a proportionate increase in the effective demand for industrial products—since any excess of supply over demand at existing prices will be absorbed in I.M.F. stocks, and any increase in the output and income of the primary producing areas will increase correspondingly their demand for manufactured goods. This element of income generation will have a powerful multiplier effect. Not only can we reckon on increased consumption in consequence (with the usual cumulation of effects because the additional income generated by that consumption will stimulate more consumption); in addition, there will be "induced investment." In particular, the manufacturing producers whose markets lie in the primary producing sector will find a market that is not only larger, but more reliable, and in consequence can expand their own facilities with confidence. For the world economy as a whole, each unit of income so generated would probably be amplified by a "super-multiplier" (allowing for induced investment) of at least four or five (indeed, the likely figure may be much larger). So long as I.M.F. reserves rise faster than the production of primary products, manufacturing areas will find that their sales rise faster than their purchases—i.e. they will experience growing export surpluses—and this will accelerate their expansion. But since every rise of manufacturing income implies a rise in the absorption of primary products by the industrial economy, this process tends to be self-balancing. The rate of growth of consumption of primary products will converge on the rate of growth of primary production; when this is achieved, the rate of growth of the reserves will match the rate of growth of the production and use of primary products. Hence the commodity reserve system provides a mechanism through which the expansion of primary production induces a corresponding expansion in manufacturing production. Thus the balance between the two sectors will be restored through an accelerated rate of industrialisation, rather than through cuts in investment and in the growth of output in the primary sectors—the latter being the adjustment mechanism that operates through prolonged periods of depressed prices.

The manufacturing sector of the world economy exists partly in the highly developed countries and partly in countries in varying stages of industrialisation, many of which do not yet export manufactures on a significant scale. The process of expansion set up by the commodity reserve system may be seen as one which will *diffuse* demand from the central to the outlying areas of industrialisation.

It is clear that the expansion of exports from the highly developed industrial countries to the primary producing areas benefits both parties so long as there is slack in the economy of the industrial countries. Then the generation of an export surplus absorbs unemployment and increases total output. But once the process of expansion in an industrial country reaches the point where output presses against the full employment ceiling, the situation changes: exports can expand further only at the expense of domestic consumption and investment. Unless the country in question adopts an austerity programme at this stage and curtails domestic consumption and investment in order to maintain its share of exports in the world market, forces will be set up which will limit the growth of its exports. Either the money costs of export goods (and of goods that compete with imports) will be pushed up as a result of the pressure of demand, or the country may choose to obviate such an inflationary process by letting the value of its currency unit rise (as countries such as Canada, Sweden or Germany have done on occasion). In either case the process will make the supplies from such countries relatively more expensive and increase the attractiveness of manufactured goods from other manufacturing areas, where expansion is not limited by full employment.

If income continues to be generated in the world's primary producing sectors by the expansion of reserves under a commodity-reserve system, each industrial country which deliberately or otherwise refuses to accept the corresponding export surplus is diverting demand to other countries. If Germany cannot expand exports further, perhaps the U.K. or the U.S.A. can; if the U.K. or the U.S.A. cannot, perhaps some of the countries like Japan, India, Mexico or Brazil, which are well past the earliest stages of industrialisation, can do so. If these economies too become fully loaded, the expansive pressure will be diverted to the industrial sectors of still less developed countries. Since the world as a whole is a vast under-developed economy—with vast reserves of under-utilised and unemployed labour which can be drawn on for employment in industry so long as raw material supplies are available and demand is expanding—it cannot be denied that it is possible to step up the growth of world manufacturing production sufficiently so as to match any likely increase in the supply of primary products.[1] It may well be true that the stabilisation of primary product prices, by reducing the risks associated with investment, will lead to a considerable acceleration in the growth of primary production. Those who fear such an expansion are thinking primarily in terms of the likely requirements of the countries already fully industrialised. But when one thinks of the needs and potentialities for growth of the world economy, such an acceleration is something not to be feared, but earnestly hoped for—provided only that we can set up a mechanism through which increased primary production will accelerate industrial growth as well.

All this presupposes, of course, that the commodity reserve will operate so as to absorb stocks and *improve* the prices of commodities in the process of doing so. It is conceivable that, in the period following the establishment of the commodity reserve system, commodity prices would show a rising trend, and the operation of the scheme might result in a release of initial reserves that would reduce world demand and hold down the terms of trade instead of improving them. The plan in the form proposed here contains

---

[1] This is not to deny that industrialisation requires other things besides labour, capital and raw materials—such as know-how and managerial ability. But the rapid industrialisation of numerous countries (notably Japan; more recently Brazil and Mexico) has shown that know-how and managerial capacity can be acquired fairly rapidly when the underlying conditions for industrial growth are favourable.

several built-in safeguards against this. In the first place, commodity stocks absorbed by initial purchases into the reserves would not be available for net sales (as distinct from turnover transactions to protect the reserve against deterioration, under which sales would be matched by purchases) until the build-up period had run its course. Secondly, experience during the build-up period would enter into the determination of the parity price for the commodity bundle. Since declared values for component commodities might be raised above their initial levels (but not reduced below them), the initial price of the commodity bundle is not likely to be set so low as to risk a major run on the stockpile at the moment when commodity bundles are first offered for sale.

If, nevertheless, it *did* happen that the system at first led to heavy destocking the remedy would be a devaluation of the currencies of industrial exporters (or of *all* currencies) in terms of bancor that would reverse the balance between the growth in demand and the growth of supply of primary products, and thus enable the I.M.F. to start accumulating stocks. In contrast to the situation under the existing monetary arrangements, a comparatively *small* devaluation could produce substantial effects under a commodity reserve system precisely because it would operate directly upon the terms of trade, whereas under present conditions the devaluation of the major currencies would leave the prices of primary commodities in their previous relationship to wages in the industrial countries. Under these conditions, the industrial countries would also have strong incentives to devalue, since the release of stocks by the I.M.F. would imply an import surplus, and a loss of reserves of the industrial countries; and exchange-rate adjustments would no longer be hampered by the existence of the "key-currency" system.

We could also suppose that the terms of trade show a trend against primary products, not on account of any tendency for production to outrun consumption of primary products, but owing to an excessive increase in money wages in the industrial sector.[1] (This would manifest itself in the rise in the bancor price

[1] This, perhaps, is not an acute danger at present, since the price level of world exports of manufactured goods, as computed by the U.N. has remained stable since 1953, despite the very considerable rise in the rate of money wages in all industrialised countries. In the case of some of these countries (such as the United Kingdom, the

level of the world's manufactured exports, while the bancor prices of primary products remained stable.) The stabilisation of commodity prices in terms of gold and bancor by means of the scheme would not itself prevent this—though it might cause some shift in primary production from the developed to the less developed countries. However, here again the operation of the commodity reserve system would make devaluation of the currencies of the industrialised countries an effective remedy, which it would not otherwise be. Since in the case under consideration, the rising trend in the prices of manufactured goods has been brought about by an excessive increase in money wages (in relation to the growth of industrial productivity) and not by excessive world demand for manufactured goods, and since the rate of growth of money wages is determined by influences which have little to do with the terms of trade, the adjustment of exchange rates, by lowering the gold prices of manufactured goods, provides an effective instrument for counteracting this trend, provided only that the reduction in the gold (or bancor) prices of manufactures is *not* offset by a similar reduction in the gold (or bancor) prices of primary commodities.[1] The latter is likely to happen under the present gold exchange standard, but it is directly prevented by the commodity reserve system.

V. CONCLUDING REMARKS

It should be evident from the foregoing analysis that the adoption of a proposal of this kind would serve a number of important and generally accepted objectives of international economic policy:

1. It would create an international reserve medium which is far more responsive to the needs of an expanding world economy

United States and Sweden) export prices have increased appreciably over the last ten years. But in the case of others (such as Belgium, France, Germany, Italy and Japan) export prices (measured in terms of gold) have fallen appreciably, so that the combined index has remained unchanged. It may be presumed that such divergent trends will continue but that on balance, barring any major upheaval, the gold price level of the world's manufactured exports will continue to be stable.

[1] Since, as we have seen, the movement in "efficiency wages" is far from uniform as between different industrial countries, and since the particular countries whose efficiency wages rose most in relation to others are likely to face acute difficulties in their balance of payments, such countries will have a strong incentive to devalue their currencies in relation to others so as to maintain their share in world trade; such individual devaluations will serve to hold down the world prices of manufactured goods in terms of gold (or bancor).

than gold, and the rules of operation of which would exert a powerful stabilising effect on the world economy.

2. It would make possible the orderly liquidation of the existing "gold-exchange standard," relieving the present strain on the key-currency countries, and obviating the risk that the system may collapse, if persistent disequilibrium in international payments at any time leads to a loss of confidence.

3. It would permit a balanced distribution of economic progress in the world, both as between the different highly industrialised areas, and as between the developed and the developing countries.

4. It would provide an effective instrument for stabilising the terms of trade between primary products and manufactured goods, and for accelerating the rate of growth of world industrial production in response to increased availabilities of food and raw materials.

On the side of monetary reform the commodity reserve proposal, as we have seen, offers substantial advantages over alternative plans. It combines reliability of the central reserve with monetary and fiscal autonomy of individual countries in a more satisfactory manner than either the plans which aim at generalising the key-currency system, or the plans which aim at establishing a credit-creating world central bank.

On the side of economic stabilisation, the prospect of creating a world currency reserve which expands *pari passu* with the production and use of primary products, offers a general support and stimulus to economic activity of the sort which in the past, the world only experienced in those particular phases of history when, by good fortune, gold discoveries were great enough to expand the monetary gold stock fairly fast. But as compared with a gold standard, or with any paper credit arrangement, a commodity reserve currency offers a far more effective safeguard in case of serious setbacks of activity in the industrial countries. Because the total world production of commodities eligible for the reserve is large (of the order of $80 billion to $100 billion a year, out of a world gross product of around $1,200 billion), there is an important segment of world income which would be protected against shrinkage in times of industrial depression. The existence of this sector would be a significant support for world markets for industrial products, and thus would appreciably raise the "floor" for any depression emanating from industrial countries. Furthermore, the maintenance of the incomes of primary producers, like unemployment insurance for industrial workers, should be seen as an instrument for preventing the effects of industrial recessions from focusing on the people who are least able to bear them.

An even more important gain is the greater steadiness of income and of investment prospects in the under-developed countries. The wide fluctuations in the prices of primary products which involve corresponding fluctuations in the profitability of investment, tend to check industrial activity in the very circumstances in which the greater availability of primary products offers scope for accelerated industrialisation. Because industrial expansion is so much a matter of effective demand, and because a weakness in the markets for primary products makes for unfavourable business conditions in industry as well, the opportunities for accelerated economic growth afforded by the technical progress in primary production tend largely to go to waste. The commodity reserve system would put an end to all this: it would induce the kind of economic growth which would operate by narrowing, instead of widening, the gap between high income and low income countries.

This is not to suggest that any monetary scheme can make economic development automatic. The use that can be made of opportunities for development depends above all, on sound policies and upon the creative initiative (both public and private) within the under-developed countries themselves. But the institution of a commodity reserve currency would certainly serve to provide a favourable financial setting for such initiatives. This is now lacking.

APPENDIX

STATISTICS RELATING TO INTERNATIONAL MONETARY RESERVES AND ILLUSTRATIVE BASE FOR A COMMODITY RESERVE CURRENCY

TABLE 1. Changes in Reserve Position and in Imports, 1952–62: United States and other I.M.F. countries.

TABLE 2. Illustrative Base for Commodity Reserve Currency: 125 per cent. of 1962 Exports if Existing Stocks exceed 125 per cent.; amount of Existing Stocks if between 90 per cent. and 125 per cent. of Exports; 90 per cent. of 1962 Exports if Existing Stocks less than 90 per cent.

TABLE 3. Movement of Index Numbers corresponding to Commodity Reserve Structure of Appendix Table 2, 1955–63.

TABLE I. CHANGES IN RESERVE POSITION AND IN IMPO▮

(Billion

Period	Total monetary reserves	Total reserves distributed by countries				
		United States	Other I.M.F. member countries			
			Total	United Kingdom	Sterling Area	A oth▮
	(1)	(2)	(3)	(4)	(5)	(▮
1952: level	*51·3*	*24·7*	*26·6*	*2·0*	*7·2*	*1*
Increments:						
1953	2·1	−1·3	3·3	0·7	0·6	
1954	1·7	−0·5	2·2	0·4	0·2	
1955	1·0	−0·2	1·2	−0·6	−0·2	
1956	2·0	0·9	1·2	−0·1	−0·2	
1957	0·5	1·2	−0·7	0·1	−0·4	−
1953-7	7·3	0·1	7·2	0·4	0·1	
1957: level	*58·6*	*24·8*	*33·8*	*2·4*	*7·3*	*2*
Increments:						
1958	1·2	−2·3	3·5	0·7	−0·4	
1959	0·5	−1·0	1·6	−0·3	0·7	
1960	3·1	−2·2	5·3	0·9	−0·5	
1961	2·0	−0·6	2·6	−0·4	0·2	
1962	0·2	−1·5	1·7	−0·0	0·3	
1958-62	7·1	−7·6	14·7	0·9	0·3	1
1962: level	*65·5*	*17·2*	*48·5*	*3·3*	*7·6*	*5*

Source: International Monetary Fund, *International Financial* ▮
istics (Washington, D.C.), December, 1963, pp. 1▮
270 and 274, and Supplement to 1963-4 Issues, pp. ▮
238, 244. Column (12), which is only implicit in▮

Dollars)

	Total reserves distributed by types				I.M.F. credit, etc.	United States: reserves minus liabilities	Total imports		
	Foreign exchange reserves						All	United States	Other I.M.F. members
	Total	United States $	Sterling	Other					
	(8)	(9)	(10)	(11)	(12)	(13)	(14)	(15)	(16)
7	*15·7*	*4·7*	*7·0*	*4·0*	*−0·1*	*20·1*	*79·8*	*11·7*	*68·1*
5	1·5	1·0	0·5	−0·0	0·1	−2·3	−3·7	−0·1	−3·8
7	1·1	1·1	0·1	−0·1	−0·1	−1·6	3·1	−0·7	3·8
7	0·5	0·2	−0·0	0·3	−0·2	−0·4	9·6	1·4	8·3
5	1·0	1·1	−0·2	0·1	0·6	−0·2	9·3	1·5	7·8
7	−0·8	−0·1	−0·4	−0·3	0·6	1·3	9·5	0·6	8·9
0	3·3	3·3	0·0	0·0	1·0	−3·2	27·8	2·9	24·9
8	*19·0*	*7·9*	*7·0*	*4·1*	*0·9*	*16·9*	*107·6*	*14·6*	*93·0*
7	0·3	0·7	−0·3	−0·1	0·2	−3·0	−6·9	0·0	−6·9
3	−0·1	0·5	0·3	−0·9	−0·2	−1·5	5·7	2·4	3·3
3	2·6	1·1	0·1	1·5	0·2	−3·2	12·8	−0·5	13·3
5	0·6	0·7	0·0	−0·1	0·8	−1·3	5·1	−0·4	5·5
3	0·2	1·0	−1·0	−0·0	−0·3	−2·5	7·2	1·7	5·5
7	3·6	4·0	−0·9	0·3	0·7	−11·6	23·9	3·2	20·7
4	*22·5*	*11·9*	*6·1*	*4·4*	*1·6*	*5·3*	*131·5*	*17·8*	*113·7*

F. data, is necessary because "total reserves" are defined by I.M.F. as plus official holdings of foreign exchange plus gold tranche positions; but old held by I.M.F. and other international institutions varies relative to um of gold tranche positions and has recently been considerably smaller.

Commodity	Exports, 1962			Stocks,
	Million dollars	Percentage of total	Apparent share of under-developed countries (percentage)	Million dollars
	(1)	(2)	(3)	(4)
Wheat *a*	1,386	7·30	10	3,422
Rice	653	3·44	69	*
Barley *a*	316	1·66	18	284
Maize *a*	892	4·70	38	3,275
CEREALS	3,247	17·10	(33)	6,985
SUGAR	1,624	8·55	78	689
Cocoa	451	2·38	100	43
Coffee	1,870	9·85	100	2,877
Tea	663	3·49	83	135
BEVERAGES	2,984	15·72	(94)	3,055
TOBACCO	1,045	5·50	49	2,758
Butter	422	2·22	0	241
Lard	88	0·46	0	7
Tallow	151	0·80	0	*
ANIMAL FATS	661	3·48	(0)	248
Soya	353	1·86	2	59
Groundnut	260	1·37	93	
Cottonseed	80	0·42	30	54
Olive	107	0·56	25	*
Coconut	258	1·36	97	*
Palm *e*	182	0·96	91	*
Linseed	102	0·54	56	*
VEGETABLE OILS	1,343	7·07	(20)	104
Cotton	2,099	11·06	56	2,33
Wool	1,781	9·38	24	29
Jute	160	0·84	97	31
Abaca	37	0·19	100	*
Agave	108	0·57	92	*
FIBRES	4,185	22·04	(45)	2,94
RUBBER (NATURAL)	1,042	5·49	100	27
Aluminium *f*	492	2·59	6	6
Copper	1,642	8·65	63	48
Lead *f*	152	0·80	72	7
Zinc *f*	160	0·84	26	7
Tin	410	2·16	87	11
METALS	2,856	15·04	(55)	80
TOTAL	18,987	100·00	(58)	17,86

Source: Column (1): United Nations, *Commodity Survey, 1962* (Sales No.: 63.II.D.3), Table A (pp.
tons multiplied by unit values, 1961 figures used where 1962 is lacking. Column (3): *ibid.* I
tages for "primary producing areas" are reduced for wheat, butter, and wool to remove A
and New Zealand. Column (4): *op. cit.*, Table A and Table 17 (p. 96). Figures of Table 17 are
formed to tons of 1962 by applying the index numbers (1960 = 100) of stocks for 1962 to 1960
in tons; then the tons are transformed to dollars by multiplying them by the unit value
in Table A. Column (6): 125 per cent. of column (1) except in lines 3 and 61, where sto
smaller than 125 per cent. of exports, and in lines where "purchases out of later productio
also entered. Column (9): 125 per cent. of column (1) in lines where purchases out of stocks are
cent.: per 90 cent. of column (1) in all other lines except 3 and 61. Columns (7-8): Excess of

62 ntage tal	Elements of proposed reserve				
	Purchases out of existing stocks	Purchases out of later production		Total reserves	
		From under-developed countries	From other countries	Million dollars	Percentages of total
(5)	(6)	(7)	(8)	(9)	(10)
·16	1,733	0	0	1,733^b	8·49
*	0	406	182	588^c	2·88
·59	284	0	0	284^c	1·39
·36	1,115	0	0	1,115^d	5·46
·09	3,132	406	182	3,720^b	18·22
·86	689	603	170	1,462^c	7·16
·24	43	363	0	406^c	1·99
·11	2,338	0	0	2,338^b	11·45
·76	135	383	79	597^c	2·92
·10	2,516	746	79	3,341	16·37
·44	1,307	0	0	1,307^b	6·40
·35	241	0	139	380^c	1·86
·04	7	0	72	79^c	0·39
*	0	0	136	136^c	0·67
·39	248	0	347	595^c	2·91
·33	59	5	254	318^c	1·56
*	0	218	16	234^c	1·15
·28	50	7	15	72^c	0·35
*	0	24	72	96^c	0·47
*	0	225	7	232^c	1·14
*	0	150	15	165^c	0·81
*	0	52	40	92^c	0·45
·61	109	681	419	1,209^c	5·92
·08	2,337	0	0	2,337^d	11.45
·64	293	314	996	1,603^c	7·85
·74	200	0	0	200^b	0·98
*	0	33	0	33^c	0·16
*	0	89	8	97^c	0·48
·46	2,830	436	1,004	4,270	20·92
·54	276	662	0	938^c	4·60
·34	615^g	g	g	615^b	3·01
·70	2,053^g	g	g	2,053^b	10·06
·40	190^g	g	g	190^b	0·93
·44	200^g	g	g	200^b	0·98
·63	513^g	g	g	513^b	2·51
·51	3,571^g	g	g	3,571^b	17·49
·00	14,678	3,534	2,201	20,413	100·00

er column (6); the proportion assigned to under-developed countries is that given in column (3)
tocks reported in source. a Exports of wheat given by the source are scaled down by 40 per cent., and
of barley and maize by 12 per cent., to remove transactions of non-commercial type (U.S. public
80). b 125 per cent. of column (1). c 90 per cent. of column (1). d Reserve determined by existing
(between 90 per cent. and 125 per cent. of exports). e Includes palm kernel. f Does not include ores,
have value per ton far below that of metal. g Calculation assumes "strategic reserves" can release
ties which with reported stocks will yield 125 per cent. of exports. The total market value of U.S.
gic stocks as of the end of 1962 is stated (Statistical Abstract of the US, 1963) at $7,484 million, of
$3,269 million is declared as "excess to stockpile objectives"; but only $864 million worth is classified
amodities. h Includes concentrates, with value per ton very close to that of metal.

TABLE 3. MOVEMENTS OF INDEX NUMBERS CORRESPONDING

(Points of to

COMMODITY	1955	1956	1957	1958
Wheat	8·94	9·21	8·76	8·25
Rice	2·61	2·53	2·57	2·75
Barley *a*				
Maize	6·85	7·59	7 09	5 57
CEREALS	*19 79*	*20 72*	*19 81*	*17·96*
SUGAR	*7·79*	*8·34*	*12·40*	*8·41*
Cocoa	3·64	2·58	2·97	4·21
Coffee	19·23	19·57	19·16	16·30
Tea	3·06	2·94	2·73	2·84
BEVERAGE CROPS	*25·93*	*25·09*	*24·86*	*23·35*
TOBACCO	*5·30*	*5·49*	*5·56*	*5·85*
Butter	2·21	2·01	1·77	1·47
Lard	0·45	0·47	0·51	0·48
Tallow	0·90	0·87	0·94	0·93
ANIMAL FATS	*3·56*	*3·35*	*3·22*	*2·88*
Soya	2·04	2·34	2·11	2·00
Groundnut	1·20	1·56	1·51	1·15
Cottonseed *a*				
Olive	0·43	0·68	0·55	0·46
Coconut	1·21	1·21	1·23	1·44
Palm	0·85	0·93	0·93	0·84
Linseed	0·44	0·58	0·48	0·47
VEGETABLE OILS	*6·52*	*7·65*	*7·16*	*6·71*
Cotton	15·18	13·33	12·82	13·04
Wool	8·93	9·44	10·44	7·43
Jute	0·87	0·91	1·01	0·97
Abaca *a*				
Agave *a*				
FIBRES	*25·62*	*24·32*	*24·91*	*22·08*
RUBBER (natural)	*6·58*	*5·62*	*5·18*	*4·68*
Aluminium	2·78	3·18	3·28	3·06
Copper	15·14	14·15	9·42	8·47
Lead	1·75	1·92	1·60	1·20
Zinc	1·32	1·42	1·18	0·96
Tin	2·07	2·11	2·11	2·06
METALS	*23·06*	*22·88*	*17·59*	*15·75*
TOTAL	*124·15*	*123·46*	*120·69*	*107·67*
TOTAL EXCLUDING SUGAR:	—	—	—	—
Points of index 1962 = 100				

Source: (Except tobacco) from United Nations, *Monthly Bulletin of Statistics* (selecting for each comm⟨ a highly representative price—in most cases for commodities delivered in British ports) tobacco (whose price is not quoted in the *Monthly Bulletin*), price quotations from *Internat⟨ Financial Statistics* have been used.
  Weights of prices (from right-hand column of Appendix Table 2 constitute the 1962 colum⟨

9	1960	1961	1962	Jan., 1962	Sept., 1962	May, 1963
28	8·16	8·28	8·49	8·67	8·43	8·49
47	2·32	2·53	2·88	2·53	2·97	2·65
			1·39			
·57	5·67	5·54	5·46	5·72	5·38	6·01
·71	17·54	17·74	18·22	18·31	18·17	18·54
·14	7·45	6·99	7·16	5·53	7·64	25·18
·45	2·70	2·12	1·99	2·13	1·86	2·93
·46	12·33	12·12	11·45	11·52	11·25	11·21
·80	2·85	2·70	2·92	2·61	3·45	2·38
·71	17·88	16·94	16·36	16·26	16·56	16·52
·09	5·99	6·33	6·40	6·40	6·25	6·02
·13	1·93	1·60	1·86	1·77	1·90	1·96
37	0·40	0·42	0·39	0·38	0·40	0·35
·79	0·69	0·76	0·67	0·73	0·60	0·67
·29	3·02	2·78	2·92	2·88	2·90	2·98
·60	1·54	1·98	1·56	1·83	1·37	1·60
·25	1·36	1·38	1·15	1·36	1·09	1·13
			0·35			
·42	0·42	0·40	0·47	0·40	0·50	0·80
·74	1·41	1·13	1·14	1·10	1·10	1·24
·89	0·84	0·85	0·81	0·86	0·75	0·83
·44	0·45	0·50	0·45	0·50	0·43	0·38
·69	6·37	6·59	5·93	6·40	5·59	6·33
·30	11·15	11·56	11·45	11·56	11·19	11·78
·60	7·43	7·52	7·85	7·18	7·52	8·85
·98	1·25	1·47	0·98	1·09	0·93	0·98
			0·16			
			0·48			
·52	20·47	21·19	20·93	20·47	20·28	22·25
·88	6·28	4·90	4·60	4·74	4·42	4·44
·99	3·09	3·09	3·01	3·09	2·99	2·99
·23	10·58	9·89	10·06	9·89	10·06	10·06
·17	1·19	1·06	0·93	0·98	0·86	1·00
·19	1·30	1·13	0·98	1·02	0·93	1·10
·20	2·23	2·49	2·51	2·65	2·39	2·53
·78	18·39	17·66	17·49	17·63	17·23	17·68
3·81	103·39	101·12	100·01	98·62	99·04	119·94
—	—	—	92·84	93·15	91·46	94·80
			100·00	100·33	98·52	102·11

Lacking price data for these items (with a total weight of 2·40 per cent.), we have treated their prices as [cons]tant. b The phenomenal rise of sugar prices would have led to exclusion of this commodity from the [tab]le during 1962, under the rule proposed in the text; consequently the relevant index for May 1963 [woul]d have been that shown in the last line of the table.

19

DUAL EXCHANGE RATES AND ECONOMIC DEVELOPMENT[1]

THE latest study by the U.N. Secretariat[2] provides ample proof, if further proof were needed, that the problem of the economic development of the low-income countries cannot be solved without these countries becoming not only producers but also exporters of manufactured goods on an important scale. At present 86 per cent. of the exports of the "developing countries"[3] consists of primary products and only 14 per cent. of manufactured goods. But the world market for primary commodities expands only slowly, owing to the low income elasticity of demand. This is partly due to the low income elasticity of food consumption in the wealthy countries and the rapid growth of their own agricultural production, and partly to economies in the use of materials in industry and the development of synthetics. Since 1938 the volume of world trade in manufactures has more than trebled, while the volume of trade in primary products has increased only by two-thirds. If the primary exporting regions were to continue to depend mainly on the exports of primary products, their export receipts to the outside world could not be expected to increase by more than 3 per cent. annually even if their export prices remained constant.[4] Their import requirements, on the other hand, would be bound to increase faster than their domestic product—mainly because their import requirements

---

[1] Published in the *Economic Bulletin for Latin America*, September 1964.

[2] *World Economic Survey, 1962, Part I: The Developing Countries and World Trade*, United Nations, New York, 1963.

[3] This term comprises all countries except those of North America, Western Europe, Japan, Australia, New Zealand, South Africa and the "centrally planned" economies.

[4] In the period 1950–61 the *quantum* of exports of the underdeveloped areas to the developed areas expanded at 2·6 per cent. a year in the case of food, 1·6 per cent. in the case of raw materials and 9·3 per cent. in the case of petroleum; the current dollar value of exports of the three categories together increased at the rate of 3·3 per cent. (see *U.N. Statistical Bulletin*, January 1964, Table B). Since the growth of petroleum exports cannot be expected to continue at such high rates, the rate of growth of the quantum of exports of primary commodities cannot be put at more than 3 per cent. a year, given the current rates of growth of the G.N.P.'s of the developed countries. (Cf. U.N. *Survey, op. cit.*, p.6.)

for capital goods increase faster than their domestic fixed capital formation, and also because their own income elasticities of demand for imports of consumer goods and raw materials are high.[1] On the U.N. estimate, the attainment of a 5 per cent. annual growth rate (the United Nations "development target" for the end of the 1960's) would require an annual increase in imports of at least 6 per cent. a year.[2] Clearly, such rates of growth of imports cannot be sustained unless the rates of growth of exports are also stepped up to the same rate. While economic aid from the "developed" countries can provide a temporary solution to the growing balance of payments problem, it cannot, even in the best of circumstances, provide a permanent one. A situation in which imports rise twice as fast as exports and in which the continuance of growth is so closely linked to the growth of imports, is bound to spell disaster in the long run.

On the basis of current trends, and on the assumption that the current rates of economic growth of the under-developed countries were to be maintained, the proportion of annual imports to be financed by external aid would rise at an alarming rate. According to the projection of the U.N. study,[3] a 4·8 per cent. average growth rate in the domestic product of the under-developed countries would entail an increase of 95 per cent. in their annual import requirements between 1959 and 1970. Their export receipts from the sale of primary products at constant prices would, on the U.N. calculations, rise by only 40 per cent. Hence their current trade gap with the developed countries (allowing for a $2 billion increase in their exports of manufactures) would rise by $11 billion, and their balance of payments gap on current current account, after allowing for a $4 billion increase in their net adverse balance on invisible account by $15 billion—i.e. from $5 billion in 1959 to $20 billion in 1970—before making any allowance for amortisation or obligations for repayment of past debt. It is unlikely that economic aid will be forthcoming on this

[1] Cf. *ibid.*, text table p. 6. Also, G.A.T.T., *International Trade in 1959*, pp. 40–56.

[2] A 5 per cent. growth rate in the domestic product, with an estimated population increase of 2·4 per cent., would generate a rate of growth of real income per head of (approx.) 2·6 per cent., which would mean that by the turn of the century real income per head of the under-developed countries would rise from the present $130 to $360. At that level it would still be only one-quarter as high as the *current* level of real income per head in the United Kingdom.

[3] *Ibid.*, Table I–5.

scale—it would imply an increase in *net* lending (i.e. in excess of debt repayments) by the advanced countries that is more than twice as great as the projected rate of growth of their national incomes—though as a proportion of the G.N.P.'s of the advanced countries, or of their defence expenditure, even the latter sum would not loom large. But even if it were forthcoming in 1970, it certainly could not be expected to be so indefinitely—the U.N. projections, if carried forward to 1980, would yield a balance of payments gap of no less than $57 billion! Unless the under-developed countries succeed in stepping up the rate of growth of their exports so as to *narrow* their trade gap sooner or later, the whole process of economic growth based on external aid is bound to break down.

Given the low income elasticities of demand for food and raw materials in the developed countries, such an acceleration in exports can only come from one of two sources: either an increase in exports (mainly primary products) to the Soviet area countries, or the growth of exports of manufactured goods to the developed countries.[1]

The volume of exports of the under-developed countries to the "centrally planned" economies (including China and Jugoslavia) is still small; in 1962 it amounted to $1·5 billion or just over 7 per cent. of their total exports to the outside world. But in recent years it has been growing rapidly; in the years 1956–62 the value of this trade increased by 170 per cent., or 16·5 per cent. per annum. If the volume of this trade continued to rise at say, 9 per cent. per annum—which is not impossible in view of the recent statements made by the U.S.S.R. delegation to the Geneva con-ference[2]—the rate of growth in the total volume of exports of primary products (given a 3 per cent. growth in their export to the developed countries) would gradually rise to 3·8 per cent. by 1980 and—if it continued—to 4·4 per cent. by 1990. Assuming, however, that import requirements of the under-developed countries would continue to grow at 6 per cent. a year, this would still leave a very considerable gap between the rate of growth of

---

[1] An improvement in the terms of trade for primary products would ease their problems in the short-run, but it could hardly compensate for an inadequate growth in the *volume* of exports over longer periods.

[2] See reference in Appendix below.

their imports and exports which could only be filled by an accelerated rate of growth of exports of manufactured goods.

At present the world trade in manufactured goods is still almost the exclusive preserve of the advanced industrial countries: the developing countries' share is only 5·3 per cent. (or 6·2 per cent., if the trade of the countries of the Soviet area is excluded from the total).[1] However, in recent years there have been welcome signs of improvement. Thus in the last five years (1957–62) the dollar value of the manufactured exports of the under-developed countries to the developed countries increased at the annual rate of 6·6 per cent. a year—i.e. at a slightly higher rate than the exports of manufactures of the developed countries;[2] whereas in the previous five years, when the value of world exports of manufactures grew at 8 per cent. a year, the exports of the under-developed countries increased only at 3·8 per cent. a year. If the growth in these exports could be stepped up to, say, 10 per cent. a year—it would be hazardous to assume any higher figure —the rate of growth in their *total* exports would attain a 6 per cent. rate by around 1985, which would enable them, from then on, to increase their current export earnings at a faster rate than their imports. Even on these assumptions it would take another twenty to twenty-five years before they could become financially self-supporting.

The Appendix (printed below) gives the results of an arithmetical exercise showing how the current balance of payments of the under-developed countries would develop in the next forty

[1] This trade at present is highly concentrated, both as to countries of origin and destination and as regards the nature of commodities traded. According to the study of the U.N. Secretariat, submitted to the Geneva conference, ten countries (India, Hong Kong, Israel, Mexico, Iran, the Philippines, Pakistan, Taiwan, Argentina and Brazil) accounted for 75 per cent. of total exports (excluding base metals), while seventy-nine other developing countries only accounted for 6 per cent. On the side of imports, 56 per cent. of the total (excluding base metals) was absorbed by the U.K., the U.S. and other EFTA countries. As regards the commodity composition of such imports, 25 per cent. consisted of clothing, textile yarn, fabrics and other textile products, almost 40 per cent. of base metals and the rest divided between carpets and leather goods (5½ per cent.), precious stones and pearls (3·8 per cent.), various chemicals (3 per cent.), machinery and transport equipment (4·2 per cent.) and all other items (18·5 per cent.). Cf. *World Economic Survey, op. cit.*, Ch. 3 and also *Trade in Manufactures and Semi-Manufactures*, U.N. document *E/Conf. 46/6.*

[2] Since textile and clothing exports accounted for a considerable part (perhaps 40 per cent.) of the increase in their manufactured expor s in the last five years and textile exports are now restricted (see belaw), there is a danger that this recent rate of growth may not be maintained in the near future.

years, assuming that their imports increased at 6 per cent. a year, their exports of manufactured goods at 10 per cent. a year, and their exports of primary products at 3 per cent. a year to the developed countries and at 9 per cent. a year to the countries of the Soviet area. The calculations also assume that the terms of trade remain constant (at 1960 prices) and that the average interest charge on all future aid received to cover their adverse balance on current account is 3 per cent. On these assumptions their trade gap, expressed as a proportion of imports, will begin to diminish after 1980, and their balance of payments gap after 1990, though in absolute terms the latter will continue to rise until the year 2000. The cumulative deficit in their balance of payments up to the year 2000 works out at $1,366 billion—a a staggering looking sum, but in fact no greater than 1·5 per cent. of the gross national product of the developed countries over the period, assuming that the latter also increases at a rate of 4 per cent. a year. More than 40 per cent. of the total deficit is accounted for by additional interest payments; if the aid to cover the current deficit was given in gifts or interest-free loans, the cumulative deficit would amount to $785 billion only or 0·8 per cent. of the cumulative G.N.P.'s of the developed countries.

No particular virtue is claimed for this exercise, except as a demonstration to show that "trade" and "aid" can in no sense be regarded as alternatives. If the under-developed countries are to achieve even a modest rate of growth in incomes per head and sustain it over longer periods, they will need every assistance to facilitate their trade as well as all the financial support which the advanced countries are ready to provide.

OBSTACLES TO EXPORTS—I. THE PROBLEM OF COMPETITIVENESS

The important obstacles to a high and sustained growth in the export of manufactures are not likely to lie on the side of production but on the side of marketing. It is not unreasonable to suppose that with 5 per cent. growth rate in their national product, the under-developed countries could increase their manufacturing production at the rate of 10 per cent. or more, so that they would be capable of achieving a 10 per cent. annual rise in exports without requiring their exports to grow at a faster rate than their aggregate output of manufactured goods.

However, the fact that they could increase their production sufficiently does not ensure that they could increase their exports at that rate. The latter depends on their ability to sell at prices which are competitive with the products of the advanced countries; and on the willingness of the importing countries to allow this to happen, and not to frustrate their efforts by the imposition of rigid or discriminatory restrictions.

Leaving the second factor aside for the moment, the main obstacle is likely to lie in the internal cost-and-price structure of under-developed countries as between primary products and manufactured goods, which militates against the development of manufactured exports. It has been well known since the days of Friedrich List that in the initial stages of industrialisation the productivity of labour in manufacturing activities is very low— so low that, even though wages are very low, manufacturing costs are high. As the scale of industrial activities expands, productivity increases and costs come down—partly because of the economies of large-scale production, but, more importantly, because of the accumulation of skill and know-how resulting from activity itself: as a result of "learning by doing". This is the basic justification of the now universally accepted principle that an under-developed country needs to protect its manufacturing activities from foreign competition by restricting imports through protective duties or quantitative import controls. The protection of "infant industries" is necessary to equalise the differences between "private costs" and "social costs"—i.e. to compensate for the fact that in the case of a less developed country, the marginal costs of production incurred by the entrepreneurs are higher, *relative to* the marginal social costs, than in the case of a more developed country. Given this fact, it follows that it is impossible to secure the best allocation of resources—either from the point of view of a single country, or the world as a whole—without interfering with the unhindered operation of the price mechanism by means of special taxes or subsidies.

This classical argument has received powerful reinforcement in recent years from the increasing recognition of the importance of "disguised unemployment" in under-developed countries. If the number who can be effectively employed on the available land is limited, there are no alternative forms of productive employment for labour employed in non-agricultural sectors, hence the true displacement cost of such employment is zero. These two arguments operate independently and powerfully, reinforce each other. Increasing returns due to learning by doing and disguised unemployment due to a surplus of labour relative to land, each set up discrepancies between money cost and social cost in manufacturing production and each therefore justifies differential taxation to promote industrialisation.

It is less generally recognised that in either case the equalisation of social comparative-cost-ratios with private comparative-cost-ratios calls for a *reduction* in the cost of industrial products (in terms of agricultural prices) by means of subsidies, rather than for a *rise* in domestic industrial prices by means of a tariff. Looked at from the point of view of the internal re-distribution of income, these two methods come to much the same thing: protective duties, by raising the prices which the agricultural sector pays for industrial products, amount to a taxation of agriculture for the benefit of industry in much the same way as if a direct levy had been imposed on the former, and a direct subsidy paid to the latter. From the point of view of their consequences for economic development, however, the two methods are by no means identical: in the one case the internal *price* structure is adapted to the *internal* cost structure, whereas in the other case the internal *cost* structure is adapted to the *external* price structure.

Import duties are efficacious in promoting industrialisation so long as there is scope for creating an internal demand for home-produced manufactured goods in substitution for imports. But once the limits of import substitution have been reached, the momentum of further industrial growth is bound to slow down—as indeed the history of many Latin-American countries has shown. Industries which have been brought into existence in the shadow of import restrictions of some kind are not competitive in the world markets precisely because they are dependent on the maintenance of an internal price ratio between industrial and agricultural products which is higher than the prevailing world price ratio. Once the scope for import substitution has been exhausted, their further expansion is limited by the growth of internal purchasing power which is ultimately governed by the growth of production in the complementary (agricultural) sector of the economy.

Unless the size of the internal market is sufficiently large to enable productivity to rise to the point at which costs, at the prevailing level of wages, become sufficiently low to become competitive with world prices—in which case the industries cease to be "infants" and are no longer dependent on protection—the kind of industrialisation which is fostered by import substitution does not make it possible to raise export capacity *pari passu* with the rise in domestic income and in import requirements. It is no accident that the cotton textile industry represents the one example in which a succession of developing countries has succeeded in attaining a strong competitive position in world markets. It is an industry which caters for mass requirements, and in which therefore the size of the domestic market, even in low income countries, is relatively large; it is also an industry where modern techniques and know-how are relatively easily acquired, and where economies of large-scale production cease to be significant beyond a certain stage. In most other cases, the establishment of a domestic industry does not raise the capacity to export because costs expressed in terms of a common currency—local cost being converted to dollar-costs at the prevailing rates of exchange—remain too high.

This is the explanation of the apparent paradox that industrialisation aiming at "import substitution" tends to cause a *rise* in import requirements relative to export capacities and hence to a chronic balance of payments problem. Although *some* imports are replaced by domestic production, the activity which is generated thereby inevitably raises the demand for other imports: partly because the establishment of new industries requires investment with a high import content; partly because there is an import component in any industrial activity connected with the use of non-indigenous materials, fuel, replacement of machinery and components, etc.; but mainly perhaps because industrial activity generates additional incomes—additional wages and profits—

a proportion of which is inevitably spent on imported goods or services.[1]

When import requirements exceed the capacity to export on account of high domestic costs, this is generally taken as evidence of over-valuation of the currency. In a sense it is; but it is essential to understand that it is not the kind of over-valuation that could be "cured" by any uniform adjustment of the exchange rate. This is because the exchange rate which would make it possible for an under-developed country to develop export markets in manu-factured products would mean a considerable under-valuation of its currency in terms of the primary commodities which form the great bulk of its exports; and the rise in export proceeds in the primary sector which follows a devaluation tends to generate an inflation in domestic costs and prices that soon neutralises any initially beneficial effects on the export costs of manufacturers.

The reasons for this are to be found (apart from the rise in the cost of imported goods) in the close link between the local currency equivalent of the main export products on the one hand and the prices of foodstuffs destined for local consumption on the other, which in turn may reflect factors operating on the side of supply or of demand, or of both. So long as primary products provide much the greater part of total exports, and so long as the bulk of such products—the so-called "cash-crops"—is destined for export rather than for home consumption, competition will ensure that the money costs of agricultural products in terms of local currency will follow fairly closely the local currency-equivalent of the prices of cash crops ruling in the world market. In such circum-stances exchange rate devaluation will, in the first instance, raise the earnings of primary producers in terms of domestic currency; it will affect the external price, in terms of dollars, only in so far as the rise in earnings induces an expansion of output, and in so far as such an expansion has an appreciable effect on total supplies in the world market. On the other hand, the rise in earn-ings from export crops will tend to raise the demand for foodstuffs from the producers; it may also tend to reduce their supply, in so

---

[1] "Import-substitution" may be efficacious in reducing the *proportion* of imports to the G.N.P. But since it also raises the G.N.P. (at a faster rate than the growth of exports) it leads to an increase in *total* imports which frequently tends to exceed the growth in export earnings.

far as there is some marginal land which can be switched from food production for local use to the production of export crops. For both these reasons, the rise in the domestic price of export crops is bound, sooner or later, to lead to a corresponding rise in the local price of food. And since, at the levels of income characteristic of under-developed countries, money wages in industry will be closely related to the price of food, a rise in *earnings* from primary exports will tend to bring about a corresponding advance in the level of money *costs* in manufacturing production. (It is, however, important to bear in mind that this interrelationship reflects the scarcity of land, and not the scarcity of labour; the rise in wages is a consequence of the pressure on food supplies, and not of any increase in the demand for labour originating in the agricultural sector.)

Hence, while, in the case of a developed country, there is a single rate of exchange which is capable of securing equilibrium between domestic costs of production and the prices, or the level of costs, in foreign markets, in the case of an under-developed country there is no *single* rate of exchange which is capable of securing this result. If the cost of producing primary commodities is taken as the basis, the appropriate rate of exchange is a much higher one than if the cost of production in manufacturing is taken as the standard. Precisely because their balance of payments problem requires an adjustment in cost-structures (the reduction of manufacturing costs *relative* to the prices of primary products) and not just a change in the general level of costs in terms of international currency, it cannot be achieved by a straightforward devaluation of their currencies.

It is mainly for this reason that the periodic efforts of international authorities such as the I.M.F. to secure an alleviation of the balance of payments problems of particular under-developed countries by the introduction of more "realistic" exchange rates, however well intentioned, have proved so misguided. In most of these cases (e.g. in the cases of Chile and the Argentine in recent years) devaluation has been followed by a new wave of inflation which has swallowed up the stimulus to exports afforded by the devaluation, within a relatively short period.[1] The diagnosis that has led to such recommendations has been based on a false analogy from the situation of industrialised countries whose export prices are cost-determined to that of primary producers whose export costs are price-determined.

But even if the subsequent inflation did not occur, it is doubtful whether devaluation would be a sensible method of raising the export earnings of countries whose exports consist so largely of primary products. No doubt any particular exporter of primary products might snatch an advantage in this manner at the cost of his competitors; but for this very reason, devaluation by any one primary producer puts his competitors under strong pressure to follow suit; if a wave of such devaluations led to any general expansion in the output of primary products the position of each would be worse than before, as a result of the subsequent deterioration in the terms of trade.[2]

There is no way out of this dilemma except by some system of dual exchange rates, or some system of combined taxes and subsidies which produce the same effect as dual exchange rates.

Both for administrative and technical reasons, a system of dual exchange rates is likely to yield as good an approximation to the Pigovian prescription of adjusting relative prices in accordance with marginal social costs as the more orthodox method involving a system of differential taxes and subsidies.

Under the dual system, a fixed rate of exchange—the "official" rate"—would continue to apply to staple exports and to all *essential* imports—i.e. to all such imports which the Government did not wish to restrict for reasons of promoting domestic industries or for other reasons such as the discouragement of unnecessary or luxury consumption. In addition, there would be a free rate (which could preferably be operated as a floating rate, though it would be open to the monetary authorities to influence the rate through varying the classes of transactions admitted to it) at which the exporters of manufactured goods would be free to dispose of their exchange receipts, and at which

[1] In the Argentine the 40 per cent. devaluation of April 1962 was offset by an equivalent rise of domestic prices (of 65 per cent.) by the end of 1963; in Chile the 42 per cent. devaluation of October 1962–January 1963 was offset by an equivalent rise of domestic prices (of 75 per cent.) within a year.

[2] Given the well-known fact that the price elasticity of world demand for primary products is considerably below unity.

the importers of all such goods which did not qualify for a currency allocation at the official rate could obtain a licence to import by purchasing the necessary amount of foreign exchange. The greater the pressure for such imports in relation to manufactured exports, the higher the free rate would tend to be, in relation to the official rate; the higher the free rate, the greater the encouragement to the development of manufactured exports. As the balance of payments pressure eased with the expansion of exports, the premium on the free rate (in relation to the official rate) would gradually diminish, and might disappear altogether when exports had risen sufficiently to balance the demand for imports at the official rate. So long as the Government can ensure that the foreign exchange proceeds from the sale of staple exports are surrendered at the official rate—which will be ensured if the marketing of such exports is in the hands of a publicly owned Marketing Board—the operation of such a system raises no great administrative difficulties. The kind of imports which are entitled to foreign exchange at the official rate can be clearly demarcated; and a system of advance deposits of local currency would ensure that the foreign exchange so allocated would in fact be spent on the goods in question.

If the obligation to purchase foreign exchange at the free rate were to replace alternative forms of import restriction through protective import duties or import quotas, the system would possess two great advantages from the point of view of the efficiency of resource allocation. The first is that it would ensure that the differential tax on imports was matched by an equivalent differential subsidy on exports—the premium of the free rate over the official rate would indeed be nothing else than a uniform *ad valorem* import duty combined with a uniform *ad valorem* export subsidy. In the second place, it would combine the advantages of free trade from the point of view of fostering international specialisation and the division of labour with the advantages of protection for the promotion of local industrialisation. (This second advantage would be obviously all the greater, the more under-developed countries adopted such a system.) For the fact that both the import-duty rates and the subsidy-rates for any one country were *uniform* in *ad valorem* terms, would mean that each country would tend to concentrate its resources on those particular branches of industry for which it had the highest comparative advantage; whilst the fact that these tax-subsidy rates would tend to vary inversely with the stage of economic development—the least developed countries tending to have the highest rates, and vice versa[1]—would mean that relative backwardness would not impose a handicap on the development of industries in any particular area. It would thus combine the advantage of regional economic integration with a balanced distribution of industrial development over the region: as is well known, economic integration through customs unions and free-trade-areas (as between countries at substantially different levels of development) invariably tends to concentrate development in the more advanced areas and to retard development in the more backward regions.[2]

As against this, it may be argued that a system of *uniform* taxes and subsidies may sometimes encourage the development of the "wrong" kind of industries—those which possess the greatest comparative advantage *initially*, but which may not be the most promising *ultimately*—e.g. those which afford the best opportunities for exploiting local natural resources; or those which possess —through linkages with other industries—external economies in

---

[1] Since the less developed a country is, the lower is its capacity to export *manufactures* relative to its import requirements in the same category, the exchange rate at which its imports and exports of manufactures came into balance (which is the rate that would tend to get established, if the supply of foreign currency in the free market came exclusively from the exporters of manufactures, and the importers of manufactures were wholly dependent on that market to obtain licences to import) would obviously be the higher, relative to the official rate, the lower the stage of development. Indeed, for countries in the early stages of industrialisation, it would be necessary to direct part of the foreign exchange earnings from the sale of staple products (or from other sources) to prevent the premium on the free rate from becoming inordinately high. Hence, irrespective of any general shortage of foreign exchange (which depends on the overall balance of payments position) the less developed country could always ensure that the premium on its free rate stood higher than that of a more developed country—at any rate so long as countries refrain from manipulating the premium upwards by *reducing* the supply of foreign currency in the free market, through open market operations. It would be reasonable, however (if this system came to be generally adopted), to fix a ceiling for the premium for each particular country—a ceiling that would take into account the varying circumstances of different countries, in particular the differences in the level of their manufacturing costs in terms of primary products—and to require the monetary authorities of each country to keep the free rate at or below this level, by sales of foreign exchange in the free market.

[2] This has been the experience with experiments in economic integration through customs unions in Africa and the Caribbean (e.g. in the East African Federation, or the Central African or the West Indian Federation) and it is the main obstacle to the establishment of such federations among newly emergent states, many of which are much too small to permit the development of efficient industries catering only for their home market.

the highest degree. The possibility of this certainly exists. However, experience has amply shown that the alternative of promoting industrialisation through differential taxes or prohibitions— giving each particular industry the protection it requires to make domestic production profitable—tends to produce the opposite evil of excessive diversification and fragmentation (with each country attempting to replace imports for as many commodities as possible) the consequences of which are likely to be far more detrimental to economic development.[1] It also tends (as experience has shown) to cause an excessive deterioration of the terms of trade of primary producers, with detrimental consequences on economic development through the discouragement of agricultural production.

A system of dual exchange rates is contrary to the prevailing economic philosophy, as embodied in the Articles of Agreement of the International Monetary Fund, and indeed the pressure of the I.M.F. has been consistently exerted to suppress such practices.[2] This again provides an example of how rules which are reasonable enough as between developed countries are applied in the context of the very different circumstances of underdeveloped countries, where they make no sense.

Failing a solution through a system of dual exchange rates, there are two possible alternative courses of action which would serve the same objectives. One possibility would be a general devaluation of currencies combined with the imposition of such export duties on primary products as would leave the export proceeds of the producers in terms of local currency unchanged. The proceeds of the export duty could then be used to subsidise essential imports so as to prevent the inflationary effects of higher import prices on the cost of living. The alternative would be to leave exchange rates unchanged but to levy a tax on the exports of primary products, the proceeds of which would be

[1] It would probably be too much to expect that the governments of under-developed countries could be induced to abolish such differential duties or prohibitions (as between different industrial products) altogether. But the institution of a free exchange rate, on the lines described, would certainly give a push in this direction; it would also open the way to regional agreements among the under-developed countries themselves which would permit their abolition in inter-regional trade.

[2] Multiple exchange rates existed after the war in a number of countries (mainly in Latin-America) though they were conceived more as an instrument of import control than of export promotion.

used exclusively for the payment of a subsidy on exports of manufactures.[1]

The first alternative has two disadvantages. For one thing, in order to deal with the problem of manufacturing costs effectively, both the general devaluation and the rate of export duties on primary products would have to be fairly high—possibly as much as 50 per cent. or more in some cases. It may be difficult for under-developed countries to impose such high export duties, since these are bound to meet with strong resistance from the primary producers. In addition, there would be a strong temptation for any one primary producing exporter to gain some competitive advantage by not imposing an export duty to the full extent of the devaluation.[2] A second disadvantage is that a large-scale devaluation is bound to upset the internal price structure of imported goods of all kinds. It may be difficult to compensate for this effectively through a policy of subsidies to essential imports.

The alternative policy of export taxes on primary commodities combined with export subsidies on manufactured goods has the advantage that it affords a large stimulus to the development of manufactured exports with relatively little disturbance to domestic or international prices. Thus for the average under-developed country which derives 90 per cent. of its exports from the sale of primary products and only 10 per cent. from the sale of manu-factured goods, a 5 per cent. duty on the exports of primary products would finance a 45 per cent. subsidy on manufactured exports. Irrespective of whether the export duty is passed for-wards or backwards, a 5 per cent. duty is not likely to make a major difference either to the position of domestic producers, taken as a whole, or to the position of the importers of primary commodities.

To be fully effective, however, the introduction of such a

[1] A third possibility of matching import duties on manufactures with equivalent export subsidies comes to the same thing (except for the possibility of differentiation), as a system of dual exchange rates.

[2] Of course it is equally open to under-developed countries to pursue a policy of competitive devaluation to gain such advantages. For political and psychological reasons, however, it is easier for a government to hold down the prices received by local producers by keeping the exchange rate high, than to balance a low exchange rate by imposing high export duties. Moreover, exchange rate devaluation is likely to be politically so unpopular as to restrain a government from employing this weapon deliberately to gain trading advantages, except under great pressure.

policy would require both the co-operation of the importing countries and general agreement on participation among the under-developed countries. The main problem, as regards the policies of importing countries, is that the case for the differential subsidy on manufactured exports of under-developed countries should be universally recognised and that this should not be regarded as a case of "dumping". As was shown earlier, the logical counterpart of the need for under-developed countries to impose protective duties on manufactured *imports*, which is now generally recognised, is that they should also be exempt from the general prohibitions concerning subsidies on *exports*, provided that the extent and manner of administering such subsidies is made subject to clearly defined rules. Such rules could take the form, *inter alia*, of limiting the amount paid in subsidies on manufactured exports to the proceeds of the special levy on exports of primary products. A ceiling percentage might also be fixed. It might further be considered desirable that the special levy on primary commodities should be at a uniform rate not exceeding, say, 5 per cent. of the f.o.b. value of the exports of commodities subject to it.

The effect of these provisions would be that the permissible rate of subsidy on manufactured exports would vary inversely with the proportion of total export proceeds derived from manufactures. Thus while a country which obtains only 10 per cent. of its total exports from the sale of manufactured products would be able to grant a rate of subsidy of 45 per cent., another country which derives one-third of its exports from the sale of manufactures would only be able to grant an export subsidy of 10 per cent.; while a third country whose exports consist as to one-half of manufactures and one-half of primary products would be permitted a rate of export subsidy of only 5 per cent. In other words, the rate of subsidy would decline as a particular country advanced to higher stages of economic development, so that the share of manufactures in its exports increased. The definition of "primary products" and "manufactures" would require careful delineation, as well as the range of countries which should qualify for the privileges of the scheme. In the case of processed materials, the 5 per cent. duty might be imposed on the value of the raw material content of the processed product, and this would be deducted from the subsidy payable on the f.o.b. value of the processed products.

Clearly, a scheme of this kind would not provide quite the same flexibility as a system of dual exchange rates; it would not ensure that the subsidies on manufactures were in appropriate relationship to the protection conferred by import duties or quantitative restrictions; or that the system of protection was rationalised through an equalisation of the rates of import duties on different commodities. And it is doubtful whether the political obstacles —the need to secure the consent of the developed countries to a scheme of export subsidies—are any less formidable than those involved in the operation of a system of dual exchange rates.

OBSTACLES TO EXPORTS—II. POLICIES OF THE IMPORTING COUNTRIES

The other main obstacle to the industrial development of the under-developed countries lies in the unwillingness of the industrially advanced countries to permit the importation of manufactured goods from low wage countries. This is based on a deep-rooted prejudice (which may have had more justification in pre-Keynesian times than in present circumstances) that such imports threaten the employment and the living standards of their own workers in a way in which imports from high wage countries do not. This view received some theoretical support from those economists who, reasoning on the basis of a peculiarly rigid interpretation of the marginal productivity theory, argued that free trade between low-wage and high-wage countries will tend to equalise "factor prices" and will therefore tend to reduce the real wage in the "advanced" country at the same time as it tends to raise the real wage in the "backward" country.[1]

It may be tedious, though not difficult, to prove that this view is based on a fallacy—at any rate in circumstances in which the "advanced" country follows a policy of economic expansion associated with full employment. Assuming that effective demand is maintained at an adequate level to secure the reabsorption of labour released from industries that are adversely affected by such

[1] Cf. W. F. Stolper and P. A. Samuelson, "Protection and Real Wages", *Review of Economic Studies*, vol. IX, November 1941, pp. 58–73, for a guarded exposition of this argument.

imports, the total flow of goods resulting from the *same* quantity of employment will necessarily be greater than before: the labour that is required to produce the exports that pay for such imports must be less than the labour that was previously engaged in producing the goods which are now imported. This means that real wages will be higher as a result, unless the goods which are increased in supply consist exclusively of non-wage goods rather than wage-goods. Since, however, the imports of manufactures from low-wage countries are likely to be consumer goods, whereas the exports paying for such imports are more likely to consist of investment goods, this is not likely to happen. It is more probable that the wage-earner will benefit from any consequential change in relative prices, as well as from any rise in wages associated with the rise in productivity.[1]

In fact, the consequences of cheap imports from low-wage countries are in no way different from the effects of labour-saving innovations. In both cases there is a threat to labour in a situation in which effective demand is static, so that the saving in labour will reduce employment rather than increase total production. And in both cases there may be serious problems of adjustment and adaptation if the changes are too swift or sudden. But, whereas the adjustments connected with the progress of technology have come to be accepted as part of the cost of economic progress that can, and must, be taken in its stride, the entirely analogous adjustments necessitated by enlarged import opportunities are still strongly resisted: despite the fact that, quantitatively, adjustments of the latter type are likely to be far less important than those connected with the former. In

[1] The fallacy in the "factor-price-equalisation" theory which suggests the opposite conclusion is that it assumes that there is, in some sense, a given amount of total capital in the country which is not altered by such a structural change, so that when labour-intensive industries contract, and the capital-intensive industries expand (it is supposed that the contracting industries are labour-intensive, since it is in these industries that the low-wage country will have a comparative advantage), there must be some offsetting change in the capital/labour ratio in *all* industries, otherwise the available amount of capital would not suffice to employ the same number of workers in the new situation as in the old situation. Hence the *marginal* product of labour will fall, even though the *average* product of labour has risen. The simple answer to this is that capital is not like "land", and its quantity cannot be treated as "given", irrespective of the distribution of output between industries. When the output of "capital-intensive" industries expands, the total amount of "capital" necessarily expands with it; the growth of output in industries with a high output per head and a high capital/labour ratio necessarily grows hand in hand with an accelerated rate of accumulation of capital.

what way does the development of a textile industry in Hong Kong differ from the invention of a synthetic fibre? A country like the United States would never dream of putting any obstacle in the way of the exploitation of a new invention, however much it may threaten some old-established industry; yet it is perfectly ready to invoke the escape clauses of the G.A.T.T. to protect its own textile industry from the threat of "market disruption", by means that are wholly inconsistent with its proclaimed economic philosophy.[1]

While quantitative restrictions on imports by the Western European countries were gradually abolished in the 1950's as regards intra-European trade and later also as regards the trade with the dollar area, such liberalisation has not extended to manufactured imports from low-wage countries: indeed, in the last few years, important new restrictions have been introduced. The U.N. Secretariat assembled an impressive amount of evidence in preparation for the Geneva Conference) of the nature and extent of such restrictions.[2] It appears that the two major member countries of the E.E.C., France and Germany, apply quantitative restrictions to most items which are of importance to the under-developed countries with the exception (in some cases) of imports from countries which are overseas associated members of the E.E.C. The United States and the United Kingdom, in contrast, pursued, until recently, a liberal policy with regard to such imports;[3] but when, in the late 1950's, there was a sudden upsurge of textile imports from Hong Kong, India and Pakistan, both countries began to apply quantitative restrictions—either by direct control, or by the indirect method of inducing the exporting countries to introduce restrictions on their own exports. On the initiative of the United States an international cotton textile agreement was concluded in 1961 which was later renewed for a five-year period. The new feature introduced by this agreement is that "market disruption", which could previously only be invoked

---

[1] Cf. U.N. *World Economic Survey, op. cit.,* p. 70.

[2] Cf. U.N. *Survey, op. cit.,* Ch. 3, and also U.N. document *E/Conf. 46/6,* pp. 40–49.

[3] This is best shown by the large differences in the share of under-developed countries in the total imports of manufactures (excluding base metals) of the various developed countries in 1962. Whereas their share amounted to 12·3 per cent. in the case of the United Kingdom and 11·3 per cent. in the United States, it only amounted to 3·8 per cent. in the case of Germany, 3·2 per cent. in the case of France and 1·3 per cent. in the other countries of the E.E.C. (Cf. U.N. document *E/Conf. 46/6,* Table 8, p. 23.)

with the authority of the G.A.T.T., can now be declared unilaterally by the importing countries, without international review.[1]

While these restrictive policies mainly affect textiles and clothing, it must be remembered that these are the only fields in which a number of under-developed countries have already attained a strong competitive position.[2] So long as the present attitudes remain, there is no guarantee that similar restrictions will not be applied in other fields as and when these also attain a competitive position.

It is to be hoped, however, that as a result of the efforts of the G.A.T.T., the Geneva Conference, and the better recognition of the fact that the adjustment problems posed by the industrialisation of under-developed countries are basically no different from those caused by other forms of dynamic change (such as the invention of television which caused "market disruption" to the motion-picture industry, or the invention of the motor-car which caused similar disruption to the railways or the horse-breeding industry) these attitudes will change in the future. In the meantime there is a glaring inconsistency between the professed aim of the developed countries to assist in the development of the poor nations through large-scale economic aid, and their commercial policies which prevent such aid from bearing fruit.[3]

[1] The long-term international cotton agreement of 1962 stipulated that countries maintaining restrictions inconsistent with the G.A.T.T. should progressively relax these restrictions and eliminate them as soon as possible; it also provided that there should be an automatic annual increase in quotas while the restraints are in force. Subsequently a number of importing countries announced annual increases of quotas for the five-year period of the agreement (by 12–19 per cent. a year) but the largest importers, the United States, the United Kingdom and Canada exempted themselves from any obligation to admit increasing imports—on the ground that their current imports are already large! Since "market disruption" can only occur as a result of a rapid *growth* of imports, it could only justify a limitation on the rate of increase in imports, not an absolute ceiling on their size. (Cf. U.N. *E/Conf. 46/6*, pp. 47–49.)

[2] Exports of textile yarn and fabrics from under-developed countries into North America and Western Europe (including E.E.C. and E.F.T.A. countries) increased from $220 to $410 million between 1956 and 1961, or by 85 per cent., whereas such imports from other sources only increased by 45 per cent. over the same period. In the latter year, however, imports from under-developed countries still accounted for only 13·5 per cent. of total imports in these categories. (Cf. U.N. *Survey, op. cit.*, Table 3–14, p. 69 and Table 3–I, p. 76, and document *E/Conf. 46/6*, Table 5, p. 15).

[3] At the Geneva Conference a number of developed countries (including Britain and France), yielding to the combined pressure of seventy-five under-developed nations, announced their readiness to accord preferences in the matter of import duties to under-developed countries. It would have been more important if they had announced their readiness to abolish quota restrictions on such imports. (The United Kingdom, did, in fact, announce its willingness to do so, but only as part of a general agreement by which other developed countries do so as well.)

LONG-TERM TRADE AND BALANCE OF PAYMENTS PROJECTIONS OF THE UNDER-DEVELOPED COUNTRIES— AN ARITHMETICAL EXERCISE

The projections shown in the attached table can in no sense be considered as *forecasts*. Their purpose is to show the long-term implications of current trends, and the requirements in terms of trade and aid if a growth rate of 5 per cent. is to be achieved in the national product of the developing countries throughout the rest of this century, on the assumption of constant rates of change in the relevant variables.

The bases on which the various assumptions have been chosen were as follows:

(1) The assumption that a 5 per cent. growth rate requires a 6 per cent. rate of growth of imports is based on detailed studies of income elasticities by the Secretariat of the United Nations.[1]

(2) The assumption that the volume of exports of primary products to the developed countries expands at 3 per cent. a year is based on an assumed growth rate of 4 per cent. a year of the developed economies (which is the target fixed by the O.E.C.D.) and an income elasticity of demand for primary products from under-developed countries of 0·75. The calculations assume constant export prices.

(3) The rate of growth of exports of primary products to the centrally planned economies of 9 per cent. a year has been chosen as the most plausible assumption in the light of recent trends and of the submission of the U.S.S.R. delegation to the Geneva Conference.[2] The latter suggested that "in the opinion of Soviet economists" the *total* external trade of U.S.S.R. might increase fourfold by 1980; and that their trade with the under-developed countries "by utilisation of the existing favourable possibilities"

---

[1] Cf. *Trade Needs of Developing Countries for their Accelerated Economic Growth.* U.N. mimeographed document *E/Conf. 46/58*, Technical Appendix.

[2] *Prospects for the Development of USSR Foreign Trade*, submission of the U.S.S.R., mimeographed document *E/Conf. 46/108*.

will increase eightfold as compared with 1963 (9 per cent. a year is equivalent to a sixfold increase in twenty years).

(4) The rate of growth of 10 per cent. in the manufactured exports to the outside world has been chosen as the highest plausible growth rate that may be sustained over a long period, assuming that the policies of both the exporting and of the importing countries are adapted so as to remove existing obstacles to such exports.[1]

(5) The net adverse balance on services account (other than investment income) is assumed to increase at the same rate as imports.

(6) The net balance of investment income is assumed to increase by 3 per cent. of the cumulative financial aid received from the outside world. This assumes that the developed countries will be prepared to make a fair proportion of aid available in the form of outright grants, or else that they will be prepared to advance loans on specially favourable terms. (At present, in the case of India, for example, the average rate of interest on aid received in all forms works out at 4 per cent.)[2]

(7) The assumption that the volume of world trade in manufactures will grow at 6 per cent. a year assumes that measures of trade liberalisation will continue as between the developed countries, as well as between the developed and the under-developed countries, and that the income elasticity of demand for manufactures, of both developed and under-developed countries, will continue to exceed unity. (The rate of growth of this trade in the past decade was over 7 per cent. a year.)

---

[1] The assumption of an 8 per cent. growth rate in manufactured exports would, *ceteris paribus*, increase the cumulative deficit up to the year 2000 by $925 millions.

[2] The assumption of an average rate of interest of 4 per cent. would add $315 millions to the cumulative deficit up to the year 2000.

PROJECTIONS OF THE TRADE, BALANCE OF PAYMENTS, ETC., OF THE DEVELOPING COUNTRIES WITH THE OUTSIDE WORLD

1960–2000

	Assumed Exponential growth rate per cent.		1960 (Actual) ($ billion)	1970	1980	1990	2000
	Per year	Per decade		($ billion, 1960 prices)			
Imports from the Outside World (f.o.b.)	6.·0	82·2	22·4	40·8	74·4	135·5	246·9
Exports of Primary Products (f.o.b.) ..			17·1	23·1	31·2	42·1	56·8
to Developed Countries	3·0	35·0	17·1	23·1	31·2	42·1	56·8
to Centrally Planned Economies ..	9·0	146·0	1·2	3·0	7·3	17·9	43·9
Exports of Manufactures to the Outside World (f.o.b.)	10·0	171·8	2·6	7·1	19·2	52·2	141·8
Visible Balance			−1·5	−7·6	−16·7	−23·3	−4·4
Transport, Travel and Other Services (net)	6·0	82·2	−1·0	−1·8	−3·3	−6·0	−11·0
Investment Income (net)[1]	*	*	−2·7	−5·8	−13·2	−26·6	−43·9
Invisible Balance			−3·7	−7·6	−16·5	−32·6	−54·9
Balance on Current Account			−5·2	−15·2	−33·2	−55·9	−59·3
Cumulative Balance in Decade			—	−102	−242	−446	−576
Cumulative Balance from 1960			—	−102	−344	−790	−1,366
Cumulative Balance from 1960, assuming interest free aid..			—	−87	−261	−534	−785
G.N.P. of Developed Countries	4·0	49·2	920	1,373	2,048	3,056	4,559
G.N.P. of Developing Countries ..	5·0	64·9	170	280	462	762	1,257
World Exports of Manufactures[2] ..	6·0	82·2	61·2	111·5	203·2	370·2	674·4
Exports of Developing Countries[3] ..	10·0	171·8	3·8	10·3	28·1	76·3	207·4
Exports of Developing Countries as percentage of World Exports of Manufactures			*Percentages*				
			6·2	9·2	13·8	20·6	30·8
AID TO DEVELOPING COUNTRIES AS PER CENT. G.N.P. OF DEVELOPED COUNTRIES							
I. Assuming average interest of 3 per cent. on loans and grants ..							
per decade			0·6	0·9	1·4	1·7	1·5
cumulative			—	0·9	1·2	1·5	1·5
II. Assuming Interest free loans and grants							
per decade			—	0·8	1·0	1·0	0·7
cumulative			—	0·8	0·9	1·0	0·8

[1] Assumed to increase by 3 per cent. of the cumulative adverse balance on current account.
[2] Excluding the centrally planned economies.
[3] Including exports to other developing countries.

PART V

COUNTRY STUDIES

20

THE GERMAN WAR ECONOMY[1]

THE waging of "total war"—the utmost concentration of resources and effort on the single objective of military victory—has always been regarded as a peculiarly German doctrine, ever since the days of Clausewitz. The proclaimed political philosophy of the Nazis was the total subordination of individual interest to the interests of the State; and State interest was conceived in terms of aggrandisement of power to be achieved by war. The "totalitarian" system of Nazi Germany was thus generally regarded—by its supporters, as well as its opponents—as one whose main purpose and *raison d'être* was the translation of Clausewitz's ideas into practice. Little wonder that the world outside Germany—the military and economic expert, as well as the man in the street—assumed, almost as a matter of course, that in the prosecution of the war the German economic system "was strained to its utmost"—that in pursuing their main objective, the Germans went as far as it was humanly possible to go. Utter ruthlessness, combined with superb organising ability—the two main characteristics with which the world credited the Germans—could lead to no other conclusion.

The collapse of Nazi Germany and its occupation by the Allies (and also the lavish scale on which Allied authorities provided for their intelligence agencies) has made possible a post-mortem analysis of the Nazi system and war effort which—regarded purely as a historical research project—is unprecedented in scope and magnitude. There can surely not have been any previous occasion in history where the defeat of the enemy in the field has been followed by such a detailed analysis of the causes of his defeat on the part of the victors—a dissection of its military strategy and

[1] Most of the information presented in this paper was acquired by the author in the course of his work for the U.S. Strategic Bombing Survey in Germany in the summer of 1945. The results of this investigation, in which a number of economists and statisticians co-operated, have been published in the United States under the title *The Effects of Strategic Bombing on the German War Economy*. The present paper was read before the Manchester Statistical Society on 22 May 1946 and published in the *Review of Economic Studies*, 1945-6, Vol. XIII (1).

tactics, of its political and social institutions, its administrative and technical practices, the technical, administrative and economic aspects of its industrial organisation. This monster "research project" is still under way and it will take years before its results are properly digested and summarised. Some preliminary results have, however, already been published and it is possible to give an account of the main features of the German war economy, as revealed by post-hostilities investigations.

The most important conclusion which emerges from these inquiries is that the picture of the German war effort which dominated Allied imagination was very largely a false one. Germany did not fight a "total war"; despite all the propaganda talk, she made no serious attempt to exploit her own war potential fully, except perhaps for a brief period in August and September 1944, when it was too late to be of any consequence. Whatever the ruthlessness she may have shown towards vanquished enemies, there is no evidence of ruthless sacrifices having been imposed upon her own people for the sake of victory; in terms of the thoroughness of the war effort, Germany lagged well behind not only Britain or Russia in the present war, but also behind her own showing in the First World War. Whatever else may be said about the German war economy it certainly was not "totalitarian."

Nor was the German war organisation particularly efficient as measured by modern standards. Although everything was "controlled" (on paper) right from the beginning of the war, the actual administration of controls was often clumsy and amateurish in the extreme. It suffered greatly from a multiplication of controlling agencies, with no proper division of spheres of influence between them; from the Nazi predilection for taking away all real power from the regular Civil Service hierarchy in favour of hurriedly erected *ad hoc* Commissariats, superimposed on the pre-existing administrative structure without any proper forethought or planning; from constant quarrels and boundary disputes between State and Party functionaries; and finally, from the Führer-principle which meant that no one below the Führer had overall co-ordinating powers or was safe from being unexpectedly over-ruled or deprived of genuine responsibility. Although certain segments of the economy—notably the industries under the control of the Speer Ministry and agriculture under the extremely able State Secretary Backe—showed highly impressive results, the problem of securing proper co-ordination of controls (a prerequisite for a total war effort), remained unresolved to the end.

Whether a really efficient and totalitarian German war effort would have fundamentally altered the course of history is not a question that can be fruitfully debated. As it happened, the reluctance or inability of Germany to engage her resources to the utmost brought her undoubted (and largely unexpected) compensations, and not only disadvantages. It was largely due to the limitations in her war effort, that the German economy proved so elastic and resilient and showed such high adaptability to unforeseen changes in requirements caused by changes in strategy and in military fortunes. The high degree of administrative and industrial inefficiency with which the German economy was initially conducted constituted a vast reserve on which to draw (a reserve that was never properly exhausted) which time and again enabled the German leaders to parry the enormous unforeseen blows to which they were subjected. It acted as a kind of shock absorber both as regards the Allied air attack and the military defeats in Russia.

I propose to devote the main part of this paper to an examination of this thesis—that Germany did *not* fight a total war—by comparing her record with that of Britain and other Allied countries. In the concluding part I shall attempt to sketch a historical explanation of the course of events.

The Meaning of "War Potential"

The question which we have to examine is not simply whether Germany's war production was large or small but how it was related to her "war potential"—meaning by the latter, the maximum war production which the country's available resources permit, once these resources have been fully adapted to the purpose of carrying on the war. On this view, the war potential of any country must be determined by at least one of the following four factors: the capital equipment of its industry, its available manpower, its supply of raw materials, and finally, the ability and skill of its industrial organisers, engineers and technicians. Some of these, however, are limited only from a short-term view-point. Assuming that there is time enough to build up the capital equipment of its industries, in all stages, to the require-ments of war, the ultimate limits to a country's war potential are set simply by the quantity and skill of its manpower, and by the richness of ores and minerals of the areas under its control or with which it is capable of trading. These two are the ultimate bottlenecks which must become operative if and when all other temporary bottlenecks have been overcome.

The experience of Britain and the United States fully bears out these generalisations. In both countries, the war effort in the early stages was limited by an extreme shortage of the requisite kind of capital equipment—particularly machine tools. In both countries there was a second stage (albeit a brief one), when expansion was held up for lack of the requisite kinds of raw materials such as steel, aluminium or rubber. And in both countries there was a third stage, when the level of war produc-tion was set neither by machine shortage nor by raw material shortage but simply by manpower. This third limit, let us be clear, though it is an ultimate bottleneck, is not a rigid one. It is relative to the extent of the sacrifices and privations which the community is willing to impose upon itself. Given the total population, the manpower devoted to war purposes can be expanded by making people work longer and harder, by calling upon women, the young and the old, and by reducing the supply of goods for civilian needs. On this test, Russia had a more total war effort than Britain, and Britain than America. But it is just this element—the extent to which the total potential labour power is concentrated on the war—which (in the absence of other, more rigid limitations) measures the seriousness of the war effort.

Which of these three main bottlenecks limited the German war effort? I shall examine the position with respect to each, only to conclude that this search after bottlenecks, in the case of Nazi Germany, is rather a futile endeavour: the German war effort was not really limited by bottlenecks, simply because German war production—except perhaps for a brief period in the summer of

1944—never reached the heights where more formidable bottle-necks would have been encountered.

Equipment

Let us begin with the question of capital equipment—generally regarded as the earliest stumbling block in the path of armament expansion. Contrary to the experience of Britain and America, the German war economy does not appear to have suffered at all from shortage of machine tools, general machinery or plant facilities—except temporarily in one or two isolated cases. On the contrary, according to all evidence, the machine tools and machinery stock were considerably in excess of actual needs, and remained so throughout the war. This is shown by the fact that almost the whole German industry worked on a single shift basis throughout the war; it left the great capacity reserve obtainable through double or triple shift working almost entirely unutilised.[1]

It is even better shown, however, by the fact that in contrast to British and U.S. experience where the machine tool industry was very much expanded and strained to the utmost to meet requirements, German machine tool production had hardly expanded after 1939; the machine tool industry itself was never subjected to close control, and remained, on the whole, under-utilised throughout the war, 30 per cent. of its capacity having been converted to direct munitions production. (The annual delivery of machine tools in 1938–44 is shown in Table 1.)

The explanation for this is to be found in the fact that both the stock of machine tools, with which Germany started the war, and her annual production of machine tools, were rela-tively large; while most of her machine tools (at the beginning, at any rate) were of the universal (multipurpose) type which could easily be converted to purposes of war production. The German machine tool census of May 1938, revealed the existence of 1,327,000 machine tools in German industry and this stock is estimated to have grown to well over 2 millions by 1943.[2] This

---

[1] According to Saur, the head of the Technisches Amt of the Speer Ministry, 90 per cent. of all industrial workers were on the first shift, 7 per cent. on the second shift and 3 per cent. on the third shift.

[2] *The Effects of Strategic Bombing on the German War Economy*, *op. cit.*, Appendix Table 36.

contrasts with an inventory of 740,000 machine tools for Britain in 1943 and 1,529,000 machine tools in the United States in the same year.[1] In Germany throughout the war, there were around 2·4 workers per machine tool in the machine tool using industries. No similar estimate has been published for Britain; but on the basis of total employment in the metal-working industries, the

Table 1

ANNUAL DELIVERIES OF MACHINE TOOLS IN GERMANY, 1938–44
(in numbers)

Type of Machine Tool	1938	1939	1940	1941	1942	1943	1944
Planes and slotters	5,179	6,582	6,636	5,522	4,402	4,214	2,742
Engine lathes ..	29,880	31,009	34,882	35,405	31,330	24,866	19,822
Turret lathes and automatics ..	9,401	10,761	12,313	12,673	11,680	9,996	6,388
Drill presses and horizontal boring mills	31,210	35,941	36,871	38,193	29,056	27,291	22,781
Milling machines	13,308	13,692	16,760	15,636	14,043	10,942	7,883
Saws and filing machines ..	7,211	7,173	7,898	7,459	5,783	4,185	3,247
Grinding and polishing machines ..	28,870	30,987	29,523	30,948	26,681	23,333	17,011
Gear cutting machines	2,127	2,106	2,490	2,435	2,639	2,297	1,921
Hammers, forging and riveting machines	6,333	6,527	5,044	4,125	2,565	2,234	1,588
Sheet metal machines except presses	33,422	38,209	29,516	30,955	23,688	20,681	11,515
Presses, mechanical and hydraulic ..	8,276	9,006	9,835	7,392	8,099	5,759	9,606
Wire bolt and nut machines ..	7,587	7,342	7,647	7,164	5,933	4,168	3,931
Machines for combined processes[2] ..	—	—	—	—	—	—	600
Heavy special machine tools[2] ..	45	26	75	53	70	118	—
Ammunition machines[2]	—	—	—	—	—	—	1,342
Total machine tools	182,849	199,361	199,490	197,960	165,969	140,084	110,377

Source.—Statistical data prepared by the Wirtschaftsgruppe Maschinenbau for the Equipment Division of the U.S. Strategic Bombing Survey, at Saalfeld, Germany, July 1945.

[1] The scope of the U.S. census is narrower than that of the German; making appropriate adjustments, the U.S. inventory compares with a stock of 1,555,000 machine tools for Germany in 1943 (*ibid.*, Table 37).

[2] These are special purpose types, but do not include all special purpose machine tools. A complete statistical separation of universal and special purpose machine tools was not possible, many of the latter being included in other categories.

corresponding ratio for Britain might well have been twice as high.

Looking at the annual production of machine tools (as shown in Table 1), we find that the maximum German output of around 200,000 metal working machine tools in 1940 was over twice as high as the maximum British output of around 96,000 reached in 1942.[1] Machine tool bottlenecks, if any, must have occurred in Germany in periods preceding the war. The machine tool industry underwent a remarkable expansion after 1934; the value of its 1938 output was two and a half times that of 1929.

With certain exceptions, the most important of which occurred in the synthetic oil and chemical industries, in the electric power system, and in the making of high grade (electric) steel, Germany's war production was at no time limited by her machinery equipment. She also had ample capacity in plant facilities. Though statistics on available factory floor space are lacking, it appears that new factory construction (apart from the industries mentioned and underground factory construction as a result of the air war) was moderate during the war, while the large industrial dispersal programmes occasioned by the air offensive were carried out without being handicapped by shortages of factory space.

Mobilisation of Manpower

It is when we come to an analysis of the German manpower figures that the limited character of her war effort is most clearly revealed. Germany, as is well known, had a remarkable economic expansion in the five years prior to the war. By 1938, her unemployment had been reduced to negligible proportions. To this extent she entered the war with fewer "man-power reserves" than Britain or America. But unlike Britain and America, she appears to have made no attempt to increase her manpower supply through an expansion of her gainfully occupied population. As Mr. Saunders has shown,[2] Britain at the peak of mobilisation in 1943 increased her gainfully occupied population, of all ages, by some 2½ millions or 12·5 per cent. of the 1939 figure, despite the stationary total population.[3] Indeed, if war losses (in

---

[1] Cf. *Statistical Digest*, C.S.O., January 1946, Table 49.

[2] "Man-Power Distribution, 1939–45: Some International Comparisons," *Transactions of the Manchester Statistical Society*, 1946.

[3] This figure allows for the decrease in domestic servants and counts each part-time worker separately.

killed, prisoners and missing) are added to the working population actively engaged (as they should be) the figure becomes
more like 2·8 millions, or 14 per cent. Similarly, the United
States increased her gainfully occupied population (including
war losses) by some 7½ millions or just under 15 per cent. in addition to the natural increase in her working population by some

Table 2

MOBILISATION OF MANPOWER IN GERMANY, 1939–44

(Pre-war Reich, including Austria, Sudetenland, Memel)

(*In millions*)

Date	Civilian Labour Force				Armed Forces			Total Germans Mobilised (3)+(5) (8)	Total Civilian Labour Force (3)+(4) (9)	Total Active Labour Force (7)+(9) (10)
	Germans			Foreigners and Prisoners of War (4)	Total Mobilised (5)	Cumulative Losses (6)	Active Strength (5)−(6) (7)			
	Men (1)	Women (2)	Total (3)							
31 May 1939	24·5	14·6	39·1	·3	1·4	—	1·4	40·5	39·4	40·8
31 May 1940	20·4	14·4	34·8	1·2	5·7	·1	5·6	40·5	36·0	41·6
31 May 1941	19·0	14·1	33·1	3·0	7·4	·2	7·2	40·5	36·1	43·3
31 May 1942	16·9	14·4	31·3	4·2	9·4	·8	8·6	40·7	35·5	44·1
31 May 1943	15·5	14·8	30·3	6·3	11·2	1·7	9·5	41·5	36·6	46·1
31 May 1944	14·2	14·8	29·0	7·1	12·4	3·3	9·1	41·4	36·1	45·2
30 Sept. 1944	13·5	14·9	28·4	7·5	13·0	3·9	9·1	41·4	35·9	45·0

Source.—Kriegswirtschaftliche Kraeftebilanz (latest edition), *Statistisches Reichsamt*
Abt. VI; O.K.W., Zusammenstellung Ueber die personelle und materielle Ruestungs-
lage der Wehrmacht; Heerespersonalamt.
Column (5) is the cumulative figure of the total numbers called up to the Armed
Forces, without any deduction for discharges, losses, etc. It does not include those
called up from outside the area of the pre-war Reich, e.g. Alsace-Lorraine, Poland
or the Protectorate.
Column (7) is the cumulative figure of losses due to deaths, personnel taken prisoners-
of-war and missing, discharges and net desertions as reported by German official
sources.
Column (2) includes "helping family members" (mainly in agriculture) who
numbered 5·5 millions in 1939, and who would not be counted as employed in
British or U.S. statistics. Thus the number of women employed on a definition comparable to British statistics, was only 9·1 millions.

3¼ millions over the war period and the absorption of some
7 millions unemployed.

The German overall manpower figures are shown in Table 2.
These reveal that the total gainfully occupied native population
of the pre-war area of Germany, not deducting war losses other
than air raid casualties, had only increased by 1 million between
1939 and the peak figure of 1943 (of which 800,000 were men and
only 200,000 women), the whole of which can be accounted for

by the natural increase in the total population of working age over the period. In terms of the percentages of occupied population aged 14 and over to the total there was *no* change. There was an expansion in the total of gainfully occupied (not deducting war losses) by 7 millions, or some 17 per cent., but 6 out of these 7 millions were provided by the importation of foreign labour and prisoners-of-war, while the remaining 1 million were the result of natural increase.

The conclusion at once suggests itself that the failure of Germany to expand her gainfully occupied population during the war must simply be due to her having already mobilised these "hidden reserves" of labour power in 1939. Indeed, the figure of 40·8 gainfully occupied, out of a total population (recorded at the 1939 census) of 79·4 millions, is extremely high; a much higher proportion than that of Britain or the United States at the same time. The difference, however, is only apparent; it is entirely due to a peculiarity of German statistical methods—the extremely generous way in which "unpaid family helpers" in agriculture are accepted into the ranks of the gainfully occupied. As the 1939 census shows,[1] out of a total agricultural population of

[1] *Statistisches Jahrbuch*, 1940–1, Sect. I, Tables 10 and 20. The distribution of the occupied population as shown by the census of population of 17 May 1939, was as follows:

GAINFULLY OCCUPIED POPULATION OF GERMANY (PRE-WAR AREA)
(*In millions*)

	Wage Earners	Officials and Salaried Employees	Ind. Proprietors	Family Helpers	Total
Agriculture	2·5	·1	2·4	5·8	10·8
Industry and Handwork ..	12·7	1·9	1·6	·3	16·5
Trade and Commerce ..	2·3	2·6	1·3	·6	6·8
Public and Private Service (excluding household) ..	1·0	2·7	·3	·05	4·05
Domestics	1·5	—	—	—	1·5
Total—Civilians	20·0	7·3	5·6	6·75	39·7
Armed Forces ..					1·3
Grand Total					41·0

The small difference between 40·8 millions shown in Table 2 and the 41·0 millions shown in the census indicates the scope of coverage of the Kräftebilanz statistics. The difference between 40·8 shown in Table 2 and 40·56 millions shown in Table 5 is due to the fact that the figures in Table 5 were taken from the 1943 edition of the Kräftebilanz, and were later somewhat revised.

14·9 millions no less than 10·9 millions, or 73 per cent.—i.e. rather more than the *whole* population aged 14 and over—is returned as occupied; and of these 10·9 millions no less than 5·8 millions represent unpaid family helpers. Moreover, the proportion of occupied to total agricultural population is equal in the case of men and women.

If both the agricultural population, and agricultural employment, are excluded from the figures, the percentage of gainfully occupied of the population aged 14 and over in 1939 was no higher than that in Britain in the same year. In both countries it amounted to 85 per cent. of the male population and 35 per cent. of the female population. (The latter figure includes domestic servants.) The degree of labour mobilisation in 1939 was therefore no greater in Germany than in Britain.

In Germany, however, contrary to Britain, America and most other belligerents, the number of native women occupied actually *fell* in the first two years of the war (by about half a million); and the subsequent increase has barely lifted it above the prewar level. If adjustment is made for the natural increase in population, the pre-war ratio of occupied women was never reached. A frequently adduced reason for this strange phenomenon is that the introduction of generous allowances to servicemen's wives induced many of the lower paid women to withdraw from employment. (Table 3, giving the distribution of employment of German women, shows that the fall was proportionately greatest in

Table 3

THE EMPLOYMENT OF GERMAN WOMEN BY INDUSTRY DIVISION
(PRE-WAR AREA)
(*In thousands*)

Date	Agriculture	Industry, Handwork and Power	Trade, Banking, Insurance and Transport	Administration and Services	Domestic Service	All Divisions
May 1939 ..	6,049	3,836	2,227	954	1,560	14,626
May 1940 ..	5,689	3,650	2,183	1,157	1,511	14,386
May 1941 ..	5,369	3,677	2,167	1,284	1,473	14,167
May 1942 ..	5,673	3,537	2,225	1,471	1,410	14,437
May 1943 ..	5,665	3,740	2,320	1,719	1,362	14,806
May 1944 ..	5,694	3,592	2,219	1,746	1,301	14,808
September 1944	5,756	3,636	2,193	1,748	1,287	14,897

Source.—Kriegswirtschaftliche Kräftebilanz, latest edition, *Statistisches Reichsamt,* Abt. VI.

agriculture, industry and handwork; while there was an increase in the higher paid occupations, services and administration.) Far-reaching measures for the conscription of women existed on paper, but they were never carried out. In January 1943, all women between the ages of 17 and 45 were registered but not more than a few hundred thousand called up.[1] A serious attempt at calling up women was only made in connection with Goebbels' much advertised total manpower drive in the summer of 1944; but owing apparently to the administrative breakdown it added only 100,000 women to the total employed.

When we turn to the length of the working week, there is again no evidence of the working population having been made to work very long hours. The "sixty-hour week" was introduced by decree only at the end of July 1944, and it is doubtful whether it was carried into effect on a serious scale. Prior to that, the sixty-hour week was worked only in the iron and steel industry; in the rest of industry, men worked 50–52 hours, women 40–44. The actual increase in hours between 1939 and March 1944 was only 4 per cent. for wage earners as a whole. At the latter date actual hours worked were affected by air raids. But as Table 4 shows, even at the time hours were longest (in the month of September 1941) they were below the average reached in Britain.[2]

There is, finally, the question of the redistribution of the labour force as a result of the war. Table 5 shows the distribution of the total labour force, in Britain and in Germany in 1939 and 1943, in terms of the British White Paper's employment categories,[3] while Table 5a shows the grouping of the civilian labour force at the two dates in terms of percentages. (Owing to the difference

[1] The question of the mobilisation of women was a subject of acute controversy among the German leaders. The Nazis (chiefly Sauckel, the Plenipotentiary for Labour Mobilisation), were against the conscription of women, in accord with their "woman's place is in the home" philosophy and insisted that all labour requirements should be satisfied out of the reserves of occupied Europe. But large-scale deportations led to the large-scale creation of guerillas and *maquis*; in the closing year of the war it proved impossible to raise the number of foreign conscripts at work.

[2] Cf. *Statistical Digest, op. cit.*, Table 107.

[3] Every effort was made to adjust German statistics so as to make them comparable with British. Owing to differences in the definition of individual categories, this may not have been completely successful in each individual case; the comparisons between broad divisions, however (such as "Group I industries"), should be fairly reliable. The scope of activities included under "Government service" is narrower in the case of Germany than Britain; the production of leather and leather goods is included under "Textiles, etc." in the German statistics, but not in the British; and there may be a few other differences of this kind.

in the definition of agricultural employment, mentioned above, agriculture was excluded from the latter Table.)

Table 4

AVERAGE WEEKLY HOURS WORKED BY WAGE EARNERS IN GERMANY

Date	All Industries	Production Goods	Consumption Goods
1929	46·0	46·3	45·7
1933	42·9	43·0	42·3
1938	46·5	47·8	44·9
September 1939 ..	47·8	48·8	43·5
March 1940 ..	47·6	48·5	43·8
September 1940 ..	49·2	49·9	45·9
March 1941 ..	49·1	49·9	45·8
September 1941 ..	49·5	50·3	45·9
March 1942 ..	48·7	49·6	45·0
September 1942 ..	48·7	49·5	44·8
March 1943 ..	49·1	49·9	45·3
September 1943 ..	47·9	48·9	43·1
March 1944 ..	48·3	49·2	43·3

Source.—Statistisches Jahrbuch, 1938–40; Ergebnisse der amtlichen Lohnerhebungen, 1944, *Statistisches Reichsamt,* Abt. Sozialstatistik.

It will be noted that the expansion in the total labour force,[1] the percentage change in the civilian labour force, and the proportion of the total occupied population in the Armed Forces in 1943 were all about the same in the two countries. But while in Britain, Group I industries expanded their employment by 68 per cent., in Germany they increased by only 19 per cent. On the other hand the contraction of Group III (civilian) industries was appreciably less in Germany than in Britain, while the expansion of Government employees was greater. The clearest test of a lack of "total mobilisation" in Germany may be found in the case of domestic servants. These show a very modest reduction in Germany; while their number in Britain was estimated to have fallen by two-thirds. As Table 5a shows, the absolute proportion of the civilian labour force in the war industries (Group I) was less than in Britain (27 against 32 per cent.) while that in Government service was considerably greater

[1] The German figures include, of course, foreigners and prisoners-of-war. The latter, therefore, secured for Germany the same expansion as the greater mobilisation of internal manpower and the elimination of unemployment secured for Britain.

Table 5
MOBILISATION OF MANPOWER IN GREAT BRITAIN AND GERMANY, 1939–43
(in thousands)

	Great Britain			Germany		
	June 1939	June 1943	Index (1939 =100)	31st May 1939	31st May 1943	Index (1939 =100)
Group I— Metal, Chemical and Allied Industries[1]	3,106	5,233	168·4	5,778	6,863	118·8
Group II— ..	5,530	5,632	101·8	18,419	19,227	104·4
Agriculture[2] ..	1,113	1,118	100·4	11,224	11,301	100·7
Mining ..	873	818	93·7	766	903	117·9
Government Services[3]	1,385	1,786	129·0	2,894	3,879	134·0
Gas, Water, Electricity	232	200	86·2	231	206	89·2
Transport[4] ..	1,273	1,191	93·6	1,624	1,799	110·8
Food, Drink, Tobacco	654	519	79·4	1,680	1,139	67·8
Group III— ..	10,477	6,779	64·7	14,969	10,757	71·8
Building, Civil Engineering ..	1,310	726	55·4	2,534	1,256	49·6
Textiles, Clothing, Boots and Shoes	1,759	1,154	65·6	2,769	2,411	76·2
Other Manufactures[5]	1,444	968	67·0	2,475	1,833	74·1
Distributive Trades	2,887	2,009	69·6	3,428	2,156	62·9
Other Services[6] ..	1,882	1,422	75·6	2,181	1,959	89·8
Domestic Service	1,200	400	33·3	1,582	1,442	91·2
Armed Forces ..	557	5,068	909·8	1,400	9,500	731·5
Grand Total ..	19,670	22,712	115·0	40,566	46,347	114·2
Total excluding Armed Forces and Agriculture ..	18,000	16,426	91·3	27,942	25,546	91·4

Source.—Great Britain—Statistics relating to the War Effort of the United Kingdom, Cmd. 6564. November 1944 for all categories except domestic service, which is an unofficial estimate.

Germany—Kräftebilanz, 1943 ed.: Handwork employment from Betriebszählung, 1939, and a report of the Planungsamt, Speer Ministry, 1944.

[1] Iron and steel and their products, non-ferrous metals and their products, machinery, transportation, equipment (aircraft, tanks, ships and vehicles), electrical products, instruments, optical goods, chemicals and petroleum products. German data cover industry groups 12–15, 20–27, 31–33 and 51, together with related fields of handwork production.

[2] German agricultural employment includes "helping family members" who numbered 5·8 millions in 1939.

[3] Government services include post office employees. German Government services *exclude* the following divisions of the Kräftebilanz: Reichskulturkammer, Gesundheitswesen, N.S.R.B. and Reichsbund für Leibesübungen.

[4] Excluding post office employees.

[5] Lumber and lumber products, paper and allied products, stone, clay and glass products and miscellaneous manufacturing. The British figures include leather and leather products other than boots and shoes. German data cover industry groups 41, 43–46, 52–54 and related handwork fields.

[6] For Britain see Appendix A, footnote 3, Cmd. 6564. German figures include divisions 10–12 and 16–18 of the Kräftebilanz.

(15 against 11 per cent.). The proportion of labour force in the distributive trades, on the other hand, was even in 1943 considerably greater in Britain than in Germany (12 against 8 per cent.).

Table 5a

PERCENTAGE DISTRIBUTION OF THE CIVILIAN LABOUR FORCE EXCLUDING AGRICULTURE. GREAT BRITAIN AND GERMANY
(1939 and 1943)

	Great Britain			Germany		
	1939	1943	Index (1939 =100)	1939	1943	Index (1939 =100)
Group I—Metal, Chemical Allied Industries	17·3	31·7	183·2	20·7	26·9	130·0
Group II	24·5	27·3	111·4	25·7	31·0	120·6
Mining	4·8	5·0	104·2	2·7	3·5	129·6
Government Services	7·7	10·8	140·2	10·4	15·2	146·2
Gas, Water, Electricity	1·3	1·2	92·3	·8	·8	100·0
Transport	7·1	7·2	101·4	5·8	7·0	120·7
Food, Drink, Tobacco	3·6	3·1	86·1	6·0	4·5	75·0
Group III	58·2	41·0	70·3	53·6	42·1	78·5
Building, Civil Engineering	7·3	4·4	60·3	9·1	4·9	53·8
Textiles, Clothing, Boots, Shoes	9·8	7·0	72·2	9·9	8·3	83·8
Other Manufactures	8·0	5·9	73·8	8·9	7·1	80·9
Distributive Trades	16·0	12·2	76·3	12·3	8·4	68·3
Other Services	10·5	8·6	81·4	7·8	7·7	98·7
Domestic Service	6·7	2·5	37·3	5·7	5·6	98·2
Total	100	100		100	100	

It is clear from these comparisons that, in the middle of 1943 at any rate, Germany's manpower was not nearly so thoroughly mobilised for war purposes as Britain's. There is no evidence, however, that her war production programme was seriously hampered by manpower shortage in that period. (Her war production was considerably higher in the following year, after the Wehrmacht had called up a further 1·8 million German men who could be only partially replaced by a further intake of foreign labour.) The explanation, as will be argued later on, is rather to be sought in the fact that the expansion of armament production, like the expansion of the Armed Forces, could only proceed with a certain momentum; and having decided on a limited war effort in the early years of the war, Germany could no more make full use of her manpower for war purposes in 1943 than Britain could in 1940.

The Supply of Raw Materials

Germany's extreme dependence on imports for all kinds of raw materials was always regarded as her fatal weakness in case of a prolonged war. Even in the case of the two chief war materials which were produced inside her territory—steel and aluminium —she was dependent on imports for almost the whole of her iron ore and bauxite requirements. The Four Year Plan of 1936 was introduced to mitigate this weakness, chiefly through the development of synthetic production of oil, rubber, textile fibres and fats, the development of home produced iron ore in Central Germany and of aluminium and magnesium production. The success of this plan in achieving self-sufficiency was very limited. At the outbreak of the war Germany was still dependent on foreign supplies for 70 per cent. of her (peacetime) consumption of mineral oil, and an equal percentage of iron ore, for 83 per cent. of copper consumption, and for her whole consumption of manganese, chrome, nickel, wolfram, tungsten, and a host of other raw materials. Apart from nitrogen and coal there was no war material of importance in which home production could cover peace-time consumption, still less any additional requirements in war. Nor did she succeed in accumulating a war reserve of any magnitude. For most commodities her stocks, at the outbreak of war, were adequate only for six months or less of peace-time consumption, with the exception of manganese, where stocks were sufficient for eighteen months and chromium, tungsten and iron ore, where they were sufficient for eight to ten months.

Yet she managed for five years without any serious embarassment to her war effort owing to lack of basic materials. This was due to a combination of circumstances. In the case of copper and ferro-alloys the Germans found that consumption could be drastically cut without real detriment to the quality of armaments, and considerable quantities could be reclaimed from scrap. Annual consumption of copper, wolfram, molybdenum and cobalt was reduced, in each case, by about two-thirds between 1939 and 1943. The victories of 1939 and 1940–1 led to the capture of considerable stocks of these materials and also to new sources of supply: chromium from Bulgaria and Greece; nickel and molybdenum from Finland and Norway; copper from Jugoslavia, Norway, Finland; manganese from Russia; mercury from Italy and Spain; bauxite from Hungary, France, Jugoslavia and Italy. Sometimes these territorial conquests were only just in time to relieve the situation at a very critical moment. In the case of manganese which is essential for steel production and the use of which could not be substantially curtailed, stocks (despite considerable captures in France) were down to four months' current consumption when the occupation of the Nikopol deposits relieved the situation for the rest of the war.

The development schemes for the home production of basic materials were discontinued after the beginning of the war, with the exception of oil, rubber, aluminium, electric furnace steel and electric power. Synthetic rubber production was raised from 5,000 tons to 134,000 tons per annum between 1939 and 1944; the latter was adequate to cover all requirements. In the case of oil, synthetic production was raised from 1·3 million tons in 1938 to an annual rate of 6 millions tons by early 1944, while crude oil production was expanded (through the development of Austrian fields) from 0·6 to 2·0 million tons. Together with the Rumanian and Hungarian supplies of about 2·5 million tons, these were adequate to meet the needs of the armed forces, whose pattern of consumption was, of course, itself adjusted to the oil situation. Oil was always short for Germany, in the sense that means of warfare involving heavy oil consumption—such as a fully motorised army, or a large force of heavy bombers—had to be foregone. But within the limits of the kind of war strategy and war equipment adopted, the oil supply was considered adequate up to the beginning of the aerial attacks on the oil industry.

The commodity which more than any other dominated the strategy of the German war leaders was steel. Steel capacity formed the basis on which the German General Staff planned the size of the army and the war production programme; and in the early stages of the war it was the supposed lack of steel which prevented the adoption of more ambitious schemes of mobilisation. This steel shortage, as it subsequently turned out, was a delusion. The officers of the Wehrmacht grossly over-estimated both the military steel requirements and the steel necessary for the maintenance of the civilian economy. Thus in 1939–40 out of a total monthly supply of 1·8 million tons, 900,000 tons were allocated to the armaments programme; but the allocations were on far too generous a scale in relation to production schedules and a considerable part of the military allocation was diverted to civilian uses and stocks. Four years later, a 50 per cent. higher monthly allocation of some 1·4 million tons was adequate for an armament production over three times as large. After the conquest of Western Europe total monthly steel supply rose up to 2·6 million tons, so that until the liberation of France, there was never any real steel shortage; in fact, considerable stocks of finished steel (an estimated 15 million tons in the hands of manufacturers) were accumulated. There was a shortage, however, from early 1944 onwards, in certain critical rolling mill products (notably heavy steel plates and tubes) the production capacity of which was relatively short and was not expanded during the war.

The other important basic commodity whose supply was considered inadequate was electric power. Here the capacity was considerably expanded during the war, but the expansion barely kept pace with growing requirements. To a lesser extent the Germans were also "tight" on coal. There was an appreciable fall in the output per man-shift, which was only just offset through the increase in labour engaged in mining.

There is no doubt that of the three main factors limiting the war potential, the raw material base was the narrowest. Steel, coal and electric power would ultimately have imposed a more severe limitation on the expansion of military output than either the man-power shortage or the equipment shortage. But even here it was a case of a potential, rather than an actual limitation; it was not operative throughout the major part of the war; it would have become a limiting factor only at production levels which were approached, rather than attained, in the critical summer months of 1944 when the combined effect of the air war and the loss of territory brought about a reversal of the trend of expansion. Throughout most of the war period German war

Table 6

COMPARISON OF OUTPUT OF PARTICULAR CLASSES OF ARMAMENTS GERMANY AND THE UNITED KINGDOM, 1940-44

	1940		1941		1942		1943		1944	
	Germany	United Kingdom	Germany	United Kingdom	Germany	United Kingdom	Germany	United Kingdom	Germany	United Kingdom
Military Aircraft:										
Fighters	3,100	4,300	3,700	7,000	5,200	9,800	11,700	10,700	28,900	10,500
Bombers	4,000	3,700	4,300	4,700	6,500	6,300	8,600	7,700	6,500	8,100
Other types[1]	1,800	1,900	2,100	1,800	1,800	1,600	2,800	3,000	1,100	5,000
Trainers	1,300	5,100	900	6,600	1,200	5,900	2,100	4,800	3,100	2,900
Total: (numbers)	10,200	15,000	11,000	20,100	14,200	23,600	25,200	26,200	39,600	26,500
Total: Structure weight (mn. lb.)	59†	59	64	87	92	133	138	185	174	208
Bombs (Filled weight 1,000 tons)	*	48	245	143	262	241	273	309	231	370
Armoured Vehicles:										
Tanks[2]	1,600	1,400	3,800	4,800	6,300	8,600	12,100	7,500	19,000	4,600
Others[3]	500	6,000	1,300	10,500	3,100	19,300	7,800	24,200	9,900	22,600
Wheeled Vehicles (thousands):										
Heavy type	*	112	62	110	81	109	109	104	89	91
Light cars and vans	*	21	*	17	29	16	36	17	26	13
Motor cycles	*	68	*	71	*	75	38	79	33	75
Heavy Guns (75 mm. and over):										
Field, medium, and heavy artillery	4,400	1,000	4,700	3,800	5,100	4,000	11,700	3,000	24,900	2,800
Tank	470	—	650	—	2,200	2	9,500	4,600	20,400	7,500
Anti-tank	—	—	—	—	2,100	500	9,900	3,300	13,800	1,900
Anti-aircraft	1,400	900	2,400	1,500	4,200	2,100	6,900	1,300	8,200	200
Total	6,300	1,900	7,800	5,300	13,600	6,600	38,000	12,200	62,300	12,400
Light Guns (over 20 mm. and under 75 mm.):										
Tank	—	240	100	6,000	3,000	22,000	900	10,400	700	1,700
Anti-tank	430	1,500	2,100	2,700	4,500	9,100	2,600	9,800	—	1,100
Anti-aircraft	*	1,100	1,200	2,700	2,100	5,300	4,600	5,600	7,700	800
Total	*	2,800	3,400	11,400	9,600	36,400	8,100	25,800	8,400	3,600

Table 6—continued

	1940		1941		1942		1943		1944	
	Germany	United Kingdom	Germany	United Kingdom	Germany	United Kingdom	Germany	United Kingdom	Germany	United Kingdom
Small Arms:										
Infantry Rifles (1000's)	1,350	81	1,358	78	1,370	594	2,244	910	2,585	547
Infantry Machine Guns (1000's) ..	170	30	320	46	320	1,510	440	1,650	790	730
Ammunition (Million rounds)⁴:										
Heavy Gun (75 mm. and over) ..	27	7	27	14	57	25	93	14	108	12
Light Gun (under 75 mm. excluding 20 mm.)	*	3	8	9	42	25	15	23	25	10
Small Arms (20 mm. and under) ..	2,950	540	1,340	1,120	1,340	2,190	3,170	3,010	5,370	2,460
Naval Armaments:										
Major war vessels completed (1,000 tons Standard Displacement)⁵ ..	**	222	162	346	193	300	221	292	234	270
Heavy Guns (75 mm. and over) ..	**	620	300	740	1,020	1,060	960	990	980	550
Light Guns (excluding 20 mm.) ..	**	860	380	1,730	1,070	2,740	1,210	2,170	2,050	400
Torpedoes	**	940	14,200	1,900	11,000	3,900	11,600	7,000	15,800	6,200
Heavy Gun Ammunition (1,000's) ..	**	840	2,450	1,150	12,640	1,510	1,680	990	1,170	800
Light Gun Ammunition (excluding 20 mm.) (1,000's)	*	3,100	4,100	5,400	35,200	8,700	3,700	7,800	7,100	4,100

Notes.—United Kingdom figures refer to United Kingdom production only. German figures include all deliveries to the Wehrmacht.
1 Including all naval aircraft, general reconnaissance, transport, rescue and other.
2 Tanks and self-propelled guns.
3 For Germany includes armoured reconnaissance cars, armoured half-tracks, armoured infantry and gun carriers. For United Kingdom includes armoured cars, scout cars and carriers.
4 Excluding naval ammunition.
5 For Germany includes submarine production only. For United Kingdom includes completions of all major war vessels.
† Estimated.
* Not available.

Source.—*Statistische Schnellberichte zur Rüstungsproduktion*, February 1945, issued by the Speer Ministry; Speer's report on Armament Production, dated 27 January 1945. (Wherever possible German figures were checked by the acceptance figures of the Armed Forces.) *Statistics relating to the War Effort of the United Kingdom*, Cmd. 6564; "The Effects of Strategic Bombing on the German War Economy." *The U.S. Strategic Bombing Survey*, Washington, D.C., 1945.

production was very much below the level which the raw material supply would have rendered possible.

War Production and Consumption

Two further comparisons between the British and the German war effort should be added to complete the picture. One refers to the comparative output of different classes of armaments, the other to the civilian expenditure on consumption.

Table 6 shows the comparative production of particular classes of armaments in Britain and Germany in the years 1940–4. It shows that in the first three years of the war, German production was less than the British in a number of important categories although it greatly exceeded the British in the final two years. In aircraft, tanks and other armoured vehicles and lorries German production was lower in each of the three years 1940–2;[1] in the case of guns in 1941 and 1942, if all guns over 20 mm. are counted together. As regards tanks, a comparison on the basis of numbers is not perhaps satisfactory, since the German types produced in those years were heavier than the British. This cannot be said, however, of aircraft, of which the British production was considerably in excess of the German already in 1940, and even more in later years.

The comparative movement of the civilian expenditure on consumption is shown in Table 7. This shows that aggregate real consumption in Germany was not really restricted as compared with 1938[2] until 1942, and even then it remained a higher proportion of the pre-war level than that of Britain, until 1944. (This estimate is based on German statistics relating to national income and expenditure. It is not inconsistent with the figures relating to the production of consumers' goods, if allowance is made for the division of consumers' expenditure between food, rent, services and manufactured goods.)

---

[1] No precise figures are available of the German production of wheeled vehicles for 1940, but it is known that production was considerably lower in that year than in 1942, which in itself was lower than the British production in this category in 1940 and 1941.

[2] Movements of war-time consumption taking 1939 as the base year are misleading, for 1939 was a "bumper year," when civilian consumption was much higher than at any previous period. The pre-depression level of consumption was regained in Germany by 1938.

War Planning in Perspective

To attempt to explain this riddle—why Germany did not have a more "total" war effort—it is necessary to go back and analyse

Table 7

CIVILIAN EXPENDITURE ON CONSUMPTION IN GERMANY AND THE UNITED KINGDOM, 1938-44

(Indices based on constant prices)

(1938 = 100)

Year	Germany (Pre-war area)	United Kingdom
1938	100	100
1939	108	100
1940	100	87
1941	97	81
1942	88	79
1943	87	76
1944	79	77

Source.—Germany—U.S. Strategic Bombing Survey, Overall Economic Effects Division Special Paper No. 1, *The Gross National Product of Germany*, Table II.

United Kingdom—*The Impact of the War on Civilian Consumption in the United Kingdom, United States and Canada*, H.M.S.O., 1945. Table IIa.

German pre-war plans and policies. The idea of preparing the country for war or at any rate for war-like "adventures" was undoubtedly dominant in the minds of the Nazi leaders right from the beginning of their régime. On the issue of rearmament they had the fullest support of the Army and of the industrialists. Sharp differences arose, however, between the Army and Hitler as to the manner in which rearmament was to be carried out, and the date by which the Armed Forces were to be "ready" for adventures. The Army leaders (chiefly among them General Thomas, who was in supreme charge of industrial rearmament) wanted to prepare the country for all eventualities; to be capable of fighting a prolonged war against a combination of major powers. This meant a steel capacity of 50 million tons, the maximum development of home-produced iron ores, of the synthetic production of oil and rubber, the accumulation of a huge war chest in all imported war materials. It would also have meant (in the Wehrmacht's estimate) ten years' preparation. In contrast to this plan of "rearmament in depth" (to use General Thomas' phrase), Hitler wanted "rearmament in width"; maximum concentration on finished munitions, the maximum rate of increase in the number of trained divisions, readiness to strike at the earliest possible moment. He further wanted to allow the civilian standard of living to rise at the same time, at least to the pre-depression level. For all this there was the labour of five million unemployed workmen to draw upon.

Hitler undoubtedly thought that Germany's main hope for achieving world domination was through superior speed, rather than superior strength. He wanted to secure sufficient lead in the international armament race to gain his ends through lightning blows delivered at the right moment, rather than await the results of full-scale war preparations which would have given time for her enemies to get prepared as well. In other words, he wanted a war, the outcome of which depended not on steel, manpower, and the other fundamental elements of war-making power, but on the number of divisions immediately ready for action.

The Four-Year Plan of 1936 was the outcome of a rather ineffectual compromise between these two view points. It provided for a certain minimum of basic war preparedness—more than enough for a *blitzkrieg* lasting for a few weeks, but not nearly enough for a war of attrition lasting for years. The rate of re-armament "in width"—i.e. the rate of increase in immediate striking power—was, in the event, limited more by the Army's own ability to grow at a fast enough rate than by the limitation of industrial resources.

The "most favourable moment, which must not be allowed to pass"[1] appeared in Hitler's view, in the closing years of the 1930's; and so after the abortive attempt of 1938, he began with the attack on Poland in 1939. At that time Germany produced but 60 tanks, 1–2 U boats, and 6–700 aeroplanes a month. But she had some 70 newly equipped divisions—fully adequate for the purposes of a minor *blitzkrieg*. The Polish campaign went entirely according to plan. The Norwegian and later the French campaigns further justified the Nazi faith in the *blitzkrieg*

[1] Words actually used by Hitler in a speech to his generals in October 1944.

conception. Both ended in complete victory within a very short time and with an unexpectedly small expenditure of resources. Indeed, from the point of view of the Nazis, it would have been far better if they had not succeeded quite so easily. For the attack on Russia was decided upon then in the confident expectation that the same experience could be repeated; and that it would not require far greater preparations than those made for the earlier campaigns.

Thus in the critical nine months that separated the decision to invade Russia from the actual beginning of the campaign, no real attempt was made to augment military strength, even though, after the conquest of France, there was no serious obstacle to an all-round expansion. The rate of armament production was continued at more or less the same level. The first three months of the Russian campaign did, in fact, go entirely "according to plan"; and at the end of September Hitler, believing the war about won, ordered a large scale reduction in armaments production. This order, even though only partially carried out, caused important reductions in stocks, particularly of ammunition, the effects of which could never be fully overcome afterwards.

The defeat before Moscow, and the entry of the United States into the war in December 1941, brought the German leaders for the first time face to face with the prospect of a prolonged war with the greatest three powers ranged against them. Hitler still hoped to finish the war with Russia in the following summer, and then have leisure to prepare for the Anglo-American assault with Russia's vast resources at his disposal. So again the cry was for a maximum short-term increase of armaments rather than an expansion of basic resources.

The means to bring about this increase were sought in the rationalisation of production and its instrument was found in Albert Speer, Hitler's architect, who, in February 1942, was appointed Minister of Armaments. Speer's administration in the course of the following two and a half years was the single great success which the German war economy can record, and the only one that will retain a more than historical interest. Speer's powers over the economy were limited. At first his control extended only to industries producing land armaments. From November 1943, this was extended to naval armaments; from March 1944, to fighter aircraft, and only from June 1944, onwards, to the armament industry as a whole. He had no control at any time over labour mobilisation, or labour allocation between war production and the civilian economy.

Speer set about replacing the existing bureaucratic machinery of control with a new organisation (consisting of "Committees" and "Rings") which was based, not on a division according to industries, but on a division according to end-products (such as tanks, guns, ammunition, etc.). On each Committee were represented all firms who were engaged in producing a particular armament, without regard to their other activities.[1] All the members were technicians and production managers attached to the various firms; directors or proprietors were only admitted if they happened to be high grade engineers. The most efficient production engineer of any industry was selected as the Chairman of the group (regardless of the importance of the firm he represented). In selecting the Chairman and members, no regard was paid to political affiliations (an important departure from a main Nazi principle)[2] but there was an upper age limit of 40. These Committees were charged with the task of increasing production by securing maximum economy of labour and materials, and optimum utilisation of capacity. This was to be brought about through simplification of designs, standardisation of components, concentration of production in the most suitable plants, reduction in the number of different armament orders given to a single firm, the exchange of patents and secret processes and the general adoption, by all firms, of the most efficient processes of production.[3] The result of this policy was reflected in a more than threefold increase in German armament production.

[1] There was a hierarchy of such Committees—e.g. to the Main Committee Tanks were subordinated the Special Committee Tank Engines which had a Sub-Committee Crankshafts, etc.

[2] Up to that time, the holders of all important posts had to be party members— a severe limitation on efficiency, as the first-class technical brains usually kept out of the party.

[3] According to Speer, "The production engineers who composed these committees became so enamoured with the technical problem of raising productivity that they were ready to overlook entirely the special interests of the individual firms they were supposed to represent."

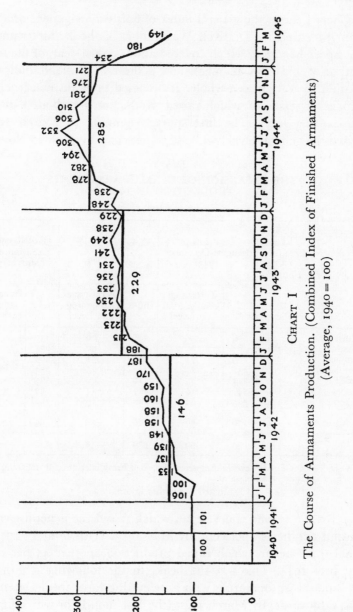

CHART I

The Course of Armaments Production. (Combined Index of Finished Armaments)

(Average, 1940 = 100)

Chart I shows the general index of finished armament production, prepared by Dr. Rolf Wagenführ, of the Planungsamt of the Speer Ministry, which covered about 90 per cent. of the total output of finished armaments and is the best available indicator of military output as a whole. It disclosed three distinct levels of expansion, each of which raised production by about half the pre-existing level. The first spurt, beginning in March 1942, raised the general level by about 55 per cent. by July. In Novem-

Table 8

THE EXPANSION OF GERMAN ARMAMENTS
PRODUCTION IN 1942–4

(1941 = 100)

Category	1st Level (July-Oct. 1942)	2nd Level (August-December 1943)		Peak Level (July 1944)		Last Recorded Month (March 1945)	
	Index	Index	Percentage change from 1st Level	Index	Percentage change from 2nd Level	Index	Percentage change from Peak Level
Aircraft	144	228	58	378	66	139	−63
Tanks	161	484	195	727	50	273	−62
Weapons	137	239	74	362	51	208	−42
Ammunition	197	251	27	313	25	154	−51
Powder	150	217	45	218	0	125[1]	−43
Vehicles	129	147	14	127	−14	37[1]	−71
Tractors	184	335	82	298	19	162[1]	−59
Naval Construction	129	176	36	126	−28	99	−21
Total	147	235	50	329	40	147	−55

Source.—*Schnellberichte zur Rüstungsproduktion*, Reichsministerium für Rüstung und Kriegsproduktion, Planungsamt.

[1] Estimated from other information.

ber 1942, a second spurt began which raised the general level of output another 55 per cent. by May 1943. With January 1944, a final spurt began which raised production another 45 per cent. by July 1944. This was the peak; in the following month the decline set in, operating with accelerating force from December 1944, onwards. By March 1945 (the last month for which figures are available), the general index was down to the level of June 1942.

In the first spurt more or less all categories participated; the second spurt was most notable for an almost threefold increase in tank production; while the last spurt showed an extraordinary increase in aircraft. (The increase in various armament categories is shown in Table 8.)

This increase was not achieved, of course, without an increase in labour engaged on armament production. But as is shown in Table 9, the increase in the labour force on armament orders was relatively modest, the total increase between December 1941, and June 1944, being only 28 per cent. Thus the bulk of the increase in production was secured through an increase in productivity. In this the simplification of designs, a rational allocation of production among plants and the introduction of mass production techniques were equally important. Curious as it may sound, German industry until recently was still largely dominated by the methods of craftsmanship, turning out high quality products with a wasteful use of skilled labour and materials; employing almost exclusively multi-purpose machine tools which required skilled labour to operate them. Outside the motor-car industry, line-assembly and the use of single purpose machine tools was practically unknown.[1] One of the achievements of Speer and his associates consisted therefore in the introduction of techniques into German industry which were used by the American and some of the British armament industries from the start.[2]

The effects of rationalisation were most spectacular perhaps in the case of the aircraft industry. This was a jealously guarded preserve of Göring, who steadily refused to allow any share of control to the Speer Ministry. At the end of February 1944, however, the Allied Air Forces succeeded, in a series of blows, in knocking out 70 per cent. of fighter assembly plants. As a result, the control of the fighter aircraft production was handed over to Speer. Extremely energetic rationalisation measures were put

[1] But even in the motor-car industry there were spectacular increases in productivity due to standardisation of types. Thus while at the outbreak of the war, there were 76 types of lorries currently produced, this was cut to 18 types by 1943 and to only 9 types by the end of 1944. In consequence, output per man-hour, over the industry as a whole, was more than doubled (in certain cases more than trebled) despite the fact that the proportion of skilled workmen in the total labour force was cut by a half.

[2] The saving of labour was accompanied by equally impressive savings in raw materials. Thus in the case of weapons, the overall ratio between the required input weight and finished weight of steel was reduced from 4 : 1 to 2 : 1, between 1942 and 1944.

Table 9

MANPOWER ENGAGED IN ARMAMENT PRODUCTION, GERMANY AND THE UNITED KINGDOM

(in millions)

	Germany							United Kingdom			
	Army	Air Force	Navy	Quarter-master Stores	Total engaged in end-products	Basic materials and com-ponents	Total	Ministry of Supply	Ministry of Aircraft Pro-duction	Ad-miralty	Total
December 1941 / January 1942	1·4	1·8	·6	·1	3·9	·8	4·7	1·5	1·3	·8	3·6
December 1942 / January 1943	1·8	1·9	·6	·1	4·4	·9	5·3	1·7	1·6	·8	4·1
June 1943 / July 1943	1·8	1·9	·6	·1	4·4	1·0	5·4	1·6	1·7	·9	4·2
December 1943 / January 1944	1·9	2·1	·5	·1	4·6	1·0	5·6	1·5	1·8	·9	4·2
June 1944 / July 1944	2·0	2·4	·5	·1	5·0	1·0	6·0	1·4	1·7	·9	4·0

Note.—British and German figures refer to December and June, British to January and July

Note.—British and German figures are not strictly comparable, as German figures refer to employment in "A" firms only, which is estimated to have taken up about 80 per cent. of the total employed in armament production. British figures refer to the numbers employed on orders for the three supply departments in the engineering, ship building, metals and chemical industries, excluding iron and steel.

Source.—Britain, Cmd. 6564, Table 2; Germany, Reichsministerium für Rüstung und Kriegsproduktion, Zentralamt, Abt. Arb. E.Wi., (Stat.).

in hand immediately: the number of models in production was severely cut, components were standardised, and designs simplified (though not, according to the Ministry's claim, at the expense of performance); while the salvaged machine tools of the destroyed plants were set up under canvas. As a result, the pre-raid level of production was exceeded by April and nearly doubled by July, with a no more than 15 per cent. increase in the industry's labour force.[1]

The picture that emerges from a study of the years 1942–4 is that of an economy rapidly trying to build up its war effort to the stage of total mobilisation, but never attaining the stage at which the country's war potential would have been fully exploited. From September 1944 onwards, the disorganisation caused by the air attacks on the railway system, and the loss of territories in the West and East caused a decline in production, followed by a complete industrial collapse in the early months of 1945. According to the officials of the Speer Ministry, war production was still expanding rapidly when these factors supervened and, in their absence, the level of munitions production would have risen by another 20–30 per cent. before capacity output, as determined by raw material supplies, would have been reached. The factors, therefore, which really limited German war production in the last three years of the war are to be sought simply in those elements of inertia in the economic system which set a limit to the rate at which adjustment and expansion can proceed, rather than in any absolute shortage either of manpower, equipment, or raw materials. No doubt, with a better system of co-ordination, a greater readiness to sacrifice civilian standards and to mobilise labour, the process of expansion could have been speeded up further. But the basic fault was the failure to plan for expansion and total mobilisation in the earlier years. It was due to a breakdown of strategy at the highest level, caused by the virtual absence of any effective machinery for thorough and systematic discussion of requirements and potentialities.

[1] No doubt this performance was greatly aided by the fact that the industry was previously highly inefficient, measured by any standard. This is evident also from a comparison of the labour force engaged on aircraft production in Britain and Germany as shown in Table 9, if account is taken of the fact that the British production was considerably in excess of the German, as measured by numbers or structural weight; and that the German figures, unlike the British, do not include all the workmen engaged on armament orders.

It would be a mistake to conclude from this analysis that the German war economy provides any evidence of the inefficiency of "planned" or "controlled" economies. Its failures were due to the absence of planning and co-ordinated control, and not to any abandonment of a *laissez faire* system. But it will stand as a monument to the inefficiency of a system of personal dictatorship. Those of us who are fortunate enough to live in a free society will take comfort from the fact that even in the matter of efficiency of administrative control and co-ordination, the "cumbrous" methods of democratic government should prove so superior to systems based on the ruthless exercise of personal power.

21

ECONOMIC PROBLEMS OF CHILE[1]

I. NATURE OF THE CHILEAN ECONOMIC PROBLEM

CHILE, like many other countries of Latin America, is apt to strike the European observer as a country of vast economic potentialities which remain unexploited chiefly on account of the inability of Government (using that term in the comprehensive sense as the sum total of political institutions) to secure the appropriate social and institutional environment for the effective deployment of resources. There can be little doubt that the combination of natural and human resources of the country—its climate and geology, its mineral resources as well as the potential fertility of its soil, the natural vitality and intelligence of its population derived from a combination of strains of European stock which in the similar climatic but different social environment of North America produced spectacular results—are as favourable, if not more favourable, than that of the economically most developed nations of the globe. By any such test Chile is as favourably placed (if not a great deal more favourably placed) for attaining a high level of material production and high standards of living as, for example, Sweden or Switzerland. Yet its income per head of around 300 U.S. dollars at current prices is less than a third of these two countries; and on account of the highly uneven manner in which wealth is distributed, the standard of living of the great mass of the population is perhaps not even one-sixth as high as that of the working population of Sweden. Unlike the vast regions of the East and some of the areas of Central America, Chile cannot by any standard be regarded as over-populated in relation to its natural resources. If it remains essentially an under-developed country—as by the test of the standard of living of the bulk of its population,

[1] A study prepared at the request of the United Nations Economic Commission for Latin America in Santiago, Chile, July-September, 1956. The author wishes to acknowledge the help of the statistical staff of E.C.L.A., particularly Mr. Bittram. A Spanish version appeared in *El Trimestro Economico*. Mexico, D.F. April-June 1959.

it must undoubtedly be so classified—this must perforce be due to predominantly social factors which hamper the free development of productive forces. It is on account of such factors that the bulk of the population of Chile has not become engulfed in that beneficial cumulative process whereby improving living standards become productive of higher efficiency—through the stimulus afforded to education, the greater incentives to progress, as well as improved vitality and physical energy—and thereby lead to further improvement of living standards in turn. Taking the last ten, twenty, fifty or a hundred years, there has undoubtedly been continued economic growth on a *per capita* basis, as well as in terms of total production. But the rate of growth lagged behind that of other more successful countries, and brought little tangible benefit to the peasantry or the lower classes of the population generally.

The immediate impression of a foreign observer is that the energies of successive Chilean Governments have been (and are still) taken up with problems of immediate emergency—problems which are not inherent in the character of the Chilean economy, or in Chile's position in relation to the rest of the world, but are largely the consequences of the economic policies pursued by the Governments themselves. The perennial problem of Chilean Governments is to keep inflation at bay and to prevent the balance of payments from deteriorating too much. It is a matter for argument whether with different economic policies both monetary stability and balance of payments equilibrium might have maintained themselves on their own, so to speak, without claiming the continuous and unremitting efforts of the authorities.

Indeed, one's general impression is that the obstacles in the path of an accelerated improvement are neither natural, technical nor economic, but essentially political—they ensue from the continued clash between the individual interests of particular groups and classes, and the social interest; and they reflect the lack of appropriate institutional arrangements for the continued resolution of conflicts, and the attainment of social compromises. It is, of course, an essential criterion of any successful society that it should have efficient arrangements for the continued resolution of such conflicts. In a competitive or quasi-competitive capitalist society, conflicts are resolved through the impersonal mechanism of the market. In a Socialist state or in a planned economy, they are resolved through the fiat of the authorities—perhaps with greater justice, but at the cost of having to exert a great deal of power and compulsion. The difficulties in countries like Chile arise from the fact that Governments, under the influence of varying political pressures, have been ready to renounce the use of the impersonal market as an arbiter without erecting any effective alternative instrument for harmonising or compromising between particular interests and the general social interest. The Chilean Governments have long ago lost any innate inhibitions against State interference in economic life, and pursued a policy of intervention with a multiplicity of detailed and complicated controls—such as quantitative import regulations, multiple exchange rates, credit controls, discriminatory tax concessions and so on—without any clear overall view of either the basic objectives which these instruments were intended to serve, or of any overall attempt to assess their efficacy in relation to such objectives.

In the circumstances, the general presumption must be that neither from the point of view of economic growth nor of social justice did these controls yield any net benefit as compared with what the situation would have been if the allocation of resources had been left to the blind operation of market forces. There can be few fields of political action where the willingness of governments to prohibit and to prescribe is so out of proportion to the intelligence at their command as to what ought to be prohibited or prescribed. The application of detailed controls in capitalist economies is often no better than quack medicine. There is a great deal of straightforward corruption which goes to nullify the intended effects of detailed physical controls and yet leaves behind an unnecessary amount of social and economic rigidity.

All this is not intended as a defence of the free market or of *laissez faire* or as an argument against economic planning—it is not a question of the choice between different "systems" but of the appropriateness of the instruments chosen for the operation of any particular system. The experience of Russia during the last thirty years, and more recently of China, provides ample evidence that centralised planning in a Socialist State can produce vigorous and sustained growth, given the use of appropriate instruments. Equally, the example of the United States has amply shown that vigorous economic growth over long periods can result from a free enterprise system in an appropriate social environment. Finally, the example of Sweden may be cited as showing that it is possible to combine private initiative and a free market system with long range overall planning by the State, and to obtain the benefits of a Socialist society in terms of social justice and stability of progress without sacrificing the benefits of a private enterprise system in terms of social and economic flexibility and the decentralisation of power.

The use of detailed physical controls is often defended on the ground that they are essential for improving an income distribution between social classes that would otherwise be hopelessly unjust; to prevent the waste of resources in unnecessary consumption; to prevent unavoidable balance of payments deficits; or to prevent inflation. I think it could be shown that in all, or practically all, such cases physical controls are inferior as compared with alternative instruments of regulation through the power of taxation. If it is objected that the administrative capability of the Government in employing the tax instrument effectively is limited, its administrative capabilities of operating a system of prohibitions and licences in the social interest must be even less.

To promote economic growth it is clearly necessary for the State to restrain the use of resources in socially unproductive activities as well as to ensure that energy and enterprise are applied at the critical points for promoting the growth of productivity. But it is idle to expect that the latter can successfully result from the operation of controls that are essentially negative in character. A system of prohibitions is a futile instrument for promoting desired activities as well as being a clumsy instrument for suppressing others.

The appropriate instruments for promoting enterprise in a mainly private enterprise economy are either of a general kind or a particular kind. Objectives of a particular kind—for example, the development of a steel industry which, however essential for long-run economic growth, would not be promoted by private enterprise on account of the amount of the investment required, the uncertainty of the long-range prospects, etc.—are best fostered through the creation of State enterprises or mixed State-and-private enterprises, using public funds and operating partially under public responsibility. (This is the one field in which the policy of active intervention of Chilean Governments in recent times appears to have been conspicuously successful. Through the creation of the Corporación de Fomento, it promoted steel and metallurgical enterprises, electricity works, etc., which have made an important contribution to the growth of the country's economic potential.)

Instruments of a general kind consist of the totality of legal and social institutions which promote the creation of a social *élite* which is effective, intelligent and dynamic in outlook; and which ensure the utmost freedom for the circulation of the *élite*. In other words the general instruments for promoting economic progress consist of all those institutions, laws, measures or policies which help in providing a capable administrative class and a vigorous entrepreneurial class—which ensure that those who take decisions on the investment and allocation of resources should be both efficient and experimental in outlook.

One of the most important instruments for promoting this end is undoubtedly education which provides opportunities for ordinary people to rise to positions of leadership which they would not possess otherwise. But apart from education which supplies the challengers, the environment must be favourable to enable the challengers to challenge successfully the positions of the established group of leaders. The true social importance of a competitive market is that it provides an opportunity for newcomers to challenge the positions of the old-established enterprises. Anything which promotes monopoly and increases the difficulty of entry must in the long run be inimical to progress.

Among such obstacles we must reckon the very social institution of inheritance which, in its economic effect at any rate, is far more important in the sphere of agriculture than in the rest of the economy. The institution of inheritance inevitably creates inequality of opportunity and thereby handicaps the newcomer in any sphere of activity. However, in the industrial sphere and in a competitive society, it does not prevent more efficient production units from gaining at the expense of less efficient ones. The more efficient enterprise can grow more quickly because it is able to reinvest more in relation to its current production, and thereby secure a more rapid growth of its own activities which narrows the market for less efficient units and may force them to contract. In the case of agriculture, however, the growth of an efficient enterprise depends not so much on the accumulation of capital but on the acquisition of land. A class of efficient farmers cannot, merely through the forces of competition, deprive the relatively inefficient farmers of their land—particularly if the latter have individual holdings large enough to enable the owners to make a living despite inefficient management and low productivity. Hence, if the land is firmly held by a class of large landowners, the forces making for efficient leadership and for a "circulation of the *élite*" in agriculture are largely inoperative; no amount of market competition can cause the efficient units to grow beyond a certain point, if they cannot force inefficient units with a stagnant outlook to surrender their land.[1]

There can be little doubt that the promotion of a vigorous entrepreneurial class in both industry and agriculture is the main long-term requirement for economic development in Chile—at any rate, so long as she remains, as she is likely to remain, a private enterprise society. In the field of industry, this has been hampered by the growth of monopolies which were powerfully supported by the foreign exchange and foreign trade policies of recent decades; and also by the continued process of inflation itself which invariably operates so as to buttress the relative position of the dominant economic groups.[2]

In the field of agriculture, progress is hampered by a traditional land-owning class going back to colonial times which owns a

[1] This is the basic technical reason why large-scale institutional reforms redistributing land are a periodic feature of all civilised societies in history.

[2] The technical reason for this is that inflation continually expropriates the lenders in favour of the borrowers. A man's or a firm's borrowing power depends on the amount of assets he owns, and not on the rate at which he increases his assets out of current production. An inflationary situation, therefore, by allowing the borrowers to expropriate the lenders, favours those particular groups which are in a position to benefit most from this process.

very large part of the total farming area.[1] Stagnation in agriculture may in itself stifle progress in the other sectors of the economy, since without marketable surpluses of food, the secondary and tertiary industries will be hampered in their expansion, both through a scarcity of food and (which is merely a different side of the same coin) through a limitation in the market for their products.

In the light of this, the main long-term requirements for promoting economic progress in Chile appear to be four in number. There is urgent need for a lasting re-establishment of monetary stability; for a reform in foreign exchange and foreign trade policies that would restore the forces of competition in the industrial field without hindrance to the general progress of industrialisation; for an administrative and fiscal reform that would enable the instruments of taxation to be used for the release of adequate resources for investment purposes both for investment in material resources and for investment in human resources, in education; and finally, for a land reform that would release the latent forces of growth in agriculture.

These are general conclusions which emerged from a broad overall view of the Chilean problem, and they are based on impressions rather than on any detailed examination of facts. In the following sections an attempt is made to analyse the long-range trends of the Chilean economy in more concrete terms in the light of the available statistics, in order to test the validity of these general conclusions and to examine how far they require to be amended or supplemented.

II. THE LONG-RANGE TRENDS IN THE CHILEAN ECONOMY

The national income estimates prepared by the Corporación de Fomento make it possible to analyse the prevailing trends in the Chilean economy over the last fifteen years in some detail.[2] To see these trends in perspective, the years 1940-2, 1946-8 and

[1] According to the 1936 census, over 94 per cent. of the farms in Chile were under 200 hectares and only 5·7 per cent. above 200 hectares, but the latter accounted for nearly 88 per cent. of the total farming area.

[2] The national income estimates of the Research Section of the Corporación de Fomento (published in the form of a book) lack nothing either in extensiveness or in the consistency and comprehensiveness of the concepts employed, in comparison with the national accounts of the U.S. or Western European countries. But the statistical error in the estimates is likely to be appreciably greater—not only on account of the comparative lack of fact-gathering sources but also of the much greater importance

1952–4 (the latter being the latest period for which figures are available) have been selected for comparison. The figures relating to the occupied population and its composition, the level of production (defined as the net internal production of each sector) and to the changes of productivity per man over the period, are shown in Table 1.

It should be borne in mind that the period 1940 to 1954 was one of a rapid increase in population. Total population increased by over 30 per cent. (from 5·06 to 6·60 millions) and the increase in the numbers of working age may have been even higher. As Table 1 shows, while the increase in the total occupied population[1] between 1940–2 and 1952–4 (from 2·39 to 3·05 millions) appears to have kept pace fully with the growth in the population of working age, the increase in the numbers occupied in the "productive" (i.e. primary and secondary) sectors of the economy (agriculture and fisheries, mining, manufacturing industries, building and construction, public utilities, and transport and communications) was only 18 per cent., while the increase in commercial, financial, Government and personal services averaged no less than 60 per cent. Among the "productive" sectors the increase in employment was confined to industry, construction and transport. The numbers employed in agriculture and fisheries remained practically stationary.

The aggregate increase in production of the five "productive" sectors over the period as a whole amounted to over 53 per cent. and among these the increase in industrial production, which approached 95 per cent., was outstanding. On the other hand, the improvement of agricultural production barely kept pace with the growth of population, so that there appears to have been no improvement at all in internal food supplies per head between 1940–2 and 1952–4. Moreover most of the improvement in

---

of price changes and in consequence the greater dependence of the results on the appropriateness of the price-indices employed in deflating the estimates in terms of current prices. I had neither the information nor the time at my disposal to make any kind of examination of how far the conclusions derived from the estimates are statistically significant, in the light of the probable margins of error. Hence my purpose here is to highlight the main conclusions that can be derived from the estimates, taking the figures as they stand—leaving it to those with a more intimate knowledge of the Chilean economy to decide how far these conclusions are probable or reasonable in the light of other available information.

[1] Comprising wage and salary earners and the self-employed.

Table 1

CHILE: NUMBER OF WORKERS, PRODUCTION AND PRODUCTIVITY IN 1940-2/1946-8, 1946-8/1952-4 AND 1940-2/1952-4

Economic sector	Number of workers (Thousands of persons)[1]			Production[2] (Millions of pesos at 1950 prices)			Production per worker (Thousands of pesos at 1950 prices)			Total percentage variation between 1940-2 and 1952-4		Cumulative annual rate of growth of productivity by periods		
	1940–1942	1946–1948	1952–1954	1940–1942	1946–1948	1952–1954	1940–1942	1946–1948	1952–1954	Production	Productivity	1940-2/1946-8	1946-8/1952-4	1940-2/1952-4
Agriculture and fisheries	1,220	1,231	1,236	15,805	18,990	22,004	13.0	15.4	17.8	39.2	36.9	2.9	2.4	2.7
Mining	95	94	94	8,270	7,288	7,771	87.1	77.3	82.7	-6.0	-5.1	-2.0	1.2	-0.4
Industry	309	410	511	12,653	19,176	24,688	40.9	46.8	48.3	95.1	18.1	2.3	0.7	1.4
Construction	56	97	112	2,538	4,196	4,395	45.3	43.2	39.2	73.2	-13.5	-0.8	-1.6	-1.2
Electricity, gas and water	8	8	9	676	730	978	84.5	91.3	108.6	44.7	28.5	1.3	2.9	2.1
Transport and communications	94	117	136	6,087	8,350	10,806	64.8	71.4	79.5	77.5	22.7	1.6	1.8	1.7
Total "productive sectors"	1,782	1,957	2,098	46,029	58,710	70,642	25.8	30.0	33.7	53.5	30.6	2.6	2.0	2.3
Trade	152	182	218	15,693	20,317	26,480								
Finance and insurance	15	16	18	1,946	2,517	3,378								
Government services	126	156	201	6,936	9,083	15,790								
Personal services	314	401	517	11,899	15,673	18,343								
Ownership of residential buildings				8,623	9,856	11,906								
Total "services"	607	755	954	45,097	57,446	75,897								
Total	2,389	2,712	3,052	91,126	116,156	146,539								

Source.—Corporación de Fomento de la Producción (C.O.R.F.O.).
[1] Including workers, employees and self-employed.
[2] Net internal income.

agricultural production occurred in the period 1940–2 to 1946–8. Between 1946–8 and 1952–4, although population increased by a further 10 per cent., the increase in food production was only 6½ per cent.[1] (See Table 2).

Another interesting feature brought out by Table 1 is that the pace of economic improvement has been slower in the period 1948 to 1954 than in the period 1940 to 1948. Taking the six productive sectors together (and these comprise all activities for which the term "productivity per head" has any definite meaning), the growth in productivity per head averaged 2·6 per cent. per annum in 1940–8 and only 2·0 per cent. per annum in 1948–54. This was due to the slowing down of the growth in industrial productivity (from 2·3 to 0·7 per cent.), and to the actual fall in productivity in construction. The only sectors which have shown an improved growth in productivity during the years 1948–54 are mining, transport and communications and public utilities. In the case of public utilities this may have been the fruit of the programme of public investment sponsored by the Government. In the case of mining, however, the growth potentialities do not appear to have been fully exploited since the improvement in productivity per head was the result of a rather modest increase in total production combined with an actual fall in employment. As measured in terms of 1950 prices output per man in mining in 1954 was 50 per cent. higher than in manufacturing industry and five times as high as in agriculture. In terms of the prices of 1954–5, the productivity of labour in mining would show an ever greater preponderance over other sectors, owing to the relative increase in copper prices in the interval. The failure to exploit the favourable opportunities for a higher export income through an increase in the volume of production in copper mining, along with the stagnation in agricultural production, thus appear as the two most immediately apparent shortcomings in the production trends of recent years.

1. *Trends in Income Distribution*

The forces underlying these economic trends become much

[1] The estimates in Table 1 relate to the net output (including depreciation) of the agricultural sector. The physical index of food production (Table 2) shows an increase of only 27 per cent. between 1940–2 and 1952–4.

Table 2

CHILE: QUANTUM INDICES OF
PRODUCTION OF FOODSTUFFS

(1940–2 = 100)

Commodity	1946–8	1952–4
Cereals	121·7	121·4
Pulses	86·9	90·8
Potatoes	125·5	121·0
Wine and *chicha*	108·8	119·9
Sunflower	596·2	1454·9
Meat	103·4	123·5
Milk	172·1	146·7
Butter	170·3	127·1
Cheese	152·7	125·1
Poultry	113·2	158·0
Eggs	115·6	141·5
Overall foodstuffs production index[1]	119·5	127·4

Source.—C.O.R.F.O.

[1] The method adopted was that of combining partial indices, the gross value of production of each of the items for which quantum indices were available being utilised for weighting purposes. Production values were obtained from C.O.R.F.O., *Plan de desarrollo agricola y de transportes* (*Agricultural and transport development programme*).

clearer when changes in the distribution of national income and in the real income per head of different classes are taken into account. These are shown in Tables 3 and 4. In Table 3 the aggregate increase in real national income and its division between different types of income are shown. The total increase in real national income in the period 1940–54, shown as 84 per cent., was considerably greater than the increase in the net national product (which was about 60 per cent.), the difference reflecting the improvement in the terms of trade. The improvement, however, was very unevenly distributed. Whilst the aggregate wage bill had only risen by 36 per cent., aggregate salaries went up by 136 per cent., the remuneration of the self-employed by 80 per cent., and profits and dividends by over 120 per cent.[1] Whilst wages and salaries taken together roughly maintained their share of the national income, this was due to the fact that the rise in the proportion of salaries went hand in hand with a diminishing

[1] The relatively greater increase in total salaries as against the income of the self-employed is entirely due (as is evident from Table 3) to the increase in the proportion of salary earners in the population and the corresponding decrease in the proportion of self-employed.

share of wages in the national income. The share of wages in the national income fell from 28 to 21 per cent. although the proportion of wage earners in the total occupied population remained constant at 57 per cent. The relative rise in the income of the self-employed (despite the fall in the proportion of self-employed in the working population) and the fall in the share of rents, may both be accounted for by the inflationary conditions. It is interesting to note also that the increase in distributed profits more than kept pace with the rise in total profits, if the element of stock appreciation is excluded from profits. Taking profits net of taxes and after deduction of stock appreciation, the share of profits in the national income in 1954 was 19·0 per cent. Of this no less than 16·2 per cent. was distributed and only 2·8 per cent. ploughed back.[1]

The trend towards increasing inequality in the distribution of income is even more evident from the changes in real income per head of different classes of the population, shown in Table 4. Real income per head of the occupied population increased by no less than 30 per cent. between 1940–2 and 1952–4. The majority of the population, who are wage earners, received, however, very little benefit; real wages per man showed only a 9 per cent. increase. As against that the salary earners' real income per head increased by 38 per cent., and the real income of the self-employed by 43 per cent. Whilst in 1940–2 the average salary was 3½ times the average wage, in 1952–4 it was nearly 5 times as high. (The increase in salaries per head occurred after 1946–8.)[2] Similarly the average income per head of the

[1] It thus appears that, allowing for stock appreciation, not more than 15 per cent. of profits were retained by enterprises. In the U.S. (as can be seen from Table 14) net undistributed profits amounted to more than 40 per cent. of the net profits of enterprises; in the U.K. to over 60 per cent.

[2] In addition it must be borne in mind that under the system of social insurance contributions in force in Chile, not only do the salary earners receive very much greater insurance benefits than the wage earners but, as a result of the method of charging social insurance contributions, the wage earners have to shoulder an appreciable part of the burden of the salary earners' contributions. This is because contributions paid by the employers are added to the price and since the salary earners' contribution is very much greater than the wage earners', the wage earners' burden (imposed on them through the rise in prices of the things which they buy) is enhanced thereby.

It should also be pointed out that the big rise in real salaries after 1948 was confined to private employees. The salaries of public employees remained very low both absolutely and in relation to the corresponding earnings in private business; and this forms one of the main obstacles to any thorough-going administrative reform.

self-employed was twice the average wage in 1952–4 whilst it was only 58 per cent. higher than the average wage in 1940–2. With regard to property owners it is not possible to show the change in income per head, since no figures are available of the

Table 3

CHILE: INCREASE OF AGGREGATE REAL NATIONAL INCOME, 1940–48 AND 1940–54

Type of Income	*Total percentage increase*	
	From 1940 to 1948	From 1940 to 1954
Wages	20	36
Salaries	49	136
Profits of self-employed	41	80
Rent	9	41
Interest	231	88
Profits	$68^1/66^2$	$126^1/56^2$
Dividends, etc.	68	124
Undistributed profits	$68^1/63^2$	$299^1/157^2$
(Undistributed profits after tax) ..	$63^1/50^2$	$402^1/232^2$
Total national income	41	84

Percentage share in National Income

Type of Income	1940–2	1946–8	1952–4
Wages	27·5	23·5	21·3
Salaries ..	16·3	16·6	20·9
Profits of self-employed ..	23·3	22·8	23·3
Rent	12·3	10·8	10·2
Interest ..	0·6	1·2	0·8
Profits ..	$23·3^1/19·4^2$	$27·1^1/21·8^2$	$26·9^1/19·0^2$
Dividends, etc.	14·7	16·2	16·2
Undistributed profits ..	$11·6^1/6·9^2$	$12·9^1/7·6^2$	$15·6^1/7·8^2$
(Undistributed profits after tax) ..	$8·4^1/3·4^2$	$9·7^1/4·4^2$	$12·8^1/4·9^2$
Total national income ..	$105·1^1/100^2$	$105·2^1/100^2$	$107·9^1/100^2$

Source.—C.O.R.F.O.

[1] Including stock appreciation.   [2] Excluding stock appreciation.

numbers comprised by this category, but the aggregate distributed income of property owners increased by 37 per cent. in real terms during the period and, whilst in 1940–2 the total of distributed profits, interest and rent was a similar amount to the aggregate wage payments, in 1952–4 it exceeded the latter by about 30 per cent. The general picture is thus undoubtedly one of increasing

Table 4

CHILE: CHANGES IN REAL INCOME PER HEAD 1940–2, 1946–8 AND 1952–4

Categories	Index of real income per head			Real income per head as a percentage of average real wage in 1940–2			Percentage of occupied population		
	1940–1942	1946–1948	1952–1954	1940–1942	1946–1948	1952–1954	1940–1942	1946–1948	1952–1954
Wage earners	100	106	109	100	106	109	57·3	56·8	57·0
Salary earners	100	101	138	374	359	472	9·8	11·2	11·8
Self-employed	100	116	143	158	172	206	32·9	32·0	31·1
Total, all groups	100	114	130	145	152	177	100	100	100
Aggregate personal income of property owners[1] ..	100	130	137	107[2]	120[2]	128[2]			

Source.—C.O.R.F.O.
[1] Includes rents, interest and dividends.
[2] Expressed as a percentage of *aggregate* wage payments in 1940.

economic inequality. The middle classes (the self-employed and the salary earners) gained both absolutely and relatively in comparison with the wage earners, whilst the property owners increased their income at about the same rate as the salary earners and faster than the self-employed. Since the average income per head of the property owners must have been appreciably higher than that of the self-employed or the salary earners at the beginning, the figures expressed in terms of proportionate changes understate the increasing differences in terms of absolute income between the upper and lower classes of society. I cannot say how far the Chilean experience in the trends of income distribution was typical of other Latin American countries during the period. But it was undoubtedly a-typical of the prevailing trend in the countries of Western Europe and North America where the period is characterised by a marked tendency towards a greater equality in the distribution of personal income.

In Table 5 a comparison is made of the structure of income distribution of Chile with that of a developed capitalist economy, that of the U.S. The differences are significant both in showing the relative preponderance of profits and property income in Chile (despite the fact that the amount of capital used in production, relative to labour, must be small in comparison with the U.S.) and also the difference in the trends of income distribution in the two countries in the period 1940 to 1953.

That the share of wages and salaries is so much lower in Chile is partly attributable to the fact that wage and salary earners account for only 69 per cent. of the occupied population in Chile and of 81 per cent. of the occupied population in the U.S. Allowance for this only accounts, however, for a part of the difference shown—just as the difference in the proportion of the population who are self-employed accounts for only part of the fact that the share of profits of the self-employed is twice as high in Chile as in the U.S.[1] The really surprising feature of these

[1] If we assumed that an equivalent proportion of the occupied population of the U.S. were transferred from the category of wage and salary earners to the category of self-employed—so as to make the percentages in the two categories identical with that of Chile—and we also assumed that those transferred earned the average income of their categories both before and after the transfer, the percentages of the national income attributable to wage and salary earners in the U.S. in 1953 would have been 58·6 per cent. and that of the self-employed 20·5 per cent. (as against the Chilean percentages of 45·2 and 24·9 respectively).

estimates is, however, that both the share of income accruing to rents and the share of the profits of enterprises is so much greater in Chile than in the U.S.[1]

Table 5

PERCENTAGE SHARES IN NATIONAL INCOME IN CHILE AND THE UNITED STATES

	1940		1948		1953	
	Chile	U.S.A.	Chile	U.S.A.	Chile	U.S.A.
I. Wages and salaries including insurance contributions	44·3	63·9	42·3	63·6	45·2	68·9
II. Profits of self-employed[1]	22·1	15·9	22·4	18·4	24·9	12·5
(a) Farm	7·6	5·6	6·5	7·6	6·5	4·0
(b) Business and professional	14·5	10·3	15·9	9·8	18·4	8·5
III. Profits of enterprises before tax[2]	19·8	11·2	23·6	13·8	19·2	12·2
IV. Direct taxes on enterprises	2·8	3·5	3·6	5·6	2·4	7·0
V. Profits of enterprises after tax	17·0	7·7	20·0	8·2	16·8	5·2
(a) Dividends	13·6	4·9	16·4	3·3	14·8	3·1
(b) Undistributed profits	6·3	3·0	7·3	5·9	7·4	2·5
(c) Inventory valuation	−2·9	−0·2	−3·7	−1·0	−5·4	−0·4
VI. Net interest	0·6	5·5	1·4	2·0	0·9	2·9
VII. Rental income of persons	13·2	3·5	10·3	3·2	9·8	3·4
Total National Income	100·0	100·0	100·0	100·0	100·0	100·0

Sources.—Chile, C.O.R.F.O; U.S.A., *Survey of Current Business*, U.S. Dept. of Commerce.

[1] Figures for Chile include only income of self-employed people, whereas for U.S.A. the figures include also profits of unincorporated enterprises.

[2] Figures for Chile include profits of all kinds of enterprises. U.S.A. figures cover only corporations; profits of unincorporated enterprises are included under heading II.

In the U.S. moreover, direct taxes of enterprises have risen sharply during the period and now account for more than one-half of total profits. As a result, net profit after tax accounted for only 5·2 per cent. of the national income of the U.S. in 1953 and was less than one-third of the corresponding Chilean figure of 16·8 per cent. In the U.S. moreover, a higher proportion

[1] The fact that the U.S. figures refer only to corporation profits whereas the Chilean figures refer to the profits of both corporate and unincorporated enterprises does not really disturb the comparability of the figures if account is taken of the fact that in the U.S. almost all business, with the exception of farms and professional services, is in the corporate form. Indeed, if the comparison were made in terms of corporate profits only, its value would be vitiated by the difference in the relative role of corporate enterprise in the two countries.

of these profits is retained, so that the share of dividends (or distributed profits) in the national income is nearly five times as high in Chile as in the U.S.

Much the same picture emerges from a comparison of the relative shares of work and property in Chile and Great Britain, as shown in Table 6. Since the proportion of wage and salary earners is considerably greater in Great Britain than in Chile

Table 6

DISTRIBUTION OF GROSS NATIONAL PRODUCT AT FACTOR COST BY KIND OF INCOME IN CHILE AND GREAT BRITAIN

(*As a percentage of gross national product*)

Kind of income	1948		1953	
	Chile	United Kingdom	Chile	United Kingdom
Wages	20·9	42·6	19·3	40·9
Salaries	14·6	20·4	18·3	20·8
Employers contribution ..	3·0	3·4	3·8	3·9
Total income from employment ..	38·5	66·4	41·4	65·5
Income from self-employment	20·4	13·0	22·9	10·7
Gross profits, interest and rent	41·1	20·6	35·7	23·8
Total	100·0	100·0	100·0	100·0

Source.—Chile, C.O.R.F.O. United Kingdom, *National Income and Expenditure*, H.M.S.O., 1956.

the percentage differences in wage and salary income tend to overstate the true differences in income distribution. In comparing the share of salaries in the two countries it should be borne in mind that the ratio of salary earners to wage earners is less than 1 : 5 in Chile as against 1 : 3 in Britain. The figures thus indicate considerably greater differences between wages per head and salaries per head in Chile. The most significant difference, .however, is the considerably greater share of property income of all kinds in Chile than in Britain.[1]

[1] The difference is shown to have been greater in 1948 than in 1953, which is partly the result of a fall in the share of property income in Chile and partly the result of a rise in the share of property income in Britain. This would appear to contradict the statement made earlier that in the countries of Western Europe the post-war period was characterised by a marked tendency towards greater equality. As compared with the pre-war situation in Britain this is undoubtedly true (particularly if the changes in taxation are taken into account) but the changes as between 1948 and 1953 were affected by the replacement of the Labour Government with the Conservative Administration in 1951, and the more liberal policies followed towards dividend distribution, etc., since that time.

Thus, whether we choose the United States or the United Kingdom as the basis of comparison, it is evident that the share of profits in the national income of Chile is relatively high. Normally this indicates a high share of savings and investment in the national income since in all countries the ploughing-back of profits provides the main source of finance of business investment. In the case of Chile, however, this has not been the case. The share of investment in the gross national income, measured by any standard, has remained remarkably low whilst the share of personal consumption has been unusually large.

2. The Allocation of Resources

The estimates relating to the distribution of the national expenditure between private and public consumption, domestic investment in fixed investment and in stocks and foreign investment are shown in Table 7.[1] This shows that during the period under review there has been an appreciable rise in the proportion of resources devoted to the current expenditure of Government (from 8·6 to 12·1 per cent.) whilst the proportion of resources devoted to personal consumption has shown only a very slight fall from 79·8 to 79·1 per cent. Gross investment and gross investment in fixed capital remained constant. They rose slightly up to 1946–8 and then fell back again to their initial levels of around 10 per cent. and 9 per cent. respectively. The rising proportion of Government consumption was offset by a corresponding change in the balance of imports and exports, largely reflecting, not a deterioration in the balance of payments, but a reduction of income payments to foreign owners. Private investment in fixed capital showed a marked improvement between 1940–2 and 1946–8 but fell appreciably between that period and 1952–4. The middle of our three periods represents therefore a peak in capital accumulation, at least as far as private investment is concerned. Net investment in fixed capital (deducting depreciation measured in terms of current replacement costs) is estimated,

---

[1] In Table 7 and subsequent tables triennial averages (for the periods 1940–2, 1946–8 and 1952–4) were chosen for comparison rather than the particular years, 1940, 1948 and 1954. It was found that the figures relating to individual years showed so many erratic variations that in order to get a more reliable picture of long term trends it was necessary to make comparisons between triennial averages.

Table 7

CHILE: COMPOSITION OF GROSS NATIONAL EXPENDITURE

(*Annual averages*)

Period	Expenditure on consumer goods			Total gross investment			Gross national expenditure	Net sales abroad	Gross national product
	Total	Public sector	Private sector	Total	Gross fixed investment[1]	Changes in stocks			
	(*Thousands of pesos at 1950 prices*)								
1940-2 ..	98,492	9,556	88,936	10,907	10,393	514	109,399	2,031	111,430
1946-8 ..	119,626	13,759	105,867	15,550	14,139	1,411	135,176	5,191	140,367
1952-4 ..	161,971	21,448	140,523	17,315	16,672	553	179,286	−1,681	177,600
	(*Percentage break-down of total real gross national product*)								
1940-2 ..	88·4	8·6	79·8	9·8	9·3	0·5	98·2	1·8	100·0
1946-8 ..	85·2	9·8	75·4	11·1	10·0	1·0	96·3	3·7	100·0
1952-4 ..	91·2	12·1	79·1	9·7	9·4	0·3	100·9	−0·9	100·0

Source.—C.O.R.F.O.
1 Gross investment in fixed capital is made up of investment by the public and investment by the private sector, as follows:

	Public sector	Private sector	Total
1940-2	6,559	3,834	10,393
1946-8	5,278	8,861	14,139
1952-4	9,074	7,688	16,762
	Percentage of gross product		
1940-2	5·9	3·4	9·3
1946-8	3·8	6·2	10·0
1952-4	5·1	4·3	9·4

as is seen from a comparison of the figures in Table 6 with those in Table 10, at the surprisingly low figure of 200 million pesos in 1940–2, at 3,000 million pesos in 1946–8 and at 2,500 million pesos in 1952–4 (all expressed in terms of 1950 prices) which was the equivalent of 0·2 per cent., 2·3 per cent. and 1·5 per cent. respectively of the net national product of these three periods.[1]

Tables 8 and 9 give details concerning the changes in the composition of internal investment. Table 8 shows that the proportion of imported capital goods in the total domestic investment in fixed capital remained constant throughout the period at around 40 per cent. of fixed capital expenditure. This makes it probable that the movement of fixed capital expenditure in individual sectors of the economy corresponded fairly closely to the movement of capital goods imports by those sectors. Table 9 which shows the changes in the imports of capital goods by the various sectors of the economy in terms of constant prices may therefore be regarded as a fair indication of the trend in fixed capital investment.

3. The Sources of Savings

Table 10 relating to the sources of savings throws some further light on the causes of the growing scarcity of investible resources. It shows that the two positive sources of national savings through the period have been the undistributed profits and depreciation allowances of enterprises and the current surpluses on the consolidated account of public authorities. The net surplus in the

[1] I understand that the estimates of depreciation are the result of a very extensive investigation of the physical assets and the current replacement costs of enterprises, and the depreciation allowances were calculated by taking the useful life of each particular asset on the basis of American data, but with due allowance for the fact that assets are used for a considerably longer period in Chile (e.g. in the case of housing of various types, the lifetimes assumed varied between 50 and 80 years as against a corresponding U.S. figure of 30 to 50 years). The resulting estimate (amounting to 8·2 per cent. of the gross national product in 1952-4) may appear somewhat high if compared with countries like the U.S. or U.K. where the amount of capital employed in relation to output is probably greater, (the comparable figure in the U.K. is 9·5 per cent. and in the U.S. around 10 to 12 per cent.) but any exaggeration in the figure is unlikely to exceed 1 to 2 per cent. of the gross national product. Even if the depreciation allowances were thus adjusted, net investment in fixed capital would still appear very low in relation to corresponding figures in the U.S. and in Western European countries. For the year 1953, the corresponding figures were: Norway 21 per cent., Western Germany 14 per cent., Italy 12 per cent., Turkey 9 per cent., France 7 per cent., Belgium and the U.K. 6 per cent., U.S.A. 7·6 per cent. (*Economic Survey of Europe in 1955*, E.C.E., Table 22, p. 44 and *Economic Report to the President*, U.S.A., January 1956).

Table 8

CHILE: COMPOSITION OF GROSS INTERNAL INVESTMENT, 1940–2, 1947–9 AND 1951–3

(*Thousands of millions of pesos at 1950 prices*)

	1940–2	1946–8	1952–4
Machinery and Equipment	4·3	5·3	7·0
Imported capital goods	3·9	4·9	6·6
Domestically-produced capital goods ..	0·4	0·4	0·4
Construction and other similar activities	6·1	8·8	9·7
Improvements	0·1	0·2	0·5
Building	5·2	7·1	7·0
Housing	3·6	5·2	5·4
Commercial and industrial buildings ..	0·9	1·4	1·0
Public buildings	0·5	0·2	0·1
Other branches of construction	—	0·1	0·2
Urbanisation and paving	0·2	0·2	0·3
Public works	0·8	1·4	2·0
Afforestation	0·0	0·1	0·2
Domestic investment in fixed capital	10·4	14·1	16·7
Changes in stocks	0·5	1·4	0·6
Gross internal investment	10·9	15·5	17·3

Source.—C.O.R.F.O.

Table 9

CHILE: CAPITAL GOODS IMPORTS

	1940–1942	1946–1948	1952–1954	1940–1942	1946–1948	1952–1954
	(Thousands of millions of pesos at 1950 prices)			(Indices)		
Special machinery for industry	0·8	1·4	1·5	100·0	186·7	200·0
Pumps, pumping equipment, engines and turbines ..	0·3	0·3	0·5	100·0	100·0	203·9
Miscellaneous machinery and equipment for general purposes	0·2	0·3	0·3	100·0	145·8	150·0
Machinery for mining ..	0·1	0·1	0·2	100·0	78·5	205·8
Tractors and agricultural machinery and equipment	0·3	0·2	0·5	100·0	66·6	189·8
Electrical apparatus and equipment	0·5	0·6	0·6	100·0	120·0	115·7
Tools, and scientific, professional and office equipment	0·2	0·2	0·3	100·0	103·7	142·8
Durable containers, durable equipment and miscellaneous accessories	0·5	0·3	0·4	100·0	60·0	77·9
Vehicles and transport equipment	1·0	1·3	1·5	100·0	130·0	150·0
Total	3·9	4·8	5·8	100·0	125·4	151·5

Source.—C.O.R.F.O.

accounts of the public authorities (which was largely the result of the surplus of the Cajas de Previsión and only to a small extent an excess of ordinary revenue over ordinary expenditure of the Central Government) only provided finance, however, for a certain proportion of public investment. As shown by Table 11, the proportion of public investment financed by public savings, which was around 40 per cent. in 1940–2, had fallen to around 9 per cent. in the period 1952–4.[1] The public sector has become therefore far more dependent in recent years on private savings for the financing of its activities. At the same time the estimates show a corresponding increase in private savings due not so much to the total savings of enterprises as to the fall in the net dissavings on personal account, which show a remarkable reduction between 1946–8 and 1952–4. The item for net personal savings has been arrived at as a residual (the difference between the estimates of personal income and expenditure) and must thus be subject to very considerable margins of error both as to magnitude and in the movement from year to year.[2] In so far as any

[1] The main source of surpluses on public account is to be found in the fact that in Chile the social security institutions accumulate funds with respect to future pension liabilities. Though the principle of charging contributions on an actuarial basis in the case of compulsory national insurance schemes is a questionable one, this practice might nevertheless have made a valuable contribution to monetary stability (and to the promotion of industrial investment) if the Cajas de Previsión had followed the policy pursued by Britain and other European countries of not utilising their savings for the purpose of direct investment. The Cajas de Previsión are anxious, however, in order to protect their funds from inflation, to utilise their surpluses in direct investment; and since these investments have been limited to particular fields which were considered appropriately safe (mostly in housing) the surpluses on social security account did not serve to relieve the strain on the rest of the economy, but merely led to an increase in particular forms of investment which would not otherwise have received the same priority. Furthermore, a considerable part of the houses built by the Cajas de Previsión were not retained by them but sold to members who financed their purchases with mortgage loans made to them by the Cajas. To the extent that this happened the policy of investing the surpluses in houses did not even have the merit of preserving the real value of the savings as a fund for future pension contributions; and the whole policy of levying compulsory contributions on the mass of wage and salary earners and consumers generally in excess of the current benefits disbursed in order to provide favoured members of these institutions with houses for which payment was only made in depreciated currency, is one of doubtful social justification. I understand, however, that in the last few years the Cajas de Previsión have abandoned the idea of calculating the contributions on an actuarial basis and are gradually changing over to a system where the current payments are financed by current contributions and not out of accumulated past funds.

[2] The reduction in private dis-savings shown in Table 10 between 1946–8 and 1952–4 from 4·3 thousand million to 1·9 thousand million pesos at 1950 prices, at the same time as the proportion of personal consumption expenditure increased in the gross national product, can be traced to the fact that the personal disposable income between these two periods rose in relation to the net internal product from 75·4 to 79·1 per cent., as a result of a reduction of the amount of income payable

Table 10

CHILE: STRUCTURE OF GROSS INTERNAL SAVINGS

(*Thousands of millions of pesos at 1950 prices*)

	1940–2	1947–9	1951–3
	Annual averages		
Private national savings	5·2	10·7	15·1
Non-profit-making individuals and institutions	−7·6	−4·3	−1·9
Enterprises	12·8	15·0	17·0
Undistributed profits	5·4	8·3	12·4
Revaluation of stocks	−4·9	−6·1	−12·6
Reserves for depreciation	10·2	11·2	14·3
Indemnification of accidental damage to fixed assets	0·1	0·2	0·2
Statistical discrepancy	2·0	1·4	2·7
Government saving	4·7	4·1	1·4
Gross national savings	9·9	14·8	16·5
Net Chilean dis-savings abroad	1·0	0·7	0·8
Gross internal savings	10·9	15·5	17·3
(Gross internal savings = gross internal investment)			

Source.—C.O.R.F.O.

Table 11

CHILE: PUBLIC INVESTMENT AND SAVINGS

(*In millions of pesos*)

	Yearly averages		
	1940–2	1946–8	1952–4
Public investment	2,784·2	9,727·9	34,626·4
Surplus of revenue on current account ..	1,206·3	2,730·7	2,978·4
Excess of public investment over public savings	1,577·9	6,997·2	31,648·0
Proportion of public investment financed by public savings	43·3	28·1	8·6

Source.—C.O.R.F.O.

conclusion can be drawn from this estimate it indicates that the personal expenditure financed out of capital gains or out of accumulated past savings must have exceeded by some considerable

abroad. Thus, in terms of the gross internal income, there was a reduction in national savings from 10·5 per cent. to 9·3 per cent. during the period, whereas in terms of the gross national income the proportion of savings remained constant at 9·3 per cent. The rise in private savings between 1946–8 and 1952–4 was thus partly the result of the smaller incidence of personal taxation and partly a reflection of the fact that a greater part of internally produced profits had been received by residents.

margin the net savings of individuals financed out of their personal incomes throughout the period.

Apart from net capital imports (which, as Table 7 shows, was a negligible item throughout) the system thus relied entirely on the savings of enterprises to finance both a rising proportion of public investment and the dis-savings out of personal incomes. As Table 10 shows, however, much the greater part of the savings of enterprises consisted of the depreciation allowances so that net savings of the community (after deduction of that part of the savings which merely represented the increase in the value of inventories due to the inflation) remained very small. We have already seen from Table 3 that the percentage of net undistributed profits in total net profits was remarkably low in Chile throughout the period; companies tended to distribute much the greater part of their increase in earnings. As Table 10 shows, even after increasing the estimate of undistributed profits by the very considerable item of statistical discrepancy, depreciation allowances took up no less than four-fifths of the gross savings of enterprises throughout the period.

The extremely low estimates of national savings, despite the high ratio of both profits and dividends to the national income, are thus to be explained by the high propensity to consume of the capitalist classes. Whilst the share of dividends in profits was very high, and the rise in dividends over the last fifteen years equalled or exceeded the rise in profits, the personal expenditure of the recipients tended to exceed their dividend income.

4. *The Burden of Taxation*

While current Government expenditure on goods and services increased appreciably between 1946–8 and 1952–4 (from 9·8 per cent. to 12·1 per cent. of the gross internal product) the proportion of income paid in taxation fell at the same time from 17·1 per cent. to 15·6 per cent., as shown in Table 12. In this table an attempt has been made to allocate both direct and indirect taxes between the three major income categories. Although the allocation has necessarily been based on broad assumptions (explained in detail in the Appendix) the possible range of error in the figures is not likely to be very large.[1] The estimates show the increasing inadequacy of the general level of taxation in relation to Government expenditures as well as the fall in the relative importance of direct as against indirect taxation —a phenomenon which is entirely explained by the reduction of the proportion of property income (profits, interest and rent) paid in direct taxation. Since the nominal rates of taxation were raised, and not lowered, during the period, this reduction

Table 12

CHILE: THE BURDEN OF TAXATION AS A PERCENTAGE OF INCOME, BY INCOME CATEGORIES

Income categories	1948			1952–4 (Average)		
	Direct taxes[1]	Indirect taxes[2]	Total	Direct taxes	Indirect taxes	Total
Personal income of wage and salary earners[3]	5·0	12·6	17·6	4·0	11·2	16·2
Income of self-employed ..	0·7	13·1	13·8	0·5	11·9	12·4
Profits interest and rent[4] ..	11·2	8·7	19·9	8·8	8·5	17·3
Net national income and stock appreciation plus transfer payments ..	6·4	10·7	17·1	5·3	10·3	15·6

Source.—C.O.R.F.O. For methods of estimation, see Appendix.

[1] Direct taxes on persons and enterprises and social insurance contributions paid by workers and employees.

[2] Indirect taxes and insurance contributions paid by employers, *less* subsidies and transfers to enterprises.

[3] Including public grants to persons under social insurance schemes, etc.

[4] The definition of profits in this table corresponds to the definition of taxable profits—i.e. includes stock appreciation and excludes depreciation.

reflects the growing inability of the tax administration to enforce the taxation of profits, as well as the fact that owing to the inflation and the absence of any revaluation of agricultural and urban properties the taxation of both agricultural and urban rents and taxation of agricultural incomes generally has gradually been reduced to insignificant amounts. Taking into account both the rates of taxation on the cedular income tax and the global tax, as well as the tax of corporate profits, the average rate of

[1] Estimates of the distribution of the tax burden were made after consultation with the experts of the Chilean Ministry of Finance. Of indirect taxation, 48 per cent. was assigned to salaries and wages, 24 per cent. to entrepreneurs' earnings and 28 per cent. to income from property; and of direct taxation, 50 per cent. to salaries and wages, 10 per cent. to entrepreneurs' earnings and 40 per cent. to income from property.

taxation on property incomes in the period 1952–4 should have been at least 40 per cent., and if the property tax had been assessed on current values it should have amounted to 45 per cent. of incomes or even more. The effective rate of 8·8 per cent. would indicate therefore that the tax administration only succeeded in bringing into assessment about one-fifth or less of the incomes liable to tax.

Though the percentage of incomes payable in direct taxes is nearly twice as high in the categories of profits, interest and rent as in the category of wage and salary earners, this is offset by the higher percentage of income payable in indirect taxes, so that the total tax burden is practically the same in the case of the income of wage and salary earners as of property owners. This is a reflection not so much of the inadequate weight given to direct taxes in the system of taxation or of the insufficient rate of progression in direct taxation (the nominal rate of progression of income taxes, taking the global tax into account, is almost as high as in the United States or in Western European countries) as of the extent of income tax evasion on profits and property incomes generally.

5. *The Distribution of Consumption*

In Table 13 an attempt is made to allocate the share of taxation, savings and consumption in the gross national income between three categories of income receivers. This estimate involved additional assumptions as to the allocation of savings, and the most reasonable assumption appeared to be to take the net savings of wage and salary earners as zero; to assume that the net savings of self-employed is 5 per cent. of their income or less, and to credit property owners with most of the savings of enterprises, as well as the net personal dis-savings, since the latter must mainly be a reflection of personal expenditure financed out of capital gains or other speculative gains that are outside the definition of "income."

It is seen that after crediting property owners with most of the net savings of the community and after deducting direct taxation on property incomes (both corporate incomes and personal incomes) as well as the appropriate share of indirect taxation,

Table 13

CHILE: ALLOCATIONS OF GROSS NATIONAL INCOME AND
EXPENDITURE BY KINDS OF INCOMES

(*In percentages of gross national income*)

Kinds of incomes	Average 1952–4			
	Income shares	Taxation[1]	Gross private savings[2]	Personal consumption expenditure at factor cost
Personal income of wage and salary earners[3] ..	44·2	7·4	0	36·8
Income of self-employed ..	21·4	2·6	1·0	17·8
Profits, interest and rent[4] ..	34·4	5·7	7·5	21·2
Gross national income and transfer payments ..	100·0	15·7	8·5	75·8

Source.—C.O.R.F.O. For methods of calculation see Appendix.

[1] Includes direct taxes, indirect taxes (net of subsidies and transfers to enterprises) and social insurance contributions.

[2] The sum of net savings and depreciation allowances.

[3] Including public grants to persons under social insurance schemes, etc.

[4] Includes distributed and undistributed profits and depreciation allowances; excludes stock appreciation.

the residual item representing the personal consumption of property owners still amounted to more than 20 per cent. of the gross national product. Given the well-known fact that there is a high degree of concentration in the ownership of property, the estimate lends statistical support to the view that "unnecessary" consumption or luxury consumption takes up an altogether disproportionate share of Chile's national resources.

The best evidence that could be adduced in support of this contention is a comparison of the position of Chile with regard to taxation, savings and consumption (as revealed in Tables 12 and 13) with the position of Great Britain as shown in Table 14.[1]

[1] The United Kingdom estimates relating to 1953 were drawn up on analogous definitions to the Chilean figures. The slight differences in the percentage distribution of incomes shown on Table B as compared with Table A of Table 14 are due to the inclusion of transfer payments which affects both the categories of wages and salaries and the category of profit, interest and rent, the latter through the inclusion of interest paid on the public debt.

The distribution of savings between income groups has been allocated on the basis of data on the institutional savings of wage and salary earners and data on the net increase of assets by individuals and partnerships (the category of self-employed) as well as the undistributed profits and depreciation allowances of companies and public corporations. The excess of institutional savings over net personal savings has been assumed to represent the dis-savings out of personal income of property owners. Hence the gross private savings out of gross property income, shown at 6·9 per cent. of the gross national income in the table, are made up of corporate savings which represent around 10 per cent. of gross national income, and personal dis-savings of around 3 per cent.

It is seen that the burden of taxation in the United Kingdom was more than twice as high as in Chile, and whilst indirect taxes are relatively almost as heavy and are equally regressive in their incidence, this is more than balanced by the heavy progression of direct taxation. Whilst the direct taxation of wage and salary earners as a percentage of income is not much different in the two countries, the percentage of gross property income paid in direct taxation is over four times as large—40·9 per cent. instead of 8·8 per cent.—as a result of which the total burden of taxation on property income at 51·2 per cent. is appreciably larger than that of the other income categories.

Table 14

UNITED KINGDOM: TAXATION, SAVING AND CONSUMPTION BY INCOME CATEGORIES, 1953

(Percentages)

A. The burden of taxation by income categories

	Income shares	Direct taxes	Indirect taxes	Total taxes
Personal income of wage and salary earners	68·7	7·6	18·9	26·5
Income of self-employed	9·6	14·2	17·3	31·5
Net profits, interest and rent ..	21·7	40·9	10·3	51·2
Net national income including stock appreciation and transfer payments	100·0	15·4	16·9	32·3

B. Allocation of gross national income and expenditure by kinds of incomes

	Income shares	Taxation	Gross private savings	Personal consumption expenditure at factor cost
Personal income of wage and salary earners	65·4	17·4	5·3	42·7
Income of self-employed	9·8	2·9	1·4	5·5
Gross profit, interest and rent ..	24·8	10·5	6·9	7·4
Gross national income excluding stock appreciation and transfer payments	100·0	30·8	13·6	55·6

Source.—*National Income and Expenditure, 1956*, H.M.S.O., London.

Note.—The definitions of the various categories of income in this table are identical with those in Tables 12 and 13. In Table A (as in Table 12) profits include stock appreciation but exclude depreciation and initial allowances (so as to reflect taxable income); in Table B (as in Table 13) depreciation is included and stock appreciation excluded. In both tables the profits of public corporations and enterprises, and interest paid on public debt are included in property incomes.

The most important difference, however, is that whilst in Chile the personal consumption of property owners appears to take up 21·2 per cent. of national resources, in Great Britain it appears to take up only 7·4 per cent. Since in Britain the category of property owners includes a relatively large number of small rentiers[1] (which does not appear to be the case in Chile) the implication is that the proportion of national resources engaged in producing goods and services for the luxury consumption of the well-to-do is at least three to four times as high in Chile as in Britain.[2]

These differences are only partly to be explained by the fact that the share of property income in total income is so much larger in Chile than in Great Britain. A quantitatively more important cause is seen in the fact that the proportion of gross property income allocated to personal consumption is only 30 per cent. in Britain whilst it is over 60 per cent. in Chile. British property owners, in addition to paying 42 per cent. of their gross incomes in taxation, save (on balance) a further 27·4 per cent., whereas Chilean property owners who pay only 16·5 per cent. in taxation, save only 22 per cent. Or, starting from the gross disposable income after taxation, British property owners appear to have saved 48 per cent. of their post-tax income and spent 52 per cent., whereas the Chileans saved 26 per cent. and spent 74 per cent.[3]

There can be little doubt that with a more efficient system of taxation (including, if necessary, special tax measures or other restraints designed to raise the proportion of profits that are retained by enterprises) it would be perfectly possible in Chile to

[1] On the basis of the distribution of the national capital derived from income tax and death duty statistics, only about one-half of the total of dividend rent and interest income in Britain is derived from large estates.

[2] This result derived from national income statistics is well supported by statistics on occupational distribution. The number of domestic servants in Chile (returned at 284,171 in 1954) is slightly higher in absolute figures than the corresponding figure in Britain, and it represents 9 per cent. of the total occupied population of Chile as against slightly over 1 per cent. in Britain. Moreover, the rise in the number of domestic servants in Chile in the period 1940–54 was 80 per cent. (in relation to a 30 per cent. increase in total employment) whilst in Britain the number has decreased by some 50 per cent. since 1939.

[3] These differences, I presume, reflect not so much differences in the savings and spending propensities of individuals out of personal incomes, but in the proportion of net profits retained by enterprises. As indicated earlier, in Chile the proportion of net profits (after tax) ploughed back was only about 15 per cent. and in the United Kingdom around 60 per cent.

reduce the proportion of property income allocated to personal consumption to a figure nearer to that obtaining in Britain.

If the proportion of consumption in gross property income were reduced to the United Kingdom percentage of 30 per cent., the personal consumption of property owners would fall from 21·2 per cent. to 10·3 per cent. of national resources; and the resources thereby released would be more than adequate to double the rate of gross investment in fixed capital and in stocks—which means, in accordance with the official estimates, an increase in the rate of net investment from some 2 per cent. to 14 per cent. of the net national income.

These estimates contradict the frequent contention that Chile, owing to its very poverty, is incapable of generating the savings necessary for an accelerated rate of capital formation. For the figures tend to show that if luxury consumption could be reduced to a more modest proportion of the income of property owners, the proportion of savings in the national income could be considerably raised without lowering the standard of living of the mass of the population. It is true that, as Table 8 shows, the import content of investment expenditure is very much greater than the import content of consumption expenditure[1]—although the import content of luxury consumption, allowing for "invisible" imports, may be considerably higher than that of consumption in general, and there are many important ways in which capital expenditure could be stepped up without requiring heavy additional imports, such as irrigation works and road building for example. The need for foreign economic assistance arises not from an insufficient capacity to save, but from the higher import requirements associated with the shift in the pattern of national expenditure, and these could only amount to a proportion of the finance required for additional investment. Moreover, the resources set free through the reduction in domestic consumption would be available for the development of export capacity out of which additional imports could be financed. This could of course also require foreign assistance over an initial period (as, for example, for the establishment of additional pulp or cellulose

[1] According to official figures the import content of investment expenditure was 42 per cent. in 1952–4 and of total consumption expenditure only 6 per cent.

mills) but once the growth of these industries provides the necessary addition to foreign income, the higher rate of investment could fully be financed out of internal savings.

Whether such an increase in internal savings and in the rate of capital investment is feasible or not is very largely a question of the possibility of imposing more effective taxation on the well-to-do classes of the community.[1] An increase in taxation relative to Government expenditure means, of course, a supplement to national savings through larger public savings—irrespective of how the taxes are raised. But it is not a matter of indifference, even from a purely economic point of view, in what manner the additional taxes are imposed and on whom their ultimate incidence falls. If the taxes imposed fall directly on the mass of the consumers, or if their incidence were shifted indirectly on to the mass of the consumers through higher prices and profit margins, additional savings through taxation could only be obtained at the cost of aggravating the inflationary forces—since the reduction in real earnings brought about through higher taxation would lead to further demands for increases in money wages and thus accelerate the wage-price spiral in much the same way as a reduction in real earnings brought about through a rise in prices. This is merely an aspect of the more fundamental proposition that additional resources can only be drawn from sources where a true surplus exists. Taxes levied on the well-to-do, and whose incidence is not shifted on to others, provide additional resources precisely because they compress that part of the claim on national resources which does not serve the maintenance or improvement of production; and which therefore could be compressed without untoward effects on social and economic stability or on economic incentives.

6. *Summary and Conclusions*

We may now attempt to sum up the conclusions which emerge from the above analysis of Chilean economic trends in the period 1940 to 1954:

---

[1] This of course is a political, and not only narrowly economic question; but the present analysis is entirely confined to an examination of the economic and technical, rather than of the political, possibilities.

(1) There has been a spectacular growth in industrial production during the period, though the growth of production and productivity was considerably less in the later part of the period than in the earlier part. The expansion of industry appears to have been concentrated more on the development of import substitutes than on the development of export capacity—as is shown, for example, by the stagnation in mining production (despite favourable opportunities in the world market) or by the lack of adequate expansion in potential export industries, like cellulose and pulp.

(2) The growth in tertiary services (commerce, Government and personal services) as shown by the growth in the numbers employed in these categories, was disproportionately large in relation to the growth in primary and secondary industries (including transport and communications and public utilities).

(3) The figures reveal a more fundamental disproportionality between the growth of food production and the growth of production (and employment) in the non-agricultural sectors of the economy. Agricultural output is estimated to have increased by 40 per cent. over the period but a considerable part of this increase reflects the change in the internal terms of trade in favour of the agricultural sector. The physical index of food production showed an increase of only 27 per cent., much the greater part of which occurred prior to 1946–8. Hence, for the period as a whole, and particularly for the period since 1946–8, the growth in food production has failed to keep pace with the increase in population, without any allowance for the increased food consumption that is normally associated with the increase in real incomes per head. Nor could the growth of marketable food supplies have kept pace with the growth in demand coming from the non-agricultural sectors. Between 1940 and 1954 the numbers occupied in the non-agricultural sectors of the economy increased by 65 per cent. Real incomes per head—i.e. money incomes in terms of a constant price level—increased by 30

cent. Hence, even if the income elasticity of demand for food were put at no higher than one-half—an estimate which is almost certainly on the conservative side—the potential demand for food by the non-agricultural sectors would show a corresponding increase of $1 \cdot 65 \times 1 \cdot 15$, i.e. by 90 per cent. If we made the extreme assumption that the food consumption in the agricultural sector itself remained constant despite higher outputs and incomes per head, internal food availabilities to the non-agricultural sectors could only have shown an increase of around 50 per cent. It is, however, impossible to assume that the income elasticity of demand for food within an agricultural sector itself is zero; and if we made the same assumption of income elasticity of demand here as in the rest of the economy, the increase of internally produced food supplies to the non-agricultural sectors would only amount to $33\frac{1}{3}$ per cent. The gap was filled (partially at any rate) by food imports which rose from U.S. $11 millions in 1940 to U.S. $70 millions in 1954 in terms of current dollars (or from 11 millions to 41 millions in terms of constant 1940 dollars). For reasons further examined below, food imports may not have been sufficient, however, to cover the food requirements which a more reasonable income distribution would have required, and which would have been the precondition to more stable monetary conditions. It must be borne in mind that food represents "wage goods" *par excellence*—i.e. the proportion of working-class incomes spent on food is both very large in itself and very much greater than the proportion of non-working-class incomes spent on food. This means that if food availabilities per head are given, real wages are also largely determined: since the working classes, through their desire to spend their incomes so largely on food in preference to other things, necessarily cause a price-wage relationship to be established, in which their wages, in real terms, become closely linked to, and can exceed only by a moderate amount, the food availabilities per head, irrespective of the increase in the availability of other kinds of goods and services.

(4) The distribution of income has tended to become more unequal, at least in the sense that while productivity and real income per head have been rising, the wage earners failed to participate. Though output per head increased by some 30 per cent. in the period, real earnings per worker remained practically unchanged, whilst the real incomes of the other groups increased more than in proportion to the increase in income per head. For reasons suggested above and which will be further examined below, these changes might themselves have been the result of the disproportionality between the growth in food production and the increase in other kinds of goods and services.

(5) Despite the growth of profits (by 56 per cent. in real terms excluding stock appreciation), there has been no increase in the proportion of savings and gross investment in the national income; and the volume of investment in fixed capital by the private sector has actually declined after 1946–8. Net investment in fixed capital has remained extremely low and, even after allowing for a possible overestimate in current depreciation allowances, could not have amounted to more than 3 to 4 per cent. of the net national income; it has tended to decline moreover after 1946–8, and the decline in private net investment in fixed capital has been considerably greater than the decline in total net investment.

(6) The reason for this is to be found in the high propensity to consume of the capitalist class who appear to have spent on personal consumption more than two-thirds of their gross income, or three-quarters of their net income after tax. In comparison with other countries, the luxury consumption of the property-owning classes appears to take up an altogether disproportionate share of the national resources, part of which would be automatically released for investment purposes if a more efficient system of progressive taxation were introduced and/or if effective measures were taken to encourage the retention of profits by enterprises. Though a higher rate of investment is a

matter of foreign exchange and not just of savings, it appears from the estimates that as far as savings are concerned (i.e. ignoring the balance of payments consequences of a higher rate of accumulation), the latent resources which could be mobilised through a reduction in luxury consumption would provide adequate resources to raise the rate of capital accumulation in Chile to a level comparable to that of the advanced industrial economies.

II. THE PROBLEM OF INFLATION

We may now turn to the specific problem which has been in the forefront of all discussions concerning the Chilean economy —the problem of monetary instability. Chile has experienced a continuing inflation for a longer period than almost any country in the world. The peculiarity of the Chilean inflation has been that while prices have been rising at a fast rate (20 to 30 per cent. per annum on the average during the last fifteen years—with a higher average rate during the last five years than in the previous ten years), she did not experience that continued acceleration of inflationary forces which, in the case of other countries which have undergone a major inflation (as, for example, Germany after the First World War, Hungary or Greece after the Second World War) brought the whole process to an end within a relatively short period through the complete collapse of the currency. The Chilean inflation has never developed into that state of super inflation where the flight from currency became so great that the rise in prices lost all relation to the increase in monetary circulation. Tables 15 and 16 show that the rate of increase in prices has not by any means shown a steadily continuing acceleration. Years of rapid inflation were sometimes followed by years of relatively moderate price increases without the process ever coming to a complete halt—at any rate during the period covered by these tables.

Indeed, considering the persistence and rapidity with which money has been losing its value the confidence of the public in the currency (at any rate up to 1949) was remarkably well maintained. The best evidence of this is the data in Table 16 showing the comparative annual percentage increases in the amount of the monetary media in circulation, in prices and in the money value of the gross national product at current prices. The inevitable manifestation of impaired confidence in the future of the currency is that individuals and enterprises reduce the amount of monetary balances held in relation to their incomes and expenditures. This is indicated by a fall in the relationship between the amount of currency in circulation and the aggregate volume of monetary payments, which in turn is closely linked to the money value of the gross national product. As Table 15 shows, whilst prices rose more than four-fold in the nine years

Table 15

CHILE: PRICES AND MEANS OF PAYMENT

Year	Means of payment (Millions of pesos)	Means of payment	Gross national product at current prices	Wholesale prices	Cost of living	Means of payment as a percentage of gross national product
			(Indices: 1940 = 100)			
1940–1	3,172	100·0	100·0	100·0	100·0	0·15
1941–2	3,850	121·4	123·1	115·5	100·9	0·15
1942–3	4,593	144·8	144·5	157·2	144·7	0·15
1943–4	5,851	184·4	184·3	175·6	168·3	0·15
1944–5	6,823	215·0	219·0	185·1	188·0	0·15
1945–6	8,028	253·1	254·2	205·6	204·6	0·15
1946–7	10,005	315·4	316·6	249·0	237·1	0·15
1947–8	12,878	406·0	366·0	316·7	316·7	0·17
1948–9	16,234	511·8	504·0	367·3	373·7	0·15
1949–50	19,659	619·8	608·5	425·8	443·8	0·15
1950–1	20,296	639·8	743·8	508·7	511·1	0·13
1951–2	27,123	855·1	914·3	634·5	624·8	0·14
1952–3	35,701	1,125·5	1,236·3	839·9	763·4	0·14
1953–4	54,160	1,707·4	1,600·6	1,049·8	956·8	0·16
1954–5	77,922	2,456·6	2,865·2	1,776·9	1,648·0	0·13
1955–6	129,367	4,078·4	5,195·1	3,133·8	2,887·1	0·12

Source.—National Statistical and Census Service (*Servicio Nacional de Estadística y Censos*), Banco Central de Chile and Corporación de Fomento de la Producción.

between 1940 and 1949, the rise in the gross national product in current prices kept strictly in step with the rise in monetary circulation; the ratio of monetary media to the gross national product remained constant at 0·15. It was only after 1949 that the national product began to rise faster than the monetary circulation. But here again, the movement was neither spectacular nor continuous; there were years when the ratio was rising again and one particular year, 1953, when the velocity of circulation even fell below its customary level. The flight from the currency therefore did not at any time attain serious dimensions.

In the light of these figures, and of our earlier analysis concerning the movements in production, income distribution, savings, etc., can any conclusions be drawn as to the fundamental cause or causes of this persistent inflationary process?

Table 16

CHILE: MEANS OF PAYMENT, PRICES AND
GROSS NATIONAL PRODUCT
(Annual percentage increases)

Year	Means of payment	Whole-sale prices	Cost of living	Gross national product
1940–1	21·4	15·5	0·9	23·1
1941–2	19·3	36·1	43·4	17·4
1942–3	27·3	11·7	16·3	27·5
1943–4	16·6	5·4	11·7	18·8
1944–5	17·7	11·1	8·8	16·1
1945–6	24·6	21·1	15·9	24·5
1946–7	28·7	27·2	33·6	15·6
1947–8	26·1	16·0	18·0	37·7
1948–9	21·1	15·9	18·8	20·7
1949–50	23·2	19·5	15·2	22·2
1950–1	33·6	24·7	24·2	22·2
1951–2	31·6	32·4	22·2	35·2
1952–3	51·7	25·0	25·3	29·5
1953–4	43·9	69·3	72·2	79·0
1954–5	66·0	76·4	75·2	81·3

Source.—See Table 15.

Can we look upon the monetary and banking authorities as having been the villain of the piece through permitting a continued and rapid increase in the monetary media, or was the monetary system the victim of forces which it was unable to control? Was inflation caused by excessive purchasing power originating from the public sector due to insufficient taxation relative to Government expenditure? Or was it simply a "cost induced" inflation due to the fact that wage and salary earners constantly attempted to secure higher real incomes than they could actually have attained in view of the amount of goods and services available for their use, their efforts being frustrated through the consequent wage-price spiral? Or was inflation simply a self-generated process whereby the forces making for the rise in prices were themselves the result of the expectation, based on prolonged experience, that the rise in prices was bound to go on?

To begin with the last question, it is well known that an inflation which has been going on for some time can generate its own fuel—i.e. the pressure causing prices to rise may originate from nothing more fundamental than the fact that prices have been rising for some time. This is the case when the expectation of continued inflation causes commodity hoarding, which is nothing else but a conversion of liquid balances which are normally held in monetary form into commodity stocks. Businesses and individuals normally keep a certain proportion of their total resources in liquid forms so as to be able to meet unforeseen (or incompletely foreseen) obligations, or to be in a position to take advantage of unexpected opportunities for profitable investment as they occur in time. In normal times such "liquid" balances are held in the form of cash, bank balances or other liquid financial investments. The commodity stocks held, on the other hand, in normal times consist mainly of those geared to the process of production. During a process of inflation an increasing amount of the liquid balances can be expected to be converted into "liquid" commodity stocks that are additional to the working capital geared to the productive or distributive activities of businesses.

Since there is no reason to suppose that the proportion of total resources of either individuals or enterprises which are held in liquid forms *of all kinds* is affected one way or another by the inflation, the reduction in the real value of monetary balances as a proportion of the national income affords an indication at the same time of the extent to which resources have been diverted into commodity hoards. There is a presumption therefore that the reduction in the one indicated the magnitude of the increase in the other. On this test, as we have seen, there is no indication of commodity hoarding in Chile up to 1949; and the extent of the conversion since that date may not have exceeded one-tenth of the balances normally held. It thus appears that whilst commodity hoarding must have aggravated the inflationary pressure during the last six years it cannot have played any significant role before that date, and even in the last six years it does not appear to have assumed major dimensions.

The monetary authorities may undoubtedly be held responsible for not keeping money sufficiently tight during this period to prevent this diversion into commodity hoards altogether. Had they imposed stricter limits on credit, the effective interest rates paid on short-term loans would have risen sufficiently to counteract the desire to switch into commodities.[1]

The fact that money incomes were rising faster than the monetary media in circulation after 1949 thus supports the view that the inflationary forces were aggravated by a certain laxity of credit policy. It would, in my view, be mistaken however to go beyond this and to make monetary and banking policy primarily responsible for the persisting inflationary trend. No doubt if the banks refused to provide credit altogether, and in consequence there had been no increase in monetary circulation at all, the rise in prices would sooner or later have to come to a halt. But if the demand for credit is not speculative in origin, but is merely a consequence of the appreciation in the value of normal working capital caused by a rise in costs, it is idle to expect the banking system to be able to withstand the pressure for more credit —it could only do so at the cost of serious interference in the normal processes of economic circulation or even of a general breakdown of contracts. It would be idle, for example, to charge the banks with the responsibility of preventing increases of money wages by refusing to grant credit to the employers, if the employers themselves regard the adjustment of money wages as fair and reasonable in the light of the rise in the prices of wage-goods that had taken place previously. It would be equally idle to expect

---

[1] Whatever the rate of inflation expected, the hoarding of commodities only appears profitable so long as the rate of interest paid for credit is appreciably lower than the expected rate of increase of prices. In a system where the Central Bank imposes credit limits on the commercial banks, but the commercial banks "auction" this credit to the highest bidder (which automatically happens when credit is granted through discounting bills of exchange and the rate of discount is determined competitively), any tightening of credit automatically causes a rise in the rate of interest; and there is always some rate of interest which is sufficient to balance the expectations of rising prices, whatever is the expected rate of increase of prices. Under a system, however, where the commercial banks themselves allocate the credit available to their favoured customers, it is difficult to ensure merely through the limitation of overall credit limits that the credits granted serve only the normal requirements of businesses and are not diverted into speculative purposes.

the banks to force businesses to reduce their normal requirements of working capital (and thereby force them to reduce the scale of their operations) in order to compensate for a rise in demand that originates from another quarter—for example, from increased spending by the Government. The responsibility of the banking system does not really extend beyond ensuring that the inflation is not aggravated through the abnormal speculative demands arising out of the process of inflation itself.

Our analysis of the movements of the components of the Chilean national income and expenditure does not really support the alternative view according to which the basic cause of inflationary pressure is to be found in excessive investment in fixed capital by businesses or public authorities. On the contrary, the figures indicate that during the very period when the process of inflation considerably accelerated—i.e. after 1947-9— there was no increase in investment in fixed capital. As a proportion of the gross national product, there was an appreciable diminution in fixed capital expenditure. There was an increase in public investment during this period which was partly offset by the diminution in private investment; if there was a reduction in the proportion of public investment financed by public savings there was a corresponding increase in the relationship of private savings to private investment.

The persistence of the inflation cannot in our opinion be adequately explained therefore either in terms of lax credit policies by the banking system or in terms of excessive investment in fixed capital in relation to the propensity to save. The fundamental cause thus appears to have been "cost induced" rather than "demand induced." At the same time, as the national income figures indicate, there was no increase in the proportion of the national income represented by wages and salaries: there was a considerable rise in the share of salaries which was balanced by a corresponding fall in the share of wages. If the maintenance of a constant share in wages and salaries in the national product involved a continuing upward pressure of money wages and salaries, this must fundamentally be due to the fact that the commodities destined for the consumption of wage and salary earners must have formed a *decreasing* share of the gross national product. And this, in my view, has been the fundamental cause of the inflation.

By the normal laws of operation of the economic system, aggregate wage and salary payments can be expected to rise more or less in strict proportion to the rise in the total value of goods and services produced—i.e. to the rise in the gross national product. If at the same time the composition of the national product alters in such a way that "wage goods" (goods which are mainly consumed by wage earners) rise less than proportionately to the total, the process would automatically involve a tendency for the prices of wage goods to rise in relation to the prices of other things, and thereby cancel (wholly or partially) the improvement in real earnings that would otherwise have resulted from the rise in production. There would thus be a tendency for "real wages" in terms of the things the workers consume to fall relatively to "real earnings" measured in terms of the things the workers produce. If the rise in productivity in industry automatically brings about a rise in "real earnings," the consequent rise in the prices of wage goods tends to cancel the effects of the latter on "real wages."

Thus if we assumed that the improvement of productivity was confined to non-agricultural goods and services, and that the wage earners' real demand for food depended only on the level of real income, and was not influenced by the relationship of prices between food and non-food items, the rise in money wage payments would cause, by a series of steps, a sufficient rise in food prices (relatively to both wages and non-food prices) as to offset entirely the increase in real earnings in terms of non-food items.[1]

[1] To illustrate this point let us suppose that output per head outside agriculture increases by 20 per cent., and wage payments per man, when measured either in money or in terms of non-agricultural output, also rise by 20 per cent. Let us suppose that wage earners previously spent two-thirds of their incomes on food; and now, with a 20 per cent. rise in income, they wish to increase their real food consumption by 10 per cent. At constant prices this would involve spending one-third of their additional incomes on food. But if food supplies have *not* increased, food prices will increase by 10 per cent. in consequence (since the food demand coming from non-wage earners may be assumed to be inelastic); this will wipe out one-third of the increase in wages in real terms, and (in accordance with our assumptions) lead to a further increase in food expenditure and food prices by $6\frac{2}{3}$ per cent., and so on. In this way food prices, and the proportion of wage earners' expenditure spent on food, would rise by a series of diminishing steps until the whole improvement in real wages was wiped out, not only in terms of food, but also in terms of other goods. Provided that the wage

As we have shown earlier, the development in Chile during the last fifteen years involved a large increase both in the volume of employment and in output per head in non-agricultural employments without an adequate increase in food supplies. The rise in the demand for food coming from the non-agricultural sectors must therefore have constantly tended to outrun the food availabilities, causing a persistent upward pressure in food prices. This would have been the case even if wages and salaries per head had remained constant in terms of non-agricultural products.

It was the rise in food prices which caused the increase in the demand for higher wages and salaries—in order to restore real wages to the level they had already, if only temporarily, attained —thereby raising the general level of industrial costs and prices. The inflation therefore was "demand induced" as far as agricultural products were concerned; and it was "cost induced" as far as the non-agricultural sectors were concerned.

On this view, the basic cause of the inflation was the disproportionality in the growth of production in the various sectors of the economy. Given the output composition of the gross national product, the inflation could only have been prevented if either (a) the rise in the production and in the incomes generated by the non-agricultural sectors had been slowed down—in which case the growing working population could not have found employment; or (b) the working classes would have been ready to put up with falling real wages without demanding (and obtaining) compensating increases in money wages. As it was, the real wages of workers tended to remain constant and the share of wages in the national income fell. Given the extent of food

earners prefer *some* increase in real food consumption to other things so long as their real income is higher, the pressure of demand on food prices will only cease when real wages have fallen back again to their initial level. This will be the case (under our numerical assumptions) when the rise in food prices has reached 30 per cent., and the proportion of food expenditure in the total expenditure of wage earners has risen from the initial 66⅔ per cent. to 72·22 per cent. At that point the purchase of the same amount of food leaves only sufficient money over for the purchase of as many non-food items as they could buy before the rise in wages had occurred; real income is therefore no higher than before, and the urge to consume food in excess of real food availabilities is eliminated. But long before that point is reached, the fall in real wages would lead to upward adjustments in money wages, and thereby ensure the continuation of the process which would otherwise converge on to a new equilibrium.

availabilities, the inflationary process could not of course prevent a relative deterioration in the position of wage earners. But it was the pressure to counteract the tendency towards this deterioration which must have been the basic force behind the wage-price spiral, and thus of the continued inflationary process.

A certain empirical support for this view is to be found in the tendency to a negative correlation between the variations in inflationary trend and the variations in food production as shown in Table 17. The 25 per cent. increase in food production

Table 17

CHILE: QUANTUM OF PRODUCTION
OF FOODSTUFFS

Year	Indices 1940 = 100	Annual percentage variations
1940	100·0	—
1941	96·9	− 3·1
1942	103·5	5·8
1943	128·3	25·2
1944	112·9	− 12·0
1945	104·2	− 7·7
1946	120·7	15·8
1947	105·9	− 12·3
1948	131·8	24·5
1949	133·0	0·9
1950	123·7	− 7·0
1951	122·8	− 0·7
1952	114·0	− 7·2
1953	131·1	15·0
1954	137·0	4·5

Sources.—See Table 2.

in 1943 (partially reversed in subsequent years) was followed by a distinct slowing down in the rate of inflation in the following two years, and the strong acceleration in the inflationary trend after 1949 coincided with the stagnation of food production after that date. Further support is afforded by the relative movement of agricultural and non-agricultural prices shown in Table 18 which indicates that apart from the depression years in the 1930's, there was a consistent upward trend in the ratio of agricultural to non-agricultural prices. Thus by 1954 food prices had risen by 42 per cent. in relation to the average of all prices (as compared with the pre-war period) which is consistent with our

Table 18

CHILE: AGRICULTURAL RELATIVE PRICES
(1934–8 = 100)

Year	Agricultural index Wholesale (A)	Overall index[1] Wholesale (B)	Relative prices $\dfrac{(A)}{(B)}$
1928 ..	56·1	49·3	113·8
1929 ..	57·4	49·3	116·4
1930 ..	45·7	42·9	106·5
1931 ..	36·2	39·1	92·6
1932 ..	54·9	58·8	93·4
1933 ..	73·6	88·4	83·3
1934 ..	74·4	88·1	84·4
1935 ..	81·9	87·8	93·3
1936 ..	98·9	97·3	101·6
1937 ..	126·4	116·3	108·7
1938 ..	118·5	110·5	107·2
1939 ..	106·4	107·8	98·7
1940 ..	130·1	118·7	109·6
1941 ..	155·4	138·8	112·0
1942 ..	196·6	188·4	104·4
1943 ..	213·2	207·8	102·6
1944 ..	232·2	214·6	108·2
1945 ..	255·2	288·6	111·6
1946 ..	302·6	263·6	114·8
1947 ..	415·6	340·1	122·2
1948 ..	490·9	390·5	125·7
1949 ..	559·0	445·2	125·6
1950 ..	638·4	522·4	122·2
1951 ..	815·0	638·0	119·3
1952 ..	1,116·4	847·3	131·8
1953 ..	1,407·3	1,042·3	135·0
1954 ..	2,325·0	1,635·4	142·2

Source.—Ministry of Agriculture, *La agricultura chilena en el quinquenio 1951–5*, p. 183, based on data supplied by the National Statistical Service.

The formula used for constructing the agricultural commodities index was that of Laspeyres $\dfrac{Pn\ Qo}{Po\ Qo}\ 100$)

Po: 1951–5.

Qo: 1946–50.

The following are the commodities included:

Cereals: wheat, barley, oats, rye, maize and rice;

Pulses: beans, lentils, chick-peas and peas;

Vegetables: all vegetables except onions and garlic, which are considered separately;

Industrial commodities: sunflower, hemp fibre and seed, flax fibre and linseed, and tobacco;

Fruit: the same procedure was adopted as for vegetables. All fruit was considered in the aggregate, and an average price, weighted by *Q pm*, was estimated;

Livestock products: beef, mutton, pork, goat's-flesh, poultry, milk, wool and eggs;

Potatoes; Wine; Apicultural products: wax and honey.

[1] Including imports.

analysis concerning the causes of the fall of real wages in relation to real income per head, given above.[1]

The relative fall in capital accumulation may have been a consequence of the stricter credit conditions imposed by the inflationary process itself; and the limitation in the rate of growth of industrial productivity (which we noted at the beginning) was in turn a consequence of this, as well as of the general adverse effects of inflation on industrial efficiency.

If this analysis is correct, no lasting cure of the inflationary tendencies of Chile can be found either in stricter monetary and credit policies or even in administrative reform which secured more effective taxation of the upper classes. No doubt both monetary policy and fiscal policy could make important contributions towards the attainment of monetary stability. Through stricter credit control the additional inflationary pressure caused by commodity hoarding could be prevented. Through heavier taxation of property owners, resources could be transferred from the production of non-wage consumer goods to investment purposes or developing export capacity, all of which would tend to remedy the disproportionality in commodity availabilities in the long run. But the lasting cure for the inflation can only be found through a more rapid increase in food availabilities— either through a more rapid increase in the productivity of agriculture (which in turn hinges upon the reform of land tenure) or a more liberal policy of importing foodstuffs from abroad.[2]

---

[1] Cf. pp. 272–3 above.

[2] As was noted earlier, the deficiency in domestic food production was increasingly supplemented by food imports during the last fifteen years. Since, however, the food import programme was itself limited to the satisfaction of essential needs which did not take adequate account of the growth in demand resulting from the rise in production, employment and incomes in the non-agricultural sectors, it could only serve to moderate, not cure, the inflationary tendencies.

THE METHOD OF ESTIMATION OF THE DISTRIBUTION OF THE TAX BURDEN AND OF SAVINGS IN CHILE AND GREAT BRITAIN

A. *Chile*

To the figures of the national income on current prices as shown in Table A (i) have been added transfer incomes to persons and depreciation as shown in Table A (ii) to yield the figures of the gross national income plus transfer payments as shown in Table B. It was thought that from the point of view of the division of the national resources, the gross national product is the more relevant concept than the net national product; and at the same time from the point of view of the percentages of income payable in taxation, income including transfer payments is more relevant than the national product.

The taxes have been divided into the following categories: (1) direct taxes on persons; (2) direct taxes on enterprises; (3) social security contributions payable by employees; (4) social security contributions payable by employers; (5) indirect taxes; (6) subsidies; and (7) inheritance taxes. Our method was to treat the employees' contributions as a direct tax whose incidence entirely falls on the payer but the employers' contribution as an indirect tax whose incidence falls on all final consumers in much the same way as the incidence of other indirect taxes. It was assumed that direct taxes on enterprises and inheritance taxes are paid entirely by the recipients of profits, interest and rent. Since social insurance contributions of employees are paid entirely by wage and salary earners this left employers' contributions, indirect taxes and subsidies as well as the direct taxes on persons to be allocated.

Indirect taxes, etc., and subsidies have been allocated in accordance with total consumption expenditure. In the case of direct taxes on persons, the division between the receipts from cedular taxation and the global tax is known, and it was assumed that the global tax is divided between the three categories in the same way as the cedular taxes. The resulting division of taxes and subsidies is shown in Tables D and E. The method of arriving at net subsidies from the accounts of the Government is shown in Table C.

Table F shows the summary results of the total burden of taxation on each of the three income categories and in percentages of the total taxes raised, whilst the burden of taxation according to income categories in percentages (derived from these figures) is given in Table G.

B. Great Britain

The method employed in the United Kingdom to estimate the allocation of the tax burden is described below. Only a brief review is required, since most of its features may be deduced from the tables included in this annex.

The figures for gross national product at factor cost which appear at the end of Table 14 in *National Income and Expenditure, 1956* (H.M.S.O., 1956), were adjusted to include transfer payments. The nature of these adjustments is shown in Table H. Payments in money and in kind made to the Armed Forces and current grants by public authorities were included for the wage and salary earning group while employers' contributions to social security institutions were excluded. In order to obtain the gross income of the property-income group, the following items were added together: rent, dividends and interest paid; undistributed income of companies and public corporations; additions to dividend and interest reserves; and residual error, the stock appreciation being deducted.

The amount of direct taxation was obtained indirectly, by deducting the figures for gross income after payment of taxes from gross income before taxes. The data were collected from the first and second part of Table 8, in *National Income and Expenditure*. It was impossible to obtain information on the proportion of direct taxes paid by the self-employed and that paid by the property income category. To this end, it was assumed that two-thirds of direct taxes were collected from the dividend, interest and rent category and one-third from the self-employed. This is because the two categories happen to have the same total, and the rate of taxation on the self-employed is 22 per cent. lower owing to earned income relief applicable to the self-employed but not to the dividend, interest and rent category.

In the same way as in Chile, the employers' contributions for social insurance were deducted from direct taxation affecting wages and salaries and added as an indirect tax (see Table I).

The total of indirect taxation, less subsidies, was also obtained indirectly, being the difference between personal consumer expenditure at market prices and personal consumer expenditure at factor cost. Such data were taken from Tables 21 and 24, respectively, of *National Income and Expenditure*.

Employers' contributions which, as already explained, have been treated as indirect taxation, were added to total indirect taxes less subsidies (see Table J).

The next problem was to allocate indirect taxation among the three income categories. The criterion adopted was that of allocating indirect taxation according to the consumer expenditure of each income category; this figure was also obtained indirectly, by deducting indirect taxation and savings from the gross income of each category (see Table K). Total savings in turn represented the difference between gross income available, consumer expenditure at market prices and indirect taxes; they were distributed among the three categories according to the figures of Tables 26 and 27 of the national income blue book.

As has already been explained, indirect taxes, less subsidies, plus employers' contributions were distributed proportionally to the volume of consumer expenditure at market prices for each of the three categories (see Table D).

As a result of summarising the operations performed in the tables mentioned above it was possible to prepare Table M of the Appendix, which shows the distribution of gross income, gross expenditure and the tax burden according to income categories. This was the basis of Table 13 of the text.

Table A (i)

CHILE: NATIONAL INCOME AT FACTOR COST

(*Millions of pesos at current prices*)

	1948	1951	1952	1953	1954
Salaries and wages	36,221	70,864	94,844	130,992	221,594
Income of self-employed	19,160	39,217	52,050	68,000	107,364
Property income ..	30,266	43,787	62,133	87,098	136,980
National income at factor cost	85,647	153,868	209,026	286,090	456,938

Source.—C.O.R.F.O.

Table A (ii)

CHILE: ITEMS ADDED TO NATIONAL INCOME AT FACTOR COST
TO OBTAIN GROSS PERSONAL INCOME

(*Millions of pesos*)

	1948	1951	1952	1953	1954
To salaries and wages: transfers to persons ..	3,492	7,471	9,291	14,642	20,352
To property income: depreciation	8,448	15,455	20,044	26,002	42,717

Source.—C.O.R.F.O.

Table B

CHILE: GROSS NATIONAL INCOME AND TRANSFER PAYMENTS, BY INCOME CATEGORIES

	1948	1951	1952	1953	1954
	(Millions of pesos at current prices)				
Salaries and wages ..	39,713	78,335	104,351	145,633	232,946
Income of self-employed	19,160	39,241	52,050	68,000	107,364
Gross property income ..	38,714	59,242	82,177	113,100	179,696
Personal gross income and transfer payments ..	97,587	176,818	238,578	326,733	520,006
	(Percentage composition)				
Salaries and wages ..	40·7	44·3	43·8	44·6	44·8
Income of self-employed	19·6	22·2	21·8	20·8	20·6
Gross property income ..	39·7	33·5	34·4	34·6	34·6
Gross personal income ..	100·0	100·0	100·0	100·0	100·0

Source.—C.O.R.F.O.

Table C

CHILE: ESTIMATES OF NET GOVERNMENT SUBSIDIES AND THEIR DISTRIBUTION

(Millions of pesos)

	1948	1951	1952	1953	1954
I. Total taxation ..	19,434	36,629	50,806	61,340	102,610
II. Current expenditure on goods and services plus surplus on current account	13,660	19,922	29,662	38,880	69,438
III. I minus II: subsidies plus transfer payments	5,773	16,707	21,144	22,460	33,172
IV. Minus: transfers to persons by the *Cajas de Previsión*	2,685	6,050	7,517	9,577	15,649
V. III minus IV: net Government subsidies	3,088	10,657	13,627	12,883	17,523

Source.—C.O.R.F.O.

Table D

CHILE: TOTAL TAX BURDEN AND ITS DISTRIBUTION BY
INCOME CATEGORIES

(*Millions of pesos*)

	1948	1951	1952	1953	1954
Direct taxes on persons ..	1,424	2,728	2,898	4,094	5,660
50 per cent. on salaries and·wages	712	1,364	1,449	2,047	2,830
10 per cent. on income of self-employed ..	142	273	290	409	566
40 per cent. on property income	570	1,091	1,159	1,638	2,264
Employees' and workers' contributions to Cajas de Previsión Social	1,250	2,756	3,419	5,338	9,054
100 per cent. on salaries and wages					
Indirect taxes and other payments	10,780	21,648	30,863	33,373	56,178
48 per cent. on salaries and wages	5,174	10,391	14,814	16,019	26,965
24 per cent. on income of self-employed ..	2,587	5,196	7,407	8,010	13,483
28 per cent. on property income	3,018	6,061	8,642	9,344	15,730
Employers' contributions ..	2,798	5,415	6,456	9,065	18,401
48 per cent. on salaries and wages	1,343	2,599	3,099	4,351	8,832
24 per cent. on income of self-employed ..	672	1,300	1,549	2,176	4,416
28 per cent. on property income	783	1,516	1,808	2,538	5,153
Direct taxes on enterprises ..	3,105	3,774	6,965	6,744	12,892
100 per cent. on property income					
Inheritance and donation taxes	77	307	205	302	425
100 per cent. on property income					
Total direct and indirect taxation	19,434	36,629	50,806	61,340	102,610
Total net Government subsidies	3,088	10,657	13,627	12,883	17,523
48 per cent. on salaries and wages	1,482	5,116	6,541	6,184	8,411
24 per cent. on income of self-employed ..	741	2,558	3,270	3,092	4,206
28 per cent. on property income	865	2,983	3,816	3,607	4,906
Total direct taxation ..	5,856	9,565	13,487	16,478	28,031
Total indirect taxation less subsidies	10,490	16,405	26,587	29,555	57,056
Grand Total	16,346	25,970	40,074	46,033	85,087

Source.—C.O.R.F.O.

Table E

CHILE: DISTRIBUTION, BY INCOME CATEGORIES, OF TAXES NET OF SUBSIDIES

(*Millions of pesos*)

	1948	1951	1952	1953	1954
Payable on:					
Salaries and wages					
Direct taxes ..	1,962	4,120	4,868	7,385	11,884
Indirect taxes less subsidies	5,035	7,874	11,372	15,349	27,386
Total	6,997	11,994	16,240	22,734	39,270
Income of self-employed					
Direct taxes ..	142	273	290	409	566
Indirect taxes less subsidies	2,518	3,938	5,686	7,675	13,693
Total	2,660	4,211	5,976	8,084	14,259
Property income					
Direct taxes ..	3,752	5,172	8,329	8,684	15,581
Indirect taxes less subsidies	2,936	4,594	6,634	8,954	15,977
Total	6,688	9,766	14,963	17,638	31,580

Source.—C.O.R.F.O.

Table F

CHILE: TOTAL NET DIRECT AND INDIRECT TAXATION, BY INCOME CATEGORIES

(*Summary of Table D*)

	1948	1951	1952	1953	1954
Payable on:	(*Millions of pesos*)				
Salaries and wages ..	6,998	11,993	19,135	21,571	39,270
Income of self-employed	2,660	4,211	5,976	7,503	14,259
Property income ..	6,688	9,766	14,963	16,959	31,558
Total	16,346	25,970	40,074	46,033	85,087
Payable on:	(*Percentage of total*)				
Salaries and wages ..	42·8	46·2	47·8	46·9	46·2
Income of self-employed	16·3	16·2	14·9	16·3	16·8
Property income ..	40·9	37·6	37·3	36·8	37·0
Total	100·0	100·0	100·0	100·0	100·0

Source.—C.O.R.F.O.

Table G

CHILE: TAX BURDEN, BY INCOME
CATEGORIES[1]

(*Percentages*)

	1948	1952–4
Salaries and wages		
Direct taxes	4·9	5·0
Indirect taxes (net) ..	12·7	11·2
Total	17·6	16·2
Income of self-employed		
Direct taxes	0·7	0·6
Indirect taxes (net) ..	13·1	11·9
Total	13·8	12·5
Property income		
Direct taxes	11·2	8·8
Indirect taxes (net) ..	8·0	8·5
Total	19·9	17·3

Source.—C.O.R.F.O.

[1] For purposes of this table the concept of gross income used in the previous tables was modified, property income being adjusted with the aim of measuring taxable income. To this end, depreciation charges were excluded and stock appreciation included.

Table H

UNITED KINGDOM: GROSS NATIONAL INCOME AND TRANSFER
PAYMENTS, BY INCOME CATEGORIES, 1953

(*Millions of pounds sterling*)

Salaries and wages		
Income from civilian employment	9,239	
Payments in cash and kind to the Armed Forces	393	
Current grants by public authorities	1,002	
Less :		
Employers' social security contributions	244	
Total salaries and wages		10,390
Income of self-employed		1,566
Property income		
Rent, dividends and interest paid	1,533	
Undistributed income of companies and public corporations	2,203	
Additions to dividend and interest reserves	39	
Residual error	118	
Less: Stock appreciation	− 75	
Total property income		3,968
Gross national income and transfer payments		15,924

Source.—*National Income and Expenditure, 1956*, Central Statistical Office, London, H.M.S.O., 1956, Table 8, page 5.

Table I

UNITED KINGDOM: COMPOSITION OF DIRECT TAXATION, 1953

(Millions of pounds sterling)

Salaries and wages		
Salaries and wages	1,041	
Less: Employers' social security contributions	244	
Total		797
Income of self-employed		202
Property income		
Rent, dividends and interest	403	
Undistributed income	948	
Total		1,351
Total direct taxation		2,350

Source.—C.O.R.F.O.

Table J

UNITED KINGDOM: CALCULATION OF
AMOUNT OF INDIRECT TAXATION
LESS SUBSIDIES, 1953

(Millions of pounds sterling)

Consumer expenditure, at market prices ..	11,399
Minus: consumer expenditure, at factor cost	9,543
Indirect taxes less subsidies	1,856
Plus: employers' social security contributions	573
Total	2,429

Source.—*National Income and Expenditure, 1956.*

Table K

UNITED KINGDOM: CALCULATION OF CONSUMER EXPENDITURE
AT MARKET PRICES, BY INCOME CATEGORIES, 1953

(Millions of pounds sterling)

	Gross income	Direct taxes	Savings	Consumer expenditure at market prices
Salaries and wages	10,390	797	845	8,748
Income of self-employed ..	1,566	202	230	1,134
Property income	3,968	1,351	1,100	1,517
Total	15,924	2,350	2,175	11,399

Source.—*National Income and Expenditure, 1956.*

Table L

UNITED KINGDOM: DISTRIBUTION OF INDIRECT TAXES,
BY INCOME CATEGORIES, 1953

(*Millions of pounds sterling*)

	Consumer expenditure at market prices	Percentage distribution	Indirect taxes minus subsidies plus employers' social security contributions	Consumer expenditure at factor cost
	(A)	(B)	(C)	(D)
Salaries and wages ..	8,748	76·8	1,866	6,882
Income of self-employed	1,134	9·9	240	894
Property income ..	1,517	13·3	323	1,194
Total	11,399	100·0	2,429	8,970

Source.—National Income and Expenditure, 1956.
(C): Applying percentages given in column (B).
(D): (A) minus (C).

Table M

UNITED KINGDOM: DISTRIBUTION OF GROSS INCOME AND
GROSS EXPENDITURE, BY INCOME CATEGORIES, 1953

(*Millions of pounds sterling*)

	Gross income plus transfers	Taxation			Savings	Consumer expenditure at factor cost
		Total	Direct	Indirect		
Salaries and wages ..	10,390	2,663	797	1,866	845	6,882
Income of self-employed	1,566	442	202	240	230	894
Property income ..	3,968	1,674	1,351	323	1,100	1,194
Total	15,924	4,779	2,350	2,429	2,175	8,970

Source.—National Income and Expenditure, 1956.

22

OBSERVATIONS ON THE PROBLEM OF ECONOMIC DEVELOPMENT IN CEYLON[1]

I. AGRICULTURE

CEYLON owes its present prosperity, in comparison with the other countries of the region, to her plantation economy. This accounts for over a third of her gross national product (and to almost one-half of the value of production excluding services) and is responsible for practically the whole of her (exceptionally large) exports. The productivity of other sectors of her economy (whether measured in terms of output per man or yield per acre) appears to be no higher than in neighbouring countries. Hence the fact that income per head and the average standard of living is twice as high in Ceylon as in India is wholly to be accounted for by the very much greater role of the plantation sector in the Ceylonese economy. This enables her to satisfy one-half of her current food consumption by way of imports in exchange for no more than one-third of her exports, which means that the one-half of food requirements which is obtained by way of international trade absorbs no more than the labour of 200,000 workers (i.e. of one-third of the labour force employed on the plantations) whereas the other half, obtained from domestic sources, absorbs the work of around 1–1·5 million adult workers.

Contrary to the widespread view according to which a "colonial" economy is necessarily at an economic disadvantage as compared with countries which do not depend on the exports of primary products for their livelihood, it seems to me that it is the further development of the plantation economy which provides the means for a rapid increase of Ceylon's national wealth. Expert opinion appears to be agreed that the scope for such development is very large—by increasing the yield on the existing estates, and also by extending the acreage under plantations; by

[1] A memorandum prepared at the request of the Prime Minister, Mr. S. R. W. Bandaranaike, in Colombo, Ceylon, in April 1958.

increasing the production of existing crops as well as by adding new products (such as coffee, sugar, cinnamon, cocoa, cotton, etc.), to those at present in cultivation. It does not appear unrealistic, assuming a vigorous effort is made, to postulate a 25 per cent. increase in the total yield of plantation crops in five years, a 50–60 per cent. increase in ten years, and a 100 per cent. increase in fifteen to twenty years. Since this would imply a corresponding increase in exports, its effects (for a variety of reasons) on both capital accumulation and the standard of living would be bound to be very much greater than that of any equivalent increase in the domestic production of import substitutes. In particular, large scale schemes for the development of food production—by means of irrigation schemes, etc.—are bound to be very wasteful in comparison with large scale schemes for the development of plantation agriculture.[1] Though with the aid of agricultural extension services, rural education, the use of fertilisers, etc., the yield of paddy cultivation could be increased considerably, large differences in productivity are bound to persist between small scale subsistence farming and large scale plantation agriculture. The superiority of plantation agriculture in Ceylon is in fact only partly to be accounted for by climatic and soil conditions; in part it is the consequence of large scale production and management. This is best shown in the case of coconuts where small scale and large scale farming exist side by side, and where the yield per acre varies from less than 1,000 nuts per acre on estates of less than 10 acres, to over 3,000 nuts in estates of over 1,000 acres. No doubt by a combination of measures involving additional expenditure in one form or another, the yield of the small farms could be considerably raised. But it is often forgotten that the same expenditure devoted to raising the productivity of the large estates might yield even more spectacular results—since even the 3,000 nuts per acre achieved on the large estates at present is only about a half of the technically optimal yield. There is in addition the fact that the increased yield of peasant agriculture would largely go into additional consumption, whereas the increased yield of plantation estates

[1] Irrigation schemes which serve the purpose of establishing commercial crops under large scale management need not of course be subject to this objection.

leaves a surplus the greater part of which automatically accrues to the Government and which could be channelled into productive investment.

The advocates of a policy of self-sufficiency in food production base their case partly on the need to find employment for Ceylon's growing population, partly on the risks inherent in the present structure of Ceylon's international trade. In the long run the employment problem in my view can only be successfully tackled through industrialisation and large-scale construction projects associated with industrial development, rather than by agricultural colonisation schemes. Indeed the latter, by absorbing large capital resources that could be devoted to more productive uses, might hinder the effective solution of the employment problem. Nor would I regard Ceylon's dependence on international trade as involving such risks as to justify a policy of self-sufficiency even at the cost of large sacrifice in her potential standard of living. It is highly unlikely that a world slump of the character and duration of that of the 1930's should recur; at the outset of a serious slump, the main capitalist countries (and particularly America) are likely to take counter measures that would limit its duration to a much shorter period, perhaps one to two years. It should also be borne in mind that whilst a serious fall in commodity prices would sharply reduce Ceylon's ability to buy manufactured goods, it would not endanger her ability to import food. In the event of a world slump the prices of food crops (and probably also the prices of cotton goods) are not likely to fare any differently from the prices of plantation crops, so that the terms on which food (or clothing) can be had in exchange for plantation crops may not be less favourable in the one case than in the other. There is also the possibility of assuring supplies by means of long-term contracts with other countries of the region on the pattern of the rice-rubber exchange with China.

The risks inherent in Ceylon's present structure of international trade arise, in my view, not from her dependence on food imports as such, nor from the exclusive dependence on plantation crops for exports, but rather from the excessive concentration of her plantation economy on a few products each subject to peculiar risks of its own (like the invention of synthetic rubber or synthetic detergents). Tea alone accounts at present for two-thirds of exports. Without any sizeable reduction of the acreage under tea, this percentage could be considerably reduced through the expansion of cocoa plantations and the introduction of coffee, sugar and other new plantations. Since these new crops may, initially at any rate, appear commercially less profitable than the existing crops, it is unlikely that development on a sufficient scale could be induced to take place under private enterprise; it will require the creation of new estates under the control of public corporations.[1]

II. INDUSTRIALISATION

The expansion of the plantation sector even at its maximum possible rate is not likely to absorb more than a fraction of Ceylon's working population. Hence the full and effective utilisation of her manpower resources is only conceivable through industrialisation and the growth of tertiary (service) industries which are based on it. There is no ultimate limit to the amount of manpower which industrial development can absorb; the pace of absorption is governed by capital accumulation and the growth of technical and managerial skills, and know-how. There appears to be considerable hesitation, however, as to the precise directions which industrialisation should take, and the methods by which it is to be brought about. The very fact that industrialisation has hardly begun means that existing trends offer little guidance to the path of future development. The relatively small size of the country, and the absence of many critical minerals, appear to exclude the kind of comprehensive development extending to all basic sectors which characterise the development plans of India or China. At the same time it would be a mistake to assume that Ceylon's industrial development need be confined to industries processing domestically produced materials, or for providing substitutes for imports in the field of "light"

[1] As the history of plantation economies (particularly Brazil) shows, the tendency to concentrate on a single product tends to be a feature of development under private enterprise, since planters prefer to concentrate on whatever crop appears most profitable in any given situation. From the point of view of the national economy, however, it is worth while to incur higher costs, and forgo some immediate advantage, for the sake of the greater stability to be gained by diversification.

industries. Though I am naturally not in a position to make detailed recommendations I feel that any development plan should bear in mind the following guiding considerations:

(1) Since hydro-electric power is the Island's main indigenous resource, the development of water power should have first priority, and the projects for building dams and power stations should be pushed ahead as fast as possible. (Latest estimates put the country's hydro-electric potential at 1,200 megawatts, and if the existing rate of development were speeded up, 350 megawatts could be provided by 1964.)

(2) The possession of an ample supply of water power suggests the development of "power intensive" industries, among which artificial fertilisers are of the foremost importance, together with cement, rubber processing (tyres) and metal refining (aluminium-making might become economical at a sufficiently low power cost even though there are no bauxite deposits on the Island). I would hesitate however to suggest the establishment of a steel industry which requires large-scale production whereas Ceylon has variegated needs and small total requirements. The arguments that can be adduced for showing the necessity of a domestic steel industry for economic development in countries like Russia, India or China do not apply in the case of Ceylon—since Ceylon is perfectly capable of generating a growing surplus of exports for the purchase of steel and machinery.

(3) Owing to Ceylon's relatively small size, it would be more advantageous to concentrate on particular fields with a view of not only satisfying domestic requirements but developing an industrial export potential, whilst continuing to rely on imports in other fields. Since neighbouring countries in the region will tend to restrict the importation of manufactured consumers' goods in the interests of their own industrialisation, this means concentrating on producers' goods, the export of which is not likely to encounter the same kind of obstacles. This consideration also suggests that fertilisers and cement are the two obvious

cases for development, since there is an almost unlimited potential demand for them in neighbouring countries. (At present Ceylon does not manufacture fertilisers, while cement production supplies only about one-quarter of current requirements. Taking into account the growth in domestic needs possibly a ten-fold expansion in cement production would be necessary for a sizeable export surplus to emerge.)

(4) The growth of power, fertilisers, cement, together with other building materials such as bricks and tiles, provides examples for the creation of large-scale units that could be undertaken under the aegis of *public enterprise*. There are other types of industrial development however (such as light engineering), which require the gradual expansion of domestic activities starting from the final assembly down to the increasing manufacture of parts and components, and these could best be fostered through the growth of *private enterprise*. The most advantageous framework for development therefore is that of a mixed economy where the public sector provides the basic products manufactured in large-scale units, and reliance is had for private enterprise in those fields in which development presupposed a gradual and organic growth in the range of manufacturing activities.

(5) An industrial development plan should therefore partly consist of an investment plan for the public sector and partly of a co-ordinated set of measures and policies designed to foster private enterprise. The latter must include the generous tax treatment of new capital expenditure in the private sector, and the introduction of a new "scientific" tariff, designed to protect domestic industries, and to facilitate the importation of capital goods and raw materials for further processing. (The existing tariff seems to be inadequate on both counts—it taxes the import of producers' goods, and it fails to protect domestic industries against foreign competition.) The working out of such a "scientific" tariff requires the setting up of a permanent Tariff Commission.

(6) Industrial development, apart from any financial limitations, is likely to be severely handicapped by the lack of technical know-how and of managerial and organisational ability and knowledge, which could only develop gradually, side by side with the growth of industrial activity itself. To speed up this process it will be necessary to draw on the knowledge and experience of foreign firms by means of long-term "management contracts" offering facilities for the establishment of domestic branches of foreign manufacturing firms on condition that after the lapse of some initial period (of the order of, say, twenty years) the parent firms should be willing to relinquish control in favour of domestic enterprises, public or private. (The introduction of a suitable protective tariff will naturally increase the willingness of foreign manufacturers to establish manufacturing subsidiaries inside the country.)

(7) The growth of private manufacturing enterprise could be further facilitated through the construction of Government-owned trading or industrial estates, leasing facilities to private firms.

III. FINANCIAL RESOURCES

An adequate rate of development requires the stepping-up of the rate of capital accumulation from the present 12 per cent. to 20–22 per cent. of the gross national product or, say, by a further 10 per cent. of the gross national product, or some Rs. 500–600 million. In my view this could be accomplished in about eight years. Some parts of the finance—that required for the purchase of imported capital equipment—should be covered from loans, etc., to be provided by international agencies. The greater part of the remainder—of the order of Rs. 300–400 million—will require additional taxation both for the financing of investment in the public sector, and for offsetting the inflationary effect of extended bank loans for development purposes in the private sector. To raise additional taxation of this order should not present any great difficulty; part of it will accrue from the increased yield of direct taxes of various kinds, and part of it by means of increased excise duties and/or the introduction of a general sales tax. The present level of taxation on articles of mass consumption appears to be rather low in relation to other countries, and the financial aspect of the problem is by no means insoluble. The danger is rather that with increased public revenue, the pressure for increasing public non-developmental expenditure will become even stronger, and an undue proportion of the additional resources raised by taxation will be absorbed in current expenditure. In recent years the level of current expenditure (on subsidies, social services, etc.), has been rising faster than desirable whilst capital expenditures have consistently fallen behind the estimates. If capital projects were pressed forward more vigorously in the various Departments this in itself might tend to slow down the growth of non-developmental expenditures.

IV. PLANNING TECHNIQUES

The most unsatisfactory feature of the present situation is the slow progress made in planning—both in the elaboration of projects at the technical level, and in working out a consistent set of targets for an overall plan, and exploring its implications on finance, taxation, foreign exchange requirements, etc. For this the lack of co-ordination between the various Government departments and the general inadequacy of the central planning machinery are largely responsible. The present conception regards overall economic planning as something divorced from departmental functions; the National Planning Council is a purely advisory body, while the Planning Secretariat serves mainly the Planning Council, and is divorced from the planning activities of individual Government departments.

In my view, since any plan must necessarily be approved by the individual Ministers and the Cabinet as a whole, whilst its execution entirely depends on the various Government departments, it is useless to entrust the task of elaborating an overall plan to an advisory body without executive functions. This should be the direct responsibility of a purely Ministerial body, the Planning Committee of the Cabinet (consisting of *all* the Ministers who have a direct responsibility for the various sectors) with the Ministers being free to delegate their responsibility to their permanent officials, in the day-to-day work of the Committee itself, or of its various sub-committees, provided only that the officials can speak with authority for their Ministers and Departments. The Planning Committee and its sub-committees should be serviced by the Planning Secretariat. The services of the National Planning Council should be retained; but instead of expecting the Planning Council to put forward individual suggestions or a comprehensive plan to the various Departments or to the Cabinet, the plans elaborated by the Cabinet Planning Committee should be submitted for airing and discussion to the Planning Council. At the same time the allocation of functions between the different Government departments needs to be rationalised. At present there is a great deal of overlapping which is a cause of both frictions and delays in reaching decisions (as e.g. between the Ministry of Lands and the Ministry of Food and Agriculture) while in other cases the responsibility for a common task is divided between various departments, with the result that progress is unnecessarily delayed. Thus matters concerning power development (as distinct from power supply) irrigation and flood control ought to be taken out of the hands of the Ministry of Transport and Works and the Ministry of Lands and entrusted to a new Ministry for Power Development, Irrigation and Flood Control.

V. THE QUESTION OF NATIONALISATION

The suggested *new* developments both in the plantation sector and in the industrial sector will require the creation of numerous public enterprises which will tax the organisational and administrative resources of the Government very severely. This managerial and administrative bottleneck is likely to impose a far more severe limitation on the pace of development than finance. In view of this it seems to me very dubious whether it is wise, at the present stage, to increase the load on the administrative apparatus even further through the nationalisation of *existing* enterprises. Ceylon's progress towards a socialist State is bound to be a gradual one, and unless nationalisation is necessary in the interest of economic development itself, it is better to provide for the growth of the public sector through new developments than through the conversion of existing enterprises. There is a case for a partial nationalisation of insurance and banking in order to obtain public control over the investment of funds of banks and insurance companies; though even here it may be wiser to allow the continuance of some private companies alongside public enterprises. But it is difficult to see the public advantage in the proposed nationalisation of estate companies. According to information given to me by the Income Tax Department, the annual remittances of dividends of the non-resident estate companies amount to Rs. 30–35 million whilst the current market value of their assets is around Rs. 1,000 million and their book value (i.e. subscribed capital plus accumulated reserves) some Rs. 350 million. Even if only the book value were taken as the basis of compensation (thus allowing nothing for the appreciation in the value of the land or for excessive writing down of assets), I cannot see that such a large outflow of capital would be justified by the consequential saving in annual remittances, quite apart from any possible damage to the further expansion of Ceylon's tea exports or on account of the reduced prospect of new foreign loans, the general discouragement to foreign enterprise, etc.

At the same time the continuance of the present state of uncertainty is bound to have unfavourable effects on the efficiency of the tea plantations, since the British tea companies are not likely to sink fresh capital in replanting or expansion so long as they are left in the dark concerning their future status. The present policy of continuing to proclaim the nationalisation of the estates as part of the Government's policy, whilst leaving it "to the last," makes the worst of both worlds. If nationalisation is decided on, there is something to be said for giving effect to it as soon as possible. If, on the other hand, it were decided to postpone it, there is much to be said for coming to an agreement with the British tea companies which would remove the present state of uncertainty, and give an incentive to them to develop their estates further. The present position is unsatisfactory, not only on account of the prospect of nationalisation, but also of the uncertainty concerning future taxation which might cut down income below the current levels, to an almost indefinite extent. (The current level of taxation including the export duty already absorbs some 85 per cent. of the profits.) Such a "gentleman's agreement," I suggest, might be possible on the lines that (a) the tea companies agree to limit their annual remittance of dividends to some agreed proportion of profits based on the present yield of exports, but with the definite prospect of being allowed to increase their remitted dividends on a certain scale depending on the increase of export proceeds, in return for an understanding not to raise export levies or profit taxation beyond certain levels; (b) the Government agrees not to nationalise the estates for a period of, say, twenty years in return for the companies undertaking to carry out an agreed replanting programme; (c) the Government states the principles on which compensation would be paid if the Government wished to take over the estates at the end of the period. Alternatively, an agreement might be negotiated for the conversion of the Sterling Companies into Rupee Companies (through the creation of resident subsidiary companies) allowing for a gradual increase in Government participation, through the parent companies agreeing to sell shares of the subsidiaries to a public corporation over a certain period, and to relinquish control (i.e. by selling the residue of the shares) at the end of that period.

I realise that the nationalisation of the plantation companies, together with the question of foreign participation in developing new industries, is an emotional issue which is not likely to be judged solely on economic considerations. Nevertheless I think it is important to point out that the pace of Ceylon's future development, at least for the next two decades or so, is greatly dependent on foreign help—not so much on account of the lack of resources for capital accumulation, as of the lack of expert knowledge in setting up and managing enterprises in new industries. It would be unfortunate if Ceylon were deprived of this help on account of a vague hostility towards foreign capital and enterprise, and the general atmosphere of distrust engendered by it—whereas it would be open to Ceylon to enlist the support of foreign enterprise without jeopardising her ultimate economic independence. I see no inherent contradiction between the growth of public enterprise in basic sectors of the economy, and the simultaneous encouragement to foreign firms in other fields where development could not take place without their participation.

23

PROBLEMS OF THE INDIAN THIRD FIVE-YEAR PLAN[1]

I

WHEN I look at the various preliminary papers drawn up in connection with the new Plan, my main reaction is one of increasing scepticism as to the adequacy, or even the appropriateness, of looking at the problem of resource mobilisation mainly in financial terms—i.e. of setting targets for investment expenditure in the light of the financial resources that could be raised by taxation, borrowings and small savings, external assistance and so on—and then inquiring in the light of assumptions concerning the possible yield from each of these sources, what sort of investment target is possible. This approach is appropriate to "advanced" economies like the U.K. and the U.S.A. (which, after all, have developed these "Keynesian" techniques of looking at the problem primarily for their own purposes) but it is not appropriate to under-developed countries like India. The important differences as I see them are due to two factors:

(i) In the "advanced" countries the only important bottleneck on increased investment, at any rate in planning for medium-range periods, is manpower. Hence deficit-financing is inflationary if, and only if, the economy is at full employment or near full employment.

(ii) In the "advanced" countries sums of money made available for particular purposes can be appropriately used to indicate a corresponding supply of real "resources," without specifying the particular basket of goods and resources which are required for the particular objectives aimed at. The reason for this is that, granted a certain period of adjustment, the market mechanism is capable of adapting the production-pattern to any given pattern of final

[1] A memorandum (not hitherto published) prepared for the planning secretariat in New Delhi in December 1958.

demand—either through the reallocation of the domestic distribution of the labour force, and/or through the conversion of goods in international trade. Post-war experience has shown that it is unsafe, even in England, to rely solely on financial planning—particular bottlenecks in steel and engineering, which set a limit also to export capacity, may make it impossible to secure continued economic expansion through the instruments of fiscal and monetary policy alone. In countries like India this technique can be very misleading in both directions—both in thinking that the required (domestic) resources will automatically be forthcoming if sufficient money is made available through the "normal" sources of taxation, the profits of public enterprises, and borrowing in the open market; and also in thinking that there is a clear limit beyond which expenditure covered by deficit financing will not cause any increase in production but will merely lead to inflation. Thus most people would agree that additional taxation of say, Rs. 100 crores, raised by means of a land tax has a very different effect on the supply of resources for investment than an equivalent tax on company profits. It is useless therefore to state the requirements in terms of so many crores of additional taxation, without specifying the character of the taxes that are to be raised. Equally, the sharp distinctions between money raised through borrowing in the open market and small savings and money raised through borrowing by the Reserve Bank seems unjustified —it assumes that the reduced liquidity of the subscribers to new loans, etc., means a corresponding reduction in their expenditure, and the increased liquidity resulting from deficit financing a corresponding increase in (private) expenditure. Finally, the extent to which increased total expenditure results in inflation depends not only on the extent to which the supply of key commodities (such as wage-goods) is unresponsive to increased demand, but also on the extent to which the allocation, and the prices, of these scarce commodities are controlled. War-time experience has shown that rationing and price-control of essential consumers' goods, and the allocation of scarce materials such as steel and cement, make it possible to finance expansion through deficit financing to a far higher degree than is possible in a free market economy.

II

I think, therefore, that the problem of resource-mobilisation should *primarily* be examined in real terms (in terms of the actual resources *required* for attaining the targets of the Plan) and financial planning should be secondary—it should be adapted to the framework of the Plan decided on in the light of the possibilities of mobilising the needed resources, rather than the other way round. These resources can be grouped under five heads:

  (i) manpower;
 (ii) wage-goods to cover the increase in aggregate wage-payments;
(iii) basic materials and fuel—i.e. steel, cement, coal, electric power;
(iv) the capacity of the (domestic) conversion industries (mainly engineering) which determines how much additional productive capacity can be created within a period, given the supply of basic materials available;
  (v) imported machinery and equipment.

Of these, (i) is not likely to prove a bottleneck—indeed the purpose of the Plan is to utilise at least a part of the vast amount of idle manpower which is constantly increasing through the growth of the population of working age. But the need for training labour for particular tasks may set a limit to the speed at which employment in particular sectors can be expanded.

However, (ii) is a major bottleneck because it is impossible to generate additional incomes through increased employment without thereby generating an increase in consumption. Sample studies show that in India, 90 per cent. of wages are spent on food and clothing and some 66 per cent. on food alone. Clothing is not likely to prove a lasting bottleneck, as there is considerable spare capacity in the cotton industry, both factory and small-scale industry at present; moreover, with full utilisation and high profits, private industry is likely to expand capacity fairly speedily. But the expansion of the food supply presents the key problem, and may require radical measures both in the field of food production and of food distribution. (I shall return to this later.) Apart from these, there is the problem of working-class housing in the expanding areas.

(iii) It is of course one of the main purposes of the development plan to expand the supply of basic materials. But at any one time the available supply may be too short for current requirements and this would necessitate some scheme of priorities in their allocation. (The best way of dealing with this is to introduce a government monopoly of wholesaling in these key commodities rather than licensing.)

(v) is a residual category in the sense that it should cover all those items which cannot be covered by (iv), and is in turn limited by foreign exchange availabilities. I think it would be a mistake however to make some assumed figure for net foreign loans (such as the Rs. 1,000 crores frequently mentioned in this connection) the cornerstone of the Plan around which all the other targets revolve. In present international circumstances there is no definite figure which can reasonably be taken to indicate the amount that India will be able to borrow in the coming five-year period—a figure of Rs. 1,000 crores may be no more or no less unrealistic than a figure of Rs. 2,000 crores. The better procedure therefore is to elaborate a Plan that is adequate and feasible in terms of the mobilisation of domestic resources and in terms of its employment target, and to work out its import requirements for plant and equipment as a residual; and to negotiate with international agencies and foreign governments on that basis.

III

It seems to me that the targets of the Third Plan should be worked out primarily in terms of the additional employment in the "organised" sectors of the economy—mining, manufacturing, construction, transport and communications—that it is desirable or feasible to create, and this should be translated in terms of the additional food, etc. requirements which the associated increase in the total wages bill is likely to involve. The Second Plan only provided "visible" additional jobs for 3 million people as against the 11 million increase in the working population. The Third Plan ought clearly to be more ambitious; indeed it ought to aim at no less than 10 million additional "visible" jobs for the end of the plan period. A part of this labour force should be engaged in construction projects, but the greater part must find employment in connection with the expansion of industrial capacity which the Second and Third Plan should have created, both in the investment goods sector and the consumption goods sector.

The main problem of an employment-expansion of this order is undoubtedly the increase in the agricultural "surplus" (i.e. the excess of food production over food consumption in the rural areas). This requires both an increase in agricultural productivity and measures that would prevent the increased production from being absorbed in increased agricultural self-consumption. I do not think sufficient thought has yet been given to the problem of how to attain these twin objectives in the quickest way. The growth of agricultural co-operatives may be the most promising approach to a solution in the long run but it is necessarily a slow-moving process under Indian conditions. There are a number of other things that can be done also—such as a rapid increase in the supply of fertilisers, improved organisation for credit, government trading in food grains, a substantial increase in land taxation, etc. One measure that springs to mind which could be expanded rapidly, and is bound to yield quick results, is that of large-scale schemes for employing surplus rural labour during the off-seasons on irrigation projects. Here I think it would be foolish to count the outlay as part of some given total, so that any increased expenditure in this direction must go to reduce outlay on other kinds of investment. For such schemes are likely to be "self-financing" well within a single plan period, so that increased expenditure on them is likely to enlarge other employment opportunities rather than reduce them. (I do not see the justification therefore for linking the scope of such projects to schemes for voluntary labour contributions. Even if the labour is paid for at the going rate, the projects will not involve added financial resources of a kind comparable to other investment outlays which do not bring quick returns in terms of wage-goods.)

IV

Some recent memoranda on the subject of the Third Plan take the figure of Rs. 7,500 crores as their starting point, and show that at the current (or prospective?) level of production there is not much likelihood of raising resources for more than one-half of this sum for the public sector plus an unknown amount for the private sector. The figure of Rs. 7,500 was chosen as the one required to maintain at least the current ratio of investment to the national income. But the difficulty with this approach is that the question of how many resources can be raised for investment cannot be answered until it is known by how much, and in what pattern, production is to be raised, and this in turn depends on how many additional people are put to work, and how far you will succeed in increasing food-production, which in turn partly depends on the investment target and its composition, and partly on other measures. The problem as a whole should be considered far more as one of increasing the production of various kinds of goods, rather than as one of attaining certain investment targets either in terms of crores or as a percentage of the national income. The rapidity with which the national income can be raised is in turn far more a matter of stepping up the rate of growth in the bottleneck sectors which keep down the rate of growth of the rest of the economy than of the rise of total investment. Thus I have little doubt that, quite apart from the existence or the size of the Plan, industrial production in India would have expanded far more rapidly during the last five years if the growth of agricultural production had been greater. Nor do I see the justification of a number of "axioms" which are sometimes advanced in connection with economic planning—such as that a plan's current outlay must be covered by taxation, and only its fixed capital investment by borrowing; that deficit financing should only be used for investment in working capital, and not fixed capital; or that the finance of private investment can be assumed to look after itself so that only public sector investment gives rise to the problem of the "gap." How much or how little can safely be left to deficit financing depends not on the character of the expenditure but on the question of how fast the national income can be expanded—the more production expands or can be made to expand, the higher is the rate of deficit financing which the economy can absorb without inflation.

V

The problem of resources mobilisation cannot be solved without knowing to what extent the country (acting through its Government and Parliament) is prepared to change its existing socio-economic framework for the sake of development. Of course experts and officials cannot *answer* these questions, but I think they ought to *pose* them, far more pointedly than has hitherto been done, in order to enable the Ministers and the legislatures to make up their minds. The questions ought to be of the "which-would-you-rather" kind, e.g. by saying that it is possible to have a Rs. 5,000 crores plan which is totally inadequate for raising living standards for the future, and a Rs. 10,000 crore plan which would alone ensure the continuance of a certain rhythm of development, but that the latter, as against the former, would involve some at least of the following undesirable consequences:

(*a*) A five-fold increase in land taxation.

(*b*) Continued inflation of the order of a price increase of 10–15 per cent. annually (Fast-growing Latin American countries like Brazil have had for many years an inflation of an order of 20 per cent. per annum, or even more.)

(*c*) Government monopoly of wholesale distribution for key commodities, including all imports.

(*d*) Food-rationing in urban areas.

(*e*) Compulsory delivery of food from farmers.

(*f*) A loophole-free tax system.

(*g*) Government monopoly of foreign trade, etc.

Until it is shown just *what* is involved in *what* plan one cannot expect that politicians or Ministers can be brought to the point of facing such disagreeable decisions. In the absence of such disagreeable decisions, it cannot be assumed that India will be capable of accelerating her economic growth to a rate which corresponds to the professed national aspirations.

24

PROSPECTS OF A WAGES POLICY
FOR AUSTRALIA[1]

1. IN recent years there has been an increasing recognition in
Britain and in the countries of Western Europe of the need for
an "incomes policy" as a means of ensuring monetary stability
under conditions of continued economic growth. This largely
reflects the acceptance of the view that the very process of growth
tends to generate a rate of increase in money wages that may be
in excess of the rate of growth of "productivity" (owing to the
complex interrelation in the growth of production and the
growth of profits on the one hand, and the growth of profits and
the growth of wages on the other) and therefore that a wage
price spiral cannot be effectively avoided by the orthodox
methods of monetary and fiscal policy—i.e., by "maintaining"
a modest percentage of unemployment. There is continued
search, therefore, for some centralised machinery of wage determination (as exists, for example, in Holland or Sweden) that
would limit annual wage increases to a percentage which is no
greater than, or at least not much in excess of, the increase in
productivity.

2. In the matter of wages, Australian experience in the last
ten years has been relatively more favourable than that of most
other high-income countries. Since 1953 the increase in award
wages averaged 3·2 per cent. a year and the increase in average
weekly earnings 4·7 per cent. a year. These are appreciably
lower figures than those of most "developed" countries with
comparable growth rates and unemployment rates. In the U.K.,
for example, in 1953-63, negotiated wages increased at 4 per cent.
a year, and earnings at 5·7 per cent. a year, with a rate of growth
of the G.N.P. per worker which was 1·9 per cent, and with

[1] A paper written during the author's visit to Australia as consulting economist to
the Reserve Bank, and published in the *Economic Record*, June, 1964. The author
wishes to acknowledge the help of members of the Economic Research staff of the
Bank, particularly Mr. Austin Holmes.

unemployment which fluctuated between 1·2–2·7 per cent. I think there can be little doubt that considerable credit for this is due to the manner of operation of the Australian arbitration system and in the absence of that system (i.e. under a system of collective bargaining similar to that of the U.K.) annual wage and price increases might have been appreciably greater.

3. Australian experience also suggests that while the annual increase in earnings is partly determined by market forces, it is *largely* a reflection of the increase in negotiated wages (i.e. "award wages"). For the figures show that while the rate of "earnings drift" varies *inversely* with the rate of increase in award wages— it was appreciably smaller in years in which award wages rose most than in years in which award wages were increased at moderate rates—the associated variation was not nearly as large as would be required to explain the movement in earnings mainly by market forces. In the period 1946-53 whilst award wages rose at 12·5 per cent. a year, the "earnings drift" was 0·9 per cent. a year. In the period 1953–62, when award wages increased by an average of 3·2 per cent. only, the "earnings drift" averaged 1·5 per cent. Even when allowance is made for the fact that the excess demand for labour (as measured by the excess of unfilled vacancies over registered unemployed) was lower in the second period than the first, there can be little doubt that the big reduction in the rate of increase in average earnings in the latter period is largely to be explained by the reduction in the rise in award wages following upon the suspension of the automatic cost of living adjustment in 1953.[1]

4. For historical reasons, which had nothing to do with the current issues of wage policy, Australia has inherited the kind of machinery for centralised wage determination which several of the countries of Western Europe are now striving to create in

[1] Keith Hancock has estimated, on the basis of quarterly data, the correlation between the increase in award wages and the increase in earnings for any *given* level of demand (demand being measured by the difference between unfilled vacancies and the registered unemployment, expressed as a percentage of the work force) and found that the (partial) elasticity of the "earnings drift" with respect to changes in award wages was around −0·2, that is to say a 1 per cent. rise in award wages was associated with a 0·8 per cent. increase in actual earnings. (Cf. his memorandum to the Vernon Committee, *Wages Policy in Australia*, June, 1963, pp. 22-24.)

an attempt to find a solution to the problem of how to combine high employment and growth with the avoidance of inflation. The Australian system, as it has operated since the abandonment of the quarterly cost of living adjustments, has not *avoided* inflation (since earnings increased at 4·7 per cent. a year whilst real income produced per worker, after allowing for the deterioration in the terms of trade, has only risen by 1·7 per cent. annually) but it has moderated wage increases to a level which under "normal" conditions of growth—i.e. in the absence of a deterioration in the terms of trade—would have been adequate to hold down the rate of increase in consumer prices to tolerable dimensions. (I think it is probably too much to hope that with continuous growth and full employment a certain upward drift in prices can be altogether avoided.[1]) The question is: Could this machinery be further strengthened and more purposively adapted for serving the objectives of growth and economic stability? The development of an "incomes policy" in Australia must necessarily be based on the adaptation of the existing system, and not on its replacement by a different kind of machinery; and the speed with which such adaptation can proceed is limited in turn by the very need to preserve the system—which presupposes continued willingness of both parties to submit disputes to arbitration and to abide by the decisions of the Court.

5. Ever since its inception the awards of the Arbitration Court were based on one of two principles, or a combination of them: the principle of "needs," which originally meant the enforcement of a certain minimum standard and which led to the principle of "automatic" adjustments to changes in the cost of living; and the principle of "capacity to pay" which was given varying interpretations in the course of time. The distinction is not a clear-cut one, since on some occasions changes in prices were

---

[1] The fundamental reasons for this are (i) that in order that the growth potentialities of a country like Australia should be efficiently exploited, the economy must be operated at a fairly high pressure of demand—otherwise the existence of unemployment will have detrimental effects on the growth of productivity, the growth of the labour force through immigration, and the growth of profit opportunities which govern both capital inflow and domestically financed investment; (ii) when demand is operated at fairly high pressure, "bottle-neck" sectors are bound to develop, giving rise to price increases (and to over-award wage increases) in those sectors, which, on account of the downward inflexibility of wages, cannot be offset by price decreases in other sectors.

themselves regarded, by the arbitration tribunal, as indications of changes in the "capacity to pay"; in others "capacity to pay" was judged on the basis of a number of indicators—such as employment, investment, production, productivity, etc., independently of prices. During the period of automatic quarterly cost-of living adjustment, clearly the "needs" criterion was predominant. After 1953 awards were based on the "capacity to pay" criterion, but in its recent 1961 judgment the Commission foreshadowed that in future it will consider adjustments in the "basic wage" on the basis of the change in consumer prices annually and adjustment in the "*real* basic wage" (presumably on the basis of the change in "capacity to pay") every three years.

6. This recent decision has given rise to certain misgivings— partly on account of the reappearance of the "cost-of-living principle" and partly on account of the fear that a single triennial adjustment to changes in the "capacity to pay" is bound to mean a large discontinuous adjustment in wages which will be inflationary in its effect, even though it may not exceed the *accumulated change* in "productivity" over the past three years. The effect of productivity changes on the *real* wage is bound to be a continuous process which is at least partially reflected in the prevailing price/wage relationship, even in the absence of an adjustment in money wages; if the money wage is then adjusted in large lumps at infrequent intervals, this is bound to de-stabilise the price level.[1]

7. There can be little doubt that in the period 1946-53 the automatic quarterly cost of living adjustments operated so as to generate a wage/price spiral of considerable dimensions and its abandonment was a major factor in slowing down the rate of price inflation in subsequent years. This is not to suggest that any cost-of-living adjustment is necessarily "inflationary"; one can think of cases (for example, when the cost of living rises on account of a rise in the prices of exportable goods and/or imported goods) when it would not generate a "spiral " inflation. However, in the period in question the real wage which the Arbitration Court

[1] This is likely to be the more "inflationary", on account of the fact that in the absence of any adjustment of award wages the increase in over-award payments is likely to be greater than it would be otherwise; a given increase in award wages is thus likely to make a greater difference to money earnings if it is awarded discontinuously than if it is awarded in smaller steps at more frequent intervals.

desired to enforce was evidently higher (perhaps only by 3–4 per cent. higher) than the *attainable* real wage as governed by basic economic forces; and the pace of inflation was considerable enhanced through the fact that the adjustment of the money wage to the rise in prices took place regularly, at *frequent* (quarterly) intervals.

8. When wages and prices chase one another in a continuing sequence, this necessarily involves some difference between the "desired" real wage and the actually "attainable" real wage—since if this were not so, the rise in prices induced by the rise in wages would be smaller than the rise in wages, thus giving rise to a smaller subsequent adjustment in wages, until, through a series of steps, both wages and prices converged on a new plateau. However, the extent to which a rise in money wages is in itself capable of raising the attainable real wage is limited, and probably amounts to only a fraction of the rise in money wages.[1] Hence in the short period when the factors determining the real wage can be taken as given, a rise in wages will tend to cause an increase in prices more or less in proportion[2] (partly as a result of the rise in costs, partly of the increase in demand generated by higher incomes), and over a period that may take no longer than a few months. The pace of inflation will therefore greatly depend on the frequency with which wages are adjusted to the change in prices. Assuming that the adjustment of prices to a rise in wages at some given date takes less than three months, the *annual* rate of increase in both wages and prices may be almost four times as high when the wage adjustment is on a quarterly basis than when it is on an annual basis—with the average real wage over the year being not much different in the one case than in the other.[3] It is quite possible moreover that when the adjustment

[1] Cf. Keith Hancock, "The Basic Wage and the Cost of Living," *Australian Economic Papers*, September, 1962, for an anlysis of this relationship.

[2] This will be the case particularly when imports are limited by quantitative import controls. In the absence of these a rise in money wages may lead to a more appreciable rise in real wages, at the cost of a deterioration in the balance of payments.

[3] This argument assumes that a given increase in wages will have exerted its full effect on prices before the next wage adjustment takes place. If this were not so, the ultimate rate of price-inflation would vary also with the length of the time lags, relatively to the frequency of wage adjustments. Thus assuming (for the sake of argument) that a rise in money wages is incapable of raising the real wage more than temporarily, but that the adjustment of prices is spread over six months (and proceeds at an even rate) then, starting with an initial increase in wages of 4 per cent. and, assuming that wages are regularly adjusted for any subsequent rise in the

is on an *annual* basis, an initial wage/price spiral might peter out altogether, as a result of the gradual rise in the *attainable* real wage, provided only that the adjustment of wages on account of the change in the cost of living and the adjustment of wages on account of the rise in productivity, are not superimposed on each other.

9. I do not think that the present Australian arbitration system could maintain itself if the Commission formally abandoned the principle of adjusting wages to changes in the cost of living— if it did, it would not be able in the long run to maintain its control over industrial relations. The Commission therefore acted wisely in resuscitating the notion (in its 1961 judgment) of a periodic revision of the basic wage in the light of the movement of the Consumer Price Index—though without committing itself to any principle of full or automatic adjustment. However, the danger of the system operating in an inflationary manner could be considerably reduced (and possibly altogether avoided) if it were more explicitly recognised that the principle of adjusting wages to changes in the cost of living is justified by the principle of "needs"; and hence it should only operate as a *supplementary* or *alternative* principle to the "capacity to pay" principle. In other words, the Arbitration Commission should only take the change in the Consumer Price Index into consideration whenever the movement of that index would indicate a greater increase in wages than would be justified on the basis of the change in "capacity to pay," i.e. whenever real wages had actually fallen.[1]

cost of living at the end of every quarter, the rate of increase in both wages and prices will converge on the figure of 2·7 per cent. per quarter, or (say) 11 per cent. per year. If the adjustment of prices were spread over four quarters (and proceeded at an even rate over this period) the rate of inflation would converge on 1·6 per cent. a quarter, or (say) 6·5 per cent. a year. (The reasons for this are that the lag in price adjustment will reduce the necessary adjustment of wages at a given date; on the other hand, the effects of the price increases following from past wage adjustments become superimposed on each other.) If on the other hand wages were only adjusted once a year, the rate of inflation would be 4 per cent. annually in both cases.

[1] Strictly speaking, the principle of "needs" only justifies a guaranteed *minimum* real wage, whereas the principle of a full cost of living adjustment is intended to maintain whatever real wage had actually been attained in the previous period. However, in a progressive economy where real income per head and the general standard of living is continually rising, "needs" could hardly be interpreted differently from the average living standard which has already been attained in the past. Barring wars or natural calamities, or some catastrophic deterioration in the terms of international trade, the mere preservation of that standard ought not to give rise to any inflationary pressures; whilst the principle offers a certain protection to the working classes against any encroachment on their living standards emanating from competing claimants on national resources.

10. This, of course, could not in practice be achieved if the Commission were to adjust wages on the cost of living basis annually and on the "capacity to pay" basis only triennially. Whilst there is a great deal to be said for the view that a comprehensive review of the economy should only be attempted at less frequent intervals "say, every three years" it would be a great mistake if such a comprehensive review resulted in a *single* adjustment of wages every three years, that would take into account the cumulative change in productivity that had occurred since the previous review. Rather, I think, the Commission should be encouraged to use the occasion of such a comprehensive review to take into account the *prospective* increases in the economy's "capacity to pay" for the next three years; and should make an award of an *annual* increase in both the basic wage and the margins for the three year period. In other words, supposing the Commission finds that "capacity to pay" is likely to increase at the rate of say, 3 per cent. a year, and the basic wage at the starting point is £15 a week, this would mean an immediate increase of 9s. in the basic wage in the first year, a further, say, 9s. 3d. to come into effect in the following year, and a further 9s. 6d. in the third year; the same principle being applied to the adjustment of margins.[1] This would have the twofold advantage of—

(a) avoiding large adjustments in the level of money wages at infrequent intervals;
(b) giving both sides of industry some assurance of the movement of wages for some time ahead.

Assuming this principle were adopted, the above suggestion concerning the annual cost of living adjustment would mean that the Commission would only take into account the rise in the cost of living in any one year in so far as the rise in the Consumer Price Index in the previous twelve months exceeded the percentage by which the money wage was to be raised on account of

[1] It might be preferable to smooth the adjustment even further—i.e. by making prospective adjustments in wages at six monthly intervals, rather than annually—but for the fact that this would also strengthen the claim for more frequent adjustments on cost-of-living considerations which, on the argument of para. 8 above, would impart an inflationary bias to the system.

the last triennial award, and the adjustment in wages would only relate to the excess of the rise in prices over that figure.

11. Apart from this, the operation of the existing arbitration system could be improved without any radical change in the system if some authoritative body—such as a permanent Economic Council which could be created in Australia on the lines of the British National Economic Development Council, though not necessarily with the same kind of constitution—made regular submissions to the Arbitration Commission. The two most important aspects in which the Commission requires expert guidance is first, in the interpretation of "capacity to pay"; and second, in getting a clearer recognition by the Commission of the extent of its powers of changing the distribution of the national income (as between broad economic classes as well as within each class) by its decisions concerning money wages. It is in these two respects that submissions by an authoritative Economic Council might gradually serve to build a body of authoritative legal interpretation that would guide the Commission's awards subsequently.

12. With regard to "capacity to pay," this clearly is nothing else than the real income of the nation out of which *all* claims on the national resources—the standard of living of the wage- and salary-earners, the consumption of the property owning classes, the needs of the Government and other public bodies, the accumulation of capital financed by domestic savings—must be met. The change in real income *per worker* comes from two sources: the increase in productivity and the change in the terms of foreign trade. If "productivity" alone were taken as the criterion governing the rise in wages (i.e. the change in domestic output per worker, measured in constant prices) real wages would lag behind the increase in real income per head in times when export prices are rising (and the terms of trade are improving), and would rise faster than real income in times when export prices are falling.[1]

---

[1] Even without a change in the terms of trade the "productivity criterion" might cause the rise in real wages to lag behind the rise in real income when world prices (i.e. both export prices and import prices) are rising: since this would cause the profits in the export trades and in industries competing with imports to increase faster than wages, which, (if it involved additional outlays on investment and consumption or a rise in the balance of payments surplus on current account) may not be offset (or not fully offset) by the slower increase in profits in other sectors.

It is more logical and equitable, therefore, to take the change in "real income per worker"[1] as the governing criterion for "capacity to pay."

13. However, reliance on this criterion also raises a number of problems, some of which are particularly applicable in the case of a country (like Australia) which mainly exports primary products and in which exports and imports take up a relatively large proportion of national income and expenditure.

(i) It does not ensure stability in the domestic price level. It will cause a certain rise in the general level of costs and prices in times when export prices are rising, without ensuring a corresponding fall in prices and costs when exports prices are falling. It can be argued, on the other hand, that a policy of *ignoring* the change in the terms of trade may have even more deleterious effects in the case of a prolonged fall in export prices, since this will cause the currency to become progressively over-valued, thereby aggravating the problem of the balance of payments. An "asymmetrical" policy which is based on productivity changes alone in times of rising export prices, but allows for the deterioration in the terms of trade in times of falling export prices is bound to operate to the disadvantage of the wage earning classes. It would be better therefore to allow wages to rise with the rise in real income, and to offset possible adverse repercussions by a periodic devaluation or by the adoption of a system of flexible exchange rates; without a system of flexible exchange rates it would in any case be impossible to isolate the domestic price level from variations in the world price level.

(ii) A more important objection is that the changes in the terms of trade provide the *unstable* element in the growth of real income; if the fall in the terms of trade is large enough, it may even cause real income per worker to fall despite a continued rise in domestic output per head. It would not in practice be possible to get money wages *reduced* in times of falling real income per worker; and even sudden reductions in the rates of increase in award wages might strain the arbitration system to a breaking-point.

[1] This is measured by the gross domestic product *plus* imports *minus* exports (all at constant prices), *plus* or *minus* the balance of payments on current account (according as it is positive or negative) divided by the number of workers employed in the year.

(iii) Irrespective of whether "productivity" or "real income per worker" is taken as the basic criterion, there is a strong case for making adjustments of wages on the basis of a forecast of the likely trend *for some period ahead*, rather than in the light of year-to-year changes.[1] The main reason for this is that short-period movements in productivity and real income per head are subject to all kinds of chance influences (such as temporary booms and recessions) which ought not be reflected in wages policy; if they were, they would serve to increase the instability of the economy, not reduce it. In forecasting future trends however (whether for a three-year period or a five-year period) it is notoriously difficult to take the movement in the terms of trade into account, since past movements (or even past trends) provide no clue to future trends. The growth in productivity can be forecast with some degree of assurance precisely because it has shown itself to be a relatively stable adjunct of a growing economy. But a forecast of the growth in real income will almost invariably involve the conventional assumption of "unchanged" terms of trade—since there is no more reason for assuming that the past trend will continue to operate than for supposing that it will be reversed. Hence whichever criterion is formally adopted, the actual forecast of the rate of increase in wages which the economy can afford is likely to be based, in effect, on a forecast of the rate of growth of productivity. The best that can be hoped is that if, as a result of a prolonged improvement in the terms of trade (or a prolonged rise of both export and import prices) the growth in real wages fell significantly behind the growth in productivity, this would be subsequently compensated for by awarding a higher rate of increase of money wages in the subsequent award period than would be appropriate otherwise.

14. Even assuming no change in export and import prices, there is no guarantee that if money wages rise at the same rate as the increase in real income produced per worker, prices will remain constant, so that real wages rise at the same rate as money wages. This will only be true if all the other claims on national resources remain unchanged, as a proportion of total income. Real

[1] The Commission has given implicit recognition to this in its recent announcement that in the future it will consider adjustments in the "basic real wage" only at intervals of three years.

wages may fail to increase in the same proportion as national real income per worker whenever—

(a) there is an *increase* in the sum of (gross) private domestic investment and net foreign investment as a proportion of the GNP;

(b) there is an *increase* in the expenditure of public authorities on goods and services as a proportion of G.N.P.;

(c) there is an *increase* in the consumption of the property owning classes *relative to* gross profits after tax.

(d) there is a *decrease* in the proportion of income saved by wage- and salary-earners.

None of the above factors can be controlled directly through a change in money wages (though wage changes may affect some of them through changing the profits in export industries or in industries competing with imports). They can, however (within limits), be controlled by the Government through the general instruments of fiscal and monetary policy, e.g. by making such changes in the balance of taxation and expenditure as would compensate for an increase in one of these items by induced contraction in others. I feel the responsibilities of the Arbitration Commission are amply fulfilled if it ensures that money wages increase, over a run of years, in proportion to the increase in "real income produced" per worker. It is the responsibility of the Government to ensure that this policy is not frustrated through any disproportionate increase in rival claims on national resources.

15. In fixing the appropriate annual increases in award wages the Commission ought ideally (i.e., in order to ensure price stability) also to take into account the probable increase in average earnings through the "earnings drift," and not only the increase in "real income produced" per worker. Thus if, in the absence of a change in the terms of trade, productivity is expected to increase at 3 per cent. a year, and the expected "earnings drift" is 1 per cent. a year, price stability would require that award wages should only be raised by 2 per cent. a year. There are however various objections to the adoption of such a rule. In the first place, it would mean the Commission acquiescing in a situation in which "award wages" become increasingly divorced from

actual earnings. In the second place, it would put too much of a strain on the system if the Commission were to limit itself to such modest awards as this policy would require; and if it were to acknowledge openly that it limits awards *because* employers are likely to pay higher-than-award wages. The problem must therefore be tackled on different lines—by discovering the causes of the "earnings drift", and adopting measures and policies which would tend to minimise it.

16. As is well known, an "earnings drift" may be the result of various factors—increased overtime and/or a change in the composition of the labour force; a general excess in the demand for labour, leading employers to make over-award payments or to "up-grade" jobs in order to attract labour; shifts in the composition of demand which create temporary shortages in some locations or industries even where there is unemployment in others; and finally, an inappropriate wage-structure (in relation to the relative attractiveness of different types of work) which causes a chronic shortage of labour in *particular* occupations or industries. Until more detailed statistics of the movement of average earnings in different industries and grades of labour are available, it is impossible to say which of these factors, if any, is the dominant one. All that one can say is that the first of these factors could only account for a temporary "drift," rather than a permanent one—it could hardly explain a *steadily growing* discrepancy between award wages and earnings. The second factor —excessive pressure of demand in the labour market—could account for a continuing drift, but it would also cause the magnitude of the drift to fluctuate with the state of the labour market, and to be more or less widespread throughout the economy. The third factor would be important if it were found that the incidence of over-award payments is likely to be concentrated in particular industries or areas at any one time and in different places at other times. The fourth factor is likely to be important if it were found that certain types of work carry a lastingly higher premium (in relation to award wages) than others, which would indicate that the existing wage structure does not ensure a sufficient *inflow* of labour to particular industries of occupations.

17. An "earnings drift" of the third type could be alleviated through measures which aim at increasing the mobility of labour —possibly through surveys of prospective man-power requirements, Government-assisted re-training schemes (offering full pay for the period of re-training), and the development of advisory services to immigrants and to new entrants.

18. The remedy for an "earnings drift" of the fourth type is likely to be found in a reform of the methods of determining relative wages within the arbitration system. Up to the present the Commission could only change relativities by increasing the basic wage by more or less than it raised the "margins"; it could only improve the position of the lower paid workers by a method which caused an overall increase in wages at the same time. A more rational system would aim at the establishment of a number of "grades" (say, 10 or 20 grades to start with) based on an agreed system of job classification according to which each of a number of attributes pertaining to a particular kind of work would carry a certain number of "points." Such a grading system would make allowance for length of training, skill, physical exertion, liability to accidents of disease, etc. so as to establish a proper valuation of what the economists call the "net advantages or disadvantages" of different kinds of work. This could be dovetailed to the existing system of differentiation through "margins" if the Commission consistently followed its present intention of determining the "margins" applicable to different grades of labour separately (instead of concentrating on a "key margin" only, as has often been the case in the past). Once the Commission adopts the policy of discriminatory awards as a matter of normal practice, and witholds increases to some grades of workers when it grants increases to others, the way would be open to evolve a system of "job classification" based on objective criteria which would serve as a *frame of reference* for its periodic review of the structure of "margins." It would, of course, have to proceed slowly and cautiously in adapting the structure of wages, since any violent or sudden change of traditionally established differentials is bound to meet with strong resistance.

19. For this reason alone, the structure of relative wages which the Commission should aim at ought to reflect the long-term

factors governing the relative supply price of labour to different occupations and not the short-term requirements arising out of the changing relative demands of different industries; it ought to aim at a scale of relative wages which is considered "fair" on equitable grounds and not merely expedient on economic considerations.[1] In the long run such a policy is most likely to be successful in minimising the rate of inflation, since it will reduce the pressure for higher wages in some parts of the system which arises in sympathetic response to wage increases granted in other parts. (The latter is a very important feature of wage inflation in countries where wages are settled by collective bargaining, and where the wage increases in certain key industries are governed by the capacity to pay of the *particular industries* concerned, rather than the growth of productivity in the economy as a whole.)

20. This still leaves the question open of how to deal with that part of the "earnings drift" which is caused by a general shortage of labour, or a shortage of labour in fast-expanding areas and industries. There is no simple answer to this since its elimination may require a degree of "excess supply" in the labour market which may be found socially intolerable, and which, for reasons described earlier,[2] may also have serious adverse effects on the trend rate of economic growth. The decision as to how much inflation the community should be ready to tolerate for the sake of a higher rate of growth—assuming that society is necessarily confronted with this choice, which is perhaps unproven, but which on our present knowledge, is likely to hold true within some critical range —is ultimately a matter of political judgment. Fortunately there are reasons for hoping that in Australia in the coming decade the choice may not present itself in an acute form. For the rate of growth of the labour force will increase considerably as a result of the higher post-war births; immigration may also increase as

[1] For such a policy to be successful (under Australian conditions) the Commission would have to take into account the existence of over-award payments, but in a different manner than it has tended to do hitherto: in order to *raise* the wages of those classes of workers who are relatively underpaid as a result of the over-award payments made to others, and in witholding increases to those whose earnings, as a result of such pay, are out of line with other wages. (So far, the Commission has tended to follow the opposite course—to consider the size of the over-award pay as one of the factors in its determination of the award increase.)

[2] Cf. para. 4, note, above.

a result of more liberal policies and a policy of continued economic expansion. With a faster rate of growth in the work force, labour shortages and bottlenecks are easier to avoid even when the rate of increase in the demand for labour proceeds at a correspondingly higher pace.

INDEX TO AUTHORS